Wally Yonamine

The Man Who Changed Japanese Baseball

Wally Yonamine

Robert K. Fitts

Foreword by Senator Daniel K. Inouye

With a new preface by the author

UNIVERSITY OF NEBRASKA PRESS

LINCOLN AND LONDON

Library of Congress Cataloging-in-Publication Data
Fitts, Robert K., 1965–
Wally Yonamine: the man who changed Japanese baseball /
Robert K. Fitts; foreword by Daniel K. Inouye; with a new
preface by the author.
p. cm.
Originally published: Lincoln: University of Nebraska Press, c2008.
Includes bibliographical references and index.
ISBN 978-0-8032-4517-4 (pbk.: alk. paper)
1. Yonamine, Wally K., 1925–2011. 2. Baseball players—Japan—
Biography. 3. Baseball players—United States—Biography.
4. Baseball—Japan. I. Title.
GV863.77.A1F584 2012
796.357092—dc23
[B]   2012008616

Set in Minion by Bob Reitz.
Designed by Ray Boeche.

Preface

Wally Yonamine died on the evening of February 28, 2011. I got the news by e-mail when I awoke the next morning, and his wife, Jane, called a few hours later. The prostate cancer had returned in the fall of 2010, and his health had gradually declined. I had spoken to Wally in early February. The telephone conversation lasted less than a minute as he was too tired to speak. Hanging up, tears had come to my eyes; I knew it would be the last time we would speak. The memorial service was on March 5 in Honolulu. It would be a long trip to spend just an afternoon, but I needed to say good-bye in person.

The service at Nuuanu Memorial Park was scheduled for 11 a.m. with doors opening at 10. I arrived a little after ten o'clock to find nearly all the seats in the chapel occupied. Chairs had been placed on the adjacent patio, and even these were filling up quickly. I squeezed into a pew near the back. A dozen large, flowered wreaths, bursting with color, covered the chapel's front wall. At five of eleven, Wally's old friend Duane Kurisu began the service: "Most of us would agree that Wally probably already walked five miles this morning, went to mass to pray for his family and for you and I, went to breakfast with friends, then probably went down to the Pearl Shop and still got here early, as he usually does, so let's start a little early." We all smiled, remembering one of Wally's endearing traits.

After prayers by Rev. Msgr. Terrence Watanabe, Wally's friends and family shared their memories. There was little need to dwell on Yonamine's exploits on the playing fields; we were all aware of his accomplishments, and that was not why we had come. We had come to celebrate a wonderful man and friend.

His old friend Satoru Hosoda recalled how his father had invited Wally to dinner when he had arrived in San Francisco as a rookie running back and how it led to a lifetime friendship. He spoke of Wally's commitment to the family, how he always wrote to Satoru's mother, and how he had flown across the world to attend her funeral.

Walter Kirimitsu, a close friend and former chancellor of the University of Hawaii, focused on Wally's "heart of gold and caring qualities." After relating personal examples of Wally's kindness, he reminded us that Yonamine's generosity extended beyond his family and friends. He never forgot his roots on Hawaii's plantations and spent most of his retirement working on charitable projects in the islands.

His brother Kenneth Yonamine shared memories of Wally's childhood—how he took care of his parents and guided his younger siblings, constantly telling Ken to study, study, study.

His children, Amy, Wallis, and Paul, recalled their favorite memories of their father, who had always made family a priority even during the rigors of the baseball season. By the time Wally's seven grandchildren said good-bye in a video, there were few dry eyes in the chapel.

In the first week of March, newspapers, magazines, and websites across the United States and Japan ran articles and lengthy obituaries on Wally. Most focused on his remarkable story as a pioneer in two sports in two countries. The *New York Times*, for example, ran a half-page obituary, detailing how Wally became the first Asian American to play for an NFL franchise, how he broke into Japanese baseball, and how he changed the game. Even *Time* eulogized Yonamine's courage for going to Japan just after the war and his hard-nosed play.

In Japan news of Wally's death spread quickly over the Internet and was covered in the sports dailies. Numerous players provided quotes on Wally's influence and career. On May 27, 2011, approximately four hundred people, including many former Japanese players, attended a memorial service for Yonamine at Tokyo's Franciscan Chapel. Among the speakers was Sadaharu Oh, who called Wally's entrance into the Japanese league "one of the milestones of the development of professional baseball." "He was my mentor for every facet of the game of baseball when I turned pro," Oh continued. Shigeo Nagashima noted, "He provided me with a lot of inspiration through his aggressive style of play. He was also a mentor that made me think of baseball as a combat sport with his violent slides on the base paths. I relied on him as a coach to help bring an aggressive style of play to the younger players during my years as manager. I pray that he finds happiness on the other side." The memorial ended as the attendees gave Wally a final standing ovation accompanied by a loud cheer and thunderous applause.

In Hawaii Wally's death was front-page news. These newspapers went beyond his sports careers to stress Wally's love for Hawaii, his support of local causes, and his gentlemanly and modest personality. Keith Amemiya told the *Maui News*, "Not only was he an extraordinary athlete whose accomplishments are unmatched in our state's storied athletic history, he was such a kind and generous person who cared so much about Hawaii and its people." Kenji Kawaguchi, a close friend who had known Wally since kindergarten, added, "He was a gentleman, and he was the same person late in life as he was when he was growing up. . . . He was a real example of what families would like their kids to grow up as."

When I first met Wally in the Roppongi Pearl Shop, I was so nervous. I had never had a real conversation with a ball player, let alone a legend like Wally Yonamine. Within minutes, Wally's easy and modest demeanor put me at ease. That meeting with Wally changed my life. His stories and friendliness led me to write *Remembering Japanese Baseball*, which led me to become a baseball writer. Without Wally, I would be a different person.

Over the next eight years, I would get to know Wally well. While writing this book, we spoke nearly weekly. I visited him in Honolulu and Tokyo and got to know his family. Wally became a true inspiration for me—not for what he did as a ball player but for how he lived his life. In short, Wally was the nicest man I have ever met. He was a true gentleman, treating people with kindness and respect, using his good fortune to help others and change the world. As hard as it is, I try to live up to his example. I will truly miss him.

In memory of William Hoffman,
because grandpops are special

And for Vera Hoffman,
who always said I should become a baseball writer

Contents

Illustrations

Following page 160

Foreword

In 1947 Wally Yonamine began his trailblazing professional sports career, first with football, and later—and most notably—with baseball. Two years earlier, World War II had ended, but the conflict was still fresh in our nation's consciousness.

When the war began, Americans of Japanese ancestry weren't permitted to serve in our nation's armed forces. We were classified as 4-C, "enemy aliens," and 120,000 Japanese Americans on the West Coast were rounded up and placed in internment camps surrounded by barbed wire and machine-gun guard towers that were located in desolate parts of the country. It was within these camps that Japanese Americans played baseball. The American pastime was a way to ease the pain of their confinement and a symbolic way of holding on to their Americanism.

As a Nisei from Hawaii, my decision to volunteer to wear the uniform of our nation was an easy choice; Hawaii's Japanese Americans were not subjected to the sort of massive roundup that occurred on the West Coast. To this day, I still wonder if I would have been so eager to serve if my parents and family members had been unjustly incarcerated.

When the war ended, Japanese Americans had proved, with much pride and sacrifice, that their courage and patriotism were beyond question and that Americanism was not a matter of skin color or ethnicity. But while we helped to win a war abroad, we soon discovered that much social progress still needed to be accomplished at home.

In 1947, when I entered politics to make Hawaii a more equitable society, Wally Yonamine became the first player of Japanese descent to make the roster of an American professional football team, the San Francisco 49ers. He immediately became a source of pride and a symbol of what Americans of Japanese ancestry could accomplish in mainstream American society. His achievement, coming so soon in the postwar years, gave much hope to the Japanese American community and opened the door to greater acceptance by all Americans.

Later, Wally would become a sports pioneer on the international stage. A wrist injury led him to abandon football and turn to baseball. In 1951 he became the first American to play in the Japanese major leagues when he joined the Yomiuri Giants, a franchise as storied as the New York Yankees. His arrival in postwar Japan came at a time when Japanese nationalists were still seething at the United States. For them, Yonamine symbolized their motherland's defeat, and he was branded a "traitor" because he was a Japanese American whose forefathers had dared to seek their future outside of Japan.

The resentment even simmered among some of Wally's teammates. Moreover, Wally's aggressive style of play unsettled many who were accustomed to Japan's gentlemanly approach to baseball that included walking to first base on a base on balls and not barreling into second base to break up a double play.

But gradually, over the course of what would become a Hall of Fame career, Wally Yonamine won over fans and teammates, just as Jackie Robinson did in breaking the color barrier on America's baseball diamonds. In Wally Yonamine's case, he opened the door of Japanese baseball to hundreds of non-Japanese and served as a bridge between Japan and the United States, strengthening friendship and understanding between the two countries. The acceptance and goodwill fostered by Wally helped to heal the wounds between two wartime foes who today are longtime allies.

On the playing field, Wally Yonamine was a fierce competitor. Off the field, he displayed humility, grace under pressure, and a deep understanding of the social advancements that could be achieved by his accomplishments on the field and by how he conducted himself in all aspects of his life.

After his stellar career as a player and manager in Japanese baseball
ended, Wally returned to his native Hawaii. He established a foundation that bears his name. It funds scholarships for student-athletes
heading off to college and sponsors the tournament that crowns Hawaii's best high school baseball team. Even in retirement, Wally has
found a way to inspire and positively influence younger generations.
"I hit a home run with my life," Wally Yonamine says. Indeed, he has.
Not only for himself, but for all of us.

Aloha,

Daniel K. Inouye
United States Senator
Washington DC
March 27, 2007

Acknowledgments

I like to joke that Wally Yonamine is the reason I don't have a job. I was a professional archaeologist specializing in nineteenth-century New York City when I first met Wally in 2003. I had planned to write only a short article when I sat down to interview him at his pearl shop in Tokyo. After listening to his riveting tales of Japanese baseball, a new idea came to me. With Wally's help, I interviewed nearly thirty other former players and edited them into narratives similar to Lawrence Ritter's *Glory of Their Times*. This became my first book, *Remembering Japanese Baseball: An Oral History of the Game*. The day after completing the manuscript, I called Wally in Hawaii and asked if I could write his biography. The project took nearly three years, but it was never a chore.

One of the great things about writing the biography of a truly wonderful person is the many people who offer to help. When I asked for an interview or a favor, the response was invariably "Anything for Wally." Accordingly, I have many people to thank.

I greatly appreciate the generosity of the following people for consenting to be interviewed: Motoh Ando, Arthur Arnold, Don Blasingame, Mac Flores, Joel Franks, Garland Gregory, Carlton Hanta, Cappy Harada, Tatsuro Hirooka, Satoru Hosoda, Tadashi Iwamoto, Dick Kashiwaeda, Walter Kirumitsu, Ryozo Kotoh, Gene Martin, Glenn Mickens, Andy Miyamoto, Bill Mizuno, Kerry Yo Nakagawa, Futoshi Nakanishi, Hirofumi Naito, Don Newcombe, Steve Ontiveros, Amy Yonamine Roper, Bart Shirley, Don Sinn, John Sipin, Lou Spadia, Shigeru Sugishita, Sumi Hosoda Tanabe, Robert Whiting, Clyde Wright, Isamu Uchio, Larry Yaji, Wallis Yonamine Yamamoto,

Akira Yonamine, Dean Yonamine, Jane Iwashita Yonamine, and Paul Yonamine.

Edited versions of many of these interviews appear in *Remembering Japanese Baseball*, but with an important difference. *Remembering Japanese Baseball* is an oral history—I allowed the players to tell their stories as they remembered them, and I corrected only obvious factual errors such as dates and statistics. For this biography, I checked the veracity of these stories and made changes as necessary. Readers who notice discrepancies between the two books should rely on the versions contained in this volume.

Many people offered helpful suggestions and pointed me to untapped sources. I would like to especially thank David Block, Philip Block, Damon Byrd, Gary Engel, Amy Essington, Lloyd Feinberg, Beverly and Donald Fitts, Joel Franks, Gary Garland, Ted Gilman, Wayne Graczyk, Ruth Hirota, William Kelly, Walter Kirumitsu, Robert Klevens, Marty Kuehnert, Bob Lapides, Kerry Yo Nakagawa, Yoichi Nagata, Ralph Pearce, Deanna Rubin, Rob Smaal, Mark Watkins and Brenda Silverman, Myrna Watkins, Michael Westbay, and Demetrius Wilson.

I would also like to thank Ryozo Kotoh for his hard work in obtaining the permissions to reproduce many of the photographs in this book. Special thanks to the Yomiuri Giants and the Chunichi Dragons for allowing me to reproduce their photographs and to Isao Harimoto, Tatsuro Hirooka, Tetsuharu Kawakami, Akira Kunimatsu, Yukinobu Kuroe, Shigeo Nagashima, and Sadaharu Oh for consenting to have their images included in this book.

I conducted my research in New York, Honolulu, and Tokyo. The staffs of the Japanese Hall of Fame in Tokyo and the Hamilton Library of the University of Hawaii at Manoa were extremely helpful. Two people in particular helped me overcome the language barrier: Takuo Yamamoto's research skills provided important sources from the Japanese Hall of Fame, and I would have been lost without Ami Shimizu, surely the greatest simultaneous translator ever.

Two others provided invaluable advice on earlier drafts of the manuscript: Rory Costello generously volunteered to edit the first draft, and Robert Whiting provided editorial comments on the second. I learned much from these fine writers and greatly enjoyed sharing my project with them.

I would like to thank the staff at the University of Nebraska Press for all their hard work, especially Rob Taylor, Sabrina Stellrecht, and Stephen Barnett.

This book would not have been possible without the Yonamine family: Wally, Jane, Amy, Wallis, and Paul. They were enthusiastic and supportive throughout the project, always making themselves available for my endless questions. They made working on this book a pure joy. I cannot thank them enough.

Finally, I would like to thank my family, Sarah, Ben, and Simon, for their patience and support.

Prologue

A Gamble

Tokyo, December 1950

Cappy Harada strode through the Ginza section of Tokyo toward Yurakucho Station. The city had changed greatly since Harada first arrived in 1945 as a U.S. Army lieutenant. Allied bombing had leveled much of Tokyo. Between March 10 and May 26, 1945, five massive air raids killed 115,000 people and destroyed 850,000 buildings, leaving only the commercial center of the city untouched for use by General Douglas MacArthur's occupying force. But now, just five years later, the area bustled. Trolley cars were crammed with commuters, and U.S. Army vehicles and delivery trucks rumbled down the street. Businessmen clad in gray overcoats scurried to and from their offices. Around the corner from the station, facing the Imperial Palace moat, was GHQ, the occupation headquarters, absorbing an unending stream of GIs and government officials. On the sidewalks, street vendors in little wooden stalls sold a myriad of wares. Harada reached the temporary headquarters of the Yomiuri Shimbun, Japan's most widely read newspaper, climbed the four flights of stairs with precision, and announced himself to Mr. Shoriki's secretary. She hastened him to a modest office.

Sixty-five-year-old Matsutaro Shoriki sat formally on the couch. A diminutive, bald man with thick, heavy-rimmed glasses, Shoriki did not seem imposing. Yet the Judo master and former police inspector single-handedly quelled angry mobs during the Tokyo riots of 1918 and 1920. He was a man of action—a risk taker with the ability to see opportunities. In 1924, after leaving the police department, Shoriki moved into newspaper publishing. Although he had no experience in the field, he borrowed 100,000 yen (roughly equivalent to $25,000 at the time) and purchased the financially troubled Yomiuri Shimbun. By cutting down on waste and adding sections on the household, radio, and other forms of entertainment, Shoriki quintupled the paper's paid circulation in three years and transformed it into one of the country's leading papers.

In 1929 a friend suggested that the newspaper extend its baseball coverage and sponsor a team of American All-Stars to play in Japan. Shoriki had little interest in the game, but he could recognize a good idea. Baseball, introduced by American teachers in the early 1870s, was the most popular sport in Japan. There were no professional teams at the time, but college games drew thousands of fans. In 1931 Yomiuri sponsored an American All-Star team including Lou Gehrig, Lefty Grove, Mickey Cochrane, Al Simmons, Frank Frisch, Rabbit Maranville, and Lefty O'Doul. The Americans won each of the seventeen games against Japanese university and amateur teams, and the newspaper's circulation soared.

Three years later, Yomiuri sponsored a second Major League tour of Japan. The All-Star's roster included Babe Ruth, Lou Gehrig, Jimmie Foxx, Charlie Gehringer, Earl Averill, Lefty Gomez, Lefty O'Doul, and Moe Berg, the famed spy. To oppose these giants, Shoriki brought together the best players in Japan to form the All Nippon team. The Japanese, however, were still no match for the American stars. The All-Stars won all sixteen contests (two games were intersquad exhibitions) and scored 181 runs to Japan's 36. Nevertheless, more than 450,000 people attended the eighteen games, and newspaper sales rose again.

Japan was becoming increasingly nationalistic, and not all of Shoriki's countrymen welcomed the American All-Stars. Ultraconservatives claimed that Shoriki had defiled Meiji Jingu Stadium, built as a memorial to the Meiji Emperor, by allowing the foreigners to play on the sacred grounds. In February 1935, a member of the War God

Society intercepted Shoriki as he reached the entrance to the Yomiuri building. A samurai sword flashed through the air and struck Shoriki's skull. The assassin fled, leaving the newspaper owner for dead. Shoriki crawled into the building and was rushed to the newspaper's dispensary where he lost consciousness. He survived, but spent the next fifty days in the hospital.

Before the attack, Shoriki had decided to keep his All Nippon baseball squad together. He renamed the team the Dai Nippon Tokyo Yakyu Kurabu (The Great Japan Tokyo Baseball Club) and sent them on a 109-game barnstorming tour of the United States in 1935 to refine their skills. Playing Minor League and amateur nines, the Japanese won 74 of the 109 contests. Their name, however, posed a challenge. On the recommendation of Lefty O'Doul, who was now advising Shoriki, the newspaper owner changed the name to the Tokyo Yomiuri Giants (at the time O'Doul played for the New York Giants). Other Japanese companies soon formed teams, and the Nippon Professional Baseball League was created in 1936. The Yomiuri Giants dominated the league, winning eight championships, before Allied bombing made the games too dangerous for the spectators, prompting officials to cancel the 1945 season.

After the fall of Japan, the Allied occupation force arrested Shoriki, along with many other industrialists and newspaper owners, as a possible war criminal and incarcerated him in Sugamo Prison. No charges were brought against Shoriki, but upon his release on September 1, 1947, he was "purged" by the occupation government until August 1951. Purged individuals were unable to hold positions that could influence Japanese public opinion. Thus, Shoriki was barred from managing the newspaper, but he could still direct the Yomiuri Giants.

The secretary glided out and soon returned with the morning snack of tea and *mochi* (a traditional Japanese sweet made from rice paste and often filled with red beans). She placed them in front of Cappy Harada first and then her employer.

Harada was a second-generation Japanese American, or Nisei,

born in Santa Maria, California. An outstanding high school baseball player, he played against the Tokyo Giants during their 1936 barnstorming tour of the United States and became friendly with general manager Sotaro Suzuki and the Giants' third baseman, Shigeru Mizuhara. Cappy had hoped to turn pro but instead was drafted during World War II. The army made good use of his bilingual ability and assigned him to military intelligence in the Pacific Theater, where he worked with the famed Navaho Ghost Talkers in New Guinea. After being wounded several times, Lieutenant Harada became General William F. Marquat's aide during the Allied occupation of Japan. Marquat, the chief of the Economic and Scientific Section of the occupation force, put Harada in charge of reviving Japanese sports to help raise morale.

The baseball stadiums stood in disarray. Most had survived the bombings, but the Allied forces were using the playing fields as motor pools and munitions dumps. Harada readied the stadiums and, working closely with his old acquaintance Sotaro Suzuki, now a league official, helped restart professional baseball. The Japanese pros played four All-Star games in the waning months of 1945, and league play resumed in 1946. In 1949 Suzuki asked Cappy to help expedite Shigeru Mizuhara's release from a Russian prison camp. Mizuhara, like many Japanese ballplayers, had served in the military during the war and was now languishing in Siberia. Harada was happy to help his old acquaintance. Soon Mizuhara was back in Tokyo at the helm of the Yomiuri Giants, and the Nisei became an informal adviser to the team.

The office door opened and Shoji Yasuda, the chain-smoking general manager of the Yomiuri Giants baseball team, entered. Once Yasuda sat down, Shoriki, speaking in Japanese, got directly to the point. The first Japan Series had just been completed, and his Tokyo Yomiuri Giants, winners of eight of the first fourteen championships under the single league format, had not made it to the inaugural series. Worse still, the Giants had finished in third place in the newly formed Central League, an embarrassing seventeen and a half games behind the Shochiku Robins.

"What can we do to bring the Giants back to the championship?" Shoriki asked. Then, before waiting for an answer he added, "Can we bring somebody in from the United States?"

Harada and Yasuda started. Although Shoriki had strong ties to the United States, he wanted to create an all-Japanese team strong enough to compete with the Major Leaguers. Importing an American ballplayer would undermine this plan. Furthermore, with anti-American feelings high in occupied Japan, importing a Yank to Japan's beloved Giants was truly risky. It could hurt the team's popularity and fuel anti-American sentiment.

Seeing their surprise, Shoriki added, "We need some help to get us back on the winning track. If I have to bring in a player from the United States, then I'll do so."

Harada thought for a second. "If we bring a Caucasian ballplayer to Japan, he might encounter problems due to the language barrier, living conditions, and different culture. It might be better to get a Nisei. Someone who can speak some Japanese, knows Japanese culture, and can also play baseball at the Major League level. I know of a fellow named Wally Yonamine, who is in the San Francisco Seals organization. He used to play football with the San Francisco 49ers. He would be perfect."

The three men understood the challenges this player would face. Japanese were especially distrustful of Nisei. Much of the population viewed them as traitors for not joining their mother country during the war. Furthermore, many of the Giants' stars were war veterans. Would they accept an American as a teammate? Even in 1950, five years after Japan's surrender, living conditions in Tokyo were still harsh by American standards. High-quality food was difficult to obtain and even fuel for heat was scarce. Would this player be able to adapt to the rugged lifestyle, or would he immediately return to his homeland? The three executives knew that it would take a special man to succeed.

Shoriki thought for a moment and announced, "Well, I guess you better see if we can get Wally Yonamine."

1

"Just a Country Boy from Olowalu, Maui"

Today, Olowalu on Maui's west coast is part of paradise. Tourists fly from around the world to relax on its pristine beaches, snorkel in its dazzling coral reefs, and be pampered in luxury resorts. But it wasn't always paradise. In the 1920s and '30s, when sugar cane plantations dominated the area, life was hard. Thousands of immigrants toiled from dawn to dusk in the cane fields for poverty-level wages. The work was dangerous, and many dreams were shattered by wayward rail cars and grinding mill machinery.

Life in Olowalu, however, prepared Wally Yonamine for the challenges of integrating both Japanese baseball and American professional football. Growing up poor on a Maui sugar plantation taught Wally how to overcome adversity, face difficult conditions, and gave him the drive to succeed. His early success in athletics prepared him for the public spotlight, while his family taught him modesty, enabling him to maintain his focus and not get sidetracked by the many diversions facing professional athletes.

Wally's father, Matsusai Yonamine, was born in Okinawa on July 31, 1890, and grew up in a small house with an attached pig sty—a common feature in rural Okinawan homes—in the coastal village of Nakagusuku near the spectacular ruins of Nakagusuku Castle. Soon after his seventeenth birthday, Matsusai's older brother married and following Okinawan custom lived with his wife at his parents' home. Custom dictated that younger brothers had to move out once they reached adulthood. Matsusai could have built his own home nearby, but he dreamed of a better life than rural Okinawa could provide. For the past few years, recruiters had been canvassing the island for laborers to work in the far-off archipelago of Hawaii. More than six thousand had already made the journey. Letters home complained of hard work and tough conditions, but they also contained much-needed cash. Matsusai didn't mind hard work—he was used to it. Deciding to start a new life, he left for Hawaii. After an arduous three-week passage spent mostly in cramped below-deck quarters, he arrived in Honolulu in late 1907.

Almost immediately, Matsusai was assigned to work on the Olowalu sugar plantation in Maui. The village of Olowalu, also known as a camp, was created by the Olowalu plantation to house its three-hundred-plus workers, most of whom were unmarried men. Japanese predominated the workforce, but there were also Puerto Ricans, Hawaiians, Koreans, Chinese, and a smattering of miscellaneous Europeans. Matsusai settled in a small house with two young Japanese men and was set to work loading sugar cane stalks onto carts to be transported to the mill.

A typical day started at 5:00 a.m. After breakfast, laborers trudged to the fields and began working at 6:00 a.m. Overseers, known as *lunas*, supervised from horseback and carried whips to drive the field hands at their tasks. Workers took minutes for lunch and then toiled until 4:30 or 5:00 p.m. Afterward, the Japanese bathed, ate dinner and socialized until the 8:00 p.m. whistle signaled bedtime. One laborer noted that "life on a plantation is much like life in a prison."

In Olowalu, the different ethnic groups lived in clusters, and nearly all of Matsusai's immediate neighbors were Japanese. A few houses away lived the Nishimura family. Isaburo Nishimura, his wife Hisano, and eldest son Tetsugi, immigrated to Hawaii in 1899 from Hiroshima. They soon settled in Olowalu, and the family grew as four daughters and another son were born. Before 1920, Matsusai Yonamine had moved in with the Nishimura family as a boarder. In early 1920, he and the Nishimuras' eldest daughter, Kikue, who was nearly eleven years his younger, eloped.

The elopement was shocking, but at that time, any marriage between an Okinawan and a mainland Japanese was unusual. Even though white Hawaiians rarely distinguished between Okinawans and Japanese, the two groups viewed themselves as markedly different. Mainland Japanese, calling themselves *naichijin* (people of Japan homeland), considered Okinawans backward and not true Japanese, as many Okinawans did not speak the standard language. Likewise, Okinawans often considered the *naichijin* to be stuck up. Although thrown together by plantation managers, the two ethnic groups rarely socialized prior to World War II.

The young couple moved next door to the Nishimuras, and their first child, a daughter named Litsuko, was born on September 4, 1920. Akira, the eldest son, came on March 23, 1923, and was closely followed by Kaname (pronounced "Ka-na-may") on June 24, 1925. Eighteen years later, Kaname would adopt the nickname Wally, the name he will be known by throughout this book. The couple had four more children, Satoru (born December 31, 1928), Noboru (born June 15, 1932), daughter Alma Harumi (born April 9, 1934), and Kenneth (born May 4, 1937).

The Yonamines lived in a small frame house with a wraparound porch. It was a typical one-story plantation home with a kitchen, living room, and three bedrooms. The bath and toilet were in a separate building. With seven children, the house felt cramped, and the youngest kids often slept in the same room as their parents. The Yonamines sparsely furnished their home in the American, not Japanese, style. For example, there were no tatami mats and the family used chairs rather than sitting on the floor. The kitchen contained just a wooden board fashioned into a table and some old chairs.

Life on the plantation was hard. Matsusai had been promoted to a bulldozer driver, but he still woke before dawn and reached the fields around 5:30 in the morning. A highly skilled operator, he was responsible for bulldozing the fallows for planting the cane, which kept him occupied until dark. With seven children to feed, he rarely took a day off. Kikue remained at home caring for the children and keeping her home spotless. To earn extra money, she did other plantation workers' laundry.

Despite the hard work, the Yonamines remained poor. Plantation wages were low and Matsusai received only sixty to seventy dollars a month. The family purchased goods at the company store on credit, and at the end of each month most of the family's income went toward their account. Wally remembers, "I didn't realize it at the time, but growing up on the plantation was so hard. If I wanted to buy a stick of candy, I didn't have any money. And my father couldn't buy it for us because he had seven kids to feed." Through frugal living, the family got by. They raised chickens and vegetables in the backyard, and Kikue cooked Japanese and Hawaiian one-pot meals, chopping up the meat and vegetables so that there would be enough to go around.

Because Matsusai immigrated alone and Kikue remained close to her family, the Yonamine children saw themselves as Japanese rather than Okinawan. They were proud of their heritage even though they adopted many Hawaiian and Western traditions. Matsusai kept a picture of the emperor in his bedroom, and the children attended Japanese language classes after their regular school let out. At home, the family spoke mostly English as Kikue was a native English speaker, and Matsusai, who spoke Okinawan, addressed the children in broken English. The children grew up thinking of themselves as Japanese-Americans, or more specifically, Japanese-Hawaiians.

By general agreement, Wally was the rascal of the family. Akira recalls Wally being a lazy child, unwilling to do his chores or homework. He once told his mother, "I don't have to study. I'm going to be a good ballplayer."

Wally was inseparable from his older brother Akira. There was not much for the boys to do in Olowalu. The family didn't have enough money for toys or commercial entertainment, and Wally wasn't much of a reader. The village didn't have a movie theater or even a library. Like adventuresome, bored boys everywhere, the Yonamine boys explored the area around the village pursuing mischief.

The two were usually hungry and often went looking for the fruit that grew throughout the island. They could regularly be seen at the tops of mango trees or along hilly trails searching for mountain apples. The most tempting treats were a nearby farmer's juicy watermelons. The farmer, however, watched his crop closely and discouraged both animals and trespassers with his ever-present shotgun. One day, Wally and Akira decided that the watermelons were ready for harvesting and crawled under the fence to help themselves. Akira picked two small ones, one for each hand and easy to carry, while Wally went for the largest he could find. As they started toward the fence, they heard the farmer ordering them to drop the watermelons. Naturally, the boys held their spoils tighter and ran. Suddenly, a shotgun blast roared nearby. Akira dropped his watermelons and sprinted over the fence to safety. Wally refused to abandon his prize, tucked it under his arm like he would a football years later, and ran with more determination. Another blast rang out and a pellet whizzed by his ear as he hurtled the fence. Safely away from the farm, the boys cracked open the watermelon to savor the fruit that they risked their lives for. It was still white inside and not even near ripe!

Stunts like this infuriated their father. "Our father got so mad at us one day," Akira remembers, "that he just picked us up and put us in the chicken coop in the back yard. He locked the door and left us there! We're 10 and 12 years old. Finally late that night, my mother unlocked it so we could come out."

In the 1920s and '30s thousands of Filipinos came to work on the sugar plantations. Most were unmarried men, uneducated and born in poverty. At times, their gatherings could get rough. Sometimes when the Yonamine boys got bored, they would wander down to the Filipino section of Olowalu. There, they met Mac Flores, a small, wiry Filipino laborer ten years their senior. Flores was one of the village's better baseball and football players, and the boys latched onto him and followed him everywhere. He played third base for the Pioneer Mill company baseball team, so the Yonamines became the team's bat boys and traveled with them around Maui. Eventually, Mac Flores would marry Kikue Yonamine's sister and become Wally's and Akira's uncle.

Like many Filipino laborers, Flores was an avid craps shooter. The boys used to watch him play, and by the time they were ten, they played alongside him. Their parents, of course, did not approve—often in the midst of a game they would hear their father bellow "Yonamines, come here!" and the boys would flee into the cane fields. On one occasion, Wally and Akira were on a roll and won nearly a hundred dollars. Realizing that this was more than their father earned in a month, they decided to take their winnings home. As the boys began to go, the gamblers snarled that they had better not leave with their money and one pulled a large knife. Coming out of nowhere, the diminutive Flores struck the aggressor with all his might and yelled, "RUN!" The future center fielder and his even faster older brother streaked home. Back at the house, they gave the money to their sister, Litsuko, to hide. "If our father found out about the money," Wally adds, "we would have been back in that chicken coop for God knows how long!"

The boys' love for sports probably kept them out of even more trouble. In a field below the village, the Yonamine brothers played softball, basketball, volleyball, soccer, and Wally's particular favorite—football. Since they didn't have enough money to buy a football, the boys took a can of Carnation creamed corn, wrapped it in newspaper, and used it instead. There were few boys their age in the village, so by the time they were young teens, the brothers joined the men in pickup basketball, softball, soccer, and even football games.

Even at a young age, Wally was highly competitive. The boys' marble games could get fierce. The older brother usually won, but Wally would not quit if he was losing, even when their parents called repeatedly for them. Akira would usually give in and let Wally win back what he lost. At eighty-one years old, Akira still argues that Wally would claim that he lost more marbles than he actually had!

Growing up in Olowalu, Wally knew little about the outside world. He remembers, "We lived in the country so I didn't know who Joe DiMaggio was. I didn't even know who Babe Ruth was. So I didn't have a favorite ballplayer. My hero was my brother, Akira. He was a good football and baseball player. He could run really fast and actually held the Maui record for the 40-yard dash until just a few years ago. I wanted to be like him."

When Wally was eight or nine years old, he began listening to the local games on the radio. The family's old box radio stood on the porch, next to where his fifty-five-year-old grandmother usually sat. Occasionally, Wally would join her. He had little interest in the serial shows or the news but could easily convince her to tune in sporting events. His favorites were the Honolulu interscholastic (high school) football games and the Hawaiian Baseball League games. At that time, high school football was one of Hawaii's most popular spectator sports; tens of thousands of fans watched the games each weekend at Honolulu Stadium. Both the Honolulu and Maui newspapers covered all the games and sometimes even practices, making the star players local celebrities.

The radio also introduced Wally to organized baseball. Formed in 1924, the Hawaii Baseball League consisted of seven semipro teams, each affiliated with a different ethnic group. Games were played at Honolulu Stadium, and the quality of ball was very high. The Asahi, an all-Japanese squad, quickly became one of the top teams—many Nisei boys dreamed of making the team. Dick Kashiwaeda, one of Hawaii's greatest players, called the first day he put on the Asahi uniform "one of the proudest moments in his life." As he listened to the games, Wally began to dream of playing at Honolulu Stadium.

Wally and Akira began playing organized sports in 1939 when Mac Flores created a softball team for the teenagers of Olowalu and entered them in an adult league. Wally had just turned fourteen years old, but his hitting led the team to the championship before they lost to a more experienced adult team in the territory finals at Hilo. Soon after, the Yonamine brothers were invited to join the Plebs Baseball Club in Lahaina. The Plebs were on the same level as an American Legion club and consisted mostly of boys fifteen to seventeen years old. At fourteen, Wally was young for the team but he was big for his age and a natural athlete. The team traveled around Maui and even to the other islands for league games. Lahaina was six miles north of

Olowalu, but the boys already attended school in town. After practice, their coach, Seke Sasaki, or their father, who now worked for Pioneer Mill in Lahaina, would drive them home. Wally played first base and pitched while Akira caught. Money was still tight for the Yonamine family, so when Wally joined the squad, he did not own a glove or spikes. The team lent him an old glove but it was for a righty and Wally threw with his left. After he caught the ball, he had to take off the glove to throw with his left hand or toss the ball with his weaker right arm. Eventually, his father bought Wally an inexpensive left-handed glove and a pair of cheap spikes.

With his constant climbing and playing sports, Wally got more than his share of childhood injuries. As plantation health care was adequate at best and often incompetent, Kikue Yonamine would take her ailing children to the town of Wailuku—an hour away by car—to see a local faith healer named Margie Carvalho. A plump mother of six, Margie was soft-spoken and genuinely kind. She saw patients at her home in a small room decorated with a large crucifix and religious pictures. As Wally lay on the bed, Margie would touch him, pray, and diagnose the problem. She would then perform the needed treatment, followed by more prayer. Patients who believed in her methods and prayed with her often recovered quickly from their ailments. Although Kikue Yonamine was a Buddhist, she found nothing unusual or worrisome about Margie Carvalho's Catholic approach to healing. Like many Japanese, who managed to incorporate Shinto weddings with Buddhist funerals, she took an eclectic approach to religion. But Margie's abilities and faith had a lasting effect on Wally. As he grew older, he became more interested in Catholicism and eventually became a devout Catholic.

The Yonamine children spent their summers working on the plantation to supplement the family's income. Wally would get up at 4:30 in the morning and work for eight hours in the fields, cutting cane with a machete. The work was arduous. At harvest time, cane stalks reach twelve to fifteen feet in height. The plant's leaves are stiff with saw-tooth edges that, if drawn quickly at the wrong angle, can slice through skin, leaving a deep gash. The supple stalks can also spring back on an unwary cutter, whipping him with their razor-sharp leaves. To protect themselves, cane cutters wore heavy clothes and hats. Although this shielded them from the plant, it made the work nearly unbearable and led to heat exhaustion. "I used to really hate that job," Wally remembers. "I got paid only twenty-five cents a day, but it was the only job that I could get. At the time, I told myself that I never wanted to work in the cane fields again. That is where my drive to always try my best and never give up came from. I never wanted to work in the cane fields again."

In 1941 Wally finished eighth grade and enrolled at the renowned Lahainaluna School in Lahaina. American missionaries founded Lahainaluna in 1831, making it the oldest continuously running American school west of the Rocky Mountains. Over the following century, the school transformed into an academy for the Hawaiian elite before becoming a public school in 1923. During the forties, Lahainaluna boarded 125 students and accepted nearly 300 day students. Each of the 125 boarders—Wally among them—worked three hours a day on the school farm. The students awoke at 5:00 a.m. to begin their chores. Wally's task was to get a hundred pounds of grass for the cows each day, and he had to climb a nearby mountain to collect his quota. The chore strengthened Wally's legs, and soon he had twenty-five-inch thighs as a high schooler, which allowed him to roll off opposing players on the gridiron.

At Lahainaluna, Wally got his first opportunity to play organized football. The school had a strong team with many big Hawaiians and Samoans, as Lahainaluna's free board attracted players from throughout the islands. Although relatively small, the speedy Akira Yonamine had starred for the team the year before, winning the Maui Interscholastic Outstanding Player Award. The team used the single wing formation, and as a freshman, Wally made second string.

In the first game of the '41 season, Wally sat on the bench hoping that his team would beat Roosevelt High and that he might see a little playing time late in the game. Early in the first quarter, however, the starting halfback broke his thumb. The coach had few options, so he sent in Yonamine even though he had never played in an organized game before. Wally approached the referee to inform him of the substitution, but his mouth—dry from nervousness—could not form the words. After several stammering attempts he got his message across and joined the team on the field. On the first play, the quarterback called for Wally to pass. The quarterback flipped the ball back to Wally, who faded to his right and threw a wobbly 35-yard pass into the end zone. The end streaked toward the ball and just managed to pull it in for a touchdown.

Wally continued to play well and in the third quarter he capped a 55-yard drive with an 11-yard touchdown run off right tackle. But the highlight came late in the fourth quarter, when Yonamine intercepted a pass on his own 30-yard line and ran in 70 yards for a touchdown.

Under a big headline reading "Yonamine Leads Lunas to 19–7 Win," the *Maui News* noted that "Kaname Yonamine . . . sparked the attack for the Lunas. Only a freshman and playing in his first interscholastic game, Kaname ran, passed and kicked the oval like a seasoned veteran as he tallied two touchdowns and passed to Joe Lopez for the first score of the contest and of the 1941 season."

Wally became the starting halfback the next day.

Although Yonamine did not dominate another game after the opener, he continued to do well as Lahainaluna put together a championship season. The team went 6-0 against its Maui league opponents and dropped only one game—against Honolulu powerhouse Farrington High School.

As Maui champions, Lahainaluna faced off against St. Louis High School, the Oahu champions, in the Haleakala Bowl. Four thousand spectators came to Kahului Fairgrounds to watch the game on November 30. The strong St. Louis team, led by running back "Squirmin' Herman" Wedemeyer, outweighed the Lunas by seven pounds per man. Wedemeyer would become an All-American sensation at St. Mary's College in California with his exciting rushing style. Later, he would become even more famous as Duke Lukela on the hit television show *Hawaii Five-O*. The smaller Lunas managed to hold Wedemeyer and St. Louis for thirty-six minutes until the visitors finally scored. St. Louis added six points in the fourth quarter to win the game 13–0. It was not the last time, by any means, that Wally and Squirmin' Herman would meet.

A week after Yonamine's football season was over and the team returned to school, the Japanese attacked the military base at Pearl Harbor on nearby Oahu Island. With the Japanese fleet in the vicinity, Hawaiian officials, worried about a full-scale invasion, imposed martial law on the island, and initiated blackouts. The following week, on December 15, the Japanese attacked Maui. A submarine began firing at the town of Kahului at 5:42 in the evening. Ten rounds fell on the town, causing minor structural damage but no casualties. After the attack, all schools on Maui were closed until further notice.

For Herman Wedemeyer and the St. Louis football team, the weeks following Pearl Harbor were quite memorable. After defeating the Lunas, St. Louis traveled to the island of Kauai to play two exhibition games. They played on Saturday, December 6, but when news of the attack reached the island, Sunday's game was canceled. Inter-island transportation for civilians was curtailed and the team was stranded on Kauai for two weeks. The visiting footballers were given guard duty at night. Wedemeyer remembered, "We had to do guard duty at night. . . . It was spooky. Everything was dark because of the blackout. My imagination was running wild. Every star looked like a ship or a parachute coming down. . . . We knew nothing of wars. All of a sudden, bang. Our whole lives changed. We matured overnight."

As the war progressed and Hawaii was no longer in immediate danger, restrictions were relaxed and the islands settled into wartime routines. Unlike on the mainland, where the federal government placed nearly 120,000 Japanese Americans into internment camps, most Japanese Americans in Hawaii remained free. Many volunteered for the U.S. Army; the 100th Battalion and 442nd Regimental Combat Team, consisting of Japanese American soldiers and Caucasian officers, served with distinction in the European Theater. Others, like

Akira Yonamine, were drafted. Akira served as an army translator with the 5th Cavalry. He spent the war in the States and went to Japan as part of the occupation forces.

After a summer working in the plantation fields, Wally returned to Lahainaluna for his sophomore year focused on the upcoming football season. He was now a projected starter and one of the pillars of the team. Once again, the Lunas had a strong team and went undefeated (5-0-1) to win the championship. Yonamine, playing halfback, was their most talented player as he could rush, receive, and pass. He also punted, place-kicked, returned kicks, and pulled down a number of interceptions on defense. Against St. Anthony on November 1, 1942, Wally scored all nineteen points in the 19–6 win as he rushed for two touchdowns, caught a pass and ran thirty-three yards for another, and converted an extra point. At season's end, the *Maui News* picked Wally as a first team All-Star.

By the end of his sophomore year, Wally had won two Maui championships and had emerged as one of the best players on the island. From exhibition games, he knew that the teams in Honolulu were more competitive than Lahainaluna, but he also knew that he had the ability to play in their league. Now was the time to pursue his dream of playing in Honolulu Stadium. Wally apprehensively approached his father and asked if he could go to school in Honolulu. Matsusai Yonamine, who came to Hawaii by himself at the age of seventeen, responded, "If you want to go, you go." With those simple words, the history of two professional leagues in two countries would be changed.

2
Football Star

In August 1943, Wally said goodbye to his family and boarded a Honolulu-bound steamer. His father had contacted Mac Flores, who now worked on the teeming Honolulu docks as a stevedore, to ask if his son could stay with him. Flores readily obliged and agreed to meet Wally at the dock.

When Yonamine disembarked, he looked to no avail for Flores. A bit apprehensive, the boy sat down on his luggage and waited. Hours ticked by. As evening came, Wally realized that Mac wasn't coming. Desperate, he counted his change. He had very little, but perhaps enough. He found a cab, handed the driver the address, and soon stood in front of a small boarding house in a run-down section of town. Nobody was at home, but the door was unlocked. The room was small, about twelve by twelve feet, with no kitchen or shower. He entered and once again waited. Finally, the teenager drifted off to sleep. In the early morning, the door opened and Flores walked in. He had worked both the day and night shifts unloading ships and couldn't leave the job site. "You couldn't imagine how happy I was to see him!" Yonamine recalled later.

In the following days, Yonamine and Flores visited the St. Louis School and Farrington High School. Wally was planning on enrolling at the St. Louis School, where he would share the backfield with Herman Wedemeyer. He toured the school and watched the football team practice, but found the players cold. Wally realized that a country boy like himself might have a tough time fitting in with the more sophisticated Honolulu students. He returned to Flores's apartment worried.

The next day, Wally and Mac visited Farrington High School. The team practiced as Wally watched from the sidelines. Soon, a few players came over, introduced themselves, and said, "Eh Yonamine, throw us some passes!" Wally, dressed in his best street clothes, ran onto the field and joined the team in their drills. The next day he enrolled at Farrington. Much of the school had been requisitioned by the military and converted into a hospital, so classes were held in two large Quonset huts built behind the school's main building. To accommodate the large number of students, school was held in two shifts—one between 8:00 a.m. and noon and another from 1:00 p.m. to 4:30.

As a transferring student, Yonamine was ineligible to play on Farrington's sports teams his junior year. "My junior year was the toughest year of my entire life. When you don't play any sports, it's really hard to make friends. On top of that, I sometimes didn't even have enough money to eat, so I know how it feels to be hungry. I couldn't ask my parents for money because they had six other kids to feed, and I couldn't even go back to Maui to see them because I couldn't afford the fare. But that experience helped me later in life."

Although Wally could not join a sports team, he practiced at the school gym. There he met Arthur Arnold, the gym's equipment manager, and the two began working out together. Arnold remembers, "He was a very shy individual. I think he was scared at first because he came from Maui and wasn't used to a big city like Honolulu, but after we broke the ice he became very friendly. I decided that Kaname Yonamine was too hard for our classmates to say. We went to Wallace Rider Farrington High School, so I suggested why don't you call yourself Wallace? He went along with that for a little while and then changed it to Wally."

Arnold sometimes stayed with Wally at Mac Flores's place. "There was a group of Filipino laborers living in the rooming house. Sometimes we had nine guys in his room sleeping on the floor. I would sleep outside on the scaffolding because there was no room inside. I had to make sure that I wouldn't fall off because the room was on the second story! There was no shower in the room so we went to the YMCA and took our showers there. We spent a lot of time hanging around the Y, but we stayed out of trouble and never went wrong. Sometimes we didn't know where our next meal was coming from, so different guys would invite us over."

At school, the shy Yonamine often felt awkward. Without much money, he dressed in Akira's hand-me-downs. But the clothes were not only old, they were also out of style. People in Maui tended to wear practical clothes—often designed for the rigors of working on the plantations. For example, many wore pants with tapered legs so that they could be tucked into work boots to keep the giant centipedes that infest the underbrush from climbing up your legs. Wally arrived in Honolulu with several old pairs of these workpants, only to find the Honolulu teens wearing twenty-four-inch bellbottoms. Since Arnold was in charge of the school's equipment room, he would help Wally by slipping him practice jerseys so that he would have clean shirts to wear to school.

In late spring, a hygienist and dentist came into the school to examine each of the students. In a back room, the dentist, a Japanese Hawaiian, looked carefully at the young kid from Maui's teeth and proclaimed that they had irreparable nerve damage. The teeth, the dentist declared, would have to come out.

In three painful office visits, most of Wally's upper teeth were pulled. That was enough, the dentist announced and constructed porcelain dentures for the young man. As years passed, Wally began to wonder if the extractions had really been necessary. His suspicions were probably correct. The dentist had told one of Wally's friends the same story, but the friend visited a second dentist who assured him that the teeth did not need to be pulled. During the 1940s, a black market for healthy teeth flourished. Dentures could be made from porcelain, but those made with real teeth commanded a premium price. Unscrupulous dentists commonly pulled teeth and sold them to supplement their meager incomes.

The school year finally ended in June. Wally could barely wait for the following August, when football camp would begin. Hopefully this past year of deprivation would be worth it. To help build his muscles for the upcoming season and to raise some much-needed money, Wally returned to Maui and took a summer job loading trucks on a pineapple plantation. It seemed like the perfect summer job, but it nearly crushed his dreams and future.

The Baldwin Packers pineapple plantation stood on a steep hill above the town of Kapalua on Maui's northwest coast. At the time, workers had a breathtaking view of the turquoise waters of the Pailolo Channel, but today the view is marred by luxury resorts, homes, and golf courses. Women field hands picked the fruit and placed them in large, heavy wooden crates. Trucks with three-man crews would collect the crates and transport them to the cannery. The trucks would drive to the top of the hill and slowly descend as the young men loaded them with crates. The three-man loading crews were paid by the box so they worked as quickly as possible. It was tiring work, but Wally enjoyed the physical activity and soon his team could load over two hundred crates in just ten minutes.

One rainy day as he was rushing to load the truck, Wally slipped on the wet pineapple leaves just as the truck began to roll forward and his foot became wedged under the tire. He tried to pull it out but the pain was unbearable. "I'm stuck!" he yelled. His companions tried to free him but the foot was wedged firmly under the wheel. The pain mounded every second. Unable to bear it, Wally screamed at the driver, "Roll the truck forward! Just roll it!"—anything to stop the pain. Fortunately, the driver was no teenager, but a seasoned worker. Ignoring Yonamine's screams, he got out of the cab, went to the front of the old vehicle and turned the transmission crank for more power. Returning to the driver's seat, he put it in reverse and gunned the motor. Mud shot out from the back of the tires as they struggled to grip the dirt path. The truck slipped again and Wally cried out, "Just roll 'em!" The driver persisted and the tires finally gripped the earth and drew the truck uphill off Wally's foot. Sure that his foot was crushed beyond repair, Wally struggled out of his boot. Already the foot was entirely black and blue.

Although Yonamine had to miss a few weeks of work and was unable to run for a while, he recovered completely before the start of the football season. He realizes now how lucky he was. A less-experienced driver might have listened to his pleas and rolled the truck forward. The truck's full weight would have crushed his foot and his sports career would have ended that day.

Wally returned to Farrington in the fall of 1944 eager for the football season to begin. He excelled during preseason practices and, as expected, became the Governors' starting halfback. Arthur Arnold remembers, "Wally used to practice so hard and was so serious that we had to loosen him up. He was strong and tough, but slightly bow-legged. So we teased him by saying that he became bow-legged from the pigs running through his legs on Maui." However, the Honolulu Advertiser wasn't joking in the least when, in a preseason preview, it described Kaname Yonamine as a "sensational halfback from Maui who is the 'sparkplug of the Govs.' The husky Yonamine is the biggest threat in pre circles this year," gushed the paper. "He is a tricky, elusive runner and fine passer as well as kicker."

The season opened on the last day of September with Farrington facing Kamehameha, one of the league's strongest teams. The winner would become the favorite for the league championship. Yonamine donned a white jersey with the number 37 emblazoned on the back and ran onto the field at Honolulu Stadium for pregame warmups. He looked up at the rows of wooden bleachers and Diamond Head towering beyond and smiled. His dream had come true.

The stadium was more than just a ballpark. It was a cultural landmark in its own right, as beloved as Wrigley Field or Fenway Park. Sportscaster Al Michaels, who began his career in Honolulu, remembers the peculiar smell of the stands: Hawaiian delicacies, such as *pipikaula* and *manapua*, mingled with beer, cigarette smoke, and old wood. For many, it was the city's social center. Longtime Honolulu resident Stuart Ho recalls, "Our society . . . was very segregated, not in a racial sense but in a social sense." Honolulu Stadium "was central to the life of the community. It was the only time the whole community really got together." The stadium held twenty-six thousand,

and on many weekends it was filled to capacity as patrons watched high school, college and professional football, Senior League and AAA baseball, rodeos, concerts, and even stock car racing.

In 1933 Babe Ruth joined local stars for an exhibition game. A year later, he returned with Lou Gehrig, Jimmy Foxx, and their Major League All-Star teammates en route to Japan. Numerous other professional teams followed, including the newly formed Tokyo Giants in 1935. But the unquestioned highlight of all these tours came in June 1944 when Joe DiMaggio, playing for an army team, had hit a 435-foot home run out of the stadium and across the street into the yard of the historic Dreier Manor. It was the longest home run in Hawaiian baseball history. That last day in September, Wally walked over to where home plate stood when the field was configured for baseball and imagined what it was like to hit a baseball that far.

Eventually, locals dubbed the slowly rotting stadium "The Termite Palace" and joked that it would crumble if the termites stopped holding hands, but on this glorious Saturday, it was in its prime as seventeen thousand boisterous fans filed into the bleachers. Farrington and Yonamine dominated the game. Wally opened the scoring with a 19-yard field goal in the first quarter, but Kamehameha struck back with a touchdown in the second quarter and would have tallied a second if Yonamine had not picked off the would-be TD pass and run it out of danger. On the first possession of the second half, the Governors marched down the field, and Wally dove over the left guard from the 2-yard line for a touchdown. He stood up and quickly converted the extra point to give his team a 10–7 lead and eventual victory. The *Honolulu Advertiser* noted, "Yonamine, 175-pound southpaw dynamite deploying from the right half position, accounted for all of Farrington's points, and also handled all the punting and most of the passing, in addition to bearing the brunt of the running attack. He played a strong defensive game also." Wally's performance in his first game at Honolulu Stadium had surpassed even his boyhood dreams.

The following Sunday a capacity crowd filled Honolulu Stadium to watch Farrington take on St. Louis. Herman Wedemeyer had graduated the previous year, leaving St. Louis a much weaker team. The St. Louis defense limited the Governors to just a safety in the first half, but led by several long runs by Yonamine, Farrington scored twice in the fourth quarter to win 15–0. The *Advertiser* again singled out Wally as the game's biggest star. For the first time in print, the newspaper referred to the Maui native as "Wallace Yonamine."

On Sunday, October 16, the Yonamine family and their close friends gathered on the porch around the old radio to listen to the broadcast of Farrington's match with Roosevelt High, a school known more for its high academic standards rather than its football team. Most of the listeners barely understood the rules of the game, but each time they heard "Yonamine" the small crowd gave a lusty cheer. They soon became hoarse as Wally was once again the star of the game, setting up several touchdowns and scoring on a 56-yard run during Farrington's 48–0 victory.

Success on the gridiron never went to Yonamine's head. He remained so shy and modest that Jimmy Murakami, a reporter for the *Maui News*, mentioned it in a November article. After practice, Wally and his friends would go for walks in downtown Honolulu or hang out at the YMCA. Although Japanese Hawaiians have often been accused of keeping to themselves, a trait that was aggravated with the suspicion other ethnic groups cast on them during World War II, Wally paid little attention to ethnicity when making friends. His closest friends included Arnold, a haole (as Caucasians are known in Hawaii), Baby Louis Castro, a large moon-faced Portuguese Hawaiian, and Bill MacWayne, a haole with Chinese ancestry. The group became lifelong friends, sharing numerous teenage adventures but avoiding serious trouble.

Farrington won again the following week, beating Kaimuki High 48–6 to improve their record to 4-0. The win set up a showdown with undefeated McKinley High School for the league title on October 28.

That Saturday afternoon, another capacity crowd of twenty-six thousand showed up at Honolulu Stadium eager to watch Farrington's powerful offense try to penetrate McKinley's superb defense. Two special guests sat on the 50-yard line. In appreciation for his star running back's marvelous season, coach Henry Kusunoki had brought Akira Yonamine and the boy's uncle Harry Nishimura to Honolulu for the game.

Wally treated his guests to a spectacular performance as he rushed for the first touchdown, kicked the extra point late in the first quarter, and, after McKinley tied the game, ran 32 yards for a fourth-quarter touchdown. The game ended four minutes later with the Governors on top 14–6. In recognition of his fantastic game and scoring all of the team's points, Coach Kusunoki gave Yonamine the game ball. Wally, in turn, handed it to his uncle to bring back to his parents in Olowalu.

After the game, some kids approached Wally and asked him to autograph the program. Taken aback, the shy Yonamine at first declined, saying, "I'm no big shot," but Coach Kusunoki intervened and urged Wally to sign. In future years, once Wally became more comfortable with his fame, he became renowned as a friendly and generous autograph signer.

Although Farrington had clinched the league title, one game remained. Two weeks later, the Governors polished off weak Punahou 33–0 to complete an undefeated season. Finally, on December 2, Farrington and Kamehameha met in the annual postseason Interscholastic doubleheader at Honolulu Stadium. Yonamine had his finest game, scoring all his team's points as Farrington won 26–20. After the game, the league's coaches and sportswriters from the *Honolulu Advertiser* named Yonamine to the All-Star team and selected him the league's most outstanding player. Overall, Yonamine had carried the ball 85 times for 557 yards, an average of 6.4 yards per carry. He had also completed 12 of 21 passes for 193 yards and 2 touchdowns. To this total, he added a field goal and 13 extra point conversions.

Yonamine's success came at an important time for the Nisei community. With World War II raging, anti-Japanese sentiment was high. Japanese Hawaiians were not treated as poorly as mainland Japanese Americans, as their sheer numbers made them vital to the economy, but they still faced discrimination and hostility. Over three thousand people, mostly community leaders, were incarcerated and many Japanese Hawaiians faced hiring discrimination as well as racial slurs. There were not many Japanese American football players—many Japanese parents, not wanting their boys to get hurt, discouraged football and pushed them toward baseball. Wally's triumphs made him a celebrity in the Nisei community and a source of pride in that troubled time. The smaller Okinawan community also claimed Yonamine as one of their own and followed his exploits closely. At the time, Wally didn't realize this. "I always thought that I was Japanese," states Yonamine, "and that Japanese and Okinawans were the same." As he would find out years later when he was courting his future wife, Jane Iwashita, the two groups considered themselves quite different.

The Governors finished off their year with a benefit game against the Maui Cardinals, an amateur All-Star team, at the Kahului Fairgrounds on December 17. Playing in front of many friends and family members, Yonamine disappointed no one, except perhaps the small number of Cardinals supporters, as he starred in the 14–0 Farrington victory. After the game, the Governors boarded a bus and went to Olowalu. Some of the city boys from Honolulu were a little apprehensive. They knew that Wally's family didn't have much money, and they didn't know what to expect. But when the team arrived, they were pleasantly surprised. The Yonamine family had prepared a giant luau and the players stuffed themselves with good country food until late in the evening.

Yonamine would turn twenty years old in June 1945, so he was ineligible to play sports for Farrington after the football season ended. Instead, Wally played basketball at the local YMCA and football for an amateur team called the Rainbows, which consisted mostly of University of Hawaii players. The team traveled around the islands, playing amateur teams and usually winning comfortably. In June Wally graduated from Farrington High School. The school held the ceremonies on a Sunday night, and the next morning Wally received a draft notice from the U.S. Army.

The draft board assigned Yonamine to Schofield Barracks, located just outside Honolulu, for basic training. Wally was projected to join the famous 442nd Regimental Combat Team. This unit, made up of Nisei soldiers with Caucasian officers, was the most highly decorated small unit in the European Theatre. Members received seven presidential citations, twenty Congressional Metals of Honor, and over eighteen thousand individual decorations for bravery. It also sustained one of the highest casualty ratings: 9,486 of the nearly 14,000 men who served in the unit received a Purple Heart. Many of the casualties came in the unsuccessful assault on Monte Cassino Abbey on January 1944 and in the subsequent drive through northern Italy. Among the dead were Sergeant Shigeo "Joe" Takata, who played baseball for the Asahi, and Goro Kashiwaeda, brother to Asahi great Dick Kashiwaeda. Had Yonamine been shipped out to the 442nd his chances of returning unscathed would have been low. Fortunately for Yonamine, by the time he was drafted the war in Europe was over and Japan surrendered six weeks after he entered basic training.

With the war over, Yonamine was assigned to the 1399th Engineering Construction Battalion stationed at Schofield. He spent much of his military service peeling potatoes and playing for army basketball, baseball, and football teams. Schofield's football team won the region's championship, and Dr. John "Jock" Sutherland, head coach of the Pittsburgh Steelers, selected Yonamine for the Honolulu All-Stars, a team made up of mostly college players serving in the Honolulu area. Yonamine's quick turns and bulldog-like attitude were perfect for Sutherland's coaching style. Sutherland had played football at the University of Pittsburgh under their famed coach Pop Warner, and after graduating with a degree in dentistry, he began his coaching career with Lafayette College in 1919. Sutherland perfected his teams' running game and avoided passing to the point that the ball never took flight during some of his games. Two years later, his team was undefeated and considered the best in the country. Sutherland returned to Pittsburgh in 1924 as their head coach and in fifteen years led the Panthers to a 111-20-12 record, including four undefeated seasons, four Rose Bowl appearances, and the 1937 national championship. He then went on to coach professionally for Brooklyn and the Steelers.

The Honolulu All-Stars were a formidable team and advanced to the Army Pacific Olympics Football Championship game held on January 27, 1946, in Tokyo. The squad boarded a military airplane in Honolulu and, after stops on Wake and Marcus islands to refuel, arrived at Atsugi Airfield twenty hours later. There, they were loaded into army trucks for the ride to Tokyo. As the team rode through the defeated nation, they saw the devastation caused by Allied bombing. Nearly forty years later, Yonamine recalled: "The city was flattened by the bombs and desolate. I was amazed at the dismal condition of the land of my forebears. Wooden shacks, old people wearing torn, cotton-padded clothes, children crowding around GIs who tossed chocolates to them."

January 27 was a miserable day—just above freezing with icy drizzle. The All-Stars faced off against the Eleventh Airborne Division Angels, a strong team that included several pro and many top college players, at the rugby grounds at Meiji Jingu. Yonamine and the other Hawaiian players had never experienced cold like this before, and it showed on the field. "I couldn't stop my legs from shivering," Yonamine commented. The Eleventh Airborne dominated the game, scoring early in the first quarter, then again four minutes later. The Angels added another touchdown in the fourth to win 18–0. Wally's impressions of Tokyo were not good. "It was pitifully poor and very cold." Also, "The food was bad and they didn't have enough. I never wanted to go back to Japan again."

Although the trip was a disappointment for Yonamine, the young Hawaiian impressed Jock Sutherland. While traveling, assistant coach Bill Hargiss spoke with Wally about the possibility of becoming a professional football player, and in May, Sutherland sent Yonamine an invitation to join the Pittsburgh Steelers and a one-year contract for three hundred dollars per game.

Wally considered the offer, but in the end declined. He wanted to attend college and had several scholarship offers from major universities including Southern California, St. Mary's (where Herman Wedemeyer was now playing), and Ohio State. He knew that if he played professionally he would lose his opportunity for a college scholarship. If he signed with the Steelers but didn't last long in the league, he would have lost his opportunity for a good education and a non-sports career. It would be better, he decided, to get an education, play collegiate football for four years, and then turn pro.

During the summer of 1946, Yonamine joined the Leilehua High School Alumni Football Club, known as the Leialum, of the Hawaii Senior League. He, of course, had not attended Leilehua High, but the team practiced near the military base, so they asked Yonamine to join. The Leialums dominated the local teams and decided to travel to the mainland to test their strength against the West Coast universities. Wally received a thirty-day furlough from the army and left with the team for Portland, Oregon, in late September.

Ten thousand spectators entered Multnomah Stadium in down-town Portland on Sunday, September 29, to see the University of Portland Pilots take on the Leialums, now renamed the Hawaiian All-Stars. Sitting among the noisy collegians was a scout for the San Francisco 49ers of the All-American Football Conference (AAFC), who came to watch Charles Kawainui Liu, a promising young Hawaiian-born quarterback for the Pilots. Liu looked good as Portland scored on the first possession, but he was soon forgotten as the Hawaiians began to control the game. The scout focused on the Hawaiians' left halfback, Wally Yonamine, who according to the *Honolulu Advertiser* "knocked off first downs right and left." The Hawaiians scored eight touchdowns that day, and Yonamine converted each of the extra points as well as handling the punting, completing several good passes, and playing outstanding defense. Yonamine's finest play came in the first half on third down and long from the Hawaiians' 40-yard line. Wally took a pitchback and started around the right end as if he was going to sweep wide, but then, still on the run, quick-kicked the ball down to Portland's 11-yard line. The crowd stood up and cheered, while the play caught Portland by surprise and led to a fumble. After the game, the scout contacted the 49ers and praised Yonamine. The report intrigued the head coach, Lawrence "Buck" Shaw, and he sent more scouts to watch the traveling Hawaiians.

The following Saturday, October 5, the All-Stars met Fresno State in front of fourteen thousand fans. Yonamine threw for a touchdown as the visitors, according to the *Los Angeles Times*, "put on a flashy display of wide-open, pass-slinging, hard-running football." But Fresno came from behind to win in the fourth quarter. Six days later, the All-Stars tied San Jose State 19–19 in front of twelve thousand. The Hawaiians were sloppy, fumbling, throwing interceptions, and receiving costly penalties. Yonamine, however, impressed onlookers with his abilities. By this time, the 49ers scouts were not alone. Scouts for several university programs and for the New York Yankees of the AAFC were watching Yonamine closely.

After the San Jose State game, the Hawaiians flew home. Wally and his teammates went directly to downtown Honolulu to grab a bite and visit with friends. Walking around town, Yonamine bumped into several soldiers from his regiment. "Hey!" they cried, "You better get back to the base! The Captain's real mad and might court-martial you!"

"What? Why?" Wally responded.

"You weren't supposed to leave the island! You're AWOL!"

Yonamine hurried back to the base and found Captain Humphreys waiting for him. The Captain detained Wally and quickly arranged for a court-martial. Guards escorted Wally into an office, where half a dozen officers sat facing him. They peppered Wally with questions, but the procedure did not last long and they soon confirmed what they had already guessed. Yonamine was unaware that he had violated his furlough by traveling more than fifty miles from the base. The officers acquitted him and allowed Wally to return to duty.

Wally later discovered that the court-martial was a mere formality. His officers knew that he played on the Leialums and that the team was touring the West Coast. They were planning to look the other way entirely, but Yonamine's performance against Portland and his name in the headlines of the *Honolulu Advertiser* forced their hands. Such a conspicuous violation of a furlough had to be addressed.

After the court-martial, Captain Humphreys told Wally that the colonel wanted to see him. "Uh-oh," thought Wally. "What have I done wrong now?"

The colonel, however, surprised Yonamine by telling him that he could arrange for a basketball scholarship to his alma mater if Wally would like to attend. Yonamine didn't commit himself, as he already had offers for football scholarships. The two discussed basketball for a few minutes before the colonel announced that the Harlem Globetrotters were coming to Hawaii and that he had arranged a game between the famed team and their regimental team.

"Wow, but I can't play."

"What do you mean?" snapped the colonel.

"The Globetrotters are professionals. I don't want to jeopardize my chances at a college scholarship," Wally responded.

The colonel tried to convince Yonamine that the game would not affect his amateur status, but Wally remained stubborn. A scholarship was his chance at college; a chance to leave the plantations and poverty behind him for good. He wasn't going to risk it. Finally, the officer resorted to threats. "Either you play, or I remove you from special service duty!" Wally remained steadfast and refused to play. For the next few months until he was discharged in December, instead of peeling potatoes and playing ball, Yonamine drove a truck.

As 1947 rolled in, Yonamine weighed scholarship offers as well as a three-year professional offer from the New York Yankees of the All-American Football Conference. Dan McGuire, a sportswriter for the *Honolulu Advertiser*, also contacted Wally to tell him that 49ers head coach Buck Shaw would like to watch him work out during Shaw's upcoming Hawaiian vacation. Wally agreed to meet Shaw, but the coach had to cancel the trip.

At last, Wally decided to accept a football scholarship that included tuition, room and board, and even a stipend, from Ohio State. In May, as Yonamine prepared to move to Ohio for the summer semester, the 49ers contacted him again. This time they invited Wally to San Francisco. He boarded a plane on May 6, telling reporters, "I still haven't made up my mind whether to attend college or turn professional. If

Mr. Shaw wants to talk to me, I'll be perfectly willing to see him because I won't be jeopardizing my amateur standing unless I sign a contract."

Shaw was impressed with the young man and offered Wally a two-year fourteen-thousand-dollar contract. He didn't pressure Yonamine to sign, but instead told him to think the offer over. Back in Honolulu, Yonamine consulted with Thomas Yoon, a local real estate developer, who read over the contract and thought it generous. It was a tough decision for Yonamine. He wanted to go to college, but fourteen thousand dollars was a lot of money in 1947, and substantially more than the other professional offers that he had declined. His parents still lived in Olowalu laboring on the plantation, so in the end, he decided that "I ought to help the folks." On May 13, Yonamine accepted the offer and signed the contract.

In a cablegram to the *Honolulu Advertiser*, Coach Shaw announced: "We consider ourselves fortunate to secure Yonamine's services. We expect him to fit into our offense very well. The club will use the T-formation again and we plan to use Wally at right half. I know he'll be a valuable addition."

The following day, the *San Francisco Chronicle* ran an article on Yonamine, noting that "Wallace Yonamine, 5-foot 9-inch, 175 pound halfback, the first American boy of Japanese parentage to break into Major League professional football . . . is expected to provide Coach Buck Shaw the climax runner needed so badly last season." Wally would never have to work on the plantations again.

3 The San Francisco 49ers

Lou Spadia waited a little nervously at the airport gate. The Pan American flight from Honolulu would arrive any minute now, and on it might be the key to a championship season. If Wally Yonamine was really as talented as the scouts claimed, the 49ers would have a dominating offense. The young man felt passionately about his team. He was only the club's gofer, but his dedication would eventually help him become the 49ers' president.

It was a typical July night in San Francisco—windy and cool. Yonamine emerged in a short-sleeve shirt shivering in the chilly air. Spadia took one look at him and declared that first they had to get him a jacket or sweater. They drove to Spadia's apartment and found something for Wally to wear. Afterward, the two men went to dinner. Wally wanted rice with his meal but to his surprise found none on the menu. It was the first of many adjustments Yonamine would have to make. Afterward, Spadia drove Wally to the 49ers' dormitory at their training camp in Menlo Park.

As Wally settled into the dorm at Menlo Park Junior College, thousands of California's Japanese Americans were reestablishing their communities after three years in U.S. government internment camps. San Francisco's Japantown, or Nihonmachi, a thriving community in the Fillmore district of the city, began in the 1860s and grew to 5,280 people by December 1941. After the attack on Pearl Harbor, both the federal and local governments worried that Japanese Americans would supply their mother country with sensitive information or take up arms against the United States. General John L. DeWitt, commander of the Fourth Army, headquartered at San Francisco, began working with local governments to remove all Japanese Americans from proclaimed "strategic areas" in early January 1942. By the beginning of February, all "enemy aliens" were required to register with government authorities, and the FBI started random search and seizures of Japanese American homes and businesses. Faced with this hostile environment, hundreds of Japanese Americans voluntarily moved away from the West Coast and settled in the more tolerant rural Midwest and East Coast. The government soon forcibly removed the remaining inhabitants of Japantown.

The army and the Wartime Civil Control Administration evacuated the first group of Japanese Americans from San Francisco on April 7, 1942. These Federal officials uprooted 644 people, including women, children, and the elderly, and carted them by train to a makeshift camp at Santa Anita Racetrack. The largest forced removals came on April 25–26 and May 6–7, when nearly half of the city's Japanese American population were taken from their homes and brought to Tanforan Assembly Center, a former horse-racing track. There they were housed in clapboard horse stalls, still smelling of their previous tenants. The small stalls were divided into two even smaller rooms—an outer with a sliding door and tiny window, and an interior without ventilation. Five people or a family shared each stall.

Officials removed the last of the city's Japanese population on May 20. The next day, the *San Francisco Chronicle* noted, "For the first time in 81 years, not a single Japanese is walking the streets of San Francisco. . . . Last night Japanese town was empty. Its stores were vacant, its windows plastered with 'To Lease' signs. There were no guests in its hotels, no diners nibbling on sukiyaki or tempura. And last night, too, there were no Japanese with their ever present cameras and sketch books, no Japanese with their newly acquired furtive, frightened looks."

The bulk of the community was transferred to an internment camp at Topaz, Utah. Located in the desert 140 miles south of Salt Lake City, the climate at Topaz was harsh. Temperatures climbed as high as 106 in the summer but plummeted to below freezing in the winter. Constant strong winds swept the camp, causing dust storms. The camp's eight thousand-plus inhabitants were packed in barracks made of pine planks and insulated only with tar paper. During the winter it was nearly as cold inside as out. Children attended school while adult internees were required to work at maintaining the camp for paltry salaries from sixteen to nineteen dollars per month. Some taught the children, some made repairs, others constructed new facilities, cooked meals, gardened, or toiled at a number of other tasks. To ensure that the occupants did not wander off, a barbed wire fence punctuated with observation towers housing armed guards encircled the camp.

While the Japanese were incarcerated at Topaz, a consortium of San Francisco developers and city officials redeveloped Japantown. Parts were condemned and rebuilt, while African Americans moved into other sections and established their own community. After nearly three years, the federal government allowed the Japanese American detainees to return to their former homes, effective January 2, 1945. Many returnees found their former homes destroyed or occupied. Although some did reestablish in Japantown, many Japanese Americans moved to other parts of the city, redefining the community as a web of social ties rather than an ethnic neighborhood.

At this difficult time, the 49ers' signing of Yonamine took on special significance. Many Japanese Americans wanted to assimilate to demonstrate that they were loyal Americans. Perhaps nothing was more American at that time in California than football. By signing with the 49ers, Yonamine became a symbol that Japanese Americans could make it in mainstream American society.

Both the mainstream *San Francisco Chronicle* and the *Examiner* ran articles on Yonamine, and the local Japanese American newspaper featured him constantly. Sumi Tanabe remembers the excitement the news caused. "It was going through the grapevine in Japantown that this kid named Wally Yonamine was coming from Hawaii to play for the 49ers. In those days, there was nobody in the Japanese American community who was really famous and the Japanese don't have a lot of famous athletes. So it was a big thing. For my father, who was a die-hard 49ers fan, having a Japanese kid play on the team was more than he could bear."

Wally was aware of his importance to the community. "It was right after the war and the Nisei had just come out of the relocation camps. So when I went to the 49ers, the Japanese Americans in San Francisco were very happy that there was a Japanese playing on the team. I was a bit of a hero to the Nisei in California." Unfortunately for Yonamine, this responsibility became more than he could manage at his young age.

The first week of the 49ers training camp was filled with meetings, conditioning, and skill contests. On the first day, the coaches handed out the playbooks. Players were responsible for learning sixty to seventy different plays as well as the various formations. For veterans, it was an easy task, but for rookies like Yonamine, all of the plays were new and required close study.

In 1947 the 49ers were just a year old. After trying unsuccessfully to receive a NFL franchise in San Francisco for five years, owner Tony Morabito cast his lot with the new All-American Football Conference for the inaugural 1946 season. Morabito hired Buck Shaw, who had guided Santa Clara College to two Sugar Bowl victories, to lead the team. Shaw decided to build the 49ers around Bay Area talent. To lead his team, Shaw signed Frankie Albert, a lightning-quick southpaw quarterback from Stanford with a strong, accurate arm. In the late 1940s, professional football was primarily a running game, but Albert would throw for over a thousand yards in each of his six seasons as the 49ers' starting quarterback.

Albert's primary receiver was Alyn Beals. Beals recalled, "Buck Shaw was a great innovator. . . . He was one of the first coaches to start spreading the ends out. We used to have the ends spread only about a foot. He kept spreading them off the tackles a little at a time. It opened up the passing game." Beals became the league's premier receiver. He was named to the All-League team three times and is the AAFC's all-time scoring leader.

Shaw's exciting offense outscored their opponents in each of the team's four seasons in the AAFC. Overall, the 49ers tallied 1,545 points to their opponents' 928. The franchise had a successful first season, finishing second to the Cleveland Browns, but Shaw realized that the missing puzzle piece was a breakaway back—a halfback with great speed who could turn a game around with long gains. He hoped that Yonamine would fill that role.

In the first week of camp, Yonamine joined the team punting contest and finished third, kicking the ball 60½ yards. When Jack McDonald, a sportswriter for the *San Francisco Call-Bulletin*, commented that Yonamine's punting abilities might have been overrated, a visiting Hawaiian quickly countered, "But you haven't seen Yonamine kick them on the fly. Just wait until you watch him start around the end as if he were going to make a wide sweep and then boot the ball down the field on the dead run. That's a trick that'll have the opposing clubs standing on their heads, to say nothing of the customers."

During camp the players stayed in a dormitory and were treated each morning to buffet breakfasts. Halfback Earle Parsons called the spread fantastic and ogled guard Garland Gregory's tray, which was piled high with six eggs, three puffy hotcakes, a side order of bacon, a box of cereal, a glass of tomato juice, two pieces of toast, and a cup of coffee. But not all of the players were happy. Wally shyly approached Coach Buck Shaw to complain. Bruce Lee, the beat writer for the *San Francisco Chronicle*, overheard the conversation and ran it in the Friday, August 1, paper under the headline "49ers Chow-Chow, Then Worry." The story poked fun at Yonamine's Hawaiian accent and grammar.

> *Wally Yonamine, the Hawaiian halfback, slid into a seat next to Coach Buck Shaw. He had a worried look on his face.*
>
> *"Coach," he said, shaking his head. "This is no good."*
>
> *"What's the matter, Wally?"*
>
> *"I don't eat. I lose twelve pounds."*
>
> *Shaw instantly was alarmed. "You bet that's not good. What's the trouble? Aren't you getting enough?"*

"No, no. That's not it. But coach, why we get no rice?"

So now Wally Yonamine is on a special diet of rice, cooked however he wants it, whenever he wants it.

It was the first time that Lee wrote about Yonamine, and his tone toward the Hawaiian would change within a few days.

The 49ers scrimmaged for the first time on Saturday, August 2. Shaw pitted the first-string defense against the offense. Although Yonamine did not play much, he carried the ball successfully, causing Bruce Lee to write, "Wally Yonamine, operating behind a second-string line, didn't have much opportunity to show his quick starting and step-and-go technique, although once he did squeeze through a hole over left tackle that promptly closed behind him, and shifted out of the grasp of three tacklers for 22 yards and justification of his Wedemeyerish reputation."

"Wedemeyerish" was, of course, a reference to Yonamine's old rival Herman Wedemeyer. After leaving high school in Honolulu, Wedemeyer became an All-American at St. Mary's College in California. His acrobatics in the backfield had made him a national celebrity. On Sunday, August 3, Lee wrote an article entitled, "Yonamine Another Wedey?" He told readers about the 1942 game between Wedemeyer's St. Louis team and Yonamine's Lahainaluna squad, before providing fans with a few facts about Wally and his background. The favorable article noted many other pundits' comments that Yonamine might indeed be another Herman Wedemeyer.

On Shaw's orders the cooks tried to prepare rice for Wally, but with little success. Yonamine remembers, "the dormitory cooks didn't know how to make rice. They didn't clean it and it would often be half cooked." Then, one day there was a knock on the dormitory door. Wally opened it and looked down on a skinny, older Japanese American man with a thin mustache.

"You don't know who I am, but I'm Frank Furiuchi," the stranger said. "I read in the newspaper that you weren't getting fed properly and are losing weight. I'd like to take you to my house for a good home-cooked meal."

The surprised young Hawaiian smiled. "I'd like to come on my first day off."

Later that week, Furiuchi picked up Yonamine at the dorm and they drove to the outskirts of the city, where Furiuchi owned a small farm with a nursery. As Wally got out of the car, he noticed a peach tree, full of ripe fruit, growing beside the house. "That was the first time that I ever saw peaches in a tree instead of in a can! So I climbed the tree and started eating them up! I must have eaten about fifteen. The Furiuchis were yelling, 'Get Down! Get Down!' They thought that I was going to get sick." The home-cooked meal was wonderful, and Furiuchi drove Wally back to the team's dormitory. Yonamine joined the family at their home many more times, and they started introducing him to other Japanese Americans in the San Francisco and San Jose areas.

Nearly four hundred Nisei joined the thirty-one hundred fans at Salinas Union High School on August 8 to watch Yonamine play in the 49ers' first intrasquad game. Coach Shaw divided the team into red and white squads with the Reds containing most of the starting offense. Shaw placed Yonamine as a substitute on the Reds to give him experience with the starting lineup. Before the game, Bruce Lee wrote: "The game tonight will present the first real test of the Hawaiian flash, Wally Yonamine at halfback. . . . Yonamine, in the practice scrimmages, has indicated that he knows what to do when he sees daylight through an opposing line, but hasn't really been tested under pressure, and . . . there'll be plenty of pressure tonight."

Yonamine responded well to the pressure. He started the scoring in the first quarter when he caught a punt on the 11-yard line, cut 7 yards to his left and sprinted down the sideline for an 89-yard touchdown. He also finished the scoring by snaring a 25-yard touchdown pass to win the game. In between, Yonamine caught three passes and racked up 20 yards on eight carries, while on defense he blocked two passes and intercepted another.

Yonamine starred again the following week in another intrasquad game. Once again he scored twice and propelled the Reds to victory. After catching a 25-yard pass from quarterback Bev Wallace, Yonamine

outran the defense for 40 yards to score his first touchdown. The
second came on a 38-yard run. The next day, the *Hawaiian Times*
proclaimed, "Wally Yonamine proved beyond all doubt [that] he will
be as dangerous as any back in the conference."

Wally and the 49ers geared up for their first preseason game against
the Los Angeles Dons on August 25. The game, however, did not go as
planned for the 49ers. Plagued by fumbles, the 49ers fell to the Dons
14–7. Coach Shaw used Yonamine sparingly on the offense, limiting
him to only three carries, and each time the Dons threw him for a
loss. Wally took the field for punt and kick returns, but his reputation
preceded him and the Dons' kickers kept the ball away from him.

Off the field, Wally' social life had begun to improve. He had missed
the Japanese community of Hawaii and wanted to recreate that
experience in San Francisco. Frank Furiuchi contacted Bill Mizono, a
young man about Wally's age who had grown up in Japantown, and
asked him to show Yonamine around. Mizono agreed and the two
young men soon became close friends.

Mizono remembers, "I was like his tour guide and his sponsor. I took
him to Japanese American picnics in Golden Gate Park and community
functions. Wally was very shy, but very nice and personable. Because he
was the first Oriental to play professional sports in the United States,
he was quite a celebrity in the San Francisco Japanese community.
That put me in a nice situation. When we wanted dates, I would just
make phone calls and all the girls said sure. I had his leftovers, which
were pretty good! When you are a celebrity, and especially in sports,
you can get anything. But Wally remained good—always a gentleman.
He was conscious about his clean cut image. He felt that if it got back
to Hawaii that he was misbehaving, it would hinder the reputation of
all Japanese Americans. I told him that he was an idiot!"

Sumi Tanabe's father, Jiro Hosoda, had also read Lee's newspaper
article about the lack of rice in Wally's diet. Like Furiuchi, Hosoda
wanted to help and asked Bill Mizuno to introduce him to Wally.
Wally visited the Hosodas for dinner and the family fell in love with
the polite young man. Sumi recalls, "He was such a nice person that

people like my parents just wanted to do things for him. So usually on the weekends, he would come over for dinner." Yonamine had been living at a nondescript hotel, but after a few visits Hosoda said, "Why are you staying in a hotel? Why don't you stay with us?" So Wally moved into Jiro's cavernous two-story Victorian home in Japantown. The majestic house with high ceilings had undoubtedly been built for a wealthy entrepreneur, but by the late 1940s it had been divided into two flats. Jiro, his wife Toshiko, and their two young children Sumi and Satoru lived on the ground floor. A separate family lived above, but both shared the front entrance and the only bathroom. Toshiko Hosoda converted the parlor into a bedroom for Wally and made him feel at home. Wally never forgot the family's kindness. He diligently wrote to Toshiko Hosoda at least twice a year for the next five decades and in every letter thanked her for helping him. When she passed away in 2002, Wally flew to San Francisco to attend the funeral despite being in the early stages of recovery from cancer surgery. Knowing Wally's physical condition, the children were deeply touched.

Going into the official start of the season, Yonamine was an incredible bundle of nerves. He worried about living up to the expectations of the Japanese American community and fretted over lingering anti-Japanese sentiment in the Bay Area. He also worried about playing in front of the large crowds the 49ers drew at Kezar Stadium, a massive picturesque oval holding sixty thousand paying customers, located next to the lush trees of San Francisco's spectacular thousand-acre Golden Gate Park.

On opening day, as the Niners and the visiting Brooklyn Dodgers took the field, Yonamine sat on the bench with the other reserves and gaped with wonder at the vast shirt-sleeved crowd, reported as thirty-two thousand but appearing much larger, roaring in the warm Sunday afternoon sun. How can anyone not get butterflies in the face of such a spectacle, he wondered. How could anyone play his best under such pressure?

The 49ers certainly had their work cut out for them. Glen Dobbs, the Dodgers left halfback, was the league's finest passer and the previous season's Most Valuable Player. Three minutes into the game, Dobbs connected with fullback Mickey Comer to put Brooklyn ahead. But that would be all for Dobbs. The 49ers' defense took over and had an outstanding game and limited Dobbs to just 8 completions in 23 attempts. On the other side of the ball, the 49ers' offense dominated the game, scoring 23 points.

Yonamine played only one down. Buck Shaw later told reporters, "I wanted to throw in a whole flock of subs and get a line on them but [I didn't] feel safe with that son-of-a-gun [Dobbs] opposing [us]." Shaw especially wanted to use Yonamine to see how he reacted under the pressure of a league game. But he noticed how tense Yonamine was.

"On the bench he [Yonamine] was all upset," Shaw told reporters. "This was the second biggest crowd he ever saw in his life—the largest was just seven days ago—and he was worrying about how the people would accept him. He is extremely conscious of being a Japanese. I try to tell him everything is okay, but he worries anyhow." In the end, Shaw decided to put Yonamine in during a low-pressure situation and chose a third down with the ball in the 49ers' territory, late in the game.

Bruce Lee surmised that the next game against the Los Angeles Dons would be Yonamine's chance to grab the spotlight. On Sunday morning, Lee wrote under the heading "WATCH YONAMINE": "Wally Yonamine, the Nisei half-back from Honolulu, may have a big share in this passing duel, too. Coach Buck Shaw plans to 'spot' Yonamine (that is, use him when his quick start and breakaway potentialities can be realized), and it would be an ideal situation to fling one of those quick flank passes to Wally and then let him take off." But once again, Yonamine saw little action. Wally carried the ball once and caught a pass but gained no yardage on either play during the 49ers' 17–14 victory in front of 31,298 fans.

The following Sunday against the Baltimore Colts, Yonamine once again remained on the sidelines for most of the game. Shaw put Wally in during the fourth quarter at right halfback and he responded with a

7-yard gain in his only carry. The *Pacific Citizen* noted sympathetically that the young Yonamine was still suffering from stage fright. He "gets all tied up on the San Francisco 49er bench and can't do his best work when sent in at halfback. Yonamine is afraid that the great big crowds at Kezar—biggest he's ever seen in his life—won't accept him as a U.S. citizen because of his ancestry. In Honolulu, yes; on the mainland, no. That's what he thinks, though he's an ex-GI." Coach Shaw, attempting to rectify the problem, focused on Yonamine during practice before the game with the New York Yankees.

Fifty-seven thousand packed Kezar Stadium to watch the 49ers challenge the 1946 Eastern Division champion Yankees. After the 49ers scored a quick field goal, the Yankees controlled the game and built up a 21–10 lead going into the fourth quarter. Yonamine carried the ball only once in the first three quarters and was thrown for a 3-yard loss. In the fourth quarter, however, Wally set up the 49ers' final touchdown as he caught a 15-yard pass from Frankie Albert to move the ball to the Yankees' 30. The 49ers scored on the next play as Albert connected with Ed Balatti.

The fine catch seemed to settle Yonamine down and help him overcome his fears. The following Sunday in Buffalo, Shaw began to use Wally on the kickoff return team. In the late 1940s, there were no special teams in professional football: teams were limited to three substitutions per play. On kickoff and punt returns, however, it was usual to put the team's best kick returners into the game. Hoping to capitalize on Yonamine's quickness, Shaw began officially inserting the Hawaiian at quarterback. Once the 49ers received the kick, star quarterback Frankie Albert would take his usual spot and Wally would return to the bench. When this occurred, Yonamine would be officially listed as the team's starting quarterback.

Over thirty-five thousand people, the largest crowd in the city's history to watch a professional sporting event, filed in to watch the 3-1 Bills challenge the 3-1 49ers. The Bills dominated the first three quarters and led 24–7 in the third quarter as they punted from deep in their territory. On the punt return team, Yonamine stood waiting for the ball. The kick was short but high. Wally ran up, caught it on the fly as white jerseys bore down upon him, cut back, and streaked through a small opening. He made it 25 yards to the Bills' 28-yard line before being pulled down. Yonamine stayed in the game for the next play. They pitched back to him, and Wally shot by the right end for a 5-yard gain. Moments later, the 49ers scored. Yonamine's punt return sparked a San Francisco comeback. The 49ers piled up 34 unanswered points in under 24 minutes to win the game 41–24. After beating the Bills, the team traveled south to Baltimore to take on the Colts, who surprised the 49ers by building a fourth-quarter 28–14 lead. Frankie Albert, however, led the 49ers back with two quick touchdowns to salvage a 28–28 tie. Yonamine saw little action but did get in the game at halfback.

Used to the ethnic diversity of Hawaii, Yonamine found traveling in the mainland United States a bit unnerving. He was surprised, for example, to see white waiters. In Hawaii, Caucasians rarely held service positions. He remembers, "We used to stay in the best hotels and go to nice restaurants, and I would be the only Oriental in the hotel—everyone else was Caucasian. At first, I felt a little funny being there, and I would kind of hold back a little bit. But after a while I got used to it. My teammates were so nice to me, especially my roommate Ed Carr. He and I went out all the time. So I was okay."

Yonamine's teammates were friendly and accepted him readily. Guard Garland Gregory remembers Wally as very congenial and liked by the whole squad. The younger players and Wally would go out to dinner and socialize together. On one occasion, the Hosodas invited some of the 49ers to their home for sukiyaki. It was probably the first Japanese food that the Caucasian players had tasted.

But on the gridiron, Wally became a target. It was just two years after the end of World War II, and anti-Japanese feelings were still high across the United States. Often the bigotry was directed toward Nisei. Bill Mizono recalls, "Wally told me things that I don't think anybody else knew. Sometimes when the opposing teams would gang-tackle him, they would punch him, kick him, or pinch him. The war was just over and they wanted to take it out on somebody, and they considered him a Jap. But he never set a word about it to the press or anybody else because he didn't want to be seen as a complainer or draw negative attention."

Returning home to Kezar, Wally finally had the game his fans were waiting for against the hapless Chicago Rockets. The Hawaiian started at right halfback and remained in the game as the 49ers scored three unanswered touchdowns in the first quarter. Playing much of the game, Yonamine averaged 4.7 yards per carry in eight attempts, including a 17-yard run, and caught two passes for 15- and 9-yard gains. Wally also played well on defense, saving a touchdown by intercepting a Rocket pass in the 49ers' end zone. The 42–28 victory gave the 49ers their fifth win of the season and moved them into a tie for first place in the Western Division with the Cleveland Browns.

On October 26, the Browns rolled into San Francisco for a first-place showdown. A sellout crowd of 54,325 packed Kezar on a cold and blustery day to cheer on the 49ers, but the Browns, led by future Hall of Famer Otto Graham, were too strong. Graham completed 19 of 25 passes for 278 yards as the Browns dominated the game. Only three fumbles kept the game close, as the Browns won 14–7. Despite his strong effort against the Colts, Yonamine saw no action in this important game.

After their loss, the 49ers began a six-game road trip. They started in nearby Los Angeles with a 26–16 victory over the Dons on November 2. Once again, Wally did not play. The team then flew to New York to play the Yankees. If Wally had been looking forward to seeing the Big Apple, he would be disappointed. The team stayed at the Bear Mountain Inn, roughly an hour north of Manhattan, to avoid the distractions of the big city. At Yankee Stadium Shaw decided to use Yonamine on the opening kickoff return team, thereby making him the official starting quarterback. The 49ers jumped out to a 16–0 lead but were unable to contain the Yankees, who narrowed the score to 16–14. In the middle of the game, Shaw decided to let Yonamine see some action.

A boisterous crowd of 37,342 was on hand at the famous stadium. Yonamine looked up at the crowd and the jitters returned. Although the temperature was only in the forties, it felt bitter cold to the young Hawaiian. As he went to the line of scrimmage for the first play, he took a deep breath and watched it stream out in front of him. He crouched down and his legs started to buckle from the cold and nervousness. Luckily, the play went off without a disaster, and Wally immediately calmed down. After a few plays, Wally returned to the bench. The Yankees scored ten unanswered points in the fourth quarter to give the 49ers their fourth loss and dashing their hopes of overtaking the first-place Browns.

The next Sunday, the Browns captured the title by defeating the 49ers 37–14 in front of seventy-seven thousand Cleveland fans. The 49ers finished up their season with wins against the Chicago Rockets and Brooklyn Dodgers and tying the Buffalo Bills. Wally played sparing in these final games, as San Francisco clinched second place in the Western Division.

Even through Yonamine did not develop into the breakaway running back that coach Buck Shaw envisioned, Wally was pleased with his rookie season. He played in 10 games, made three receptions for 40 yards, and carried the ball 19 times for 74 yards for a respectable 3.9 yards per carry average. A mainstay on kickoff and punt returns, Yonamine ran back seven kickoffs for 127 yards and two punts for 29 yards. On defense, he made one interception.

"At the end of my rookie season, I felt that during the next season, I would get a chance to play and that it would be my year. In the first year, I had to get used to the league and learn all the plays and formations, and I didn't do too badly. Back then, they hardly used the rookies. So the first year was really just a learning experience for me. Once I had some experience and knew the formations, I thought I would get more chances to play." As it turned out, however, fate had something else in store for him.

4 Lucky Breaks

At the end of the 49ers' campaign, Wally returned to Honolulu with one goal: to make himself stronger for the following season. He took a job at a trucking company, figuring that lifting and carrying cargo would help build his muscles, and rejoined the Athletics, a Senior League baseball team that he had played for the previous spring, to keep himself in shape.

The Athletics, previously known as the Asahi, were the elite Japanese American team in the Hawaiian Islands. Founded in 1905 as a team for Japanese thirteen- and fourteen-year-olds, the Asahi soon dominated the AJA (Americans of Japanese Ancestry) Oahu Junior League. Finally, in 1920, league organizers decided that the team was too strong and moved the youths into the adult AJA Honolulu Baseball League. Three years later, the Asahi won the championship.

In 1924 the multiethnic Hawaii Baseball League was formed with six teams. Original members included the Portuguese Braves, the All-Chinese, the All-Hawaiians, the All-Filipinos, the Elks (made up of haoles) and the Asahi. With no age restrictions, Asahi recruited the best players from the AJA leagues throughout the islands. The Japanese team fared well, winning championships in 1925, '26, '29, '30, and '38. Japanese Hawaiians followed the Asahi's triumphs closely, and Hawaii's two Japanese-language newspapers, the *Hawaii Times* and *Hawaii Hochi*, covered the games and players in detail. The ballpark also became a meeting place for the community as thousands of ethnic Japanese came to Honolulu Stadium for each game.

With the outbreak of World War II, Japanese Hawaiians strove to show their loyalty to the United States. Many, including Asahi owner Dr. Katsumi Kometani, volunteered for the armed forces. With Kometani's permission, the team downplayed its Japanese affiliation. John A. Burns, the future governor of Hawaii, ran the team in Kometani's absence, while future Honolulu mayor Neal Blaisdell managed. The two haoles changed the team's name to the Athletics and added several non-Japanese to the roster. The club did well and captured the 1942 championship. Kometani returned in 1945, reestablished the team's all–Japanese American roster, and appointed Allen Nagata as manager. The team, however, remained the Athletics until it retook the Asahi name after the 1949 season.

On the Athletics, Wally formed two friendships in particular that lasted a lifetime and helped change the history of Japanese baseball. Jyun Hirota, known to his friends as Curly on account of his full head of wavy hair, was the team's catcher. Hirota grew up on Ewa Plantation near Pearl Harbor, excelled at both academics and sports, and enrolled at McKinley High School in 1937. There, he played varsity baseball but was cut from the football team because he stood just 5 feet 6 inches tall and weighed only 130 pounds. After high school, Hirota entered the University of Hawaii, paying tuition through a variety of odd jobs and working on the plantations during summers. He continued to play baseball in college and joined the ROTC.

One peaceful Sunday morning, Jyun and his teammates were preparing for a scrimmage in the hills overlooking Pearl Harbor when loud explosions and smoke attracted the team's attention. They looked down to see the naval base in flames and Japanese airplanes flying above. Immediately after the attack, the university summoned its ROTC cadets, armed them with rifles, and had them guard public utilities. Jyun joined the Varsity Victory Volunteers, a group of University of Hawaii Nisei students, and was stationed at Schofield Barracks. There, Hirota played baseball and football for regimental teams. He even played against Joe and Dominic DiMaggio and caught future Yankees' star pitcher Joe Page. After the war, Hirota returned to the University of Hawaii—this time on baseball and football scholarships. He starred at both sports and was named captain of the football team his senior year. During school breaks, Hirota played for the Athletics and quickly became known as one of the most talented and toughest catchers in the league.

Wally also became friendly with the team's third baseman, Dick Kashiwaeda. Dick was the youngest of seven children from Makaeli, Kauai, and both of his older brothers starred in the AJA leagues. The eldest, Kenneth Goro Kashiwaeda, was offered a professional contact from the Hanshin Tigers of Osaka, Japan, immediately before the outbreak of the war. Unable to accept the offer, Goro joined the 442nd Infantry and died in Italy.

Because of Goro's ability, coaches kept their eyes on young Dick, and he began playing in the AJA leagues at only thirteen years old. He was soon recruited by the St. Louis School in Honolulu and played high school ball with football sensation Herman Wedemeyer. In 1943, directly after graduating high school, he joined the adults on the Asahi. Kashiwaeda could hit for power as well as average and was superb defensively. Carl Machado of the magazine *Nisei* couldn't avoid clichés to describe his smooth fielding. "His cat-like pouncing on ground balls with the grace and rhythm of a ballet dancer, stamps him as poetry in motion."

The Athletics/Asahi excelled at small ball. Knowing that outslugging the larger non-Japanese opponents would be difficult, the smaller and more agile Nisei perfected their defense, practiced bunting and the hit and run, and ran the bases aggressively. The team played for one run at a time and tried to pressure their opponents' defense into mistakes. They always tried to score first, luring their opponents to abandon their game plans and swing for the fences in an effort to catch up. The coaches instilled the philosophy "if you score one run, they have to score two to beat you."

When Wally Yonamine came to the Athletics, Dick Kashiwaeda remembers him as a raw player, but a hustler and strong. Under the tutelage of Allen Nagata and the other Athletics coaches, Wally learned many of the skills that would make him a star in Japan. Yonamine soon became a superb bunter and a master of the hit and run, but with his football background Wally was even more aggressive than many of his Nisei teammates. He asked coaches to hit fly balls over his head and practiced running back, football-style, to catch them over his shoulder. This skill allowed him to play shallow, thereby turning would-be line-drive singles into outs. Within a year, he became a fine defensive outfielder and a feared hitter.

By the 1948 season, the Hawaii Baseball League had grown to nine teams. A second Japanese American team, known as the Rural Red Sox, was added in 1946 and became the Athletics' chief rival. Both teams started fast in 1948. On June 13, the Athletics and Red Sox were tied for first place with 7-1 records. Yonamine was playing well, batting leadoff and playing center field. In the last two weeks of June, Yonamine saw the ball particularly well, gathering seven hits in twelve at bats, but the Athletics dropped two games to the Red Sox and fell into second place.

In the first week of July, the Athletics traveled to Hilo on the Big Island for an exhibition game. Yonamine led off as usual and stroked a hit into the outfield. He rounded first and decided to try for second. As he approached the bag, Wally realized that the throw would beat him. His only chance was a fade-away slide to avoid the tag. He purposely slid away from the bag and reached for the base with his left hand. He missed and his hand slammed into the dirt. As Wally got up and jogged back to the bench, his hand began to throb. Soon, it started to swell. After the game, Yonamine went to the hospital, and an X-ray revealed a small fracture in the back of his hand. The doctors put on a cast and sent Wally home. The injury ended Yonamine's baseball season, but more importantly, preseason camp for the 49ers started in just two weeks.

At midnight on July 17, Wally boarded a Pan American Clipper bound for San Francisco. His hand still bore the cast, but he was optimistic about his chances. The previous evening he told a small gathering in his honor, "I'm going to do my best to make good this season. I know my hand will be okay before we start the intersquad games."

Yonamine arrived at Menlo Park Junior College for the start of training camp on July 19. Alarmed at his injury, the 49ers quickly had the club physician examine the hand. It had begun to heal but the cast was still needed for another three to six weeks. Although Yonamine could run, the cast made passing impossible, and scrimmaging was out of the question. Wally would not be ready to practice until just before the season began.

During the off-season the 49ers had made significant changes. They signed seventeen rookies and eventually brought back only sixteen members of the 1947 squad. Their most important pickup was an African American running back with a granite build named Joe Perry, who had been playing for Alameda Naval Air Station. He was a powerful man, capable of bowling over tacklers, but more importantly he was a quick starter with an uncanny ability to find tiny holes in the opponent's defense and bolt through them. By the time he retired in 1963, "the Jet" had rushed for more yards than any other man in the history of the NFL and would eventually make the Football Hall of Fame. Perry's acquisition made Wally Yonamine expendable.

About two weeks into camp, Wally was summoned to the coach's office. Head coach Buck Shaw and owner Tony Morabito sat waiting for him. The two explained to a downcast Yonamine that the team had a wealth of running backs and that he was one of the most inexperienced. They couldn't keep him on the roster while he healed and then just throw him into the regular season games without practice. Morabito pointed out that Wally's contract stipulated that he had to be physically fit at the start of preseason camp. With his hand in a cast and unable to practice, Wally was obviously not physically fit and thus had violated the contract. Therefore, Morabito continued, the 49ers were voiding the second year of the contract and giving him his unconditional release. He was, however, welcome to return to camp the following year as a nonroster player if he wanted to try to make the team and gain a new contract.

Yonamine left camp the next day and returned to Hawaii. "I was naturally very disappointed, really sad. Football was the sport that I really loved. In the off season, I just fooled around with baseball.

Moreover, I wouldn't receive the other seven thousand dollars and that was a lot of money back then. A cup of coffee at a San Francisco restaurant was only five cents. But I didn't blame the 49ers. I was the one who got injured."

Within a week of his release, the Hawaii Warriors contacted Yonamine and made him an offer for the 1948 fall season. Wally accepted and began preparing. He took a job with Wilson Sporting Goods and after his hand healed joined the team's workouts, held in the evenings as most players had daytime jobs. The Warriors were the reigning champions of the Pacific Coast Pro Football League (PCPFL). Founded in 1940, it was officially a minor league, but before the NFL and the AAFC came to California in 1946, the PCPFL was one of the most important professional leagues in the country. As the only professional league on the West Coast from 1940 to 1943, the PCPFL games drew well. The league fielded strong teams filled with West Coast players and African American stars barred from playing in the NFL because of their race. After NFL and AAFC franchises moved to the West Coast in 1946, the popularity of the PCPFL declined, and the league was thrown into a financial crisis. Several teams were unable to stay afloat and ended the season early.

Although attendance waned on the West Coast in 1946, the new franchise in Honolulu boomed. The Hawaiian Warriors played all of their games at Honolulu Stadium, with visiting franchises playing both of their league games during the same visit to save on travel expenses. The Warriors finished second to the Los Angeles Bulldogs during their inaugural season, and in 1947 captured the title with a 7-2 record. But a week after the season ended, four Warriors, including Buddy Abreu, the league's leading scorer and rusher, were permanently suspended for betting on the outcome of the final game. With the scandal and the unrelated failure of two of the league's five teams, the PCPFL tottered on the brink of extinction. In 1948, however, the Hollywood Bears rejoined the PCPFL after sitting out the 1947 season, thus bringing the league up to four teams and saving the upcoming season.

The Warriors were scheduled for six league games, starting on October 1 and ending on November 28. Most of the media doubted that Warriors could overcome the loss of star running back Abreu, and picked the L.A. Bulldogs as the preseason favorites. The Warriors, however, believed that Yonamine would bring the team back into contention. In a preseason exhibition game with the L.A. Rams, Wally turned his ankle and had to sit out the opening game of the regular season against the Bulldogs. Without Yonamine, the Warriors scraped by with a 7–6 victory.

"Wally Yonamine, a sturdy lad capable of breaking up any football game, will be the Hawaiian Warriors chief running hope when they meet the Los Angeles Bulldogs in a Pacific Coast Football League rematch at the Stadium tonight," the *Honolulu Advertiser*'s lead paragraph blared on Friday, October 8. But Yonamine's comeback was short-lived. During the opening kickoff, Wally received a blow to the head and had to be helped off the field. Team doctors examined Wally in the dressing room and determined that the injury was not serious, but to prevent further mishap he remained on the sidelines for the rest of the game. Once again, the Warriors faced the Bulldogs without their first-string back. This time they did not escape—the Bulldogs crushed the Hawaiians 34–7. It was the franchise's worst defeat since joining the league.

The Warriors had two weeks off before welcoming the Hollywood Bears to warm Hawaii for a pair of games on October 30 and November 5. The break allowed Wally's ailments to heal, and he started at right halfback against the Bears on October 30. Only four thousand spectators filed into Honolulu Stadium—the smallest crowd ever to attend a professional football game there. The Warriors handled the Bears easily, defeating them 28–12. Yonamine played much of the game and scored a touchdown on "a neat double reverse" in his first full game as a Warrior.

The following Friday night, the Warriors crushed Hollywood 75–21. "Yonamine sparks locals to one-sided pro grid victory," proclaimed a *Honolulu Advertiser* headline. Wally seemed to rush up the field at will, setting up three touchdowns with long gains, completed two touchdown passes, and scored twice himself, one a 40-yard run on a Statue of Liberty play.

The PCPFL postponed several games in mid-November while officials pondered the league's financial stability. In late November, games resumed and the San Francisco Clippers arrived in Honolulu. Excited by the Warriors' powerful offense, eleven thousand fans came to the stadium to watch the game on November 28 despite driving rains. As strong winds intensified the rain, Yonamine "whirling and squirming" ran for 63- and 34-yard touchdowns and threw into the end zone for another touchdown. Wally also made two interceptions, returning one for a touchdown.

A week later, the Warriors pummeled the Clippers 45–7 in the final game of the season. Wally rushed for two touchdowns and set up another with a 56-yard scramble after catching an 11-yard pass. The Warriors finished with a 5-1 record to clinch a tie for the league championship with Los Angeles, which had three wins and a loss with two games remaining. The Warriors waited for the outcome of the final two games, but they were never played. Attendance on the West Coast had been dismal—one Bulldogs game held in Long Beach drew only 850 spectators—and the Pacific Coast Pro Football League folded without completing the schedule.

Yonamine entered 1949 with the future of his football career uncertain. Although the PCPFL was defunct, the Honolulu Warriors remained intact. Hopefully, the league would reform or the Warriors would join another league. Also, Wally still had the invitation to try out for the 49ers. He had shown that he was among the top players in minor league football, and perhaps he would fulfill his potential with the 49ers in the upcoming season. In the meantime, Wally played winter baseball with Waialae of the Honolulu AJA League. He won the league's batting title and, along with teammate Dick Kashiwaeda, was named to the All-Star team.

In early March a letter arrived from the 49ers officially inviting Yonamine to Menlo Park on July 25 to try out. Although there could have been little hesitation in Wally's mind, he did not announce his acceptance for several months. In the meantime, he finished up the AJA winter season and joined the Athletics for the summer baseball season.

The Senior League season began on May 8 with the Athletics easily defeating the Tigers 8–4 as Yonamine smacked a double in a four-run fourth-inning rally that sealed the game. The Athletics dropped the next game to the rival Red Sox, but more importantly for Yonamine's future, the Hawaiian Warriors' board of directors met the same week to decide the team's future. The board agreed to officially end their affiliation with the PCPFL and join another viable league in the near future. In the meantime, the Warriors would tour the East Coast in the fall of 1949 and play teams in the American Pro League.

Wally continued to hit well in the Senior League, but the Athletics slumped despite his efforts. In early June, with the Athletics in fifth place, the 49ers sent Wally another letter encouraging him to attend the preseason tryout. A couple of days later, Wally announced that he would accept the 49ers' offer and try out for the team. "This time I feel that I'll make the grade," is all he told reporters. Two days later, the *Honolulu Advertiser* ran an editorial suggesting that if Wally didn't make the 49ers, he should stay on the West Coast and try out for a Pacific Coast League (PCL) baseball team. "Yonamine is just as good a ballplayer as he is a gridder. He is a long hitter, a brilliant fielder with a swell arm, and in general a mighty fine ballplayer," editor Red Mc-Queen gushed. "He would be worth money to a team like Sacramento, if only for his appeal to California's many Japanese fans." McQueen also added, "The P.C.L. has already lifted its ban against colored players, so there shouldn't be any racial barriers against Yonamine."

Wally remained with the Athletics until it was time for him to leave for San Francisco. In his last game, he went 2 for 3 on July 17 as the Athletics beat the Fil-Americans 10–1. A week later, Yonamine was at Menlo Park. The first two weeks of camp were uneventful. Wally went through the usual preseason training sessions and learned the new plays. In his third year at camp, Wally knew most of the players and was comfortable with the team's routines. The competition was tough as the 49ers' starting backfield all returned. The team's reserve running backs from the 1948 season were in camp, and so were three promising rookies, Sam Cathcart, Don Garlin, and Bob Lund, who were actually challenging the veterans for starting roles.

On Saturday, August 6, the scrimmages began. Assigned number 94, Yonamine joined the veterans' Red team as a substitute. The more promising younger players and the experienced reserves started on the opposing White team. Despite the sunny, warm afternoon only 11,154 of the expected 20,000 spectators watched the Reds cruise to a sloppy 30–0 victory. The overall poor play hampered Coach Buck Shaw's ability to evaluate the younger players. He had hoped to cut his squad to a more manageable size based on the performances in the scrimmage, but after the game he announced that he would cut only half a dozen players and would need another scrimmage to evaluate the other rookies. The rookie backs Cathcart and Garlin distinguished themselves in the contest, almost guaranteeing themselves a roster spot.

Wally played much of the game at left halfback. At times, "he shot through the openings like a bolt of lightning" and looked uncatchable. Late in the fourth quarter, he grabbed a Frankie Albert pass on the 27-yard line and streaked into the end zone. Unfortunately, the touchdown and flashes of brilliance could not outweigh several fumbles Wally committed, each time dropping the ball before reaching the line of scrimmage. The following day, Shaw cut ten players, including Yonamine. It seemed that nervousness had once again plagued Wally and undermined his dream of playing for the 49ers. Columnist Hal Wood wrote, "There have been thousands of other athletes who had all the courage in the world—but got stage fright when they took the spotlight before a big crowd. It just happens that Yonamine falls into that category—otherwise he might have become one of the great football players of the time."

Despondent, Wally returned to Honolulu and rejoined the Athletics. He finished out the Senior League season and, along with teammate Jyun Hirota, was given honorable mention in the postseason All-Star selection. Dick Kashiwaeda made the All-Star team.

In mid-August, Yonamine rejoined the Hawaiian Warriors, who were preparing for a month-long tour of the East Coast. The Warriors met the local semipro All-Stars at Honolulu Stadium on August 19 in a warmup match. Nearly eleven thousand fans watched a dull game as the Warriors fiddled away scoring chances with fumbles and what one writer called downright weird signal calling. With four minutes left on the clock, Yonamine took the ball directly from the center, shot through the left guard, cut to his left, and outraced two defenders for a 21-yard touchdown. The game ended with a 7–0 Warriors victory, but the team's play was not encouraging.

Three days later, the Warriors boarded an 8:30 Pan American flight to the East Coast. They arrived exhausted and lost three of their first four games to teams from Jersey City, Bethlehem, and Richmond. The Hawaiians took a break and stayed in New York City for five days, taking in the sights, before tackling the Paterson Panthers on September 18 in Bloomfield, New Jersey. Far from home, tired, nursing minor injuries, and coming off five days without practicing, Yonamine and his teammates were not enthusiastic about the upcoming game. It did not seem an important exhibition contest—yet it became one of the most crucial football games of Wally's career.

A "Sad Afternoon" the Honolulu Advertiser's headline proclaimed over the brief article describing Paterson's 34–6 drubbing of the Warriors. At the time, nobody realized the game's true consequences. Yonamine was playing defense when he picked off an errant pass near the sidelines. He ran down the line looking for a hole to cut back through, but the field ahead was crowded. Wally knew that the intended receiver was still behind him, but the end, a lumbering giant, surely wouldn't be able to catch him. All of a sudden, Yonamine was hit hard from behind. The behemoth end slammed Wally to the ground. As Wally got up, he knew that something was wrong. His left shoulder throbbed. On the sidelines, it became obvious that it was dislocated.

The Warriors stayed another week on the East Coast before ending the tour early and returning home. A few weeks later, the team disbanded. Yonamine was unable to lift his left arm for nearly three months. Even after it healed, its strength had been sapped. Before the injury, he could throw a football sixty-five or seventy yards. Now, his arm was weak. The injury would change the future of Japanese baseball, but it would also block Yonamine from becoming the first ethnic Japanese in the Major Leagues.

In late October 1949, the players on the Warriors held a farewell party at a house in Haleiwa, on the other side of Oahu from Honolulu. The host invited several young women from Hawaii Business College, including an attractive nineteen-year-old named Jane Iwashita. Wally arrived late to the party and noticing Jane, asked her for a dance. Jane recalled, "I rarely saw a football game, but the name Wally Yonamine was famous. I didn't imagine that such a famous football player would pay attention to a little girl like me. He asked for a dance but I had to refuse, because all fifteen dances on my card were filled."

The two were invited to several other parties at Haleiwa, and Wally volunteered to drive Jane and her classmates. Soon, Wally and Jane had become friends. In December, Wally needed a date for an engagement dinner and decided to ask Jane. Jane agreed and the two started dating regularly that month.

Jane was born in Kamuela on the Big Island of Hawaii on May 18, 1930. Her father, Migaku Iwashita, worked on Parker Ranch as a carpenter after emigrating from Kumamoto, Japan, when he was just sixteen years old. In 1938 the Iwashitas moved to Honolulu, where Jane's father became a successful contractor. Bright and studious, Jane excelled at school and attended the prestigious Roosevelt High School before entering Hawaii Business College.

As Wally was a celebrity and an eligible bachelor, people soon noticed that the couple were dating. To their surprise, the news upset many. Wally had always considered himself Japanese American, but with an Okinawan father and last name, many Hawaiians categorized him as Okinawan. Soon Jane's family started receiving anonymous telephone calls. "You leave that Okinawan boy alone! Okinawan marry Okinawan and Japanese marry Japanese! Tell your daughter to leave him alone! Don't bother him!"

Jane's grandparents also didn't approve. They felt that Jane should not be dating an Okinawan. Jane explained to her mother that Wally's mother was from Hiroshima and that only his father was from Okinawa. But she said, "It doesn't matter because his name is Okinawan!" Wally remembers, "For two years, I wasn't allowed into her house! When I went to take her out to see a movie or something, I had to meet her in the yard."

As he nursed his injured shoulder, Wally realized that his professional football career was probably over. The Warriors were defunct, the rival teams of the Pacific Coast Pro Football League disbanded, and he was unlikely to make a NFL or All-American Conference team with a weak arm. Bethlehem, Richmond, and Paterson of the American Pro League were interested in him, but Wally did not want to move to the East Coast to play in a low minor league. He needed other options. Perhaps, he thought, he should try professional baseball. After all, he had always done well without really focusing on the sport. What if he concentrated on improving his skills? Could he really make a Pacific Coast League team?

In a lucky coincidence, that December the San Francisco Seals of the Pacific Coast League stopped in Honolulu on their way home from a seven-game goodwill tour of Japan. The Allied Occupation Headquarters, in conjunction with the *Yomiuri Shimbun*, had invited the Seals in an effort to raise Japanese morale. The tour had been a resounding success, partly because of the popularity of the Seals manager Frank "Lefty" O'Doul, but also because of the Seals themselves. The Japanese interpreted their presence as a sign of respect, which helped reestablish baseball's popularity after the war.

O'Doul had an unusual Major League career. After failing as a pitcher in parts of four seasons from 1919 to 1923, he returned as a thirty-one-year-old outfielder in 1928. Over seven more years, he went on to hit .349 lifetime, winning the 1929 batting title. A strapping, gregarious character, Lefty is perhaps better known for his affiliation with the PCL, where he played, coached, and managed for thirty years. For years, fans have unsuccessfully petitioned the Baseball Hall of Fame at Cooperstown to induct O'Doul; for his contributions to Japanese baseball he has been inducted into the Japan Baseball Hall of Fame in Tokyo.

O'Doul first went to Japan in 1931 as a member of the visiting Major League All-Stars. He fell in love with the country and befriended the *Yomiuri Shimbun*'s owner Matsutaro Shoriki and his deputy, Sotaro Suzuki. Lefty returned to Japan in 1932 and 1933 to coach players from the Tokyo-area universities, and again in 1934 as a member of the Major League All-Star team. He became an advisor to Shoriki when the newspaper owner decided to create the Yomiuri Giants in late 1934 and helped organize the Giants' trips to the United States in 1935 and 1936. The war prevented O'Doul from traveling to Japan for ten years, but in 1946 he returned, paying his own way, to reestablish his ties with Japanese baseball.

When the Seals goodwill tour began in September 1949, the morale of the Japanese was low. The nation was still rebuilding from the war's devastation, good food and electricity were scarce, and the victorious Allies occupied the country. Cappy Harada, then a U.S. Army lieutenant acting as O'Doul's guide, recalled: "When Lefty arrived in Tokyo, we had a parade through Ginza. It was amazing! There were so many people! I was in the same open car as Lefty. He yelled, '*Banzai! Banzai!*' but nothing happened. 'Usually before the war when you yelled *banzai*,'" he commented, "'they would yell *banzai* back. How come they don't yell *banzai*?' And I said, 'That's the reason you're here, Lefty. To build up the morale so that they will yell *banzai* again.' He understood. By the time he left, people were yelling *banzai* again."

When the Seals and Harada arrived in Honolulu, Katsumi Kometani, the Athletics' owner, contacted Harada and explained that one of his players named Wally Yonamine wanted to try out for a PCL team. Soon afterward, Paul Fagan, the Seals' owner, held a party for his team at his vacation home in Honolulu. Wally was also invited. There he met Lefty O'Doul for the first time. "Somebody must've told him that I was a pretty good baseball player," says Yonamine, because when I met him, he said, "Wally, why don't you take a chance and play baseball?" I said, "Well, if you think that I'm good enough, I'd be glad to try."

A month later, O'Doul wrote to his friend Yets Higa in Honolulu and authorized him to officially invite Yonamine to the Seals training camp at El Centro, California, in early February 1950.

5

Of Seals and Bees

The Bay Area writers huddled around Lefty O'Doul at the San Francisco Seals' practice ground in El Centro, a resort town located in the heart of Southern California's Imperial Valley. They could always count on the gregarious Lefty for a colorful quote or tidbit that could be turned into a story. On the first day in camp, for example, the Seals manager had brought a football to the field and posed for photographers with the Seals' three ex-footballers. "No Sir, No Football!" ran the caption below the eye-catching photo of O'Doul with former 49er Wally Yonamine, former All-American Herman Wedemeyer, and a former University of California fullback named Rube Navarro.

Yonamine had spent a full month with the Seals at El Centro. The Seals practiced between 8:30 and noon to avoid the heat and had the afternoons off to relax. The first week consisted mostly of calisthenics, throwing, and games of pepper. Wally was in top shape, having played throughout the winter with Moiliili of the AJA Senior League in Honolulu. "Everything was first class," Wally remembered, "You could eat all the food you wanted—you just signed the check and the team picked up the tab. I could eat so much in those days!"

Wally was surprised to meet his old rival at camp. Wedemeyer had been playing for the Los Angeles Dons and Baltimore Colts of the All-American Conference, but as with Wally, his professional football career never really took off. After leaving the Colts, "Squirmin' Herman" decided to try professional baseball. He had played in high school and also at St. Mary's College, where he was considered good, but not a pro prospect. Wedemeyer approached the Seals and asked to try out for the team as a walk-on. Management quickly agreed, and he joined Wally and the other players.

Yonamine and Wedemeyer impressed O'Doul. After watching his new Nisei, he observed, "Wally has a perfect swing and great power." In exhibition games he did well enough to merit ink in various dispatches, including the *Los Angeles Times*, *The Sporting News*, and the *Pacific Citizen*. Roger Williams of the *San Francisco News* wrote, "Yonamine has impressed Manager Frank O'Doul with his all-around play. Wally really shines with his throwing, fielding and hitting and we particularly like his deft sliding ability." Despite his strong showing, Wally was unable to break into the Seals' lineup. On March 25, O'Doul announced that both Yonamine and Wedemeyer would be signed to contracts but would not make the Seals' main roster. Instead, they would be seasoned with the Yakima Bears, a Class B team in the Western International League.

Wally balked at going to Yakima, at the time a small city of 135,000 in Central Washington State. Instead, Wally requested to be sent to the Salt Lake City Bees, an unaffiliated team that had a working agreement with the Seals. Salt Lake City had a large Japanese American community and several of Wally's friends had relocated there. The Seals acquiesced and the Bees' management, hoping to attract the city's Japanese Americans to the ballpark, readily agreed.

As Wally worked to make the Seals' roster, rumors spread that he might play in Japan instead. On March 18, 1950, the *Pacific Citizen* ran an article entitled: "Yonamine Has New Offer from Tokyo." After explaining that Yonamine would have a difficult time breaking into the Seals lineup, the article stated that the Nisei star had been offered three hundred dollars a month plus his room and board to join the Tokyo Giants. According to the *Citizen*, the offer would have made Yonamine the highest-paid player in Japan and indicated how much Wally impressed Tokyo Giants scout Richard Uehara.

The report, however, was unfounded. Both Yonamine and Cappy Harada categorically deny that the Giants made such an offer in March 1950. Harada, who was advising the Giants at the time, says the idea of hiring a foreign player was not even discussed until nine months later. The article does suggest, however, that Richard Uehara was already scouting Nisei players and had guessed that they would soon be sought after by Japanese professional teams.

Wally met the Bees at their spring training camp in Palo Alto, California, on April 2, and three weeks later, Wedemeyer, who was demoted because of trouble hitting the curve ball, joined him. The Bees now had an abundance of outfielders but a hole at first base. Learning that Wally had occasionally played first base with the Athletics, Bees manager Earl Bolyard had Wally practice the position as the Bees geared up for their season opener against the Ogden Reds on April 29.

It was cold and snow threatened in Ogden as Wally stepped to the plate in his first professional baseball game. Roughly five thousand fans sat shivering in the night air. Acclimated to the gentle Hawaiian breezes and the scorching heat of El Centro, northern Utah seemed arctic to Yonamine. Although it was his first game, the jitters didn't overwhelm Wally as they did with the 49ers. Officially, he went 1 for 4 with 2 RBI, but he was on base five times as he walked twice, and his speedy running caused the Reds infielders to muff two grounders.

The next day, the snow—the first the Hawaiian had ever seen—arrived from the north. It forced the remaining two games at Ogden and six of the Bees' first ten to be postponed. Playing in the frigid weather, Wally caught a bad cold and was bedridden for several days. As he lay there wondering what he had gotten himself into, he listened doubtfully to friends explain that snowstorms in May were highly unusual even in Salt Lake City. The city, however, was beautiful. Snow covered the ground as cherry blossoms bloomed overhead.

As the weather warmed in mid-May, Wally recovered. By May 20, he had a team-high .341 batting average, and manager Bolyard moved him from fifth to third in the lineup. Bolyard also moved Wally back into his natural center field position.

Wally wrote Jane Iwashita every day. She remembers, "I never heard him complain or grumble about anything in Salt Lake. I think he was perfectly happy there." As the stream of letters arrived at Jane's home in Honolulu, her family started to soften on Wally and the romance. One day, sitting in her bedroom, Jane heard her mother and aunt talking in the backyard. "The guy can't be that bad because he writes to her every day," said her mother. "I don't know what he's writing about, maybe the cockroaches crossing the street and getting run over or something!" responded the aunt. "How could anybody write a letter every day?" "That's when I knew that we were all right," remembers Jane.

After traveling with the 49ers and attending the Seals' camp at El Centro, the living conditions with the Bees were a shock. "They didn't pay very much in Class C. I think I made only a hundred and fifty dollars per month and we had to get our own apartments. I was fortunate that I knew a couple of Hawaiian Nisei and I stayed with them. When we went on the road, they gave us only two dollars for meal money each day. That didn't take us too far. We would often skip lunch to save money and just have a good dinner. There were also long bus rides. It took fifteen hours to go from Salt Lake City up to Montana, and we didn't have a nice bus like they have today. We had this third-rate old bus with no heat or air conditioner. In April and May, when we went up into the mountains it would get so cold that we would put our uniforms on over our clothes just to stay warm! Those days made me appreciate what I have today."

On the road, Wally roomed with Herman Wedemeyer. After being a star in the AAFC, Wedey found the poor pay and tough living conditions particularly hard. Wedemeyer could run and throw extremely well, but was still having trouble with curve balls and struggled at the plate. His frustration continued to mount as his average dipped. By late May, he was hitting just .250 in eighty-four at bats with no home runs and just eight RBI, when he finally snapped.

The Bees were owned by Bert V. Dunne. The broad-shouldered, square-jawed advertising executive from San Francisco had just purchased the team the previous November. Dunne had played baseball for the University of Notre Dame in the 1920s and considered himself an authority on hitting. He had written several books on baseball fundamentals for children, and the most famous, entitled *Play Ball, Son*, remained in print for decades. Dunne's friend, Hall of Famer Joe Cronin, wrote the foreword and called the little pamphlet the "best technical book on baseball ever written for boys." It included a famous inspirational essay entitled "Don't Die on Third" that challenged readers to take initiative in their lives. Dunne understood the game and would often sit in the dugout giving the players and manager advice and occasional orders.

One day, in the third week in May, Wedemeyer, slumping and testy, was due up. As Squirmin' Herman was about leave for the on-deck circle, Dunne called him over to issue some instructions. Wedemeyer bristled, but the orders continued. Finally, Wedey couldn't contain himself and yelled at Dunne to stop interfering. He claimed that Dunne's comments were driving the players crazy, "Even Wally Yonamine hates you!" he shouted. Dunne fired Wedemeyer right away and considered firing Wally as well. But he reconsidered. Yonamine was the team's leading batter, and at least a hundred Nisei fans came to each game to watch him. He could not afford to let Wally go.

On May 29, the Bees faced off against the Reds at John Affleck Park in Ogden to make up the earlier snowed-out game. A large group of Nisei and Issei from the Ogden area were on hand for the festivities. Wally didn't disappoint his fans. Stepping to the plate in the top of the first inning, the Hawaiian smashed his first professional home run, driving the ball 345 feet over the right-field fence. Later in the game, Ogden's catcher, future Major Leaguer Ed Bailey, purposely tipped Yonamine's bat during a swing to disturb his stroke. Bailey got away with the trick and Wally grounded out.

The following day, the Reds were leading the Bees 5–2, when Yonamine came to bat with the bases loaded in the seventh and hit a sharp line-drive single to score two runs and bring the Bees within one. In the ninth, the Bees threatened again. With a runner on first and one out, Yonamine strode to the plate. He steadied himself, waiting for the pitch. The ball came right down the middle and Wally swung hard. At the last moment, Bailey reached in and tipped Wally's bat with his

glove again. Wally got a piece of the ball and the trickler became an
easy game-ending double play. This time, however, the umpire had
noticed Bailey's interference. Wally was awarded first base. The next
batter, Dick Treat, lined a single past third base, tying the game and
moving Yonamine to third. Wally scored the winning run moments
later when the Reds' shortstop couldn't handle a hot grounder.

A couple of days later, Earl Bolyard installed Wally as the lead-off
batter. At the time, Yonamine was hitting .337 with 5 doubles, 4 stolen
bases, and a team-leading 23 runs scored. Wally thrived in the one-
spot, and after ten days his average shot up to .351. Many of these hits
were classic Texas-leaguers—bloop singles that fall between the infielders and outfielders. By midseason, opposing teams started calling
them "Yonamines" or "Japanese Hits." Yonamine, however, is adamant
that he did not experience prejudice or anti-Japanese sentiment in the
Pioneer League. Glenn Mickens, who played on the Billings Mustangs
and later in Japan, also does not recall racial slurs at Yonamine.

Wally hit Mickens and his fellow Mustangs particularly hard. In
early June, he garnered seven hits in eleven at bats during a two-game
series in Salt Lake City. Mickens later tried to convince the Brooklyn
Dodgers veterans that Yonamine was one of baseball's greatest hitters. The incident was immortalized in an April 8, 1953, *Sporting News*
article by Bill Roeder entitled, "No. 1 Hitter? Mickens Knew Him: Jap
Out West Named Yanamini":

> *Ben Wade, a Ted Williams man, and Preacher Roe, a Stan Musial*
> *man, and their respective backers, were getting nowhere in an ar-*
> *gument over who was the best hitter any of them had ever seen.*
>
> *So Glenn Mickens, the rookie who seldom pipes down, piped up,*
> *"Wally Yanamini," he said. "That's what it sounded like, anyway."*
> . . . .
> *"What was that, son?" Asked Preacher Roe.*
> *"You're talking about the best hitter," said Mickens, "so I'm giv-*
> *ing you the best hitter I ever saw. Wally Yanamini."*
> *"How do you spell it?"*

*"Heck, I don't know. Y-a-n-a-m-i-n-i, maybe. Something like
that. He's a Jap; I think he's back there playing in Japan now. He
used to give me a rough time when I was up at Billings. He was a
left-handed hitter for Salt Lake."*

*"That's funny," Pee Wee Reese said. "I should know the name.
What league is that?"*

*"Pioneer League," said Mickens. "He was one of those guys that
poke the ball. He'd punch the ball and foul it off 'til I either threw
him his pitch or he struck out."* . . .

*[Pee Wee] Reese laughed, "Wally Yanamini," he said. "I'll buy
that."*

"I'll still take Ted Williams," Ed Wade said.

In early July, Yonamine had his only slump of the season. His average slid from .328 to .305 as Idaho Falls and Ogden used their left-
handed starters against the Bees. Wally's batting picked up as he faced
Mickens and the Mustangs again a week later, but in the first of many
such instances, it took Jane Iwashita to inspire Wally.

Jane decided to attend the International Business Women's Conference in San Francisco as a delegate for Honolulu. Over five thousand
women from around the world congregated in San Francisco from
July 3 to 7 to discuss world affairs and the role of women in business.
After the conference, Jane flew to Salt Lake City to visit Wally. As she
cheered him on from a third base box seat during the July 18–20 series
against Billings, Wally banged out a succession of hits. Her presence,
however, did not go unnoticed to the press. On July 22, 1950, the *Pacific
Citizen* ran the following news blurb: "Incidentally, that pretty Nisei
girl who occupied a third base box seat during the Billings Series at
Derks Field in Salt Lake City was Jane Iwashita of Honolulu who flew
from San Francisco to watch Wally Yonamine play. Jane was a delegate
from Honolulu to the International Business Women's Conference in
San Francisco. On her first night at the park Wally got three for five,
including a rousing triple."

Jane remembers, "The story not only came out in the Salt Lake papers but it was also picked up by the *Star Bulletin* in Honolulu and my mother read it! Of course, Japanese girls are not supposed to visit a boy's house. The boys can come and visit you, but you never go to the boys' houses. I got selected as queen of the convention. That was also reported in the paper and the whole school was at the airport to greet me when I came back. But there was my mother in the back fuming! She was just embarrassed to heck."

Jane explained to her parents that she had stayed in a separate hotel and that she only met Wally in public places, but her parents were still upset. Jane's father was president of the Kumamoto Kenjin Kai, an organization of Japanese Americans whose families emigrated from Kumamoto Prefecture in Japan, and members had been calling the Iwashitas to object to Jane's choice in men. Members of the Okinawa Kenjin Kai (the organization for emigrants from Okinawa) also called to complain.

Just when it seemed that Jane's family had given their grudging approval of Wally, the incident caused them to object to her boyfriend again. Jane's father would preach to her in the car, "I wouldn't allow a dog or cat to pair off on their own. All the more, that you are my precious daughter." Besides being an Okinawan, Wally was also a ballplayer. In Jane's mother's eyes that translated to a grown man, without a real job, loafing around playing games for fun.

Inspired by Jane, Wally went on a tear. From July 15 to 20, he rapped out 15 hits in 36 at bats. The hot streak contributed to the growing esteem with which the Bees players, fans, and press held their Hawaiian lead-off hitter—as did Wally's preternatural congeniality. A dispatch filed by Jack Schroeder of the *Salt Lake Telegram*, on July 20 went:

> *Baseball players are pretty serious about getting their hits. And, as a consequence, it's not unusual for a player to accost an official scorer on his call of a specified play.*
>
> *Since it's their livelihoods—this hit business—it's not unusual then for them to want to count every blow in their collection. A slight slip can drop a batting average below the .300 mark very easily. . . .*

On occasions, since box scores are so difficult to set, there are some typographical errors in the contents. They're not official until they're sent in by the official score to the league statistician.

The other night we were sitting in the Bee dugout before the game, [when] Wally Yonamine, that likable guy who plays all over the outfield for Salt Lake, came churning up to us breathlessly.

"You made a mistake in the box score that was in this evening's paper," said Wally, who is among the six top hitters in the league. "You had me at bat four times and I was actually up five," he complained.

There's a new twist for you from a darn swell guy.

In late July and early August, Yonamine began honing the aggressive style that would make him a superstar in Japan the following year. In the outfield, he used his speed to chase down long drives and dove for balls when he couldn't track them down on the run. His already good bunting improved—he could often turn sacrifices into infield hits. On the base paths, Wally became more aggressive, challenging for the league lead in steals. On July 24, for example, Yonamine stole three bases in one game, and a week later he tried to steal home as a Boise Pilots pitcher was winding up. Wally and the pitch reached the plate at the same time, but the umpire called him out.

By mid August, Yonamine was second in the league in hits, runs scored, and stolen bases. His .330 batting average was also among the league leaders. Having proven that he could excel in the Pioneer League, the San Francisco Seals sent a scout to watch him. Wally hoped that he would get called up to the Seals for the remainder of the season, but despite his strong play, he did not.

As Wally played out the last month of the season at Salt Lake, he made a serious bid for several league titles. By the end of August, he raised his batting average to .338, ranking fifth, and he remained runner-up in stolen bases, runs scored, and hits. During the first week in September, Yonamine went 6 for 14, moving into the lead in both hits and stolen bases, and up to fourth in the batting race. The lead didn't last long, however. In the last week of the season, Wally gained only two hits in twelve at bats and lost the race in each category. He finished the season with a .335 batting average (fourth in the league), 165 hits (second), 118 runs scored (third), 30 stolen bases (second), 24 doubles, 10 triples, and 3 home runs.

Wally said his farewells to Salt Lake at the September 8 fan appreciation night before the final game against the Pocatello Cardinals. Special events included a race around the bases between Yonamine and Pocatello pitcher John Romonosky, considered one of the fastest runners in the league. Romonosky finished in 14 seconds flat with Wally just behind him at 14.3 seconds. After the game, Nisei fans presented Wally with a "transoceanic portable radio," while the Issei community gave him cash and a pen and pencil set.

Three days later, Wally left Salt Lake City and flew to San Francisco for a week. He visited with the Hosoda family, Bill Mizono, and other old friends. He also paid his respects to Lefty O'Doul. They spoke about Wally's success at Salt Lake and Lefty told him that he would be promoted the following season and should once again attend the Seals spring training camp. Wally boarded the plane to Honolulu confident that he would eventually become a member of the San Francisco Seals.

6

A Winter of Uncertainty

Wally returned to Honolulu, happy to get back to warm weather, family, and Jane Iwashita. He joined the fire department at Pearl Harbor and signed up for the winter Nisei basketball league to keep in shape. Playing guard for Russell's, Yonamine led the team in scoring and was named to the Honolulu Nisei All-Star Squad.

In late October, Lefty O'Doul and Joe DiMaggio arrived in Japan on a month-long goodwill tour. They visited American servicemen in Japan and Korea, coached Japanese players, and made celebrity appearances. During their travels to and from Japan, O'Doul and DiMaggio stopped in Honolulu. On one of the stopovers, O'Doul contacted Wally and invited him to join them at the elegant Lau Yee Chai for dinner. Founded in 1929 by P. Y. Chong and still in business, many considered the restaurant to have the best Chinese food in America. During dinner, O'Doul asked, "Wally, have you ever thought of playing in Japan? The Japanese would love your style." They spoke about the prospect for some time. There were no concrete offers from Japanese teams, but Lefty felt that it was time for them to begin importing players.

Wally considered the idea. He was not a power hitter, but instead hit for average and relied on speed. After dislocating his shoulder in the Warriors game against Paterson, his arm was weak compared to most Major League prospects. A power hitter might make the grade with this deficiency, but a singles hitter needed superb defense to make the Majors. If he stayed in the States, he would be lucky if he could play Triple-A ball. And he wasn't going to make good money there! So, he concluded that he would just be wasting his time playing ball in the States.

"Okay," he told Lefty, "I'll go if there's a chance."

Lefty promised that he would look into it, but Wally heard nothing more about the prospect for months and soon dismissed it as a remote possibility.

In January the Honolulu AJA Senior Baseball League 1951 season began. Wally once again joined the Moiliili team, playing right field and batting second. Wally usually excelled in the Senior League—entering the 1951 season, he was hitting .438 over two and a half seasons. Yet, he started off slowly in '51 and was not among the top ten batters in mid-February. Perhaps Wally had things other than baseball on his mind as he and Jane Iwashita announced their engagement in February.

While he played for Moiliili, the *Pacific Citizen* speculated about Wally's future in pro baseball. The Salt Lake City Bees wanted to retain Yonamine for the 1951 season. Eddie Leishman, who purchased the team after the 1950 season, noted that Yonamine was valuable to the team because of his ability, his popularity with the fans, and also because he was exempt from the Korean War draft, having already served in World War II. Nevertheless, Leishman said that he would attempt to trade him to a Class A or B team as "Yonamine should have the opportunity to play in faster company."

While Leishman was shopping Yonamine, Cappy Harada flew from Tokyo to San Francisco. Officially, Harada was in San Francisco to arrange for several of Japan's brightest stars to train with the Seals in March. Harada met with Paul Fagan, the owner of the Seals, and with Lefty O'Doul. As always, Lefty was happy to help improve the quality of Japanese ball. They agreed that Yomiuri Giants' captain Tetsuharu Kawakami, Osaka Tigers' star Fumio Fujimura, and Nagoya Dragons' ace Shigeru Sugishita would join the Seals for spring training at their Modesto, California, camp. Harada was, of course, also in town to discuss Yonamine's availability. As O'Doul had already concluded that Yonamine would make an ideal ambassador to Japanese baseball, he readily agreed to secure Wally's release so that the Yomiuri Giants could sign him.

Leishman, however, was not informed of the agreement and suc-

ceeded in trading Yonamine to the Salem Senators of the Class B
Western International League for Bobby Cherry, one of the Senators'
leading hitters, in the final week of February 1951. Like the Bees, the
Senators also had a working relationship with the Seals, which would
allow Yonamine to move up to San Francisco in due time. The Senators' manager, Hugh Luby, quickly mailed Wally a contract with "a
salary substantially above the minimum for Class B baseball" and a
note to report to spring training in Napa, California, on April 1.

At the end of February, Kawakami, Fujimura, Sugishita, and an ad-
ditional player named Makoto Kozuru left Tokyo for the Seals' training camp. During the trip, Kawakami remarked to Sugishita that the
Seals had a Nisei player named Wally Yonamine who played American
football as well as baseball. Kawakami also confided that the Giants
were interested in signing Yonamine. Not finding Yonamine at camp,
Kawakami asked the Seals where he was but did not get a straight
answer.

On Sunday, February 18, the Mainichi Orions, winners of the 1950
Japan Series, arrived in Honolulu for spring training. Tadashi "Bozo"
Wakabayashi, the Hawaiian-born Nisei assistant manager, led the
club during the trip. Wakabayashi hailed from the Wahiawa pineapple
plantation. Born in 1908, he learned baseball as a child from servicemen at neighboring Schofield Barracks military base. He played for
McKinley High in Honolulu and in 1928 toured Japan with a Nisei
team from Stockton, California. Impressed with Wakabayashi's pitching, Hosei University tried to recruit him, but the other Big Six Universities objected to enrolling a foreigner purely for his baseball skills,
and Hosei supposedly dropped their plan. Yet Wakabayashi did not
give up. After a brief return to Hawaii, he arrived in Tokyo declaring his intentions to enroll at Hosei. A compromise was reached, and
Wakabayashi attended preparatory school for nine months until he
attained the university's minimum entrance requirements. In 1935, a
year after graduating, he signed with the Osaka Tigers, surviving the
Tigers' rigorous preseason training camp—which included lessons
by martial arts masters on how to walk barefoot atop the upturned

edge of a samurai long sword as a demonstration of mental strength. Wakabayashi became one of the top pitchers in Japanese baseball. He stayed with the Tigers for fifteen seasons, winning twenty or more games six times, but with the creation of the Pacific League in 1950, he left to become a player-coach of the newly created Orions. With Bozo, the expansion team won both the pennant and the inaugural Japan Series.

For their Hawaiian excursion, the Orions supplemented their squad with three players from other Pacific League teams: Hiroshi Oshita, Tokuji Iida, and Jiro Noguchi. The Japanese stayed in Hawaii for thirty days, playing eighteen games against various AJA clubs, All-Star squads, military teams, and the University of Hawaii. Overall, the Japanese club won fifteen, losing only to two AJA all-star teams and the AJA Senior League Waialua club.

Several of the Japanese players attracted Major League scouts. Bill Veeck, at that time the owner of the Cleveland Indians, flew to Hawaii in mid-March to watch the Orions. He was particularly impressed with Atsushi Aramaki, Kaoru Betto, and Hiroshi Oshita. Betto and Oshita were interesting characters. Known as the "Gentleman of Baseball," Betto starred in high school and college ball but was reluctant to turn pro because he found the idea of playing for money repugnant. He overcame this aversion in 1948, becoming a twenty-seven-year-old rookie, and stayed in baseball for nearly forty years. Oshita, on the other hand, was outgoing and a noted drinker and connoisseur of the opposite sex. He was also a feared slugger who had used a trademark blue bat until colored bats were banned in 1948. According to newspaper reports, Veeck wanted to sign the players to contracts with either Dayton of the Class A Central League or Oklahoma City of the AA Texas League. Veeck's plans, however, did not materialize, and the three stars returned to Japan to have Hall of Fame careers.

During most of the Orions' stay, Yonamine and his Moiliili teammates were busy with AJA Senior League games, but on March 4 the two teams met. It was Wally's first chance against a professional Japanese team, and he did well. The Orions beat Moiliili 6–2, but Wally went 2 for 4 with an RBI off submariner Kiyoshi Nomura and Atsushi Aramaki. Even through Wally played only one game against the Orions, Moiliili played in the opening game of six split doubleheaders when the Orions played in the second game. So Wakabayashi, who was actively scouting Japanese American talent, had plenty of opportunity to watch Wally play. In an interview published in the March 13, 1951, *Hawaii Times*, the Orions acting manager stated: "Wally's got everything. He's a finished player who's got natural ability plus a lot of baseball savvy. Not only that, I understand he knows how to take care of himself, especially off the field. . . . I'm highly confident that he'll make an instant hit in Japan. He'll hit and field with the best of them, [and] . . . be a standout . . . in base running. We have some fleet men but they don't measure up to Wally's all-around ability. Wally has had minor league experience on the mainland, and for this reason he will be a valuable man on our staff in instructing our players."

In the second week of March, Wakabayashi asked Yonamine if he would consider playing in Japan, and Wally quickly responded that he would be glad to go. Wakabayashi promised to contact the president of the Mainichi newspaper and get back to Wally. Later that week, Bozo told the press, "A letter is on its way to the Mainichi office. I've recommended that we pay Wally a certain sum, and if the home office agrees, I'll wrap up Wally even before our departure. . . . Wally himself is anxious to play for us."

In late March, Kawakami, Sugishita, Fujimura, and Kozuru had finished their training with the Seals and flew to Honolulu. The four stars practiced with the Orions and joined the AJA All-Stars in the final two games against Mainichi. Here, Kawakami and Sugishita finally saw Wally Yonamine. Because of the language barrier, they never actually spoke, but Yonamine's speed impressed Sugishita, who could not see a flaw in the Hawaiian's game. After the game on March 29, where Sugishita pitched six shutout innings for the AJA All-Stars, the Orions and the four Japanese stars boarded a 10:00 p.m. flight back to Tokyo.

In Honolulu, Yonamine waited and waited for a contract from the Orions, but none came.

Years later, Yonamine discovered that several of the Orions players had informed the president of Mainichi that Wakabayashi was overestimating Wally's ability. On their advice, the president decided not to send a contract. Perhaps these players were not keen on having an American teammate.

While Wally waited for Mainichi's offer, April 1 came and went without Wally reporting for spring training with the Salem Senators. Deciding that he wanted to play in Japan, Wally had not signed the contract Luby mailed him. He was now committed to playing in Japan or playing semipro ball in Hawaii for the 1951 season. In the meantime, Wally accepted a job in the public relations department of Coca-Cola in Honolulu. It was a well-paid position and meant to be permanent if professional baseball did not work out.

On Tuesday, April 16, Wally received a telephone call from Sam Uyehara, owner of the Smile Café and a sponsor of sports, particularly baseball, in Honolulu. Sam's genial personality and his importance to the local sporting scene made the Smile Café a ballplayer hangout that even attracted visiting Major League teams.

Uyehara had welcome news—the Tokyo Yomiuri Giants had offered Wally a contract. Sam suggested that Wally come down to the café to discuss the details. The news surprised Wally as he didn't know the Giants were interested in him. Wally, who had been to the Smile Café many times and especially enjoyed the spare ribs, hurried down to Waikiki to learn the details.

Unbeknownst to Yonamine, Uyehara and his cousin Richard Uehara had been scouting him for the past three years. Richard had moved to Tokyo after World War II, but during a visit home in 1947, he had watched Wally play in an AJA game. Uehara contacted the Yomiuri Giants and repeatedly told them about Yonamine. The Giants, however, remained uninterested until Shoriki summoned Cappy Harada to his office in December 1950.

At the restaurant, Uyehara laid out the details. The Giants would pay Wally one million yen (about $3,000) as a signing bonus and 100,000 yen (about $300) per month as salary, plus travel expenses and living expenses during the season. By Japanese standards it was a generous amount. The average office worker drew only 6,700 yen per month in 1951. Uyehara also explained that the Giants were Japan's most popular and successful team. Wally quickly agreed to the terms and the Honolulu papers announced the signing the next morning.

The Yomiuri Giants' 1951 season had started on March 29, so Yonamine prepared to leave for Tokyo at once. He informed Mr. Adams, the president of Coca-Cola Hawaii, of his decision to leave Hawaii. Adams supported Yonamine's decision and told him "Go to Japan and get baseball out of your system. If you make it, great, but if you don't, you can come back here and have your job back."

In the first week of May, Wally flew to Tokyo and met Richard Uehara at the airport. Uehara took him to his home and put Wally up for a few weeks until his contract was officially signed. One final obstacle remained. The Allied occupation forces had been using baseball to boost morale and to forge closer ties between the United States and Japan. Thus, the Giants signing Yonamine was an important event. As members of the nation's most popular team, Giants players were in the spotlight, with thousands of fans and dozens of reporters scrutinizing their behavior both on and off the field. The inclusion of the right American player could help U.S.-Japanese relations, but the wrong player could be disastrous. Tensions between the occupying forces and the Japanese were still high. If the American player was perceived as arrogant or disrespectful, the popularity of the Giants could help fuel anti-American sentiment. Accordingly, before Yonamine's contract could be finalized, the SCAP (Supreme Commander of the Allied Powers) needed to give his approval.

Given Cappy Harada's influence within the SCAP office and Yonamine's genial personality, his approval should have been a quick decision. SCAP, however, was in flux. On April 11, President Truman relieved General Douglas McArthur of command for criticizing his Korean War policies and appointed General Matthew B. Ridgway as the Supreme Commander of the Allied Powers. In the midst of the Korean War and with plans to strengthen Japan's security against the perceived threat of communism, the new commander was fully occupied. Baseball, despite its importance to Japanese morale, was a low priority.

Yonamine would not be the first American to play professionally in Japan. Prior to World War II, sixteen Nisei, two Caucasians, and an African American had joined the league. The most prominent were Bozo Wakabayashi and Andrew Harris McGalliard, who, playing under the name Bucky Harris, won the 1937 fall MVP award and led the league in home runs in the 1938 spring season. Several of the Nisei players, including Wakabayashi, stayed in Japan throughout the war and continued to play during the occupation. In 1948–49, three other American-born Nisei joined the league. Jyo Furutani, a Californian, signed with the Nankai Hawks in 1948 but saw only four at bats before being released. The following year, the Hanshin Tigers signed Hawaiian-born Isao Odate. After hitting just .213 in eighty at bats, Odate followed Wakabayashi to the Mainichi Orions in 1950 and spent the next six years with them as a backup outfielder. Odate was not considered a *gaijin* as he had attended a Japanese high school and was fluent in the language. Like many Nisei who returned to Japan, he probably had dual American and Japanese citizenship.

Also in 1949, California-born Isamu Uchio joined the Hankyu Braves. Uchio, a graduate of Los Angeles High School, traveled with his mother to Japan immediately after the war to search for his two brothers, who had been drafted into the Imperial Army while living with their grandfather in Japan. He located both brothers alive but imprisoned in a Russian POW camp. As Isamu waited in Japan for their release, he took a job as a translator. In 1948, he attended an open tryout for the Hankyu Braves and made the team's roster the following year. He played seven seasons, mostly as a reserve infielder. Although he had not attended a Japanese high school, Uchio was not considered a foreigner as his grandfather had registered him at birth as a Japanese citizen.

Although these three American-born Nisei preceded Yonamine, Wally was at the time, and is still, considered to be the first foreigner to play in Japan after the war. The Japanese did not consider either Odate or Uchio to be foreigners as both were fluent in the language and citizens, and Furutani's four at bats made little impact on Japanese baseball and were quickly forgotten.

There was little for Yonamine to do in Tokyo while he waited for the SCAP to make a decision. Luckily, Dado Marino, the flyweight champion of the world, was in Tokyo to fight Yoshio Shirai. Marino was also from Olowalu, but since he was ten years older than Wally, the two had never met. The men from Maui became acquainted and Wally joined Marino on his morning runs through Meiji Jingu Park. Henry "Dose" Teshima and his wife, Ethel, Nisei acquaintances from Honolulu, also contacted Wally. In Hawaii, Henry led a big band called the Top Notchers, but in Japan he worked for the Allied occupation forces. Ethel Teshima, fluent in English and Japanese, helped Wally field questions from reporters. She also took Wally on a tour of Tokyo to acquaint him with his new home.

Tokyo had changed greatly since Wally played in the army's Pacific Olympic championship game in January 1946. The miles of flattened landscape had been transformed into bustling neighborhoods of homes, office buildings, and even small factories turning out materials needed by the United States for the conflict on the Korean Peninsula. Ginza, the city's main shopping center, was rebuilt, and multistory buildings and shops once again lined the avenue. The previously poverty-stricken inhabitants, who had been wearing rags, were now back at work, neatly dressed.

But Tokyo in 1951 was not the clean and efficient city of today. Yonamine was struck by the dirt, chaos, and crowds. The city was still rebuilding and poor. Many houses had neither electricity nor gas, and the smell of fish and soy sauce from backyard charcoal grills permeated the air. Small wooden stalls lined the streets as few shop keepers had enough capital to rebuild their stores. Cars were scarce; most automobiles belonged to the occupation forces. Many of the Japanese-owned vehicles had been converted to run on charcoal instead of the expensive and difficult-to-obtain gasoline. Drivers stoked charcoal in a rear compartment to allow their cars to lurch along, spewing smoke. To climb hills, drivers needed to get out and push. It was the crowds, however, that were most surprising. Wally looked around in disbelief at the throngs of people shoulder to shoulder on the sidewalks and crammed into trolleys. The sidewalks constantly looked as though people were just leaving a theatre or sporting event. Wally realized that negotiating daily tasks in Tokyo, such as shopping, might be harder than adapting to Japanese baseball.

At last, in the second week of June, General Marquat and the Japanese baseball commissioner met to discuss Yonamine. They agreed that a less-experienced Nisei would be a better candidate for the first American ballplayer than a Caucasian former Major Leaguer or Triple-A ballplayer. As one of America's best Nisei ballplayers, who was known for his exciting style of play and quiet demeanor, they agreed that Wally Yonamine was ideal for the task.

After the meeting, the Giants called Yonamine to tell him the good news and asked him to come down to the Yomiuri offices to sign the official contract as soon as possible. Yonamine remembers: "Before I left for the office, people told me that I should take a bag with me because I was going to get so much money. I thought they were kidding me. But I took a small bag anyway."

At Yomiuri's headquarters, Wally met with Shoji Yasuda and Cappy Harada in a small institutional-looking office. The men sat around a three-foot circular folding table. Somebody had covered it with an ill-fitting rectangular white tablecloth in an attempt to make the atmosphere more formal. Wally, wearing a Hawaiian shirt open at the neck, sat comfortably between Harada and Yasuda. Dressed in suits, the two Giants' representatives were warm, so the two windows were cranked open. The breeze occasionally flapped the thin white curtains, cooling the office so there was no need to use the electric fan on the end table by the window.

Yasuda chain-smoked, flicking the ashes into a heavy glass ashtray, as they talked. When it was time to sign the contract, a photographer arrived. Wally picked up a silver pen in his right hand and signed as the camera flashed away. Wally and Yasuda then posed, shaking hands, for the camera. Before he left, Yasuda presented Wally with his signing bonus. One million yen—all in red and white one-hundred-yen notes! Wally's friends had not been kidding after all. "I was so surprised," Wally recalled, "and I had to fit all those notes in my little bag. So I came home with one million yen in this little bag. In those days I never used the banks, so I hid it all in my friend's house."

The following day, when the Giants were playing the Kokutetsu Swallows on the outskirts of Tokyo, Cappy Harada took Wally to meet his new teammates. As Harada introduced him, the nervous Yonamine leaned his arm casually against the railing next to the dugout and bent his leg forward. In Hawaii, the pose would have suggested a relaxed friendliness, but in Japan, where you stood at attention during introductions, it was almost insulting. Wally's new teammates surveyed him and thought to themselves, "What a cocky little guy." Tetsuharu Kawakami, the team's captain who had seen Yonamine play in Hawaii, was especially annoyed. "Another insolent American," he thought. It was not a good beginning for Yonamine. The thickset, bespectacled Kawakami was known in Japan as "The God of Batting." He had joined the team in 1938 and would win five batting titles, two home run crowns, and two MVP awards by the time he hung up his *fundoshi* (traditional loincloth). He was so revered that he would even go on to star in a movie about his own life. He was the team leader, and irritating him had confirmed the other players' views that Americans were generally arrogant and without manners. At the time, Yonamine did not realize that anything was amiss, but months later, when he got to know some of the players well, they told him about the poor first impression he made.

The Giants left the next day for a three-game road trip to Osaka. Yonamine stayed behind, waiting nervously for his Japanese baseball career to begin when the team returned on June 19.

7
Debut

Wally Yonamine sat at the end of the Giants' bench. June 19 was a pleasant evening—in the upper 70s—but his new white flannel uniform made it feel hot. The Giants had given him number 7, his lucky number, without him asking for it. A good sign, he thought.

Not wanting to be late on this first day, he had decided to take a cab to Korakuen Stadium even though he lived nearby. The traffic was terrible, so Wally promised the driver a one-thousand-yen tip above the usual sixty yen fare if they got there quickly. With a half-week's wages at stake, the cabbie made sure that they did. The Giants' home park was the most modern ballpark in Japan—the only one, people said, that resembled a Major League ballpark. It was a double tiered stadium with porthole windows, seating a reported forty-eight thousand fans. The upper deck stands and stairways were so steep that they often induced vertigo. The higher rows, however, offered a stunning vista of the city, especially at night, when Tokyo's ubiquitous neon signs were turned on.

After some introductions, Yonamine went to the locker room to change. The room was small and bare, lacking even hangers for the players' clothes. As the team came in to change, there was no room for the players to sit down. They all dressed standing up. Once he was in uniform, there were photographs—a lot of them. All the sports papers were there to cover Yonamine's debut. Afterward, the team held their daily team meeting to go over the opposition, and Wally was handed a *bento* (traditional Japanese boxed lunch). The food looked unappetizing, but he hadn't really eaten yet and wanted to make a good first impression, so he ate and waited for his turn at batting practice.

In the early 1950s, batting practice lasted just forty minutes. The stars hit first, with Tetsuharu Kawakami, Japan's most feared hitter, taking center stage. In his heyday, Americans called Kawakami "the Lou Gehrig of Japan," but "the Ted Williams of Japan" would have been more accurate. Like Williams, Kawakami made hitting into a science. Tadashi Iwamoto, who roomed with Kawakami in the mid-1950s, remembers being awakened in the middle of the night by a swooshing sound, only to see Kawakami practicing his swing over his head in the small room. But also like Williams, Kawakami focused solely on hitting, never perfecting his defense or base-running skills. Contemporaries recall that he had a range of only one or two steps at first base. Kawakami also had a prickly personality. He usually kept to himself and jealously guarded his position as Japan's most popular player.

After Kawakami came the 5½-foot tall, 140-pound Shigeru Chiba. Chiba joined the Giants in 1938 and quickly became the league's best second baseman. Rock solid but unspectacular on defense, Chiba made his reputation with the bat. He was a superb contact hitter who rarely pulled the ball but instead purposely hit into right field. In general, he was reserved and a bit gruff, but all who knew him swear that he was among the most kind-hearted men in baseball.

The power-hitting Noboru Aota usually hit next. The star center fielder, known for his verbosity, was one of the league's top hitters, usually posting a .300 average with thirty home runs. After the stars, the other starters took a few hacks. By that time, thirty of the forty minutes had passed. The rookies, like Wally, and the guys on the bench only had time for a couple of swings each.

Before the game started, the Giants honored Wally and Kazuo Higasa, whom the Giants had just acquired from the Hiroshima Carp, with a brief ceremony. The stadium lights were on and the writer for *Sports Hochi* noted that the stands glowed white. The announcer introduced Yonamine to the forty thousand fans while Miss Hawaii, Lillian Tanaka, presented him with a bouquet. The starting nines then took the field and Wally went to the bench with the other reserves.

Wally sat back and watched the game. The opposing Nagoya Dragons were in second place, just four and a half games behind the Giants. Hiroshi Nakao, a lefty, started for the Giants. The future Hall of Famer had pitched two no-hitters—the first as a rookie in 1939, the second against the Dragons in 1941—but although only thirty-two years old, he was now past his prime. Three years in the Japanese Imperial Army had taken their toll. Nakao calmly dispatched the visitors in the first, and the Dragons took the field behind Nobuaki Miyashita, whom the Giants had traded to Chunichi in 1948. Yomiuri greeted their former teammate with a quick run, but the lead did not last long as the Dragons responded with one in the top of the second.

Wally knew little about Japanese baseball, and as the game progressed, he realized that he had much to learn. The game was different here. Americans often assumed that the smaller Japanese would play a fast game emphasizing speed and quickness, much like the Japanese American Asahi. Wally soon saw that this was not the case. The game was painfully slow. Players strolled to and from their positions. Pitchers did not challenge hitters, but instead nibbled at the corners, making full counts common. Even when the ball was in play, players rarely hustled, and much to Wally's surprise, they seldom ran out ground balls. Instead, they slowly jogged to first, putting no pressure on the defense. When sacrificing, batters did not run toward first base since logic dictated that they would most likely be out. On the base paths, they were not aggressive and hardly ever tried to take an extra base. Instead of breaking up double plays, runners would politely turn into the outfield, allowing the pivot man to throw unmolested. Outfielders also took few chances. They let balls fall in front of them, playing them on the hop, rather than risking a diving catch. Hirofumi Naito, the Giants' reserve infielder, summed it up: "In those days, we played in a uniquely Japanese way. It was rather easygoing. There wasn't much fighting spirit."

In the fourth inning, Aota slugged one over the outfield wall to give the Giants a 2–1 lead, but two innings later, the Dragons scored three off Nakao. The manager, Shigeru Mizuhara, barked something toward the dugout. Jiro Miyamoto leaned over and translated. Miyamoto was also a Nisei. Born in California but also a Japanese national, he had been with the Giants minor league club for three years. He had been called up this week solely to interpret for Wally. Hideo Fujimoto, one of the Giants' usual starters, left the bench and began warming up. Soon he replaced Nakao. The Giants struck back in the bottom of the sixth as Chiba singled and Aota hit his second home run to tie the game.

Wally looked up into the packed stands, surprised at the noise the fans created. Unlike in America, where fans usually cheer as individuals, Japanese appoint fans (usually men) to lead group cheers. In the 1950s, the cheerleaders stood right on top of the dugouts. Throughout the game the players could hear the thumps and creaks as they jumped overhead. The cheers were often accompanied by brass instruments, drums, and noisemakers.

Mizuhara brought in another of the Giants' ace starters, Takumi Otomo, in the top of the seventh. The Dragons hit him hard, scoring twice, and Mizuhara went to the bullpen again. This time Takehiko Bessho, the number-one starter with large, bushy black eyebrows, emerged. Bessho had pitched a complete game in a frustrating 4–2 loss against the Hanshin Tigers just two days before and was itching to make amends. The intense Bessho stopped the Dragons' rally.

Wally was still learning his teammates' names and was unaware that Mizuhara had used four of his five starters in the game. By American standards, it would have been an unusual, even reckless, managerial decision. In Japan, however, it was the norm. During the 1950s, Japanese managers had no set rotations. They chose their starters based on performance in pregame practices or on hunches. Pitchers prided themselves on always being available. Not until Yonamine became a coach would Japanese pitchers be separated into starters and relievers. As a result, ace pitchers in the 1950s could appear in three or four consecutive games.

Nagoya now led 6–4. In the bottom of the seventh, the first two Giants reached base. The Dragons responded by bringing in their lanky ace, Shigeru Sugishita. Although most Americans thought of Japanese as short, Sugishita stood just over six feet tall. Weighing just 155 pounds, the bespectacled hurler looked a bit comical in his baggy flannel uniform. But could Sugishita pitch! He had obviously benefited by training with the Seals. He would lead the Central League in wins in 1951 while lowering his ERA nearly a full run from the preceding season. In fact, after training at Modesto, Sugishita's ERA never rose above 2.84 for nine consecutive seasons. Tadashi Iwamoto, who joined the Giants in 1953, remembered, "Sugishita would throw these slow curves. I would think, 'Oh, I can hit a home run!' I'd swing and it would go close to the wall, and then go foul. I'd get two strikes like that. He was just baiting me. Then he'd throw a high fastball or his forkball that weaved as it came over and then finally dropped. Even Kawakami-san couldn't hit that one!"

The weak-hitting catcher, Toshiaki Takemiya, was due up. Down by two, Mizuhara wanted to move his runners into scoring position. He looked at his bench and asked, "Does anybody have enough guts to lay down a bunt?"

Other than the two or three swings at batting practice, Yonamine hadn't faced live pitching since coming to Japan, but he believed that he could do the job. Hirofumi Naito, one of the team's youngest players, recalls, "All the players were looking down at the ground, avoiding Mizuhara's eyes. It was a really important game." Naito looked at the end of the bench and "there was Wally, in his first game after coming to Japan, twirling his bat, appealing to the manager." Chiba noticed too and offered, "Let Yonamine try."

Mizuhara looked at Wally and said, "Hey Wally, can you bunt?"

"Okay, I'll try!" Wally declared as he bounded off the bench.

Yonamine walked toward the plate and calmly took a few practice swings. Matsutaro Shoriki, Shoji Yasuda, and Cappy Harada watched intently from the first row directly behind home plate. Wally stepped into the batter's box and heard the noise of forty thousand fans. "When I got into the batter's box, my knees started shaking! Shaking like a leaf! It was the first time that I ever played baseball in front of 40,000 people. In football, I played at Yankee Stadium with 40,000 and at the Los Angeles Coliseum with 54,000, but in baseball the most I had played in front of was about 6,000. The first pitch, I bunted down the first base line. When I started to run, I was shaking so much that I fell down." Luckily, the ball rolled foul.

Before Yonamine got back in the box, Mizuhara walked over and told him, through his interpreter, to bunt down the third base line. Wally nodded and headed back to the plate.

In Japan, both in 1951 and today, batters ordered to sacrifice hold the bat in the bunting position as soon as they enter the batter's box. Bunting is difficult, they reason, so they assume the proper bunting position before the pitch is made to increase the odds of a successful sacrifice. Of course, by doing this, the bunter loses the element of surprise. Yonamine readied himself for the second pitch. His feet were shoulder width apart with his front foot about two inches closer to the first base foul line than the back foot. The lefty stood almost erect with his weight placed slightly on his back leg and his knees relaxed. He held his hands at shoulder height with the bat angled back over his left shoulder. It looked like he would swing away on the second pitch.

On the mound, Sugishita assessed the situation. He remembered Yonamine from Hawaii. "I had a pretty good idea that Yonamine was going to bunt toward third base," he later recalled. "Tsuguhiro Hattori was playing third base and I told him, 'Move up a little bit because he's going to bunt!' But he wouldn't listen to me!" As Sugishita went into his delivery, Yonamine stayed in his batting stance.

The ball hurtled toward the plate. At the last possible moment, Yonamine squared, bent his knees, pushed the ball down the third base line, and streaked toward first base. The ball rolled slowly up the line. Hattori charged in, but instantly gave up. He had no chance. Instead of loitering near the plate, Yonamine was already near first base. The Japanese had never seen a batter get up the line that quickly. The crowd roared with delight as the bases were now loaded with no outs. Turning to Yasuda and Harada, Shoriki proclaimed, "I think we got the right guy!"

In the Giants' dugout, the players stared with surprise and admiration. They had rarely seen a bunt so deftly executed or such quick running. Kawakami later said that his eyes were glued to Yonamine's footwork as he laid down the bunt and ran to first. The Giants ended up losing the game, but it was overshadowed by Wally's at bat. Mizuhara smiled to himself, realizing that he could take the Giants to an entirely new level. With that first plate appearance, Wally Yonamine had begun to change Japanese baseball.

8

The Jackie Robinson of Japan

On Wednesday morning, June 20, 1951, Ryozo Kotoh met his friends as usual before classes began on the roof of the Bunkyo Ward Junior High School Number Two. It was already hot, so they had left their black, military-style jackets at home and lounged in the school's summer uniforms of white button-down shirts with black trousers. As always, the thirteen-year-old boys discussed the latest baseball game. Korakuen Stadium was about two hundred yards away, so they were avid Giants fans. That morning all they spoke about was Yonamine's debut. "Last night was amazing! Yonamine was so fast, I couldn't believe it," Hideo Kuroyanagi exclaimed. "The bunt was unbelievable. I've never seen anything like that before," Akio Sakaino added. Young Ryozo hadn't seen the game, but vowed to go watch the Hawaiian as soon as possible.

Later that day, Yonamine prepared for the game against the lowly Hiroshima Carp. The Carp were in last place, fourteen and a half games out of first place, with a record of 11 wins, 26 losses, and a tie. A tie? Yes, as Wally was surprised to learn, there were ties in Japanese baseball. Umpires declared a day game a tie if a score was knotted after twelve innings. There were no extra innings for night games or the opening games of doubleheaders. If the score was equal after the bottom of the ninth, the game ended in a draw. The rules for ties would be tinkered with over the ensuing five decades, but ties are still a part of the Japanese game.

Manager Mizuhara informed Wally that he would be starting in left field and batting seventh. Yonamine startled the crowd and his teammates by sprinting out to his position as the Japanese players dutifully walked on to the field. Although the Giants were the wealthiest baseball club in Japan, not a blade of grass grew in Korakuen Stadium. The Giants had planted grass prior to the 1950 season, but through wear and tear the field soon reverted to dirt. The infield was rolled as smooth as a billiard table and the grounds crew raked the base paths between innings. But they ignored the outfield. Small rocks, ruts, and even holes made the surface unpredictable and sometimes dangerous.

On the mound for the Giants was Kiyoshi Matsuda, a rookie like Yonamine. He was just twenty years old but practically unhittable. He had already won eight games in the young season, but that day Matsuda lacked his best stuff and gave up three runs in the first inning. After the third out, Wally sprinted back to the dugout, reaching the bench before several of the Giants infielders. Impressed with his hustle, the crowd cheered. His new teammates were less pleased as they believed the American was trying to show them up.

On the bench Yonamine watched the Carp's battery carefully, looking for flaws in the pitcher's delivery and the catcher's defense. He noticed hesitations in both the delivery and the catcher's return and knew that he could exploit them. Wally reached base twice, slamming a double and a single, and swiped two bases easily. By the end of the 8–3 win, Yonamine's aggressive style had begun to win over his teammates.

Wally's first week in a Giants uniform was busy as Yomiuri hosted the Carp for another game and the Hanshin Tigers for a pair. The Giants won all three with Wally continuing to impress. In his first week, Yonamine played in five games, knocked out ten hits in seventeen at bats, including three doubles, stole three bases, and drove in three runners. On June 24, Wally turned twenty-six years old. He got three hits and a couple of RBI against the Tigers that afternoon, but with the excitement of finally playing and without his friends and family to remind him, Wally forgot his own birthday.

The hometown fans enjoyed Wally's hustle, but they were unprepared for the first time he was forced at second base. Yonamine took his lead off first base as usual, attempting to distract the pitcher. The hurler ignored him, threw to the plate, and was rewarded with perfect double-play ball to short. Fielding it cleanly, the shortstop tossed it to the second baseman, who stepped on the bag, pivoted and prepared to throw to first. To his surprise, there was Yonamine, a few yards away, bearing down at him at full speed! The Hawaiian had not turned into right field as a Japanese would. Instead, the former San Francisco running back was about to knock him flat. At the last second, Wally slid hard, spikes high, directly toward the second baseman's pivot leg. The second baseman panicked and jumped out of the way, still clutching the ball. The crowd was stunned. They had never seen such a dirty play. The second baseman glared at Yonamine in disgust, but said nothing and the game continued.

The Giants teammates and fans soon became accustomed to Wally's aggressive style. Shigeru Chiba commented that Yonamine's "dynamic speed with his weight was terrifying. The speed of a Japanese running can be likened to a squirrel, but Wally was different, nothing cute like a squirrel. He reminded us of a leopard or a tiger. He didn't run with the wind. He charged ahead generating wind."

Spectators packed the stadium to see the new sensation for themselves. Young Ryozo Kotoh came many times, and Yonamine soon became his favorite player. One afternoon, Ryozo spied Wally walking past his house. The boy soon discovered that his new hero lived in a nearby inn. Ryozo would often wait near his home after day games and watch for Yonamine, but, like many boys his age, he was too shy to approach. When he eventually got up the nerve to speak, Kotoh was a thirty-three-year-old sports reporter covering the Chunichi Dragons for *Sports Hochi.* The two men eventually became close friends.

There was more to Yonamine's game than just hustle. In 1951 there were no Japanese "five tool players"—baseball lingo for a player who excels at the five basic aspects of the game: to hit for average, to hit for power, to run well, to field well, and to throw well. Japanese fans and players tended to regard hitting and pitching as the only criteria for stardom. Consequently, most great hitters paid little attention to fielding or base running. Yonamine was one of the first players to play all aspects of the game well. Knowledgeable fans realized this right away and came to watch him play.

The first week was lonely for Yonamine as his new teammates were reluctant to approach him. Not being able to speak Japanese, he could only converse with Miyamoto, his translator. "To tell the truth, I got so homesick after a week in Japan that I wanted to go straight back to Hawaii. I wanted to talk to my heart's content in English with my friends and family. In Japan, I was deaf and dumb and uneasy about what my teammates thought of me. I knew that some guys on the team had fought against the United States during World War II, and I was concerned how they would react toward me, but they didn't mention anything about the war. They were outwardly friendly, and they bowed to me and things like that, but they didn't try to get to know me."

A week after Yonamine's debut, the entire team took an excursion for a few days to a hot spring resort on the Izu Peninsula. Just as they would be in the United States, midseason vacations were highly unusual in Japan. Yomiuri management had, however, carefully planned the trip. They believed that the Giants had lost the pennant the year before because of bad team chemistry. The trip to Izu, although disguised as a welcoming party for Yonamine and a celebration of the anniversary of Hideo Fujimoto's perfect game, was designed to break up the long, tense season and improve team morale.

The evening the team arrived at the inn, they had a party to honor Yonamine and Fujimoto. They served sukiyaki and other traditional Japanese dishes, but no alcohol. It was the first time that Wally had had sukiyaki in Japan and he loved it. In the relaxed atmosphere, Wally and his teammates interacted more. The older players were still reserved and distant, but the younger players became friendly. Although he couldn't speak more than a handful of Japanese words, Wally stayed up most of the night talking to Hirofumi Naito and a few other players with hand movements and baseball terms.

Naito, one of the youngest players on the team, had signed with the Giants straight out of high school in 1948. At the time, a rigid hierarchy based on seniority dictated Japanese social relations. Younger individuals (known as *kohai*) had to serve and obey their seniors (*senpai*). In return, the *senpai* were expected to guide and use their influence to help their *kohai*. As the youngest player on the team, Naito was responsible for collecting the equipment after practices and games and running errands for the established stars like Kawakami, Chiba, and Aota.

Under the *senpai-kohai* system, the older players received many special privileges. For example, they entered buses first, and ate before the younger players. After the games, the team would bathe in a communal tub in the clubhouse. Here too, the *kohai* had to wait until their seniors finished before bathing. By the time the younger players entered, the bath was usually cold and the water dirty. During his rookie year, Naito would often skip the bath and only take a shower.

One day the visiting team went straight back to their hotel after the game, so the bathtub in their clubhouse was unused. A janitor found Naito and told him, "Hey, come on over. This is your chance to take a nice bath." The rookie obliged and for once enjoyed a hot, clean bath, but the older players found out. Noboru Aota smacked him on the head and scolded him, "Were you playing in the game today?"

"No, I wasn't," Naito responded.

"How many of the people who came to watch the game came to see you?"

"Probably nobody," the rookie said meekly.

"So the fans came to see the regular members of the Giants. Therefore, it's the regulars' sweat and hard work that provide your monthly pay. To take a bath before the starters, who were working hard for you, is not the proper thing for a human being to do."

After many hard lessons, Naito learned that the Giants expected more from their players than other teams did. It was not enough to be a good player, one also had to respect tradition and develop the proper "Giants' spirit." Naito rarely played in his first few years, but eventually developed into a good utility infielder. From that first night in Izu, Naito and Yonamine became friends and also roommates on road trips.

On the second day at the Izu resort, the team had a fishing contest and visited the hot springs. The trip had the desired effect and the Giants returned relaxed and ready to play a Saturday game in Osaka against the Kokutetsu Swallows before the twelve-day All-Star break. It was Yonamine's first look at Masaichi Kaneda, the Swallow's left-handed ace who threw over ninety miles per hour. The hot-tempered Kaneda would become Japan's greatest pitcher. By the end of his twenty-year career, he would be the all-time leader in victories (with 400), innings pitched, complete games, and strikeouts, as well as losses and walks. He had an unusual way of loosening up each inning: he would throw his first warmup pitch from second base and gradually work his way toward the mound with each successive throw. An ethnic Korean, Kaneda was just over six feet tall, making him among the league's taller players. It was only his second professional season in 1951, and the eighteen-year-old had not learned the pinpoint control that he would possess later in his career. At this point, batters needed to be wary of the kid's blazing fastball, as he led the Central League in strikeouts, walks, and hit batsmen. Many Americans who later played against Kaneda claimed that he would have been a Major League star. Indeed, in the fall of 1955, he would strike out Mickey Mantle three times in one exhibition game, but in truth, the Yankee center fielder was seriously hung over after enjoying Japan's nightlife a bit too much. In their first encounter, Kaneda got the best of Yonamine, holding him hitless for the first time since coming to Japan. Despite Yonamine's off day, the Giants won 2–1 as Hideo Fujimoto outdueled the Swallows' ace.

The Giants entered the All-Star break in first place, three and a half games in front of the second-place Dragons. During the long break, the Central and Pacific League All-Stars played three games: one at Koshien Stadium in Osaka and two at the Giants' home Korakuen Stadium. The starting All-Stars included five Giants: Bessho, Kawakami, Chiba, Aota, and the shortstop Saburo Hirai. Yonamine was not included on the team as he had only played in six games, but because of his success and fan appeal, league officials considered adding him to the squad. In the end, however, they decided against the idea.

Following the All-Star break, Yonamine lapsed into his only slump of the season, going hitless in his next four games. The cause of the slump is lost to time, but it was likely an injury, as Yonamine sat out the next three games. He returned on Saturday, July 22, with a hit and an RBI in a win over the Tigers that increased Yomiuri's lead over the Dragons to seven games.

On July 23 the Giants congregated at Tokyo Station and boarded a train for the ten-hour trip to Osaka. It was Yonamine's first extended road trip and an experience he would never forget.

Arriving in Osaka, the team settled in at their usual abode. Ball clubs did not stay in luxury western-style hotels but instead at Japanese inns called *ryokan*. These inns were furnished in the traditional fashion with a large common space and communal bath. The guest rooms, separated from the hall by sliding paper doors, were also large but contained no beds or furniture. Instead, guests slept on futons placed on the straw mat floors (tatami). Several players occupied each room. The toilets at the ryokan were barely sanitary. The sewer system in that section of Osaka had not been completely restored after the war so flush toilets were not installed. Instead, the *ryokan* guests used open holes. Yonamine remembers, "I would wrap my face firmly with a towel to fight the stench and charge in and out of the toilet."

The team assembled for dinner. Following Japanese custom, the players sat on the floor and were served a traditional Japanese meal on low wooden tables. Unlike the food served at the Izu resort, Wally thought the fare both looked and smelled unappetizing. The smell of raw fish and *natto* (fermented soybeans) revolted him and the fatty veal cutlet was particularly unpleasant. But Wally wanted to make a good impression on his teammates. He worried that if he declined the meal, or left it uneaten, his Japanese teammates might think that he was stuck up or felt himself above them. Wally also wanted to show that he could adapt to Japan, so he forced the food down.

Yonamine soon figured out how to avoid the unsavory meals. At first, he would sit next to a window. As Japanese summers are hot and sticky, the windows were always open. He would slowly pick at his meal and move it around the plate; then, when nobody was looking, he would quickly empty his plate out the window.

Soon, however, he tasted *tamagomeshi*, raw eggs served on top of hot rice. Adding Japanese pickles, Wally found a dish that he enjoyed and was predictably fresh. During road trips, he ate it three meals a day. He lost a lot of weight that summer, and his teammates must have thought him a bit odd. "Surely, nobody could like *tamagomeshi* that much!"

Later in the summer, when Yonamine visited cities with U.S. Army bases, GIS would introduce themselves and invite him to their bases for American-style meals. There, Wally could eat steaks, which were unavailable to the Japanese, and dessert. When asked what he would like, Wally always responded with enthusiasm, "Pie à la mode!" One of his favorites, it was completely unavailable in Japan outside the military bases.

On Tuesday, July 24, the Giants began a three-game stint at Osaka Stadium against three different teams. They beat the Robins 8–5 on Tuesday, the lowly Carp 22–2 on Wednesday, and Sugishita and the second-place Dragons 7–6 on Thursday. Yonamine hit well in all three games, going a combined 5 for 10. As always, Wally ran on and off the field and hustled on the base paths. Early in the three-game series, he broke up a double play by going hard into the pivot man. Once again, the slide shocked the crowd, but this time there wasn't stunned silence. Instead, the crowd started hurling insults at him. "YANKEE GO HOME!" and "GO BACK TO HAWAII!" were slung often, but there were many others in Japanese that Wally could only guess the meaning of. Whereas Giants fans loved his hustle and aggressive style of play, many opposing fans regarded Yonamine as a dirty player who typified the bullying American occupiers.

The fan abuse got worse when the Giants played at Koshien Stadium at the end of the week. Built in 1924, it is Japan's oldest and most famous ballpark. "Koshien is massive," Brian Maitland writes, "with an iron framework and girders that are truly imposing. One section of the stands is so steep that it is called the Alps. In the summer the place is like an oven; ice is sold or handed out to cool off potential sunstroke victims." Every summer and spring, Koshien hosts the high school baseball championship tournaments. The games, usually just called "Koshien," pit the champions from each prefecture against one another in a single-elimination tournament and are Japan's most popular sporting events.

Koshien Stadium is also the home of the Hanshin Tigers, the Yomiuri Giants' fiercest rivals. The two teams finished in first and second place in each of the first seven seasons of professional baseball. But the rivalry transcends baseball. The Giants are by far the most popular team in Tokyo, the country's political, intellectual, and economic capital. Amid the top universities, trading companies, and government, Tokyoites consider themselves urbane and sophisticated. The Tigers are the favorite of Osaka, the country's second most populous city, known for its manufacturing and tough, gritty inhabitants. The two cities are natural rivals, and in the early 1950s local pride was especially strong. As the importance of Osaka declined in the postwar years, its inhabitants flaunted their resentment toward Tokyo at the baseball park. One former Giant recalled that the two teams and their fans "just didn't like each other. You could feel the tension in the stadium when we got together."

When Yonamine trotted out to the field for Sunday's game, the Koshien crowd was ready for him. The taunts started immediately. "Yankee go home!" "Hawaii e kaere (Go Back to Hawaii)!" Others yelled insults in Japanese, while a few yelled the only English they knew, "One, Two, Three!" Something whizzed by Yonamine's ear. A rock. Wally ignored it and concentrated on the game. From time to time, small objects would shoot from the left-field bleachers toward him, but luckily none found its mark. Yonamine knew that he could not react. Not only would a response send the crowd into a frenzy, but as the only foreigner in the league he was closely scrutinized. An inappropriate response might prevent other foreigners from playing in Japan.

Instead, he channeled his anger into the game, smacking a double and triple, and running the bases with abandon. As the Giants poured on the runs, the crowd grew more belligerent. Late in the game, a fan vaulted over the wall surrounding the field and ran toward Yonamine. He stopped a few feet away and yelled at Wally in Japanese. Security guards quickly removed the intruder and the game continued. By the end, the Giants had pounded out nine runs while their rookie ace Kiyoshi Matsuda held the Tigers to a single tally. It was Matsuda's thirteenth win and his eighth in a row.

After the game was over, Wally questioned himself: "Perhaps I am a dirty player. Maybe my style is too aggressive for Japan." He approached his manager, Shigeru Mizuhara, and asked his advice. The leathery-faced Mizuhara was a legend in Japan. He had been a star third baseman at Tokyo's prestigious Keio University and had been an aggressive player in his own right. He was famous for the "Ringo Jiken" (apple incident). During a tense moment in a game versus archrival Waseda University's nine, a Waseda fan had thrown a partially eaten apple onto the field at Mizuhara's feet. Mizuhara picked it up and threw it right back into the stands, igniting a riot. Several years later, Mizuhara played against Babe Ruth and the All-Stars in 1934 and played in over one hundred games against American teams during the Giants' 1935 U.S. tour. He had seen American baseball and wanted to bring the more aggressive style to Japan. He looked at Yonamine and said, "Don't let the fans bother you. What you did in the States, what you learned there, you do that in Japan." Wally smiled. "Okay!" he thought "He's backed me up now!" He vowed to not hold back and became even more aggressive on the base paths.

Yonamine had been in Japan for about two months and was picking up the language. He had become friendly with many of the younger players, especially Naito, but the older players mostly remained distant, and some were even a little cold. As a rookie, Wally ate, roomed, and bathed with the younger Giants. But unlike the other youngsters, Yonamine was a starter. He was also a foreigner and he knew that the rules and customs that bound the Japanese didn't always apply to him. He was learning which customs he must respect and which he could test. Maybe it was the fan abuse, maybe the oppressive heat of Osaka in the summer, but during the road trip Yonamine finally had enough of the dirty, cold baths.

"I said to myself, 'I'm going to go in with the old timers.' So I put my head down and walked into the room. I could see the guys poking each other. I knew they were thinking, 'What is this rookie doing in here?' I just got in the tub and they didn't say anything to me. I knew that they wanted to tell me to get out, but I was playing every day and I'm a foreigner, so they wouldn't say anything directly to me."

What seemed like a small action was the first step in a larger process. Wally had asserted himself as one of the regulars and he had also challenged the *senpai-kohai* structure. Strong cultural practices do not collapse instantly, but slowly the club's rigid social structure began to change. Over the next few years, many of the Giants' hierarchical traditions would break down.

After the ordeal at Koshien, the Giants headed home for a couple of games, easily defeating the Whales and Carp. The Giants had now won fourteen straight games and were 15-1 since the trip to Izu. About this time, Wally moved out of the *ryokan* where he had lived for the past six weeks. Dose and Ethel Teshima had a large house with five bedrooms, and they invited him to live with them. Wally readily agreed. As employees of the occupation forces, the Teshimas could shop at the military PX and commissary, where fresh American vegetables and meat were available. Yonamine's fare became instantly better. He had heard that the Japanese used human manure on their fields, so, fearing worms, he dared not eat fresh vegetables in *ryokan* and he missed these terribly.

With the stress of adapting to Japanese culture, Wally realized that he missed the soothing familiarity and peacefulness of church. Although he was not yet a baptized Catholic, the rituals of the Church and prayer helped him relax and find inner peace. Locating a military Catholic church in downtown Tokyo, near GHQ, he started to attend Mass.

Tokyo in August is hot, sticky, and unpleasant. In the days before air conditioning, Tokyoites survived by dressing in light cottons, eating shaved ice, and escaping to the nearby mountains. Each August, the Giants left the city on a long road trip to the cooler northern regions of Japan. The excursion was also designed to bring professional baseball to the rural sections of Japan, thus increasing the Yomiuri Giants' fan base.

The Giants journeyed to the northern tip of the main island of Honshu and to the island of Hokkaido. The trek took about fifteen hours by train, and the team traveled third class. The seats were uncomfortable wooden benches, making sleeping difficult. Many players slept in the dirty aisles as teammates and passengers stepped over them. Others brought along boards and made rough beds by laying them between two facing benches. Saburo Hirai, the shortstop, found a novel solution. Only 5 feet 5 inches tall and weighing just 132 pounds, Hirai would climb onto the luggage rack to sleep. To protect himself from the swarms of mosquitoes that fed off the passengers, he brought netting and placed it over his perch.

In the August heat, the cars soon became unbearably hot. The players, dressed in their compulsory jackets with neckties, opened the windows. The rushing air brought relief, and another problem. The trains were not the modern diesel or electric models, but old-fashioned steam engines run on coal. The open windows drew in the soot and soon a fine black dust covered the players, benches, and luggage.

Once north, the team stayed at *ryokans* and, in Wally's opinion, were once again served inedible fare. During the long trip, Yonamine got to know his teammates better, and many were warming up to him. Hiroyoshi Komatsubara and Noboru Aota in particular went out of their way to be friendly. Komatsubara was only a year older than Yonamine, but he had been playing in the league since 1942. He had started as a pitcher but was the regular left fielder before Wally joined the team. Although Wally had replaced him in the lineup, Komatsubara showed no resentment and frequently helped the Hawaiian. After the games, he would often take Wally out to eat. Aota, the star center fielder, stood just 5 feet 7 inches, but his strong wrists gave him incredible power. During the war, Aota supposedly could toss a grenade seventy meters. An extrovert, Aota invited Wally out several times, but their personalities were too different for a strong friendship to develop. Aota enjoyed the fast life. A heavy drinker and sometime brawler, he mixed with a rough crowd.

The Giants played seven games in six different northern cities, winning five against the Whales, Dragons, Carp, and Swallows but dropping two to Chunichi. Yonamine played hard during these games. Following Mizuhara's advice, he ran the base paths even more aggressively, knocking down any opponent in his way. In the outfield, he played shallow, using his football skills to go back and chase down long drives. Unlike Japanese outfielders who often played balls on one hop rather than risking the ball getting behind them, Yonamine ran full speed for shallow hits and dove to reach them. The fans had never seen fielding like this before.

The long, uncomfortable train rides and the poor food were taking a toll on Yonamine. He thought about returning to Hawaii but didn't want to return a failure, so he persevered. Mizuhara, realizing that Wally wasn't used to the long train rides and cramped conditions in third class, quietly offered him a second-class ticket, where he would have his own seat. "I was tempted," Yonamine recalls, "but . . . one thing I had learned from being the new guy—first at Farrington, then at San Francisco and Salt Lake—was that your teammates had to respect you before they'd accept you. I really wanted to be accepted so I tried to do everything the way they did."

After eleven days in northern Japan, the road trip continued in Nagoya, where Mizuhara decided to shake up the Giants lineup and move Yonamine to the lead-off spot. Wally was pleased.

"As a lead-off batter, I had to get on base any way I could. I would try to work out at least one walk every game. Sometimes if it was a tie game, or we were one run behind, I would stand right on the plate. If the pitcher threw inside, I would just stick out an elbow and get to first base. I learned to use the whole field. If the pitch was from the middle of the plate out, I'd hit it back to the box or into left field. If it was from the middle of the plate in, I used to pull the pitch. If I was going to hit it back through the box, I tried to swing down and hit the ball at the pitcher's legs or past him for a base hit. I didn't have a lot of power, so if I tried to hit the ball to center field, it was going to be caught. I always tried to think when I was hitting. For example, I was a good bunter, so the third baseman would often play way up on me. Sometimes I would purposely show them the bunt, and when they charged in, I would push the ball over the third baseman's head with a swinging bunt."

Noboru Aota noted that Yonamine's batting style differed from the Japanese form. "Wally would swing from where he held his bat ready. A Japanese batter would always pull the bat back to start his swing and hit with the momentum of the swing. Wally would not move his body but would pivot on it to swat the ball. This was an unusual style never seen in Japan. . . . He didn't shift his weight, and so he could let the ball come to him to be hit. . . . Later on, when the Cardinals came [to Japan in 1958], the ace hitter Stan Musial batted the same way."

Yonamine excelled in his first game at the top of the lineup, getting two hits and an RBI in five at bats as the Giants won a squeaker, 6–5, over the Dragons. Nagoya remained twelve games behind as the two teams faced off again the next day.

The Dragons started lanky Sugishita while the Giants went to the bushy-eyebrowed Takehiko Bessho. On and off the field, Bessho was one of the most aggressive pitchers in Japan. Instead of nibbling at the corners like most Japanese pitchers, Bessho came straight after hitters with a blazing fastball and a nasty curve. Many American opponents believed that Bessho could have been a Major League star, but by staying in Japan, he became one of the country's greatest pitchers. He still ranks among the all-time leaders in wins, innings pitched, complete games, shutouts, and earned run average. Off the field, Bessho drank hard and would fight on the slimmest excuses. Often Bessho and Aota, who had attended the same high school, would close down the local bars and on more than one occasion, end the evening in a fistfight.

In the third inning, the Dragons' star first baseman Michio Nishizawa stepped into the box with a 2–1 lead. Bessho was in his windup when somebody yelled, "Fire! Fire!" The Chunichi ballpark was old and made of wood. Patrons sat on long wooden benches rather than individual seats, and the small gaps between the floor and benches were always stuffed with newspapers, trash, and personal belongings. Many fans smoked and water buckets stood at the end of each aisle, just in case a fire broke out. Several small fires had already disrupted the game. Each time, a fan had grabbed a water bucket and quickly extinguished the flames.

This time, the threat was more serious. A fire had broken out directly behind home plate, a number of rows behind the wall and netting that separated the fans from the field. The flames spread horizontally. Soon the entire stands behind the backstop were ablaze. Flames leapt up twenty feet, igniting the second tier.

In left field, Wally heard the alarm and ran toward the pitcher's mound. Mizuhara intercepted him. "Get out of here!" the manager screamed at his new star, "Go! Run!" and he pointed toward the outfield. Obeying, Yonamine retreated. On the managers' orders, the dugouts emptied and the players moved toward the outfield. Fans leaped out of the stands and stampeded into the outfield. Shigeo Sugishita remembers, "It was like a mudslide of people coming on to the field."

Immediately behind home plate the blaze raged, surrounding and trapping fans. Some climbed the netting behind home plate, and dropped nearly twenty feet to the field. Fans eventually threw down the netting and jumped over the low wall onto the field. Seeing an escape route, the people closest to the fire surged forward, sandwiching the fans in front against the wall, crushing their chests. Sugishita and several other players ran to help pull spectators from the stands. Many were "crushed and bleeding from their eyes and ears. The fans closest to the fire jumped on the people in front of them and used them like steppingstones to get on to the field." Three people died at the scene. Another died later and about three hundred others suffered injuries, most trampled by the stampeding crowd. The fire had also destroyed the stadium, forcing the Dragons to finish the season at nearby Na-rumi Stadium.

During that long road trip, Wally's mornings were usually spent relaxing in the *ryokans* with his roommate Hirofumi Naito and writing letters to Jane. One morning, a young maid entered the room and spied Yonamine writing. "Wow!" She gushed. "He's writing in English!"

"He's not Japanese," the fun-loving Naito responded. "He came over from America and he doesn't understand any Japanese. Watch." He turned to Wally and said, "Baka" (stupid) and other profanities.

"You shouldn't say such bad things to him," admonished the maid.

"Oh, he doesn't understand. You try it."

"Baka," whispered the maid. Yonamine didn't react and continued to ignore them. The maid tried again with the same result. Finally, she shouted a variety of bad words at him. At this, Wally turned around and yelled in Japanese, "What are you saying?" The terrified maid ran barefooted out of the hotel and did not return until the Giants left.

The Giants finally returned home on August 29 for a four-game series. They won three of the four, dropping one to the Hanshin Tigers. In the third inning against the Tigers, Yonamine slid into third base, eluding the tag with a beautiful hook slide. The Japanese rarely used the hook slide, where a player aims the slide a few feet beside the bag and then catches the bag with the top leg at the last moment, but Wally successfully used the difficult maneuver so often that they soon began practicing it. In the final game of the home stand, against the Taiyo Whales on September 3, Yonamine hit his first home run.

Before and after each game, a crowd of children would wait near the Giants' dugout, hoping to meet their favorites or get autographs on thick cardboard squares known as *shikishi*. Occasionally, a star stopped and signed one or two, but usually the famous Giants players ignored the youngsters. Wally was different. He rarely turned down an autograph request. He has always believed that as a professional athlete it is his honor and duty to sign for fans.

One day, perhaps on this home stand, an eleven-year-old boy stood in the crowd. He had tried many times to get players to sign, but, as he remembered later, "The players would walk past me as though I didn't exist. My brother would tease me because I always wound up feeling so hurt that I wanted to cry." On that day, too, the players walked by him. Then the last player, Yonamine, stopped, looked directly at the boy and smiled. "He took my board, asked my name—which I could barely get from my lips—and signed his autograph."

Sadaharu Oh still treasures that *shikishi*. When Oh joined the Giants in 1959, he was too embarrassed to tell Wally the story, but years later, after Oh had broken Babe Ruth's and Hank Aaron's lifetime home run records, he recounted the story in his autobiography. Oh commented, "When I became a player it was always remarked how readily I gave autographs—which is true—but I did so for the best of reasons: because of the joy Wally Yonamine brought into my life one afternoon in my boyhood."

The home stand was over quickly and the Giants packed their bags once again. This time it was a short trip to the mountains west and northwest of Tokyo, where they played a total of six games in the small cities of Niigata, Nagaoka, Shimosuwa, Matsumoto, and Nagano against the Whales, Swallows, and Robins. Yomiuri thrilled the rural fans by winning all six contests as Yonamine stole a base in all but one game. Although many fans still did not completely approve of Wally's scrappy style, they flocked to watch him play.

With Yonamine in the lead-off slot, the Giants developed an aggressive attack. If Wally reached first safely, he would try to steal second. Chiba would then take the ball the opposite way into right field, scoring Wally or moving him to third. The power hitters, Aota and Kawakami would then bring in Yonamine and Chiba, too, if they could.

On September 11 against the Swallows and their ace Masaichi Kaneda, the Giants played this new style to perfection. Yonamine led off the game with a walk. Chiba singled up the middle and Wally raced to third and slid around the tag with a deft hook slide. Aota followed with a sacrifice fly to center, scoring Yonamine and giving the Giants a 1–0 lead. After the Swallows tied the game in the top of the second, the Giants pounded out five more runs in the next three innings.

Yonamine led off the sixth inning against reliever Teru Takahashi with the Giants leading 7–2. Wally drew another walk and took a large lead off first. Chiba swung and hit a routine grounder to Sakae Nakamura at short—easy double play. With Yonamine barreling toward second base, Nakamura knew he needed to hurry. Flustered, he looked up for a split second, but that was enough. The ball glanced off his glove and rolled behind him. Yonamine raced to third and Chiba reached first safely. Next, Aota strode into the batter's box. With the pitch, Chiba ran toward second. As the catcher, Kazuo Satake, threw down, Yonamine broke for the plate. The Swallows cut off the throw and threw home to get Wally, but they were too late. In a perfectly executed double steal, Chiba was standing on second as Yonamine slid home with the Giants' eighth run. Aota followed by doubling home Chiba. Before the inning ended, Aota would also score on a double by Uno.

After Nakao grounded out to start the Giants' seventh, Yonamine came to the plate to face the Swallows' third pitcher of the game, Shinichiro Inoue. For the fourth time, Wally walked. Yonamine had been watching Inoue's motion since he came in to relieve Takahashi in the sixth inning and had noticed a flaw he could exploit. Chiba was up next. As Inoue began his delivery, Yonamine streaked toward second base, stealing it easily. Inoue turned his attention back toward Chiba, ignoring Yonamine, who was now leading off second. Wally ran with the next pitch, sliding into third ahead of the throw. Rattled, Inoue walked Chiba. With Yonamine on third, Chiba at first and Aota up, the Swallows' manager signaled to the bullpen again. Rookie Jyun Hakota emerged.

In 1954 Hakota would move into the Swallows' starting lineup as a talented middle infielder, but this year he was an ineffectual reliever. The righty took his warmup tosses and focused on Aota. Aota had hit his thirtieth home run of the season the day before. He was a challenge for anyone, much less the green Hakota. At third base, Yonamine saw the hurler concentrate on Aota, barely looking at the runners. Wally lengthened his lead—still no reaction. Once again Chiba and Yonamine tried the double steal. Chiba broke for second and on the throw, Wally took off for home. Again the Swallows cut off the throw to second and relayed the ball home to nab Yonamine. Wally came in hard, spikes in the air, kicking up dust, and beat the throw by inches. The stadium erupted with cheers. Wally had stolen all three bases in the inning, and had stolen home twice in the game. Both feats were Japanese records. By the end of his career, Yonamine would steal home six times—another Japanese record.

On September 17, the Giants boarded the train to Hiroshima for the final road trip of the regular season. They were now seventeen and a half games up on the Dragons with only two weeks left on the schedule. With the pennant clinched, the Giants relaxed and fell to the Carp's twenty-one-year-old ace, Ryohei Hasegawa. Hasegawa threw underhand with a graceful motion that made him look "like he was dancing." In 1951 the submariner's pitching was the only bright spot in the Carp's dismal season. The team ended up winning only thirty-two games, and Hasegawa won seventeen of them. He pitched for fourteen seasons with the Carp, during which the financially strapped team had only one winning season. In 2001 Hasegawa became the only modern pitcher with a sub-.500 mark elected to the Japanese Hall of Fame.

The Giants and Carp traveled together to Osaka, where the Giants bested Hiroshima 9–2 on Saturday before meeting the Tigers on Sunday. The Hanshin fans were once again waiting for Yonamine. The usual chants started the minute Wally took the field. "Yankee go home!" "Hawaii e kaere!" Occasionally, small objects were hurled in his direction, but none came close to hitting him. Takumi Otomo started for the Giants. The submariner had one of the best curve balls in Japan—it supposedly buzzed as it broke—but this Sunday, Otomo was quite ordinary. The Tigers hit him hard, and soon Hiroshi Nakao entered in relief. As the Tigers and Giants battled back and forth, the crowd became more enthusiastic. Late in the game, while the Giants were in the field, the stadium lost power. Yonamine remembered, "I was playing left field when the lights went out. Since I was close to the fans, I thought that I had better start walking toward the infield. When the lights came on, I went back to my position and there was a big rock right where I had been standing! Somebody must have thrown it in the dark, trying to hit me."

The Giants lost to the Robins 5–6 the next day at Koshien before returning to Tokyo for a four-game home stand. Yonamine played in all four games but did not join the team for the pair of away games that finished the season on October 2 and 4. Instead, Wally remained in Tokyo resting for the Japan Series against the Nankai Hawks.

The Hawks dominated the Pacific League in 1951, finishing eighteen and a half games over the second-place Nishitetsu Lions. The Osaka-based club, owned by the Nankai Railroad Company, was founded in 1938 as simply Nankai. Before the end of World War II, the franchise had little success, but its fortunes changed after the team changed its name to Kinki Great Ring in 1946. Led by Takehiko Bessho on the mound and an intelligent player-manager named Kazuto Tsuruoka at second base, the Great Ring beat out the Yomiuri Giants for the pennant by one game. The name "Great Ring" referred to the ring-shaped Osaka railroad system, but the American GIs soon nicknamed the team "the Ringers," which, at the time, had a double meaning. Historian Joseph Reaves explains, "Ringers, of course, referred to extremely talented players who were slipped in against unsuspecting opponents to ensure victory. But 'ringer' also was slang used by U.S. servicemen to refer to especially good-looking Japanese women because they were most likely to get an engagement ring—and an engagement ring at that time essentially was a free ticket to sex, regardless of whether marriage eventually resulted. When officials of the club eventually caught on to the saucy dual meaning, they changed the name of the team to the Nankai Hawks."

The Hawks won the pennant again in 1948, this time topping the second-place Giants by five games. Bessho remained the team's top pitcher, but he was joined by a group of young pitchers including rookie Susumu Yuki, who won 19 with a 1.89 ERA, and Nobuo Naka-tani, who won 21 with a 1.98 ERA. Immediately after losing the pen-nant to the Hawks, the Giants lured Bessho away from Nankai after the ace tried to hold out for more money. For not honoring his com-mitment to the Hawks, the league suspended Bessho for two months, but he joined the Giants in June 1949 and helped Yomiuri capture the pennant. The following year when the professional teams split into two leagues, league officials separated the Giants and Hawks, but both failed to win a pennant in 1950.

An exuberant crowd of 29,074 packed the tiny Namba Stadium in Osaka for the series opener on October 10. Wily Shigeru Mizuhara brought a supply of brand-new lively balls for batting practice, and the Nankai players watched in wonder as the Giants hitters pounded them into the stands. The ruse worked and the already nervous Hawks became even tenser.

Hideo Fujimoto started for the Giants and scattered ten hits as he shut out the Hawks speedy lineup. The Giants, on the other hand, hit the Hawks' starter Tadashi Eto hard. Relievers Nobuo Nakatani and Takeo Hattori fared no better as the Giants racked up fifteen hits and won the game 5–0. The game's highlight came in the sixth inning. With two outs and pitcher Hideo Fujimoto on first, Yonamine sin-gled, moving Fujimoto to second. Mizuhara called for a hit and run, and as the runners took off, Chiba singled to right field, scoring Fu-jimoto. Right behind the pitcher came Yonamine, racing at full speed toward the plate. It would be close. Keizo Tsutsui, the Hawks' catcher, set up to block the plate as the throw came in from the outfield. The throw came in wild. Tsutsui leapt for it, missed, and came crashing down, face first into the dirt. Wally slid across the plate, spikes up and dust flying. Clicking cameras immortalized the play. Newspapers ran the pictures the next morning, and the images have been reprinted numerous times. They portray Yonamine at his best—hustling, slid-ing aggressively, knocking down anyone in his way, vividly capturing the essence of the man who changed Japanese baseball.

The Giants shut out the Hawks again the next day as Takehiko Bessho limited his old team to just six hits and doubled in three runs in a 7–0 victory. It was a tough day for Yonamine, who went hitless in five at bats. The series moved on to Tokyo as 35,066 watched the Giants take the third game 3–1. Yonamine sparked the Giants' attack by leading off the bottom of the first with a single and scoring when Tetsuharu Kawakami lashed a long single to right field. Wally, however, went hitless in the remaining eight innings.

With their backs against the wall, the Nankai Hawks put nineteen-year-old Takeo Hattori on the mound three days later for Game 4. Hattori held the Giants to just one hit for the first eight innings, while his teammates scored four off Hiroshi Nakao and Bessho. In the bottom of the ninth, however, Hattori suddenly lost control of his pitches. After Kawakami singled and Aota walked, Mizuhara brought in the rookie Takeo Higasa to pinch hit for Mitsuo Uno. On a 1-2 count, Higasa homered into the left-field stands to bring the Giants within one run. Susumu Yuki immediately came on in relief and set the Giants down 1-2-3 to save the game. It was another disappointing game for Yonamine, who went hitless in four at bats.

Only 15,519 fans came to Korakuen Stadium on Wednesday, October 17, for Game 5. Many diehard fans gathered in Ginza instead to welcome Lefty O'Doul, Joe DiMaggio, and a team of Major League All-Stars. Sponsored by the *Yomiuri Shimbun*, the Major Leaguers had come to Japan for a sixteen-game tour that would start directly after the Japan Series. The team landed at 4:30 p.m. at Haneda Airport and went to their hotel in a motorcade, but nearly a million fans jammed the streets to catch a glimpse of the stars, tying up traffic for hours.

At Korakuen Stadium, Hideo Fujimoto started for the Giants and Mizuhara rewarded Kazuo Higasa by starting him in left field instead of Yonamine. Despite closing the night before, Susumu Yuki started Game 5 for the Hawks. He lasted just three innings. Fujimoto, on the other hand, shut down the Hawks for the first eight innings. In the bottom of the eighth with a runner on and up 4–0, Mizuhara decided to let Yonamine pinch-hit for the hitless Higasa. Left-hander Nobuo

Nakatani delivered and Wally slammed the pitch into the right-field seats for a two-run homer, sealing the Hawks' fate. Following Japanese tradition, the victorious Giants ran on to the field, hoisted manager Shigeo Mizuhara above their heads, and tossed him several times into the air.

The Major League All-Star team arrived the next afternoon for practice at Meiji Jingu Stadium. O'Doul had brought a strong squad. Joe DiMaggio was the premier attraction, but his brother Dominic, AL batting champ Ferris Fain, eighteen-game-winner Mel Parnell, Billy Martin, Eddie Lopat, and Bobby Shantz accompanied him. Journeymen players and minor leaguers (such as Joe Tipton, Bill Werle, and Dino Restelli) filled out the roster. Nearly five thousand fans watched from the stands as the All-Stars took fielding and batting practice.

After practice, the team made several social calls, including one to Supreme Commander General Matthew B. Ridgway at GHQ. In the evening O'Doul called Wally and suggested they join Joe DiMaggio at the Latin Quarter nightclub. The Latin Quarter was a notorious nightspot that was owned jointly by the infamous Yoshio Kodama, a former member in the wartime Tojo cabinet and ex–war crimes suspect, and his partner, a Meyer Lansky cohort and Mafia gambling kingpin named Ted Lewin. A secret casino operated in an adjoining room. Wally dressed in his finest and met the two visiting Americans at the crowded club. After pleasantries, Lefty asked Wally how his baseball skills were progressing.

"Well," said Yonamine, "I'm having trouble hitting the inside pitch."

"Get up and show me your batting form," commanded O'Doul.

Wally stood up, found some room, and got into his stance. O'Doul and DiMaggio watched intently as Wally took a few shadow swings, his dinner jacket catching on his shoulders as he swung. Soon many of the patrons stopped their conversations to watch. Standing there in his suit, taking practice swings, Wally felt more than a bit silly.

"The reason why you can't hit the inside pitch," said O'Doul, "is that your hands are too forward. You have to move your hands back by your back shoulder."

The next morning, before the Giants played the All-Stars, Yonamine went to the Giants training ground at Tamagawa and practiced over and over until the new stance felt comfortable and he could hit inside pitches.

On Saturday, Korakuen's gates opened at 8:00 a.m. so that the standing-room-only crowd could enter safely. Nearly fifty thousand Japanese fans and American GIs packed the stadium. Not satisfied with standing, two young men climbed the light tower in right-center field and watched the game from the crossbars high above the diamond. At 11:40 the All-Stars and Giants began their pregame warmups. Spectators immediately saw the difference in size, power, and speed between the Major Leaguers and the Giants. In a pregame interview, Mizuhara "readily admitted [that] his championship team didn't have a chance, but he promised his ballplayers will be hustling all the way to put up a good fight."

Johnny Price, the famed baseball comedian, warmed up the crowd with pantomimes and acrobatics prior to the pregame ceremonies. Price's most popular feat was his one-handed catch of a baseball shot high into the sky by a mortar while driving a jeep across Korakuen's dirt outfield. At 1:45 the announcer introduced the two teams and numerous dignitaries as they lined up on the field. Just as the pregame ceremonies and long-winded speeches seemed endless, General Marquat yelled "Let's get on with the ball game!" A few minutes later, Lefty O'Doul and his translator Cappy Harada confirmed the ground rules with Shigeru Mizuhara and the umpires, and the home-plate umpire signaled for the teams to play ball.

After Joe DiMaggio put the All-Stars up by one with a timely single, Mel Parnell, a left-hander with one of the nastiest breaking balls in the Majors, took the mound. Most of the Giants had never heard of Parnell, but Yonamine had and was nervous facing such a top-level star. Nevertheless, Wally fared well, drawing a walk to lead off the first, singling sharply between short and third in the third inning, and hitting a strong fly ball to left field that Dino Restelli nearly misjudged in the fifth. The All-Stars won the game 7–0, but Yonamine was pleased with his performance. As a left-handed batter, he should have been particularly susceptible to Parnell's breaking balls, but he had hit one of the top lefties in the Majors well. Nevertheless, Wally had no regrets about coming to Japan. He knew that Parnell was not in midseason form and that his own shoulder injury would have prevented him from excelling at the Major League level.

The Major Leaguers stayed in Japan for another month, playing a Japanese All-Star team and other league franchises (Joe DiMaggio would hit the last home run of his career—a towering fly ball into the left-field stands—on November 10 against Shigeru Sugishita of the Central League All-Stars). Yonamine was not chosen for the Japanese All-Stars, but his exclusion did not perturb him. He was eager to return home to Hawaii.

Yonamine's first season had been more successful than Matsutaro Shoriki could have imagined, hitting .354 and slugging .519 with 17 doubles, 5 triples, and a homer. He also stole 26 bases and was caught just 4 times. In only 54 games Wally reached base in 45, scoring a remarkable 47 runs.

With Yonamine in the lineup, the 1951 Giants jelled into one of the best teams in the history of Japanese baseball. Before Wally joined the team, the Giants had won 32 of their 55 games, for a .640 winning percentage. They scored an average of 5.1 runs per game. With the Hawaiian, this output jumped to 7.2 runs per game, winning 47 of their remaining 59 contests—a sizzling .810 mark, even more notable because 5 of the 11 losses came after the pennant was clinched.

But Yonamine's impact on the game was even more important than the extra lift he gave his club. As Takeshi Iwamoto succinctly put it, "He changed Japanese baseball forever." His tactics on the base paths, in the batter's box, and in the outfield unraveled the passive Japanese approach. Players and fans alike now realized the need for a higher level of play. The next few years would see dramatic change.

American writers often called Wally Yonamine "the Jackie Robinson of Japan," "the Nisei Jackie Robinson," or "the Oriental Jackie Robinson." Like Robinson, Yonamine was a pioneer in breaking down ethnic barriers. Both had to endure hostile fans without complaint and win over their fellow ballplayers. Both were also former football players who played baseball aggressively. Both were part of larger social experiments, with the future of their ethnic groups in baseball riding on their performances. If they failed either on the field or, more importantly, off the field, other members of their ethnic groups would not receive offers to play. And both Robinson and Yonamine overcame their difficulties to change the game.

The modest Yonamine notes, "Although I had it rough, Jackie Robinson had it much rougher. You see, my skin is yellow just like the Japanese." Yet, being racially Japanese and culturally American posed its own problems. On the field, few forgot that he was an American, but away from the ballpark, where Yonamine was less recognizable, people were easily annoyed by this clueless man who could barely speak the language and couldn't read the signs. Often, they assumed he was either an idiot or a smart aleck and had little tolerance for him.

After the Giants won the championship, Shigeru Chiba took fifteen of the younger players to the nightclub Mimatsu to celebrate. Partway through the pleasant evening, Chiba pulled Yonamine aside and quietly said, "Wally, I was first opposed to having a foreign player on the team. I didn't want to grip hands with a player from the victor nation. As a whole, we don't like Nisei, but you did everything we did. You slept with us. You ate the food. You didn't grumble. You're one good Nisei. So go back to Hawaii, get married, and bring your wife. I'll back you up one hundred percent from here on in."

9

Settling In

Wally returned home to Honolulu and followed Chiba's advice. On February 2, 1952, he married Jane Iwashita. After a ceremony at Harris Memorial Methodist Church, between twelve hundred and fourteen hundred guests celebrated at the Chinese American Club—one of the few clubs in Honolulu large enough to handle the party. Hundreds of uninvited guests crashed the reception, but somebody put a large calabash bowl by the door, and following an old Hawaiian custom, people without invitations placed donations in the bowl to defray the cost of the party. There was food for all. Guests dined on a traditional Hawaiian buffet and a four-hundred-pound roasted pig—brought by Wally's Okinawan friends—as a band played the current hit songs.

Wally and Jane took a brief honeymoon on the islands of Maui and Hawaii before boarding a plane for Tokyo on February 20. Before they left, Jane's father sat her down and lectured her on Japanese etiquette. He told her, "Don't dye your hair. Japanese women don't do that. And don't drink beer outside of the house. Japanese women don't do that either." The list of what Japanese girls didn't do was long, but well intentioned. "But when I arrived in Japan everything was different!" Jane recalls. "The girls were out in the beer halls drinking beer and their hair was dyed. Everything my father told me that I wasn't supposed to do was being done! The Japanese who were in Hawaii never saw the changes in Japan. They remembered what it was like forty years before."

Jane wasn't apprehensive about the move. "I was only twenty-one. When you're that young, you don't really know what's out there, and if you don't know, then there is nothing to worry about. I didn't think about it that deeply. I just thought that if I'm marrying Wally then I have to go where he is going, and if we don't like it, we can come back."

Accompanying the Yonamines was Jyun Hirota, Wally's former teammate on the Athletics, who was joining the Yomiuri Giants for the 1952 season. Wally's success in the 1951 season had convinced many Japanese teams to sign American players. The Giants once again acted first. In early 1952 Cappy Harada contacted Wally to ask him if he could find a good Nisei catcher. Yomiuri's starting catcher, Yasuo Kusunoki, had a weak arm and it was time to search for a replacement. Wally instantly thought of Hirota and helped bring him on board.

Other Japanese teams were also busy scouting and signing Hawaiian talent. By midseason, six of the fourteen Japanese teams had American players. Bozo Wakabayashi's Mainichi Orions, undoubtedly regretting letting Yonamine slip through their fingers the year before, signed Dick Kitamura and Masato Morita. The Hanshin Tigers picked up Nisei Katsuji Kojima, while the Kintetsu Pearls imported Tomoharu Kai. Kai was particularly successful, finishing second in the Pacific League batting race. He was, however, not another Yonamine. Kai fizzled in the 1953 season and the Pearls quickly released him. The Nishitetsu Lions, led by the maverick manager Osamu Mihara, took a risk and signed two Caucasians as well as Hawaiian Nisei shortstop Larry Yaji. Marion O'Neil and Billy Wyatt thus became the first Caucasian Americans to play in Japan after the war. Their integration into the Japanese leagues was smooth without recorded protest, but neither player contributed much to their team's success. The Hankyu Braves were even more daring, signing Jimmy Newberry and John Britton, two African American players.

Newberry, a pitcher, had starred for the Birmingham Black Barons of the Negro American League from 1942 to 1950. Britton (a.k.a. Brittain) had also played for the Black Barons as well as the Ethiopian–Cincinnati Clowns. On the Clowns, Britton was an accomplished shadow-ball player and would often play in a wig that he would throw in mock disgust when arguing with umpires. The two players were instant celebrities in Japan. Although stereotypical racist caricatures of them appeared in Japanese magazines and newspapers, most Japanese fans seem to have embraced the players. Newberry won eleven games for the fifth-place Braves, and Britton hit .316. Newberry left after the 1952 season, but Hankyu hired four more African Americans in the subsequent four years.

Wally and Jane arrived in Tokyo in dead winter. It was Jane's first winter ever, and during the taxi ride from Haneda Airport she pointed to the bare trees along the road and asked, "Why do they leave all those dead trees standing that way?" Wally explained that he was also puzzled the first time he saw them, but learned that the trees lose their leaves in the winter. "Unbelievable," Jane responded.

The couple was unaware that Tokyo was filled with tension and unrest. Just days before the Yonamines arrived, on February 21, three thousand students and radicals rioted to mark Anti-Colonization Day (the anniversary of the Indian Navy Mutiny of 1946). Armed with sticks and rocks, the protesters attacked police stations, injuring twenty policemen before five thousand officers quelled the riot.

With the poverty and newly found political freedoms of postwar Japan, many workers and students flocked to join labor organizations as well as the Communist and Socialist Parties. Augmenting these Japanese were several hundred thousand Koreans—many of whom had been brought to Japan as forced labor in the prewar years—who sympathized with the politics of relatives living in what had become communist North Korea. These groups protested both the perceived injustices of Japanese capitalism as well as the policies of the occupying Americans and the Japanese government.

Communist and student groups were planning further demonstrations for later in the week. On February 24, one thousand students and laborers protested and attacked three police boxes. Once again a large police force brought order. A week later, there were widespread disturbances throughout Japan as Korean leftists clashed with police on the thirty-third anniversary of the Korean Independence Movement. In Tokyo, sixty thousand labor unionists rallied, but the event and city remained peaceful.

Wally brought Jane to the rented rooms at Dose Teshima's house. Although the house was nice, it was unheated. Jane felt frozen to the bones. "The room had tatami mats. Tatami are designed so the air comes through to keep you cool in the summer. But in the winter, it was so cold! They didn't have rubber hot water bottles, but they had these metal cans, shaped like turtles. You put water in them and heated them on the stove. Then, you put them in the bed to heat it up. Wally was really sweet. Wally would iron the whole bed for me; or go upstairs first, jump into the freezing bed, warm it up, and then yell for me to come up."

A few days after arriving in Tokyo, Wally left for spring training in Akashi, a coastal town near the city of Kobe. Wives were prohibited from attending spring training, so Jane stayed in Tokyo. Knowing only a handful of people in the cold, foreign city, Jane quickly became lonely. After a week, she telephoned Wally.

"May I go back to Hawaii?" she asked. "I'm lonely and will wait in Hawaii."

"I'm lonesome too," said Wally. "If you want to go, you can, but I won't meet you [in Hawaii]." Wally explained that he had to remain with the team and she would have to travel alone.

Daunted by the prospect of traveling by herself, the twenty-one-year-old decided to stay and got up her courage to explore the city. Every tourist knows that difficulties arise when one doesn't speak the language of the country they are visiting. Yet not speaking or reading the language but looking like a native causes even more problems. For example, one afternoon Jane wanted to go to a shop in Ginza called Shinbi-do. She took a taxi to Ginza and asked the driver in simple Japanese directions to Shinbi-do. The driver exploded, "Bakayaro [You fool]! Didn't you go to school!" as he pointed to the sign directly in front of them. Jane apologized in English, as she didn't know enough Japanese to apologize in the driver's language, and the embarrassed driver pointed gently again to the sign. "When we were in Hawaii, we felt that we were Japanese," Jane recalls. "But once I came to Japan, and I couldn't communicate—I thought I knew Japanese but I really didn't—then I didn't feel like I was really Japanese."

Down in Akashi, Wally focused on spring training. American teams usually travel to warm resort spots for spring training. There, players gradually get into shape and sharpen skills during morning workouts, scrimmage in the early afternoon, and spend their late afternoons relaxing by a pool or playing golf. Japanese spring trainings were, and still are, entirely different. Teams trained in secluded areas to avoid distractions. Often these areas were not far enough south to escape the cold. Akashi was frigid that March. Players wore long underwear beneath their uniforms and burned charcoal in giant metal cans to warm their fingers. The cold tightened the players' muscles and led to injuries.

Japanese spring training is often likened to military boot camp. Training starts close to dawn and continues late into the evening. Mornings are usually spent on conditioning—long runs, calisthenics, sprints, and baseball technique. Teams scrimmage in the afternoons or focus on batting. Players often spend the evening in meetings, listening to the manager discuss strategy or reviewing opposing teams.

This attitude toward training dates to the late nineteenth century. Soon after American teachers introduced baseball to Japanese elite prep schools in the 1870s, the country's premier school, the First Higher School of Tokyo (known simply as Ichiko) incorporated baseball into the traditions of the martial arts. The team purposely created a philosophy based on the concepts of *budo* (the military and martial arts) that emphasized extensive training to achieve perfect form and the development of inner strength—often called fighting spirit. Ichiko quickly dominated their baseball rivals and even defeated American adult teams by lopsided scores. Soon, other Japanese schools adopted Ichiko's approach. As this system both led to victories on the field and conformed with the traditions of Japanese athletics, such as sumo and judo, it became an integral part of Japanese baseball. In a modified form, the approach survives today and helps explain many of the differences between the Japanese and American game.

Managers designed drills to build endurance and toughen the players' spirits. The most infamous is the one thousand ball drill, where coaches hit grounders at an infielder until he drops or successfully fields one thousand. Outfielders face a similar ordeal. Two coaches alternate hitting fly balls to a player's right and left until he collapses with exhaustion or catches a hundred. In 1952 Wally strove to complete this drill, but in subsequent years he learned to feign exhaustion after twenty or thirty balls and lie unmoving on the grass. The coaches would amuse themselves by hitting balls at the prostrate Hawaiian for a few minutes before losing interest. According to Yonamine, these drills were actually counterproductive, as tired fielders often forgot about fundamentals and lapsed into sloppy habits.

Now that Yonamine was familiar with Japanese baseball, he arrived at spring training with a plan. He was determined to become one of the league's top players, if not the best. He asked himself, "Who is the best hitter in the league?" It was obviously the Giants' captain, Tetsuharu Kawakami, who had batted .377 to capture the Central League batting crown in 1951. "If I can beat Kawakami," Wally thought, "then I would have a good chance of winning the batting title, and even if I can't beat him, I would probably hit over .300." Wally kept his idea a secret, but from then on focused on outplaying Kawakami.

As usual, the Giants were the favorites to win the pennant. All of the key players from the 1951 championship team had returned, and Jyun Hirota boosted their catching. Hirota hit well in spring training, but manager Mizuhara decided to use him sparingly once the season started until the Nisei catcher had a better grasp of the pitching staff and the Japanese game.

The Giants' season started poorly as they lost the opener, 5–4, to the Kokutetsu Swallows in the ninth inning. Yomiuri was on the verge of losing again the following day, when Yonamine won the game in the bottom of the ninth with a sacrifice fly. The funk continued as the Giants lost four of the next seven games and fell into sixth place.

The mood in the cramped team clubhouse was foul. The Giants were under excruciating pressure to win as numerous reporters and fans followed the team, dissecting each game. Despite their incredible talent and experience, the team wasn't playing well. On April 3, another loss threatened. The Giants were locked in a seesaw contest with the Shochiku Robins when Kiyoshi Matsuda gave up a run in the top of the ninth. Matsuda, who had been so brilliant in 1951, had already lost twice and blown a ninth-inning lead in the opener. The sparse crowd sat glumly with little hope as Yomiuri batted in the bottom of the ninth. "Where were their great Giants?" they asked themselves.

But then a Giant reached base and Yonamine strode to the plate. Perhaps there was a chance after all. Wally had been swinging the bat well this season. Although not a power hitter, Wally came through with a long drive over the outfield fence. It was the Hawaiian's first sayonara home run as the Japanese call "walk-off homers." Excited teammates ran onto the field to mob Wally as he jogged home grinning. The come-from-behind victory energized the team. They won four of the next five and moved into fourth place. April ended with a streak of eleven wins in twelve games, catapulting the Giants into first. Good news also came out of Hawaii. Cappy Harada had just signed a young pitcher named Bill Nishita.

Wally had played with Nishita briefly in 1949 while with the Athletics (Asahi). A few months later, the young righty attracted the attention of Clint Evans, the coach at the University of California, while the Bears were playing in Hawaii. Evans recruited Nishita, but before attending Berkeley, Nishita needed a year sharpening his academic skills at Santa Rosa Junior College. There, he dominated the Northern Conference, and his 14–1 record led the Bear Cubs to the championship. Major League scouts labeled him a can't-miss prospect, and one commented that "He's got baseball sense plus a good fastball and a sidearm curve that's rarely hit."

Nishita rejected pro offers in the summer of 1950 and decided to attend Berkeley, where he had a stellar 1951 season. That summer he toured Japan with a Hawaiian AJA team and grabbed headlines with a three-hit win over Tokyo Big Six champions Waseda University. After the 1951 season, Yonamine spoke to Cappy Harada and suggested that Yomiuri make Nishita an offer. Although Nishita was still sought after by American professional clubs, Harada went to work and lured the prospect to Japan with the highest contract in the history of Japanese baseball—two years at ten thousand dollars per annum.

The size of the pact surprised and even outraged many. Jane was especially upset since the sum was more than three times her husband's salary. But Wally remained unperturbed. He was truly happy for Nishita's good fortune, but he also knew that the high salary would eventually benefit him as it raised the ceiling on the Giants' payroll. If he out-performed Nishita, Wally could possibly double or even triple his pay.

Nishita's sizable contract further increased Yonamine's desire to become Japan's top player. He now knew that if he succeeded in Japanese baseball, he could provide for his family for many years. Yonamine set up a training regimen that was tough even by Japanese standards. He explains, "In my forty years of baseball in Japan, I never took a day off during the season. We had no games on Fridays and Mondays, so I'd go out to the Tamagawa practice fields and train. The Giants players trained hard, so to outdo them I had to train on the off-days. I set a clear objective each time, such as hitting curve balls or sliding. I also neither drank or smoked and didn't drink much coffee. After nights when I went 0 for 4, the next morning I would go down to the farm team to practice. I would arrive about ten o'clock and practice for about an hour and a half. Then, I'd go home, sleep for about two hours, and eat before going to the stadium for our game."

Yonamine wasted little time and found novel ways to work in practice time. After night games in Hiroshima, the team would usually catch a 1:00 a.m. train and arrive in Tokyo the next afternoon. Wally would occasionally get off the train in Osaka, go to the airport, and pay six thousand yen to fly to Tokyo. Arriving about 10:00 a.m. he would go straight to the Giants' dormitory at Tamagawa, sleep a few hours, have a bowl of *udon*, and practice with the farm (minor league) team.

Other times, Yonamine would disembark at Tokyo Station after an all-night train ride, pull Hirofumi Naito aside, and say, "Hey, let's go!" "And where did he invite me to?" Naito recalls. "To practice at the Tamagawa grounds. He'd ask me to pitch to him, and he'd bat to his heart's content! He'd think it over, muttering, 'No, that isn't the right way.' When he was finally satisfied, we would switch roles and he'd pitch to me. Nowadays it's taken for granted that somebody in a slump would have special batting practice or special fielding practice, but this was something that Wally brought to Japan."

Yonamine's intense training paid off. He was driving the ball better than ever. Although normally a singles and doubles hitter, Wally was hitting for power. He homered on May 5, and then in both games of a May 11 doubleheader against the Taiyo Whales. He now led the team with six home runs. The increase in power did not, however, lower his average. Toward the end of May, he was fifth in the Central League batting race, hitting .327.

By now, Jane was adapting to Tokyo. She would take a cab to Ginza and just wander. When she wanted to return home, she would find another cab and give the driver her home address. Eventually, she began to know her way around the city. Jane found Japan fascinating, but there wasn't much for her to do. With her limited Japanese, she couldn't travel far or truly enjoy the museums or theatre. Even finding a restaurant was difficult. Good-quality food was still scare and many buildings still lacked modern plumbing. The U.S. military put little stars outside restaurants considered sanitary enough for Americans, but acceptable restaurants were few and far between. So most of the time, Jane ate at home. Luckily, the Teshimas had good food purchased at the military PX.

On April 28, the Allied occupation of Japan officially ended. Japan was now a fully independent nation, although there was still a large American military presence. Three days later, the Teshimas warned Jane to stay inside.

In the prewar Taisho period, Japanese workers had joined laborers around the world by observing May Day to express worker solidarity. The practice was outlawed from 1936 to 1945 but was reestablished under the occupation in 1946. The day was marked with demonstrations that sometimes turned violent. On May 1, 1952, a large demonstration was planned for downtown Tokyo.

Four hundred thousand Japanese marched along five approved routes that morning. Most of the demonstrators were peaceful, but approximately six thousand attempted to rally in the plaza across from GHQ, the occupation headquarters. Five thousand riot police blocked the demonstrators. Fighting broke out and the police used tear gas, truncheons, and pistols on the crowd. A mile away in her room, Jane could hear the noise from the clash. Rioters overturned cars and set several on fire. By the end of the battle, two demonstrators had died, roughly twenty-three hundred were injured, and over a thousand rioters were arrested. Perhaps most surprisingly, only a mile from the thick of the riot, the Yomiuri Giants were playing the Chunichi Dragons at Korakuen Stadium.

On May 10, Bill Nishita arrived in Tokyo. Mizuhara wasted no time and put his new prize on the mound three days later against the Hiroshima Carp. It was a smart move by the crafty skipper. The Carp were having another dismal season. Their anemic offense would hit only .233 with just twenty-nine home runs during the entire season. It would be a good confidence builder for Nishita as well as a chance for Mizuhara to test his new pitcher in a game that the Giants should win. Nishita didn't disappoint. He shut out the Carp for three innings, giving up just two hits, before giving way to a reliever. The pleased Mizuhara announced that he would probably allow Nishita to pitch a full game in his next start. "His drop and fast ball are fine weapons," the manager stated after the game. "When he gets accustomed to the weather and living conditions here, he should develop into one of the mainstays of the Giants."

With three Nisei on the Giants, the team's dynamics had changed greatly. Yonamine was no longer the lone outsider desperate to conform. He had proven his resolve the previous year and he was now accepted by nearly all his teammates. Shigeru Chiba lived up to his word and went out of his way to support Wally. The two soon became close friends, going out to dinner and socializing on the road. When traveling, Wally roomed with Jyun Hirota, Bill Nishita, and Hirofumi Naito. Wally found it comforting to speak English with his roommates and express his thoughts accurately. Naito's English improved greatly, but without the constant immersion, Wally's Japanese deteriorated. He would never fully master the language. Even fifty years later, Yonamine still speaks with a Hawaiian accent and endures teasing about it from Naito.

Yonamine explained the team's rules and customs to Hirota and Nishita, and the Japanese-born Giants accepted the new Nisei without issue. Tadashi Iwamoto, who actually joined the Giants the following year, states, "There was no tension between the Nisei and the Japanese players. In fact, many of the Japanese were friendlier with the Nisei than they were with each other. Everybody valued them because they were motivated and had a lot of ability. And they didn't do anything other than baseball! We played mah-jongg, pachinko, we'd go out with girls, but they didn't do anything! They only did baseball. They had a strong sense of responsibility for what they needed to do."

Jyun Hirota fit into the team easily. Unlike most of the Nisei who came to play in Japan, Hirota could speak and even read Japanese. He remembered, "My teammates were wonderful and accepted me into their family." His play on the field, however, cemented his popularity. He hit Japanese pitching well. In mid-May his average was over .300 despite battling a case of the mumps, which he caught from his son. More importantly, behind the plate Hirota introduced the Japanese to a new style.

At the time, a typical Japanese catcher would receive the ball from the pitcher, take two steps forward, crank his arm back, and throw it back to the mound. In the midst of that routine, Yonamine would sometimes steal second base, sliding in safely just as the pitcher caught the ball. Hirota brought American receiving to Japan. He had a strong arm and used to return the ball to the pitcher while still in his crouch. The fans loved it as much as opposing base runners feared it. Soon, Japanese catchers began mimicking Hirota and their mechanics changed. The average number of stolen base attempts in the Central League dropped from nearly 3.0 per game in 1952 and 1953 to 2.6 per game after Hirota's second season in Japan.

Hirota particularly impressed his teammates with his mettle. When asked about Jyun Hirota, his former teammates always begin, "He had guts!" In one game, an errant pitch ripped open his hand between his two fingers. Hirota calmly bandaged the wound and continued playing, despite his teammates' pleas for him to come out of the game. Later, he needed six or seven stitches to close the gaping cut. "Even with such an injury, he wouldn't take a day off," recalls Iwamoto. "I was shocked when I saw that. I thought he was even tougher than the old guys like Aota and Kawakami, who had fought in the war!"

By mid-June the Giants had built their lead in the Central League to five games and were looking forward to the All-Star break. But the break gave them little rest. Seven of the Giants' starting position players, four pitchers, and Jyun Hirota made the squad. Yonamine was hitting above .300 and had carried the Giants for much of the first half of the season, but he still remained unpopular with opposing fans. He received only 4,360 fan votes on the All-Star ballot, finishing eighth among the Central League outfielders, well behind Noboru Aota's leading 31,867 votes.

Luckily for Wally, Shigeru Mizuhara, as the skipper of the 1951 champions, was managing the Central League team. Mizuhara put Wally on the squad and inserted him into the lead-off spot for the first game at tiny Nishinomiya Stadium near Osaka. Thirty thousand fans filled the stadium for the 1:00 p.m. game. Pitching dominated the day and at the top of the seventh the score was knotted at two. Shigeru Sugishita, the Dragons' ace, entered the game for the Central League in the seventh, and Tokuji Kawasaki of the Nishitetsu Lions took the mound for the Pacifics. Each pitcher was unbeatable, matching scoreless innings. The game entered the tenth, still tied. Takao Fujimura of the Tigers relieved Sugishita and threw three scoreless innings. Giichi Hayashi of the Daiei Stars matched him. The game wore on and on. Pitchers came and went, but Mizuhara had kept all but one of his starting position players in the game even though the Central Leaguers had not gained a hit since the tenth inning.

In the eighteenth inning, a weary Yonamine stepped to the plate with two outs. So far he was 0 for 7 with two strikeouts. Toshinobu Sueyoshi of the Orions looked in and threw one down the middle. Wally pounced on it and drove it deep off the wall. He cruised into second. "Maybe this would be it," he thought as his friend Shigeru Chiba stepped to the plate. Chiba and Sueyoshi battled hard before Chiba drew ball four and ambled down to first. Now it was up to the great Yoshiyuki Iwamoto. Iwamoto was forty years old but only in his seventh year of pro ball. He had lost three years to the Japanese military and after being discharged, elected to play in the industrial leagues for three seasons. When he did return to the pros, he became an instant star and became the first Japanese to hit four home runs in a single game. Unfortunately for the exhausted players, Iwamoto was not destined to be a hero this day. He grounded weakly to short, ending the inning.

Two more innings whizzed by. Yonamine led off the twenty-first inning. On the mound stood the blond-haired, blue-eyed, 6-foot 3-inch Victor Starffin, who had been in Japanese professional baseball since the league's inauguration in 1936. From the Urals, the Starffins were forced to flee Russia during the revolution. After a harrowing escape, which included traveling in a freight train packed with typhoid patients and hiding from the Red Army in a truck carrying corpses, the family settled in the city of Asahikawa in Hokkaido, Japan, in 1925. Young Victor picked up baseball quickly and soon became a regional star. He had hoped to play college ball at prestigious Keio or Waseda, but in 1933, his father was convicted of murdering a young Russian woman who worked in his teashop. Yomiuri approached Victor and promised to use their influence to help his father if he would sign a professional contract. Starffin agreed and pitched briefly against the Major League All-Stars in 1934 before becoming an inaugural member of the Giants. He quickly emerged as the premier power pitcher in the prewar years, leading the league in wins for five consecutive seasons and capturing the 1939 and 1940 Most Valuable Player Awards.

During the war, Starffin was forced to take the Japanese name Hiroshi Suda and eventually was interrogated for being a Russian spy and placed into a detention camp. Upon release, he became an interpreter for the occupying forces and continued to play professional baseball with several different teams. He had returned to his old form and won twenty-seven in 1949, but now at thirty-six years old, he was beginning to lose his arm strength, while his fondness for the sake cup was affecting his conditioning. But this evening, he looked like the Starffin of old. He dispatched Wally and his teammates easily—his pitches barely visible in the dwindling light of the unlit stadium. At the end of the twenty-first inning, the umpires looked at the darkened sky and mercifully ended the ordeal. It was one of the longest games in the history of Japanese ball, yet because of the stellar pitching had taken only four and a half hours.

With the summer weather, Yonamine's hitting improved. In early August, his average rose to .336, surpassing Tetsuharu Kawakami by two points. Kawakami had never been fond of Yonamine, but Wally now noticed that the haughty Giants captain was especially cold.

"It was very unusual for Mr. Kawakami to hold anybody as a rival, but against Wally there was a very strong rival spirit," Naito remembers. "When Yonamine came, he immediately attracted lots of fans and brought new plays into the game. Maybe there was a sense of jealousy on the side of Mr. Kawakami. Kawakami was also an old-fashioned guy, he felt that titles should be won by Japanese players. When he was competing with Wally for leading hitter or MVP, there was a more severe and harsher expression on his face. Neither of them showed this rivalry in their words, but inside it was all there." Over time, the rivalry would increase and would influence Japanese baseball for decades.

The summer of 1952 was a special time for Wally and Jane. Jane went to all of the Giants' home games. "Now they have family seats but they didn't back then," Jane recalls. "The wives weren't supposed to go to the games, because Japanese wives don't go to their husbands' offices and for the ballplayers the stadium was their office. But I acted the dumb American and went anyway. I sat right in back of the dugout by myself. I might have been the first wife that ever went to the ball games. Several years later, some of the other wives came to keep me company. Takehiko Bessho's wife came once. It was the first time she had come in eleven years. She purposely came after the game started and left before the game ended. And she never told her husband that she had come! After the games, I would wait in the alleyway behind the stadium, where the players would come out, and Wally and I would go to dinner or go home together."

Jane and Wally were also expecting their first child. The baby was due in December and the hot, sticky August weather was making Jane uncomfortable. "It was so hot that you would only sleep one per bed because you didn't want to touch anybody else! To keep me cool, Wally got a big tin wash tub, put blocks of ice in it, and set up a little fan to push the cold air toward the bed. That was our air-conditioner. But, it was fun. When you are young, you can try anything. I don't think I could stand it now!"

Yonamine maintained his .336 batting average throughout August. As competitors faltered, he moved up to second in the batting crown race. Only the Dragons' first baseman, Michio Nishizawa, stood in front of him. But Nishizawa was well ahead, hitting .360 on August 27. The Giants were in first place by a comfortable six games and the players were relaxed and playing well.

On a train to Nagoya, Wally pulled out a piece of chocolate and began nibbling on it. Naito and the rookie pitcher Masanori Iratani looked up and noticed the snack. "Wally, give us some too," they begged. Wally tried to tell them that it was chocolate flavored Ex-Lax, not candy, but he couldn't explain it in Japanese. His friends continued to beg and he didn't want them to think he was being stingy so, feeling mischievous, he acquiesced. In Nagoya, the teammates went to a movie. Part way through, Wally could hear his teammates' stomachs rumbling. Finally, they both stood up simultaneously and ran to the bathroom. Wally couldn't help laughing.

The incident started a string of practical jokes. Wally was usually the instigator. During a 2003 interview, the seventy-two-year-old Hirofumi Naito leaned over toward me, pointed at the seventy-eight-year-old Yonamine, and said, "He was a real prankster! He looks so quiet now but he was such a bad boy!"

Wally still found much of the *ryokan* food unpalatable, but when he saw a dish he wanted, he would pull out his false teeth and toss them into the serving bowl. His teammates would yell out, "That's disgusting!" and Wally would smile as he ate the dish by himself. The ploy worked several times before his teammates put an end to it by just picking out the teeth and helping themselves to the dish anyway.

During long train rides when the players slept, Wally would sneak from seat to seat tying his teammates' socks in knots and stuffing them back in their shoes. He would let his victims sleep until they arrived at the station and then yell, "Get up! Get up! We're at the station!" Disoriented, the players would have to rush out of the train but they couldn't get their shoes on because their socks were all knotted up. So the image-conscious Yomiuri Giants would emerge from the trains barefoot with their bags on their backs.

Practical jokes, an important part of American locker room camaraderie, were not practiced in Japanese baseball. The Japanese players took their jobs too seriously to act so frivolously, and the rigid social structure and mutual responsibilities of *senpai-kohai* precluded the type of lighthearted hazing common on American sports teams. But the Nisei were more relaxed and outside of the Japanese social structure. The jokes were targeted only at the friendly younger players. Yonamine commented, "We just did them with the guys we hung around with. Not to the veterans. You didn't dare do things to the veterans."

In early September, Yonamine boosted his average to .341 and now began to seriously challenge Nishizawa for the batting title. Opposing fans still hurled insults at the Hawaiian but he was no longer the target of projectiles. Jobo Nakamura, a Nisei visiting Hiroshima, wrote to the *Pacific Citizen*: "The Japanese fans seem to have a healthy respect for his hitting and running prowess and for this reason he was singled out to be jeered by the Hiroshima crowd. His being a Nisei was an excuse for ridicule. My neighbor yelled using pidgin Japanese, 'Oi, Yonamine, Nippon-go wakaranai ka? [Hey Yonamine, don't you speak Japanese?]' As the game progressed, in favor of the Giants, Wally Yonamine pounded the ball all over the park and stole bases with ease, 'Yoku hashiro no! [You run well, don't you!]' 'Yoku utsu na! [You hit well, don't you!]' were some of their reluctant praise for the Nisei player."

"Thank God we didn't speak Japanese!" says Jane. "We couldn't understand half the things they were saying. And the things they wrote in the papers, we couldn't read. If friends read you an article, they would only read you the good parts. I think that not understanding Japanese that first year was a blessing in disguise."

The Giants lost seven of their eighteen games in September, and their lead dwindled to three and a half games over the second place Hanshin Tigers. But on October 3, with only a week remaining on the schedule, Yomiuri beat the Kokutetsu Swallows 15–2 to clinch the Central League pennant. With the championship settled, fans focused on the batting race. Yonamine trailed Nishizawa by nine points with just a handful of games remaining. On the fifth, Wally went 4 for 4 in a 4–3 loss to the Tigers, closing the gap to just a few points. Realizing that Yonamine might catch him, Nishizawa sat out the few remaining games to ensure that his average would not drop. Wally knew that he would have to be near perfect to win the title and began to press. Consequently, hits became harder to come by and his average dipped in the final few games, allowing Nishizawa to capture the batting crown.

In September, Jane, now six months pregnant, returned to Hawaii. The grueling trip took eighteen hours with a two-hour stopover to refuel at Wake Island. Wally would join her at the conclusion of the Japan Series.

The Giants were once again pitted against the Nankai Hawks, who had won the Pacific League pennant by just a game over Bozo Wakabayashi's Mainichi Orions. The Hawks fared better than the previous year, winning twice, but Yomiuri captured the title in six games. Wally hit well, picking up ten hits and a homer in 24 at bats to win the top hitter award with a .416 average. As a prize, he received a small amount of cash and a bicycle. Besides hitting well, Wally had been outstanding in the field, robbing the Hawks of several sure hits. After the series, the Hawks' manager Kazuto Tsuruoka approached the Hawaiian. "Wally, we lost to you," he said.

Wally's performance in 1952 moved him into the league's elite players. Besides finishing second in the batting race, Yonamine led the Central League in hits, runs scored, and doubles. He was also third in the league in stolen bases with thirty-eight. Many thought that Wally might win the Central League Most Valuable Player Award, but the honor went to Takehiko Bessho, who led the league with thirty-three wins and posted a nifty 1.94 ERA. Perhaps it was too soon for a foreigner to be given the coveted award. Yonamine was, however, selected for the Best Nine—an annual award given to the best player at each position.

Jyun Hirota and Bill Nishita also had good seasons. Hirota ended with a .277 batting average, but more importantly had solidified the Giants' defense with his strong arm and handling of the pitching staff. Nishita did not become the dominant pitcher the Giants had expected. A sore arm limited him to just a few starts, but he did pitch seventy-five innings—mostly out of the bullpen. His 3.20 ERA was respectable, but the highest among the Giants' pitchers with fifty or more innings pitched.

At the end of the '52 season Wally's original contract was up. It had been a tough year for Jane, so Wally thought seriously about returning to Honolulu for good. The job offer from Coca-Cola was still open and the salary was more than he was making with the Giants. Yonamine discussed his predicament with Shoji Yasuda, the club's president. Yasuda looked shocked. He had assumed that Wally would be staying in Japan for years to come. "No, no, no, don't go home!" he pleaded. "We will take care of you."

"Well, I'll have to go back and talk it over with my wife," Wally responded.

"No need to do that. Wally, you can earn a lot more here. Don't go back to Hawaii."

The two agreed to discuss a new contract before Wally left for Hawaii. Richard Uehara, who had helped Wally get his original contract, negotiated with Yasuda on Wally's behalf. They quickly reached an agreement. Yonamine signed a three-year deal for eight million yen (roughly $26,000), plus Yomiuri agreed to pay the rent on a single-family house for the Yonamines in the Meguro neighborhood of Tokyo. Wally was very pleased. He had tripled his salary. Before Wally flew back to Honolulu on October 28, Yasuda asked him to try to recruit another Nisei player. Wally knew exactly who he would try to get—the third baseman of the Athletics, his old friend Dick Kashiwaeda.

The year ended even more happily for the Yonamines. On December 27, 1952, their first child, Amy Shizuko, was born at Queen's Hospital in Honolulu.

10
Lessons from Santa Maria

Matsutaro Shoriki was pleased with how the Yomiuri Giants had improved. Yonamine had showed them how to be more aggressive and brought techniques such as drag bunting and hook sliding to Japan. Jyun Hirota had introduced the American style of catching and shown a fighting spirit that surprised even many of the Japanese veterans. The Giants were doing well, having won both the 1951 and '52 pennants and Japan Series titles easily. Yet, Shoriki knew from watching the Major League All-Stars during their 1951 tour of Japan that his Giants were still not up to big-league standards. Early in the 1952 season, he summoned Cappy Harada into his office to discuss the problem.

"I want to get our ballplayers to play at the same level as they do in the States. How can we do that?" he asked.

Harada thought about it. "The best thing would be to send them to spring training in the United States," he answered. "We should open up a spring camp for the Tokyo Giants and play games against Pacific Coast League teams and perhaps a Major League team."

Shoriki nodded approvingly. Harada suggested that they hold the camp at his hometown of Santa Maria, California. The town had a large bilingual Nisei community and also a ballpark large enough to hold the games. Shoriki gave his approval and suggested that they contact Lefty O'Doul to help organize the camp. The planning continued throughout the season.

In mid-October 1952, O'Doul officially announced that the Yomiuri Giants would train in Santa Maria the following spring. Lefty told the San Francisco *Call-Bulletin* that he had arranged with the federal government for the Central League champions to make the trip and was scheduling games with both Major and Minor League clubs. It would be the first time a professional Japanese team would visit the continental United States since the Giants' last tour in 1936. O'Doul "hailed the impending visit . . . as a new milestone in goodwill between Japan and the United States," and added brightly, "I know of no better way of fighting communism than batting the ball!"

Before the Giants left Tokyo in early February 1953, they made several important changes to their roster. The Giants' management believed that Noboru Aota, their power-hitting center fielder, was washed up. Although just twenty-eight years old, he had served two years in the military during the war and enjoyed Tokyo's raucous nightlife. The abuse to his body may have caught up to him during the 1952 season, as his average plummeted from .312 in 1951 to .260. His power numbers also fell. His Central League–leading thirty-two homers in 1951 dwindled to just eighteen, and his extra-base hits, RBI, and stolen bases slipped as well. The Giants traded him to the Taiyo Whales and signed Tadashi Iwamoto, the star of the Tokyo Big Six University League.

From the early twentieth century until the late 1950s, the Tokyo Big Six University League was the pinnacle of Japanese baseball. They usually played in front of sold-out crowds and stole the newspaper headlines from the pros. Historically the top two university teams were the archrivals Waseda and Keio. Iwamoto led Waseda to four of the six possible championships between 1950 and 1952. The promising rookie allowed the Giants to reconfigure their outfield defense. Mizuhara gave Iwamoto the starting left field job and moved Yonamine to his natural center field position.

On their way to California, the Giants stopped in Honolulu. There, they met Yonamine, Hirota, Nishita, and their new Nisei teammate— Hawaii's top third baseman, Dick Kashiwaeda. Kashiwaeda had enthusiastically accepted Yonamine's offer to join the Giants and had signed a two-year contract. The Giants, however, already had Mitsuo Uno, an All-Star, at third base so Kashiwaeda would be used primarily as a utility player and pinch-hitter.

During the off-season, Yonamine and Hirota had briefed Kashi-waeda on the Giants' players and their customs. "So when I actually got to meet the players, and started to play with them in spring training, I was pretty comfortable. I knew what I should be doing and what not to do. In the Japanese League, that's the most important thing."

The Giants touched down in San Francisco on February 16 and were "given a rousing welcome from the Japanese community," including the Japanese consul general. They then traveled in a motorcade to downtown San Francisco and spent the night at the Eddy Hotel. The next morning, they continued on to Santa Maria to begin training.

In Santa Maria, the roles of the Nisei and Japanese players became reversed. Now it was the Japanese who were trying to adapt to a foreign culture in a language they didn't understand, and the Nisei who were their guides. "We stayed at a good hotel and a lot of movie actors and actresses were staying there," Yonamine recalls. "One day we went down to breakfast and they served soup. When Japanese drink soup they slurp very loudly. So they started making all this noise! The Americans were wondering what was going on and were looking all around. We had to teach the Japanese how to eat soup in America."

Dick Kashiwaeda adds, "Before our first breakfast at the Santa Maria Inn, all the ballplayers were standing outside because Mr. Mizuhara hadn't come down and been seated yet. In Japan the manager has to go in first and sit down, before anybody else can enter. The maitre d' came over and said, 'Hey, this is going to foul us up if the manager comes in late every morning!' So he asked us to talk to the owners' representative to make sure that whoever came down first would go in the restaurant first. This was one way the Giants' ballplayers became more Americanized. It was the same thing with the bus. The manager and the starting players would go in first and then the rookies, but the rookies had to sit in the back. In those days, everybody carried his own equipment bag and bats, so once the front was filled up, getting to the back was difficult. The bus driver put a stop to that."

At first most of the Giants enjoyed their trip to California, but after a while they became bored. Not speaking English, the Japanese could not even enjoy a movie. They had nothing to do there in the small town and after practice just went back to the hotel. After a month, most were ready to go home.

With the help of O'Doul, acting General Manager Cappy Harada had set up a challenging schedule. The Giants warmed up with two games against the Valley All-Stars, a strong semipro team managed by Kenichi Zenimura, the elder statesman of Nisei baseball in California. A fine player in his youth, Zenimura had faced Babe Ruth and Lou Gehrig during their 1927 barnstorming tour and had brought his Fresno All-Stars to Japan in 1924, 1927, and 1937. He maintained close ties to Japan and would help a number of Nisei players sign with pro teams there. After Zenimura's All-Stars, the Giants faced the Hollywood Stars, Sacramento Solons, San Diego Padres, and Oakland Oaks of the Pacific Coast League. The Central League champs were also able to test their skills against the New York Giants, St. Louis Browns, and a group of the younger Chicago White Sox.

Wally knew that the Giants faced stiff competition. In a feature article in the *Call-Bulletin*, Yonamine explained, "Japan's baseball championship team is not ready to engage the New York Yankees in any world series. As a matter of fact the [Pacific] Coast League plays faster baseball than we do. Our pitching is not as good, our hitting is not as long or as sharp and we haven't mastered the technique of base running like the Americans. But we are learning. For one thing, we have given up trying to whack the ball out of the park. It has improved our hitting."

Wally was right. The Yomiuri Giants did not fare well against the American professional teams. They lost 12 of 15 games against Pacific Coast League teams, and a couple of their wins were not meaningful victories. For example, in the Giants' 2–0 March 8 victory over the Hollywood Stars, the Giants did not get a hit for the first eight and two-thirds innings before scoring two runs in the top of the ninth on a walk and two hits. At that point, the Stars had pulled their regulars and were fielding a rookie team. Yomiuri also lost three of the four games against their Major League opponents, and their 9–7 win over the New York Giants was not truly legitimate as Leo Durocher, New York's manager, sat in the Yomiuri dugout analyzing every play and giving the Japanese pointers.

Nevertheless, Cappy Harada claimed to be pleased. Many of the games were close—Yomiuri lost six games by just one or two runs. Harada enthusiastically, if perhaps somewhat unrealistically, told the *Hawaii Times* that "the Tokyo team is good enough now to finish 'fourth or fifth' in the Pacific Coast League . . . ahead of Sacramento, San Francisco and 'maybe Portland' over a full season."

One of the most enduring questions of international baseball is how the quality of the Japanese leagues compares to the U.S. Major and Minor Leagues. Many baseball experts consider the Japanese leagues at the present time to be "4A"—that is, better than Triple A but not equal to the Majors. In 1953 the gap was even broader. The Giants were undoubtedly Japan's best team, but they were unable to match Pacific Coast League teams, even during spring training. The game results suggest that the club was probably equivalent to class A competition. Some of the Giants, however, could have played at a higher level. Takehiko Bessho particularly impressed PCL managers; San Diego reportedly tried to buy his contract from Yomiuri. Lefty O'Doul also noted that Yonamine could move into the PCL if he was interested in returning to the United States.

Despite their poor record, the trip to Santa Maria was a resounding success. "We certainly learned a lot during our spring training," proclaimed Harada, "and I can truthfully say that this is an entirely different ball club now. The Major League . . . managers especially, briefed us thoroughly on how to play the national pastime properly. The many so-called inside hints that they offered us went a long way toward improving all of our players." The managers helped the Giants with all aspects of their game. Kawakami learned to hit with more power by cocking his wrists. Chiba worked on fielding fundamentals and getting his body in front of the ball. "He doesn't make those one-handed catches he used to make," Harada commented approvingly. Mizuhara adopted Leo Durocher's style of leaving the dugout and managing from the third base box. He also learned how to direct base runners and use signs like the American managers.

Perhaps most importantly, the Giants experienced the aggressiveness of American baseball firsthand. Early in the trip, Shigeru Chiba, attempting to turn a double play Japanese-style by standing on second base, was taken out with a hard slide and was spiked. He quickly learned how to move off the bag and avoid a slide while making a double play. The Japanese realized that Yonamine was not particularly rough or dirty, but just played hard-nosed American baseball. Some of the Giants began to adopt a more aggressive style and learned to slide hard with their spikes up.

In the third week of March, Bill Nishita received an ominous message. His draft number had come up and he had to return to Hawaii for an April 13 induction into the U.S. Army. For two years his professional baseball ambitions would be put on hold. Naturally, he was disappointed. "I certainly wanted to play ball this season because I figured I could do a great deal, especially after all that learning I received from the Major Leaguers who were kind enough to instruct us in our spring season games, but duty is duty, so I'm ready to serve my country." It was a big blow to the Giants, who expected Nishita to become a star in the upcoming season. Wally told *Hawaii Times* reporter Wallace Hirai, "Bill would have been a cinch twenty-game winner this year. Bill really has the stuff to go far in Japan pro ball."

A few days later, bad luck hit the Giants again. Only 2,789 came to watch the Giants face off against the Hollywood Stars at Gilmore Field on Friday, March 20. Stars shortstop Johnny O'Neill led off the bottom of the first. A small man, O'Neill had not hit a home run since 1942 and had tagged only four in his fifteen-year professional career. Naturally, his teammates nicknamed him Slugger. O'Neill hit a deep fly to the gap in right center off Takehiko Bessho. Both Yonamine and Fukashi Minanimura gave chase, each convinced they could catch it. They converged on the ball at full speed, colliding viciously. Both collapsed to the ground as the ball scooted past them. Slugger raced around the bases and, according to the *Los Angeles Times*, "puffed up like a pouter pigeon as he strutted across the plate." The Giants raced over to the prostrate players. Minanimura was just shaken up, but Yonamine had a deep spike wound in his foot and was helped off the field. The following day, the Giants sent Wally home to Hawaii to recuperate. He would rejoin the team during their stopover in Hawaii on their way back to Japan.

Before the Giants left Santa Maria, Cappy Harada and Horace Stoneham, the owner of the New York Giants, agreed that the New Yorkers would try to visit Japan at the end of the 1953 season.

The Yomiuri Giants left California on March 27 and arrived in Honolulu for a series of exhibition games before returning to Japan. The Giants beat most of their island opponents but their play was lackluster. "We've had a most strenuous schedule and we're dog tired. All this traveling and playing with little rest in between is a killing business," a player told the *Hawaii Times*. Shigeru Chiba was so exhausted that he collapsed on his bed after the first game and could not be roused for a reception at the Kanraku tea house.

When the Giants finally returned home on April 4, the Japanese pro season was already in its second week. The tired team rested for several days before opening the new season at Korakuen Stadium against the Swallows. The lessons learned in Santa Maria paid off immediately. Masaichi Kaneda, the Swallow's fiery left-handed ace, mowed down the Giants for eleven innings, but Takehiko Bessho matched him. Entering the bottom of the eleventh, the score remained 0–0. Fukashi Minanimura led off with a walk and moved to second on a sacrifice bunt. Kaneda looked in and threw his best heat to Jyun Hirota, who grounded it meekly to second. Minanimura ran on contact, reached third easily, and as the Swallows' second baseman nonchalantly fielded the ball and tossed it to first, streaked home. The Swallows blinked with surprise as Minanimura's teammates crowded around him, celebrating the win.

With this first win, Yomiuri moved into first place. They continued to play aggressively, winning their first five games, then going 13-3 in

April and 16-7 in May. As the weeks passed, the Giants' lead grew. According to Dick Kashiwaeda, the hit and run helped the Giants win many of these games. At the time, Japanese teams rarely used this play, but the Giants had mastered it in California. In "Santa Maria we saw how Major Leaguers executed the hit and run for the first time. Nobody did that in Japan. We adopted it because our lineup started with Wally Yonamine and up to the sixth or seventh batter everybody could run well. I think we did it better than some of the Major League teams."

Although the Giants were playing well and winning, Wally was stuck in a slump. The injury he received in Santa Maria was healing slowly, causing him to miss games and hampering his game when he played. Wally was also having difficulty adapting to a new slot in the batting order. Without Noboru Aota, the Giants lacked power, so Mizuhara decided to move Yonamine into the third spot in the lineup to bolster the middle of the order. However, the approaches of a third and lead-off hitter are different. Lead-off hitters are expected to get on base any way they can. A clean single, a walk, beating out an infield hit or a bunt, getting hit by a pitch—all get a lead-off man on base equally well. Lead-off batters are also expected to work the count to both tire the pitcher and to expose a hurler's repertoire of pitches. Third hitters, on the other hand, are expected to drive in runs. Rather than work a count, they are expected to jump on the ball and hit for extra bases. In a key situation, a walk for a third or cleanup hitter is viewed as "passing the buck"—a failure to produce. Furthermore, third batters often have runners on base when they hit, making it more difficult to beat out a ground ball or bunt for a hit. With these new responsibilities, Wally's average plummeted. By mid-June, he was not among the Central League's top twenty batters.

Yomiuri's other Nisei, however, were having strong seasons. Jyun Hirota had finally supplanted Yasuo Kusunoki as the Giants regular catcher. Hirota was handling the pitchers well and in mid-June was twelfth in the Central League batting race with a .280 average. Dick Kashiwaeda provided the Giants with power and clutch hitting off the bench. "I had an advantage over the rest of the players because when you go in as a pinch hitter if you get a hit, you look great. If you don't hit, it's just one of those situations." Dick adjusted to pinch-hitting amazingly well. On May 12 he slammed a pinch-hit grand slam against the Hiroshima Carp during an 11–1 Giants' rout. But his true heroics came four days later. The Shochiku Robins were in the process of handing the Giants their second straight loss when Shigeru Chiba doubled home the tying runs in the seventh inning. The next two Giants' batters reached base and Kashiwaeda emerged from the dugout to pinch hit. He promptly homered to give the Giants a 7–5 lead and the eventual victory.

Although Yonamine had debuted only two years earlier, Japan had changed greatly since 1951. Good food and sanitary conditions were no longer scarce, allowing Kashiwaeda to adapt easily to Japan. "Even though we were foreigners, our problems were not that severe or critical," he recalls. "We just had to adjust to the Japanese style of living. For example, there weren't many hotels in those days so we stayed in Japanese inns, and the food was a little different. I was fortunate that Mr. Yonamine and Mr. Hirota . . . clued me in. They have a set menu at the inns but you can deviate from it if you pay the difference. So, we all did that. If we had a doubleheader, the Japanese players would take a box of sushi for between the games, but we'd order sandwiches. We'd have to pay for the sandwiches because they were more expensive than sushi. The Yomiuri Giants were very generous. The management felt that the players should be well cared for, so we traveled special second class, where you would get a reclining seat, or in sleepers if there was a game that day. The other teams usually traveled third class. Mr. Chiba told me when I first arrived, "Look, Yomiuri will give us everything first class but at the same token you have to respect that and don't take advantage of it."

As Kashiwaeda was already twenty-eight years old, he mixed well with the veteran players. Chiba especially gave him advice, took him out to dinner, and helped keep up Dick's spirits when he was riding the bench. Kashiwaeda even got along well with Tetsuharu Kawakami.

The usually austere loner, who guarded his baseball knowledge closely, shared his secrets with Kashiwaeda.

"In Japan, rookies don't talk to the veterans, but I felt differently because in Hawaii you learn from the old-timers. The Giants' veterans were glad to talk if you approached them. They wouldn't come to you, but you could go to them. The younger ballplayers were afraid of Tetsuharu Kawakami, but he was such a nice guy that if I had problems I would go to talk to him."

Although all the Giants liked Dick, they couldn't get used to his constant chatter from the dugout. Japanese dugouts at the time, and even today, are quiet places. Players are expected to watch the game and study the opposition. Riding the opposition was unheard of, and even friendly calls to support one's own team were rare. Kashiwaeda, however, came from a different tradition. Asahi players were taught that the more you supported your team, the better they would play. Both on the field and on the bench Asahi players kept up a constant barrage of chatter to encourage their players. The comments were always positive and not directed toward the opposing team. Dick continued this tradition from the Giants' bench. At first his Japanese teammates looked at him in disbelief. They had no idea what the crazy Nisei was blabbering about as he yelled only in English. But they liked Dick and let him chatter away, occasionally yelling at him, "You're noisy, aren't you!"

One the road, the Nisei players would usually hang out together. None of them drank, so they would stay at the *ryokan* and write letters or go to the movies. Often, they lounged around and talked baseball. Wally and Jyun knew every opposing pitcher well, so they would act through potential games and practice swings specifically tailored for each pitcher in different situations.

Jane and Amy arrived in Tokyo in May. Jane had learned the previous year not to leave Honolulu until Wally returned from spring training. They settled into the new house in Meguro. At the time, few foreigners lived in the neighborhood. There were no English-speaking neighbors for Jane to socialize with, but she remained busy caring for five-month-old Amy. Baby food was not available in local Japanese stores, but Jane found a black market shop in Shibuya that sold Carnation milk and American baby food. The shopkeepers told her matter-of-factly not to come on Thursdays because that was when the police raided the store.

The extensive black market was tolerated in postwar Japan as a necessary means of making much-needed goods available to Japanese consumers. American military personal would buy items at the PX and sell them for great profit to Japanese black marketers, who in turn sold them to the public. Such shops operated in the open but were subject to raids and fines. Nonetheless, fortunes were made by many prominent Japanese and Americans in this arrangement.

The prices at the black market shops were far above the original prices of the items at the military PX, but they were the only places that Jane could get the American-made items she needed. The exchange rate of 360 yen per dollar also made Tokyo an inexpensive place for Americans to live. When Jane decided to hire a maid, the going salary was just thirty-five hundred yen per month plus room and board. But for the Japanese maids, the nonmonetary compensation was more important. At the shop in Shibuya, Jane bumped into an old classmate, who was now living in Tokyo. Through this friend, Jane met other American moms and soon developed a social network—Tokyo started to be fun.

In one game in late May or early June, Mizuhara put Yonamine back in the lead-off spot. Wally reached first and looked over at Mizuhara standing in the third base coach's box. As Chiba stepped to the plate, the manager gave Wally the steal sign. Yonamine sprinted toward second on the pitch, but Chiba fouled it off. Wally returned to first. On the next pitch, Wally went again. Once more, Chiba swung and fouled off the pitch. The Hawaiian jogged back to first. They repeated the play again, and again Chiba fouled off the pitch. During the at bat, Wally tried to steal second six or seven times, but each time Chiba stuck out his bat and fouled off the pitch. Finally, Yonamine had enough. "Hey," he called to Chiba, "I'm tired, you know!"

After the inning, Wally approached Chiba. "Chiba-san, were you doing that on purpose or what?" To Wally's surprise, Chiba said yes and explained that he felt that Wally wasn't getting a good jump, so he had purposely fouled off the pitches.

"Teach me how to do that?" Wally asked.

After the game, Chiba explained that a left-handed batter should roll over his right hand as he stepped into a ball that he didn't like. Thus, preventing the bat from swinging fully and causing the ball to scrape the bat and fly backward. The next day, Wally began to practice the tactic. It took a lot of work and he didn't fully master it until spring training the following year.

During this time, Wally continued to go to Mass each Sunday. In Tokyo, he attended a military chapel at Hardy Barracks. The chaplain, Father McDonald, was a baseball fan, and Wally often gave him tickets. The two soon became friends. When the chaplain found out that Wally wasn't baptized, he suggested that Wally learn about the Catholic doctrines. Wally agreed and began studying with Father McDonald. Later that year, he took the sacrament.

When the Hiroshima Carp came to Tokyo for their June 22 game with the Giants, they brought along three new players. Kenichi Zenimura had helped the Carp sign three of California's top Nisei players: his own sons Harvey and Howard Zenimura, along with Ben Mitsuyoshi. Over thirty-five thousand fans came to Korakuen Stadium to watch the new players. Howard Zenimura started in left field and batted third but went hitless in four at bats, and Mitsuyoshi pitched an inning in relief, showing "a streak of wildness" but holding the Giants scoreless. Only Howard Zenimura, a pitcher, did not play. The three Carp were among the thirteen new *gaijin* to join Japanese teams in 1953, making a total of twenty foreigners in the leagues.

By late June, Yonamine's foot had finally healed and he was getting his swing back. His batting average shot up to .326 and he began to make a run for the batting title. Hirota and Kashiwaeda also continued to hit well. On June 24 Hirota was hitting around .300, while loquacious Kashiwaeda led all rookies with a .346 average. Since Dick was a pinch-hitter and utility player, he did not have enough at bats to qualify for the batting race.

For the second year in a row, the fans did not select Yonamine as a member of the Central League All-Star team. He received just 1,012 votes, the lowest of the six outfield candidates. Makoto Kozuru of the Carp, who at the time held Japan's single-season home run record with 51 in 1950, led the pack with 5,723. Jyun Hirota placed third among catchers with just 2,103, nearly 9,300 votes behind the winner, Akira Noguchi of the Dragons. Ill feeling toward Nisei was still strong in 1953. Later that year, the Honolulu-based magazine *Nisei* ran an article entitled "Anti-Nisei Fever Rising in Japan." As both Yonamine and Hirota were among the best players at their positions, if not the top, their lack of popularity was probably due to their American citizenship. Shigeru Mizuhara once again managed the Central League team, so once again he added both of his Nisei stars to the roster and used them as substitutes in each of the three All-Star games.

On July 22 the Giants came to Osaka for a two-game series with a four-and-a-half-game lead over the Chunichi Dragons. Wally continued to hit well and was now third in the batting race with a .333 average. Tetsuharu Kawakami, hitting .351, led the league. The third-place Tigers took the first game and the two rivals squared off again on Thursday, July 23.

Hideo Fujimoto took the mound for the Giants, while Shozo Watanabe threw for the Tigers. Behind the plate was rookie umpire Minoru Yamashita. Yamashita had been a star high school and college player in the 1920s. He led the Tokyo Big Six University league in batting average and home runs and represented Japan against the 1931 and 1934 Major League All-Star teams. Before the war, he starred in the first few seasons of the professional league, winning the fall 1936 home run crown, but after entering the army in 1942 he did not return to professional baseball until becoming an umpire in 1952.

The game started off normally enough, except that the fans seemed more raucous than usual, even by Osaka standards. The score remained deadlocked until the Giants scored three in the top of the fifth. The Tigers answered back in the bottom of the inning, loading the bases with just one out. At bat stood the shortstop Choei Shirasaka, a good hitter who would end up with eight home runs that season. Fujimoto reared back, lifted his left leg straight up in the air, and threw. With a crack, Shirasaka hit a bouncer toward Chiba at second base. The Tigers' speedy captain Masayasu Kaneda broke from first and quickly approached second as Chiba gloved the ball. Chiba tagged the passing Kaneda, whirled, and threw to first to complete the double play. But the throw went wild, sailing past the first baseman Tetsuharu Kawakami. The Tigers' fans roared, and quickly fell silent as the umpire began pointing and signaling. They roared again, this time in anger, as Yamashita ruled that Kaneda had interfered with Chiba's throw and thus Shirasaka was out. Kaneda and Chiba exchanged words before rushing at each other to exchange blows as fans screamed and pelted the field with bottles and seat cushions. Yamashita finally restored order and medics entered the stands to carry away an injured spectator on a stretcher.

Chiba came to bat in the top of the seventh, greeted with shouts and jeers from the crowd, and relief pitcher Takao Fujimura promptly drilled him with an inside pitch. As Chiba stomped toward first, he barked at Fujimura, and flung his bat toward the pitcher. Masayasu Kaneda rushed in from right field to protect his pitcher. He first protested to the umpire before going after Chiba again. The two scuffled as the fans threw more bottles on to the field. Again order was restored and again medics carried away another injured fan on a stretcher.

The Giants scored twice in the inning as Yonamine doubled, but the Tigers tallied for two of their own in the bottom of the seventh. Down 5–2 in the bottom of the ninth, the Tigers had runners on second and third with two outs. Hideo Fujimoto was clearly tiring but as complete games were the norm in the early '50s, Mizuhara stuck with his starting pitcher. It was nearly 9:20 and almost dark. A light mist had settled over the outfield, making it even more difficult to see. With the game on the line, none other than Masayasu Kaneda strode to the plate.

It seemed like a storybook ending. Kaneda blasted a deep line drive that looked as if it would clear the fence for a game-tying home run. As the ball shot into the gap in right-center, Yonamine and Iwamoto converged. Wally turned his back on the infield and sprinted to the wall, but couldn't catch up to the ball. It was just out of reach. At least it would stay in the park. Wally stretched out his glove, but the ball dropped, took a big bounce, hit the fence, and fell back into Wally's still outstretched mitt. He whirled and threw to second base to hopefully hold the fleet Kaneda to a double or triple. As he threw, Wally heard the umpire Yamashita shout, "Out!" "Queer," thought Wally. Chiba took the throw and stepped on second base for the game-ending double play. The Tigers' runners, assuming correctly that Kaneda's hit couldn't be caught, had already crossed home plate, and couldn't get back to their bases.

The Tigers ran on to the diamond to protest as irate fans jumped over the outfield walls and chased the Giants into their dugout while shouting, "You cheaters! That wasn't a catch!" "The stadium was like a disturbed beehive full of angry bees," Yonamine remembered. "We picked up our equipment and did a fast retreat. Outside where the bus was waiting, the furious fans surrounded it in a threatening mood. Pushing our way through, we climbed into the bus, but the crowd began bashing the windows. I shielded my head and crouched down low in my seat." The bus pulled away toward the Giants' hotel. In the meantime, thousands of fans had invaded the playing field and chased Yamashita into the stadium's office. Rioters threw bottles and smashed windows before the police finally cleared the stadium an hour and ten minutes later.

Another crowd of angry fans greeted the Giants at their hotel, but the players reached their rooms unmolested. Wally immediately went to Mizuhara's room. He entered and closed the door behind him. "I have to confess," said Wally. "I didn't catch that ball."

"What!" bellowed Mizuhara. "Alright," he said more calmly, "if anybody asks, tell them you caught it."

The Giants packed and left for the train station. More angry fans waited in front of the station. The players had to push their way through and just made the train before it rumbled out of town. On the train, Chiba asked Wally what had really happened. Wally confessed to Chiba, who also told him, "Don't tell anyone. Keep quiet about it for ten years." At Kyoto Station, reporters entered the train.

"They are still shouting at Osaka Stadium," they informed the team. "What really happened?" they asked.

"I caught it," Wally lied.

But a couple of days later, Yonamine accidentally bumped into Masayasu Kaneda.

"Tell me the truth," he asked.

Wally couldn't lie to Kaneda. "I didn't catch it," he responded.

Kaneda nodded and said nothing.

The Tigers officially protested the game, but to no avail. Yamashita—perhaps realizing his mistake, or perhaps shocked by the fans' attack—retired immediately from umpiring and left professional baseball completely. In 1987 he was elected to the Japan Baseball Hall of Fame for his accomplishments as both an amateur and early professional player.

After the so-called Namba Riot (Namba is the section of Osaka where the stadium was located), Wally continued to hit well. He moved into second place in the batting race on July 27, the same day a truce in the Korean War was signed. Yonamine's average was now up to .342. He had surpassed Kawakami and trailed Michio Nishizawa of the Dragons by only .001. With Wally's success, his rivalry with Kawakami intensified. "He always used to needle me. If I didn't get a hit, he would come up to me, and say, 'Oh, Yonamine-san you didn't get a hit. Oh, you looked terrible.' But that was his mistake because it would really get me mad. I would think to myself, 'Okay, I'm going to show you!' And the next day, I'd get two or three hits."

Shigeru Chiba remembered, "Wally and Kawakami were not only rivals but also on bad terms. They mutually tried to steal techniques from each other. Wally learned to hit the way Kawakami did by letting the ball come to him. Kawakami learned base running from Wally.

They competed as they fought." Several American writers have labeled Kawakami as a Japanese nationalist and have attributed his dislike of Yonamine to a general hatred of all Americans or Nisei. For example, James Floto of the *Diamond Angle* magazine's Web site wrote in 2001, "Yonamine's success further fueled the hated of his ultra-nationalist teammate, Tetsuharu Kawakami. . . . Here was a young American upstart [Yonamine] with his disrespectful ways and his badge of what Kawakami considered dishonor—his parents had turned their back on the fatherland." Yet, Yonamine, Cappy Harada, and Dick Kashiwaeda all emphatically state that this interpretation is incorrect. The dislike was personal and directed at Wally, not the other Nisei on the team.

During the next week, however, Wally's average plummeted by fifteen points as he battled a stomach flu. The illness became severe, forcing him to miss five games during the annual August trip to Hokkaido. In the meanwhile, Kawakami moved back to the top of the batting leaders. At the end of August, Yomiuri beat Hanshin 6–2 at Korakuen Stadium in Japan's first televised baseball game.

Television had only come to Japan recently. The country's first station, the publicly funded and government-run NHK, began broadcasting at 2:00 p.m. on February 1, 1953, with a message from the station's president followed by the news. A second station known as NTV (Nippon Television), Japan's first private station, began broadcasting on August 28 1953, the day before airing the Giants-Tigers game. NTV was the brainchild of Yomiuri owner Matsutaro Shoriki, who realized the potential of adding a television station to his media empire. At the time, fewer than one thousand households in Japan owned televisions, as the new Sharp model TV3-14 cost 175,000 yen (about $500), roughly thirty times the monthly salary of an average worker. To increase the viewing audience, Shoriki had forty-two NHK-owned televisions set up in public places throughout Tokyo. Thousands gathered on street corners, department stores, and train stations to watch the Giants-Tigers game. In some areas the crowds became so great and chaotic that small riots occurred.

A television craze hit Japan the following year when NHK broadcast the first international professional wrestling match on February 19, 1954. The event featured a tag team contest between a retired sumo wrestler named Rikidozan and the amateur judo champion Kimura Masahiko on one team and the American Sharpe brothers on the other. Ben and Mike Sharpe each stood 6 feet 6 inches tall and weighed roughly 250 pounds. They were the reigning world tag team champions and had dominated opponents for five consecutive years. To the Japanese, still stunted by the prewar diet, the Sharpe brothers looked like giants. In contrast, Kimura stood 5 feet 8 inches tall and weighed just 170 pounds, while Rikidozan was the same height but fifty pounds heavier. Much to everybody's surprise, Rikidozan pummeled each brother in succession with a furious series of karate chops before forcing Ben Sharpe to the ground and pinning him for the win. The victory, which was watched by ten to fourteen million television viewers, set off celebrations throughout Japan. People cheered wildly and wept with joy as many saw the match as symbolic of Japan's struggle against the mightier foreign powers. Shoriki stated, "Rikidozan, by his pro wrestling in which he sent the big white men flying, has restored pride to the Japanese and given them new courage."

Rikidozan became a national hero, and NTV quickly organized a Friday night wrestling program called the Mitsubishi Diamond Hour. Although the Yonamines would not own a television for another year or so, Wally enjoyed watching the Fightman Hour whenever he could. His favorite was Rikidozan, whom he had met on numerous occasions. Before he became a big star, Rikidozan had spent time in Honolulu learning the finer points of the sport. Jane's father, then president of the Honolulu Sumo Association, befriended the wrestler. But Wally had another reason to be fascinated by the sport. In the late 1940s, a successful wrestling promoter named Al Karasick approached Yonamine about becoming a wrestler. Karasick figured that Yonamine's popularity with Japanese Americans could be turned into large profits. "The wrestlers were so big and I was just 180 pounds, but he told me not to worry about being small because he would teach me how to wrestle," Yonamine recalls. "I'm glad that I decided not to become a wrestler. I might have been killed!"

Kawakami increased his lead in the batting race on September 9 as he went 4 for 4 during the first game of a doubleheader against the Swallows, and then got three hits in his first three at bats in the second game. The Giants won both games as Dick Kashiwaeda hit his sixth home run of the season to help win the nightcap. Yomiuri now had a ten-game lead over the Tigers and Dragons in the Central League standings.

With the pennant race almost wrapped up, Mizuhara decided to give Kashiwaeda more playing time. Dick responded with a home run tear. He hit number seven on September 15 and hit another and drove in five the following day. Number nine came a week later in a 3–0 victory over the Robins. Yonamine, on the other hand, entered the longest slump during his first three years in Japan. His average fell to .310 on September 23, dropping him to fifth in the batting race. Wally tried to break the slump with extra workouts at Tamagawa, but when that didn't help he devised ways to practice at home. Before he went to bed, he would swing his bat four hundred times. Some nights he even asked Jane to play shadow ball. Jane would stand on one side of their longest room, go into a wind up and pretend to pitch. Wally would stand with his bat ready at the other end and try to imagine the ball coming toward him and take a swing.

A week later, the Giants clinched the pennant by sweeping the Tigers in two doubleheaders. Yomiuri ended the season with an 87-37-1 record, finishing sixteen games in front of the Tigers. Wally, however, didn't regain his batting form and ended the season with a .307 average. Kawakami won the batting crown with a .347 average, twenty points above his nearest competitor.

Yomiuri faced the Nankai Hawks once again in the Japan Series. The first two games, held in the Hawks' bandbox park in Osaka, were thrillers as the Hawks won Game 1 in the bottom of the twelfth and the Giants bounced back to take Game 2 with consecutive home runs by Yonamine, Chiba, and Minanimura.

It rained on October 12, but league officials decided to play Game 3 despite the poor weather. Cappy Harada had successfully arranged for the New York Giants to come to Japan for an exhibition series, but only a single day separated the end of the Japan Series and the start of the goodwill games. The Giants and Hawks struggled to play through torrential rain. The ball was slick, rain obscured the players' vision, and their feet stuck in the oozy mud of the all-dirt infield. Wally scored a run and batted in Jyun Hirota for the Giants' second run, but entering the top of the ninth the score was 2–2. The Hawks quickly got two runners on with just one out when the rain intensified. With the Hawks on the edge of victory, the umpires called the game due to the downpour. The game ended in a tie and would have to be replayed despite already finishing eight and a third grueling innings.

The Giants won the next two games easily to take a 3–1 lead in the series. Wally hit well in the victories, going 3 for 7 with a double and triple. With their third consecutive Japan Series defeat to the Giants looming, just 6,346 fans showed up to root for the hometown Hawks in Game 6. Taketoshi Ogami treated the faithful fans to a sparkling 2–0 shutout of the mighty Giants.

The series moved back to Korakuen Stadium for Game 7 on October 16. The New York Giants had already arrived in Tokyo and had begun working out for their first game with the Giants scheduled for Saturday, October 17. Before Game 7, Ryuji Suzuki, the chairman of the Central League, and Michiaki Hashimoto, the business manager for the *Yomiuri Shimbun*, met with Shigeo Mizuhara to emphasize the importance of winning that day. If the Hawks forced an eighth game, it would create an embarrassing situation as either the Japan Series or the games with the New York Giants would have to be postponed. In either case, the Japanese would look disorganized and unprofessional.

The scoring began with a play that helped define Yonamine's career. Leading off in the bottom of the first, Wally stepped in against right-hander Masaki Obata. Obata was far from the Hawks' best pitcher. A rookie, he had pitched just thirty-five innings in professional baseball, but with his ace Taketoshi Ogami tired from Game 6 and his other pitchers hit unusually hard by the Giants in earlier games, Hawks' manager Kazuto Tsuruoka decided to give him a chance.

Obata came inside, but Wally quickly turned on the pitch and pulled it into right field for a clean single. From the third base box, Mizuhara gave Chiba the inevitable bunt sign, and Chiba dutifully laid down a sacrifice moving Yonamine to second. Fukashi Minanimura then hit a hard drive to the left of third baseman Kazuo Kageyama. The ball handcuffed Kageyama and squirted off his glove further to his left. Seeing the loose ball, Yonamine sprinted toward third. Chusuke Kizuka, the Hawks' lithe shortstop, went into the hole and quickly retrieved the ball. Instead of throwing to first, he threw to Kageyama. Wally saw Kageyama's glove stretch out as the throw reached him. "I was out by three or four steps. Kageyama had the ball in his glove and was waiting for me. Well, I wasn't going to give up easily!"

Kageyama brought the glove down to tag Yonamine's lead foot, but he made a mistake. Wally could see the ball in the palm of the glove. Yonamine didn't try to elude Kageyama's tag, but slid right at the glove. As he made contact, Wally kicked the back of the mitt. The ball flew out and rolled into left field as Wally upended Kageyama. Struggling to his feet, he tagged third and tried to race home, but Wally felt something holding him back. He soon broke loose and scored.

From the stands, it looked like Kageyama had just dropped the ball from the impact of the collision. But in the dugout, the Giants players realized what happened and appreciated the difficulty of the play. "It was the first time that we saw such base running," Naito remembers. "Once we saw that play, we started practicing sliding more seriously." Years later, Wally made an interesting discovery. "On August 26, 1990, my friends held a retirement party for me in Honolulu. They made a video that included that play. The video showed Kageyama frantically grabbing both my feet trying to prevent me from scoring!"

As the game progressed, it seemed that the Giants might only need the one run to win. Starter Takehiko Bessho put down the Hawks in short order in each of the first five innings. In the top of the sixth, however, the Hawks' weak-hitting catcher Jun Matsui and shortstop Chusuke Kizuka both homered to give the Hawks the lead. Mizuhara promptly removed Bessho and brought in Takumi Otomo, who shut down the visitors.

Tsuruoka removed the rookie pitcher, Masaki Obata, after five innings. He had done well, giving up just three hits and a single run. Taketoshi Ogami took the mound for the Hawks. Ogami had been the Hawks' most effective pitcher during the series, surrendering only one run in sixteen innings, but he had pitched a complete game the day before. After Otomo grounded to lead off the seventh, "Yonamine ripped a line drive inches inside the first base line into the right-field corner." Right fielder Teruo Shimabara reached the ball quickly. Most players would have stopped at first, but Wally rounded the bag at full speed and sprinted toward second. The throw came in just ahead of him, but with a "beautiful hook slide" Wally eluded the tag and reached second safely. After Chiba made the second out, Minanimura singled into short left. Wally darted to third, and according to the *Hawaii Times*, "Manager Shigeru Mizuhara coaching at third waved him home in a desperate attempt to score. It would have been an easy out but Hawk left fielder Kazuo Horii's throw was 10 yards off the plate and Yonamine tied the score at 2–all." Minutes later, Kawakami singled home Minanimura to secure the win and the Giants' third straight championship.

After the game, the Hawk's manager Kazuto Tsuruoka congratulated Wally and praised him for his aggressive play. Leo Durocher, who had been watching the game from the stands, came on to the field and sought out Yonamine. After shaking his hand and congratulating him, he added, "You're the kind of ballplayer I want on my team!" Wally cherished the praise.

At a ceremony in the center of the field, league officials presented the trophies and awards. They honored Wally with the Fine Play and Home Run awards, but the series Most Valuable Player Award went to Tetsuharu Kawakami. Leslie Nakashima of the *Hawaii Times* wrote: "Many, including [this] writer, thought Yonamine whose brilliant all-round playing and rally starting hits, was more deserving of the honor." Kawakami led the Giants with a .481 batting average (13 hits in 27 at bats) and five RBI and was a perfect 4 for 4 in Game 5, but Yonamine contributed more to the Giants' victory. Wally banged out twelve hits, one less than Kawakami in the same number of at bats, but also walked five times (three times more than Kawakami) for a .630 on-base average. Yonamine scored six runs and had three RBI from the lead-off slot, while Kawakami scored twice and batted in five from the clean-up position. Yonamine's hits, however, were more timely. His two-run homer in Game 2 provided the game-winning RBI; his fifth-inning RBI single provided the run that ended Game 3 in a tie; his lead-off double and daring base running gave the Giants the winning run in Game 5; and his timely hitting and aggressive base running gave the Giants the victory in the final game. Kawakami had no game-winning RBI, nor did he score a winning run. It seems that Nakashima was correct: Yonamine should have won the MVP Award.

The next day, the Yomiuri Giants squared off against the New York Giants at Korakuen Stadium. Although both teams were determined to play their best, the Japanese knew that they were outclassed. The *Nippon Times* wrote: "The Japanese fans, of course, won't be expecting the local Giants to win against their big league opponents. They will be primarily out to see what Japan's best players can do against Major League pitching and how long its hurling aces can hold up against the National League sluggers before the roof falls in." Roughly forty-five thousand fans, including thousands of Americans, packed Korakuen for the game. The New Yorkers dominated the game, rapping out twelve hits and scoring eleven to Tokyo's one. Yonamine scored the Giants' sole run in the seventh inning. As Shigeru Chiba doubled to right field, Wally came into the plate sliding hard and knocking the ball from catcher Wes Westrum's grasp.

The New York Giants remained in Japan for another three weeks, playing thirteen more games against All-Star teams, the Hanshin Tigers, the Chunichi Dragons, and Yomiuri. The New Yorkers dominated the series winning 12, losing 1, and tying 1. They outscored the

Japanese 98 to 30 and held the Japanese batters to a .195 average. Wally did particularly poorly. In 22 at bats, he failed to get a single hit. The Major Leaguers meanwhile feasted on Japanese pitching with a .304 average and 20 home runs.

Yomiuri did manage to beat the New Yorkers in one game. On Halloween, thirty thousand watched as Takumi Otomo faced off against Al Worthington at Korakuen Stadium. Prior to the game, Lefty O'Doul, who came to Japan to watch the tour, explained that the Japanese had no chance against the Americans, because they always pitched low in the strike zone. They did this because Japanese tend to be high-ball hitters, but O'Doul told them that Major League power hitters preferred low pitches. "Pitch higher. Throw high," O'Doul suggested. During the game, Jyun Hirota crouched only halfway down to keep his target high, and Otomo held the Giants to just seven hits and won 2–1.

Otomo particularly impressed the visitors. In 25 innings, he struck out 15 and posted a 2.88 ERA—nearly 3.5 runs under the Japanese pitchers' ERA for the series. The New Yorkers attempted to acquire Otomo, but were told the price would be ten thousand dollars plus two or three good American ballplayers. Finding the sum too high, the Giants abandoned the idea. The Majors would have to wait another eleven years before fielding a Japanese player.

The famed Negro League oral historian John Holway tells an amusing tale from the New York Giants' visit to Japan. In *Japan is Big League in Thrills*, published in 1954, Holway writes: "In the New Yorkers' first game in Japan, Leo [Durocher], coaching at third, called across the diamond for the runner on first to steal. [Jyun] Hirota played dumb like the rest of the Giants, quietly called for a pitch-out and nailed the astonished New Yorker by 20 feet. They didn't know Jyun is a graduate of Hawaii University!"

Unfortunately, the story is just that. Durocher knew the Yomiuri Giants well from spring training in Santa Maria and had spoken to Jyun Hirota prior to the first game. The New Yorkers knew Yomiuri's Nisei players, as they were some of the few Japanese that the visitors could communicate with. Both Yonamine and Kashiwaeda also state that the event did not occur. Actually, nearly the opposite happened. According to Yonamine, Durocher, who was managing from the third base coach's box, was able to steal Jyun Hirota's signals and taught the Nisei how to better hide his signs.

In late November Yomiuri's three Nisei returned home. Each had had a strong season. Despite the slump at the end of the season, Wally still hit .307, good enough for fifth place in the batting race. He was named to the Central League Best Nine team. Jyun Hirota's average had also dipped late in the season and ended at .242, but he had become the league's top catcher and was also selected for the Central League Best Nine squad. Although only a part-time player, Dick Kashiwaeda had the most successful season of the three. Dick hit .341 with nine home runs. His 57 RBI were the fourth highest on the Giants, even though he had only 220 at bats, roughly half of the starting players. The Rookie of the Year honors, however, went to pitcher Masatoshi Gondo of the Robins, who posted a 15-12 record with a 2.77 ERA. Yomiuri management was very happy with the Nisei's success and signed Hirota and Kashiwaeda for the 1954 season. Yonamine, of course, was already signed.

When Wally arrived in Honolulu, instead of going home to see Jane and his daughter Amy, he took the next available flight to Maui. He hired a car and drove to Olowalu to see the old house he grew up in and the field where he cut cane. "I wanted to remind myself how fortunate I was to be making a living playing baseball. I told myself that I'd better not forget what I went through to get there. I knew what it felt like to be hungry. I did this after every season for the next ten years, so that when I went back to Japan I would try harder."

1. Wally (*far left*) playing for Farrington High School in 1944. *Courtesy of Wally Yonamine.*

2. Wally as a San Francisco 49ers running back in 1947. *Courtesy of Wally Yonamine.*

3. Wally playing center field for the Salt Lake City Bees in 1950. *Courtesy of Wally Yonamine.*

4. Shoji Yasuda and Cappy Harada look on as Wally signs with the Yomiuri Giants in June 1951. *Courtesy of Wally Yonamine and the Yomiuri Giants.*

5. Wally shows off his prize for being named the 1952 Japan Series Top Hitter—a bicycle! Pitcher Takehiko Bessho is on Wally's right. *Courtesy of Wally Yonamine and the Yomiuri Giants.*

6. Wally with Hirofumi Naito at a *ryokan* in 1951 or '52. *Courtesy of Wally Yonamine.*

7. Wally uses his famous hook slide to
score in 1951. *Courtesy of Wally Yonamine
and the Yomiuri Giants.*

8. Always trying to fit in, Wally wears a *yukata*
and *geta*. *Courtesy of Wally Yonamine.*

9. Wally marries Jane Iwashita on February 2, 1952. *Courtesy of Wally Yonamine.*

10. Wally scores with a hard slide as Nankai Hawks catcher Keizo Tsutsui goes flying in Game 1 of the 1951 Japan Series. *Courtesy of Wally Yonamine and the Yomiuri Giants.*

名古屋ドラゴンズ　杉下投手　　国鉄スワローズ　金田投手

11. The Giant killers (*left to right*): Chunichi Dragons ace Shigeru Sugishita
and Kokutetsu Swallows ace Masaichi
Kaneda. *Courtesy of the author.*

12. Giants captain and longtime rival
Tetsuharu Kawakami eyes Wally warily.
Courtesy of the Yomiuri Giants.

13. The Yomiuri Giants Nisei players in 1955. *Left to right*: Yonamine, Jyun Hirota, Dick Kashiwaeda, and Andy Miyamoto. *Courtesy of Wally Yonamine and the Yomiuri Giants.*

14. Yomiuri Giants stars, circa 1956. *Left to right*: Yonamine, Tetsuharu Kawakami, and Andy Miyamoto. Tatsuro Hirooka is squatting. *Courtesy of Wally Yonamine and the Yomiuri Giants.*

15. Wally in the mid-1950s. *Courtesy of Wally Yonamine and the Yomiuri Giants.*

16. Wally with his family at the Tamagawa training grounds, circa 1958. *Courtesy of Wally Yonamine.*

17. Wally instructs the Chunichi Dragons. *Courtesy of Wally Yonamine and the Chunichi Dragons.*

18. Wally is tossed by a sea of fans after winning the Central League pennant in 1974. *Courtesy of Wally Yonamine and the Chunichi Dragons.*

19. The Yomiuri Giants in 1978. *Left to right*: Tsuneo Horiuchi, Isao Harimoto, Sadaharu Oh, Yukinobu Kuroe, Yonamine, Shigeo Nagashima, and Akira Kunimatsu. *Courtesy of Wally Yonamine and the Yomiuri Giants.*

20. Wally and Jane with their grandchildren, circa 2000. *Courtesy of Wally Yonamine.*

11

Gaijin Dageki Oh—Foreign Batting Champion

In January Wally, Jyun, and Dick began training for the 1954 season. Douglas Mitsuo Matsuoka, who had signed with the Giants during the winter, joined them. The twenty-two-year-old pitcher had been a star at Iolani High School in Honolulu. The Giants hoped that he would replace Bill Nishita, who had one more year to serve in the army. The four met at Moiliili field in Honolulu for general conditioning and baseball drills. They played a lot of pepper. "Anybody who fouled the ball back over the backstop had to buy the rest of us shaved ice from this shop across the street," recalls Dick Kashiwaeda. "If you did it twice, you had to pay for ice cream in the shaved ice. If you hit a third one, then we added sweet red beans. That would be red beans, ice cream, and shaved ice all in one container. You know who paid? Doug Matsuoka—every single time we practiced. He was a pitcher so he didn't hit as well."

In mid-February the four packed their bags and joined the Giants at their frigid spring training site in Akashi. The Japanese had arrived two weeks earlier, but the Hawaiians had been given permission to come late, providing they arrived in shape and ready to play. During the off-season, Yomiuri had signed Tatsuro Hirooka, Waseda University's star shortstop. Hirooka was a slap hitter but a slick fielder. He was not expected to supplant All-Star shortstop Masaaki Hirai, but instead give the Giants more depth on the bench. The Giants also hired full-time coaches for the first time in their history. Previously, managers designated certain veteran players to help run practices, but team president Shoji Yasuda decided that veterans should concentrate on playing and not be distracted with coaching responsibilities. Accordingly, Yasuda hired Daisuke Miyake as head coach, Goro Taniguchi as pitching coach, and Kyoichi Nitta as farm team coach. All three men were former collegiate stars prior to World War II.

Sportswriters openly questioned the wisdom of choosing these men. All three were older than manager Mizuhara, and Daisuke Miyake had been the Giants' general manager when Mizuhara was a player. Thus, in Japanese social hierarchy, Mizuhara was Miyake's *kohai*. The experts wondered if this inverted hierarchy could work on the field. Would Mizuhara feel comfortable telling his coaches what to do? Would the coaches follow the younger man's plans, or would they ignore him and do what they wished? The fears were unfounded—the coaches behaved professionally and respected Mizuhara's authority.

The Giants' biggest personnel move came two weeks into spring training when they sold starting third baseman Mitsuo Uno to the Kokutetsu Swallows. The news shocked the players and their fans. Mizuhara spoke out against the sale, but Shoji Yasuda wanted Dick Kashiwaeda inserted into the starting lineup. Kashiwaeda had proved that he could hit Japanese pitching in 1953 and his defense had always been outstanding, but there had no open position for Dick to play every day. With both Hirofumi Naito and Tatsuro Hirooka as reserve infielders, Yasuda felt that Uno was now expendable. Uno reacted angrily to the transfer, but the Swallows pacified him by making him the assistant manager and announcing that he would eventually take over the helm. As things turned out, the sale was a colossal blunder.

As spring training progressed, Kashiwaeda and Hirota looked strong, but Yonamine was often behind in the count and hitting poorly. Close observers would have noticed that Wally was hitting an inordinate number of foul balls. "During the intersquad and exhibition games I started practicing how to hit foul balls," Yonamine said. "I would take two strikes purposely and then try to hit them foul. I didn't get a hit for about ten games, but I didn't tell anybody what I was doing. They were just exhibition games and I knew I could get a hit if I wanted to. I ended up getting pretty good at it. I once fouled off sixteen pitches in one at bat. I would just foul off the hard pitches and wait for one that I wanted. Together Chiba and I would sometimes make the opposing pitcher throw over twenty pitches in just the first inning."

The Giants season opened at Korakuen Stadium on April 3 against the Kokutetsu Swallows and their ace, Masaichi Kaneda. Prior to the game, Wally strode over to the bullpens and watched Kaneda warm up. The southpaw looked tired and did not have his best stuff. Wally had been studying Kaneda for three seasons and knew his pitches and style well. When Kaneda felt fatigued, he fell into a predictable pattern. He would start batters with curve balls until he got two strikes, then he would rear back, mass all his energy, and release his ninety-seven-mile-per-hour fastball.

By the second inning, Kaneda was struggling. Runners stood on first and second with two outs as Yonamine came to the plate. Wally guessed that Kaneda would start with a curve. It came in high and broke toward the inside. Wally waited for the break and drove it into the right-field bleachers for a three-run homer. It was a great start to what would become a great season.

The following day, forty-five thousand packed Korakuen to watch a doubleheader against the Swallows. The Giants took the first game 3–0, but in the second game Mitsuo Uno began to show the difficulties he would cause his old team. Uno's revenge started in the field. Throughout the series Uno had been watching Mizuhara as he flashed signals to the Giants' batters from the third base coach's box. Mizuhara became convinced that Uno had stolen his signs. His fears were confirmed in the second inning of the third game, when he called for a bunt and Uno charged toward the plate with the pitch. The Giants' manager immediately stopped using signs for the remainder of the game.

Uno also suggested that the Swallows alter their rotation to start Masaichi Kaneda as many times as possible against the Giants. Previously, opponents often saved their aces for sure victories against weaker teams and started less experienced pitchers against the mighty Giants. Uno pointed out that this strategy helped the Giants win pennants. Other teams soon followed the Swallows' lead. During the 1954 season, Kaneda had eleven decisions against the Giants, while the Dragons' ace Shigeru Sugishita had sixteen.

Despite the trouble Uno caused in the third game, the Giants recovered and swept the next seven. During a 16–6 thrashing of the Hiroshima Carp, Jyun Hirota hit three home runs and added another the following day in a 21–6 victory over the Robins. Yomiuri led the Central League by a game and a half over the Dragons on May 1, but unlike in the previous three seasons, the Giants could not build on the early lead. Each time the Giants threatened to pull away, they would face the Swallows. Led by Uno, the Swallows won eight straight encounters, knocking Yomiuri into second place on June 1. Wally also struggled. On May 14 his average stood at .350, but it plunged rapidly, and two weeks later he fell from the league's top ten batters. "I focused on swinging my bat and tried to recall my form when I was doing well, but even this didn't help." As the slump continued, Wally became sullen.

"We didn't have a television," Jane recalls, "so my maid and I used to have a signal. She would look through the garage doors and look at Wally's face when he came home to see how he did. She'd give me one signal if he was fine or a different signal that meant go cook because he's not looking so good. When he had a bad day, he wouldn't yell or anything. He just wanted to go over the game, so he would go into the bath. I would think he was going to come out soon so I would get his food ready, but then I would wait and wait and he wouldn't come out. So I would put the food back in the oven. I would end up taking it in and out, in and out, for two hours, and he would still be in the tub going through every pitch. Finally, he would come out and he would be fine."

The Giants' luck began to change in early June. On June 5, Takehiko Bessho outdueled Shozo Watanabe of the Tigers for a 2–1 victory. It was Bessho's two hundredth career victory. At the time, only three other pitchers in the history of Japanese baseball had won as many. Hawaiian Bozo Wakabayashi and Jiro Noguchi of the Hankyu Braves

had each retired with 237 wins, while Russian-born Victor Starffin, who was still pitching with the Takahashi Unions of the Pacific
League, needed just a few more wins to become the first to reach three
hundred. The thirty-two-year-old Bessho had struggled in the spring,
losing five of his first nine decisions, but reaching the milestone energized him as he won twenty-one more games that season.

The first-place Dragons came to Tokyo for a two-game series
on June 8. The Dragons started their gangly ace Shigeru Sugishita,
while the Giants went with aging Hiroshi Nakao. Nakao pitched a
brilliant game, limiting the Dragons to a single run, but Sugishita's
forkball baffled the Giants as usual, holding them scoreless through
seven. The Giants rallied in the bottom of the eighth as Yonamine
clobbered a forkball into the right-field stands with two runners on
to win the game. Even the normally reserved Kawakami joined the
ecstatic Giants celebrating around Wally. "Yonamine! Hey Yonamine,"
Kawakami called. "You're pretty good, really good!" He proclaimed as
he gripped Wally's hand.

The Giants beat the Dragons the following day in a 13–0 romp. Wally
homered again as did Kashiwaeda, Hirota, and Hirooka. With the two
wins, Yomiuri retook first place. Wally had overcome his slump and
the hits now came in bunches. "It is impossible to hit well all the time.
There are always ups and downs. So when I was hot, I tried to get as
many hits as possible." With this approach, Yonamine had numerous
multihit games. In the doubleheader against Hiroshima on July 20,
for example, Wally went 3 for 4 against ace Ryohei Hasegawa in the
first game, and then 5 for 5 in the nightcap. By the end of June, his
average rose to .348, and he trailed only Hiroyuki Watanabe of the
Tigers and Kawakami in the batting race.

When many batters get on a hot streak, the ball seems larger than
normal and thus easier to hit. After Mickey Mantle hit his famous 565-
foot home run in 1953, he stated, "I just saw the ball as big as a grape-
fruit." A study by Jessica K. Witt and Dennis R. Profitt of the University of Virginia psychology department empirically demonstrated
a correlation between how well a player hits and the perceived size

of the ball. At the end of several games, Witt and Profitt asked softball players to choose one of five pictures that most closely resembled the size of an actual softball. Players who had hit well that afternoon picked a diagram larger than the actual ball more often than players who had hit poorly. For other professionals "in the zone," the ball seems to come to them in slow motion. When Tetsuharu Kawakami was hitting particularly well, the ball seemed to stop—presenting a stationary target—just before he made contact.

Wally's experience during a hot streak was different. Yonamine studied opposing pitchers in detail. He knew their deliveries, their repertoire, and tendencies. He knew when certain pitchers were likely to throw a curve and its likely location. When Wally became hot, he could predict the pitch and its location with amazing accuracy. "The ball wasn't necessarily bigger or slower, I just knew what was coming," he noted. With that information, the pitcher lost the element of surprise and Wally could focus better on the ball and in the words of American Hall of Famer Wee Willie Keeler "hit 'em where they ain't."

At the All-Star break, the Giants led the second-place Dragons by three games. In the past two seasons, Japanese fans seemed reluctant to vote for Nisei players on the All-Star ballot. This ethnocentricity passed away in the 1954 season as over 150,000 voted for Jyun Hirota as starting Central League catcher. The next highest total went to the 1953 winner Akira Noguchi of the Dragons, who received just 45,576 votes. Wally placed second among outfielders with 116,439, only 287 votes behind the popular Tigers' captain, Masayasu Kaneda. The other Central League starters were pitcher Takumi Otomo of the Giants, first baseman Tetsuharu Kawakami, second baseman Shigeru Chiba, third baseman Mitsuo Uno now of the Swallows, shortstop Yoshio Yoshida of the Tigers, and Giants' outfielder Fukashi Minanimura. Once again, Wally had a disappointing All-Star series, going hitless in six at bats with two walks. As Yonamine relied on studying pitchers and figuring out their weaknesses, he often had trouble hitting pitchers he didn't know well. Accordingly, he hit only .163 in his seventeen career All-Star games.

Immediately after the All-Star break the Dragons returned to Tokyo for a three-game series. Sugishita won the first game with five scoreless innings in relief as the Dragons broke a 2–2 tie with two runs in the tenth inning. The Giants returned the favor the next day by scoring in the bottom of the tenth to win 3–2. Sugishita came in once again in relief and held the Giants for two and two-thirds innings. In the third game, the Giants and Dragons were tied again going into the bottom of the ninth. Sugishita came in for the third consecutive day to preserve the tie, but Wally homered with two outs in the bottom of the ninth to win the game and give the Giants a four-game lead over the Dragons.

Throughout July, Wally continued to hit well. His average remained in the .340s, and on the twenty-ninth, he took the lead in the batting race. Two days later, the Giants left for their annual trip to northern Honshu. They began by facing the Carp in a doubleheader at Sendai. Yonamine rapped out a single in his first at bat and then, inexplicably, the hits dried up. He could no longer predict which pitch was coming and soon felt lost at the plate. A week went by without a hit.

Wally tried everything to break the drought, including prayers, but to no avail. By the time the team reached Fukushima on August 8, his average had fallen to .336. In truth, Wally was only 0 for his last 14 at bats, but after the hot streak in June and July, the slump felt endless.

"I was going crazy. Even though I was slumping, Mizuhara didn't use anybody else. I played every game. We had a doubleheader that day, so before the first game I went to see the head coach, Daisuke Miyake. 'Mr. Miyake,' I said, 'I was at bat fourteen times and I didn't get a hit. Can I rest one game?'

"'Well, let's go see Mr. Mizuhara,' he said.

"But Mizuhara gave me a good scolding. 'What you talking about!' he yelled. 'You're getting paid from the Giants. You play!'

"I got so mad, but I didn't say anything to him because I respected him. Inside, I was thinking, 'Mizuhara, you *yaroo* [fool]! I'm going to show you now! I'll show you!' I was just so mad.

"I was batting third—a guy who couldn't hit at all. I thought Mizuhara was just being mean. I flared up. On my first time at bat, I furiously swatted at the ball and got a hit. In the fourth inning, I hit my ninth home run.

"I ended up going four for four in the first game. In the second game, I got three hits and a walk in four plate appearances. Eight times at bat, eight times on base! After the game, Mr. Miyake, the head coach, came to me. He was so mad! 'Yonamine, do you think that I'm a damn fool or what!' And he gave me a good scolding! 'Eight for eight and you wanted to sit down!' But that's what I needed, somebody to kick me in my pants.

"A lot of times when you're in a slump, you go into the batter's box thinking, 'I'm not going to get a hit.' You need to get more aggressive. I learned that if something gets you mad then you get more aggressive at the plate. So from then on, when I started to slump I became even more aggressive on the base paths. If anybody was in my way, I'd just knock them down."

After the double-header, Wally set his uniform and socks aside unwashed. He would wear them as long as the hot streak continued. From that August onward, Wally refused to wash his "lucky" clothes when he got on a hot streak. "It always happened in the summer when it's hot and sweaty," Jane laments. "The socks would stand up on their own from all that grime. Sometimes, we had to hang the uniform out the window because it smelled so bad." Unfortunately for his roommates, Wally remained hot for over a week. His batting average climbed into the .350s before settling around .348 for most of August and early September.

The Giants felt confident as they returned from northern Japan on August 10: they led the Dragons by four games and Wally had broken out of his slump. Following a five-game series against the Swallows and a single match against the Tigers, the Chunichi Dragons would come to town for three games. The experienced Giants knew that this was their chance. A hot streak could put them far in front of the Dragons and sew up the pennant. And that, of course, is when the season fell apart.

Mitsuo Uno and the Swallows once again toppled the Giants from first place, taking two of the five games. The Dragons, meanwhile, started to win. During the first half of the season, Michio Nishizawa, Chunichi's star first baseman, experienced a prolonged slump, hitting just .280 at the All-Star break. In August, however, Nishizawa found his stroke. As his batting average climbed so did the Dragons' winning percentage. By the time, Chunichi arrived in Tokyo for the three-game showdown, the two teams were tied for first place.

Once again, the bespectacled Shigeru Sugishita dominated the series, winning the first match with a five-hit complete game and pitching thirteen innings on just one day's rest to win the third game of the series. The two rivals met again on August 31 and September 2 in Nagoya. The Dragons' manager, Shunichi Amachi, devised a perfect battle plan: put Sugishita on the mound. On August 31 Sugishita pitched a complete game and shut out the Giants on just two hits—a double by Wally and a single by Jyun Hirota. The teams took September 1 off before meeting again the next day. Once again, Amachi turned to Sugishita, and once again, Sugishita responded with a complete game shutout. Yomiuri left town two and a half games behind the Dragons.

Yomiuri climbed back during the first two weeks of September. During this stretch, Wally hit well and on September 9 caught up with Hiroyuki Watanabe of the Tigers to share the lead in the batting race. Each had a .347 average, but Michio Nishizawa of the Dragons, still in the middle of a hot streak, was only a point behind them. When Nishizawa and the Dragons arrived in Tokyo for a doubleheader on September 19, the teams were even in the standings.

Amachi started Yasushi Soratani against the Giants in the first game but turned to Sugishita in the second inning after the Giants hit Soratani hard. The lanky Sugishita held the Giants scoreless for the remaining eight innings, while his team scored four to win the game 6–2. Game 2 followed a similar pattern. When the Dragons pulled ahead in the sixth inning, Amachi called on Sugishita once again. It had been just a few hours since he had pitched eight innings in the first game, but the Dragons' ace shut out the Giants for three more innings as the Dragons scored twice. In the bottom of the ninth, down 4–6, the Giants loaded the bases with two outs. With a big hit, the two teams would remain tied for first place. If the Giants failed to rally, Chunichi would leave Tokyo with a two-game lead. The players knew that the next batter might decide the fate of the pennant race. As Sugishita starred at the catcher for his signs, Wally stepped into the batter's box. Yonamine had gone hitless so far and wanted to make amends.

Sugishita bore down and threw with all his might. Ball one. He was tired now but knew that the game and season depended on him. Again he challenged Yonamine with a fastball, but it missed outside. Ball two. Sugishita stood back and collected his thoughts. He knew Yonamine's batting style well. When Wally was ahead in the count, he changed his batting style and tried to drive the ball. A home run or extra base hit here would be disastrous. He couldn't give Wally something to hit. He hated the idea, but he saw only one choice.

Wally steadied himself. He knew that Sugishita would have to put one over the plate or risk a 3-0 count. Now was the time for a home run. He shifted his batting stance slightly, allowing him to bring the bat through the strike zone faster, thus generating more power.

Akira Noguchi, the Dragons catcher, suddenly stood up and stuck out his right arm. Wally stared in disbelief as a murmur went through the crowd. They were going to intentionally walk him with the bases loaded! Sugishita purposely threw two wide pitches, and Wally jogged to first base as the runner on third trotted home.

For Sugishita it was a difficult decision. In his last thirty-six innings against the Giants, he had held them scoreless. He was proud of this accomplishment, but he sacrificed his personal record for the win. With the dangerous Yonamine out of the way, Sugishita focused on Shigeru Chiba. The star second baseman hadn't been swinging the bat well, and Sugishita believed he could take care of him. A few pitches later, Chiba flied weakly to center field for the final out of the game.

After the two losses to the Dragons, the Giants went south for four against Hiroshima. The Carp took the first game 5–4 and jumped out to an early lead in the first game of a doubleheader the next day. Tempers in the Giants' dugout frayed as the players watched their chances for the pennant slipping away. In the fifth inning, Wally reached first with a single and immediately decided to swipe second. He took his normal lead off the bag and slowly extended it as Carp pitcher Noboru Matsuyama remained in the stretch. The pitcher stepped off the mound and threw to first, but Wally read the pick-off attempt clearly, slid back, and easily beat the throw to first. "Out!" hollered the first base umpire. Wally couldn't believe his ears. As he stood up, the frustration boiled over. "I'm safe!" he yelled. But the umpire just shook his head impassively. Wally snapped. With both hands he shoved the umpire, knocking him over backward.

"Get off the field!" retorted the ump as he threw Wally out of the game. It was the first time the gentlemanly Yonamine had ever been thrown out. At first Wally didn't budge, but the Hiroshima fans grew angry and several leapt from the stands onto the field. One with gold-capped teeth strutted directly to Wally. "If you do that again, I'll kill you," he barked. Several of the Hiroshima players, including Nisei Harvey Zenimura, recognized the man and came to Wally's rescue. "Leave him alone. He's a friend," they said as they escorted Yonamine off the field. Later, they told Wally that the man with the gold teeth was a well-known *yakuza* and a dangerous man. For the remainder of the game, Wally sat in the stands behind the home plate screen guarded by ten policemen.

Yonamine returned in the second game of the doubleheader, but the Giants lost anyway, falling four and a half games behind the Dragons with thirteen games left in the season. Although not mathematically eliminated, the Giants had little chance of overtaking Chunichi. Yonamine's chances at the batting title were also slipping away. Nishizawa had surpassed both Wally and Watanabe with a .354 average. Watanabe dropped into second, hitting .350, while Wally stood three points behind him in third place.

The Giants had a week off after their disastrous trip to Hiroshima.

The rest calmed Wally and his teammates and they won three of their next four but couldn't gain on Chunichi. Wally seemed especially revitalized, gaining 12 hits in 21 at bats during the four games. His average rose to .357, catapulting him to the top of the batting race as Nishizawa began to slump.

Wally's hot streak continued and his average stayed at .357 as the Giants took four of the five from the Tigers. Watanabe, in the meantime, had a poor series against the Giants, getting just 5 hits in 21 at bats. The batting race was virtually over. Watanabe could only hope that Yonamine would slump in the remaining six games, but Wally didn't. He boosted his average to .361 before sitting out the last two games of the season. Watanabe finished at .353, while Nishizawa faded to .341.

Wally was the first foreigner to win the batting championship, but he had to share the honor. In the Pacific League, a young African American on the Hankyu Braves named Larry Raines beat Hiroshi Oshita by sixteen points for the batting championship. Raines had been playing with the American Giants of the Negro National League when the Hankyu Braves asked the team's owner Abe Saperstein, who also owned the Harlem Globetrotters, if they could acquire several good American players. Saperstein convinced Raines and Rufus Gaines to try their hands at Japanese baseball. Both played for the Braves during the 1953 season, but only Raines returned in '54. With a season under his belt, Raines was clearly the best player in the Pacific League. Known as "Mr. Brilliant" in the Osaka sports papers, Raines's batting average stayed in the .350s for much of the season before settling at a league leading .337. He also led the Pacific League in at bats, runs scored, hits, and doubles, and was only 1 RBI behind the league leader. On top of that, he stole 45 bases and hit 18 home runs and 8 triples. Despite Raines's gaudy numbers, Hankyu finished a dismal fifth, twenty-three and a half games out of first place. Without the pennant, Raines had no chance of winning the Pacific League MVP award. His success, however, led to a better reward. In late November, the Cleveland Indians invited him to attend the rookie training school at Daytona Beach the following March. Two years later, Raines made the big league club.

The Giants played well during the final weeks of the season, winning ten and losing just four, but the Dragons did better and won the Central League by five and a half games. Chunichi went on to beat the Nishitetsu Lions four games to three in the Japan Series. Shigeru Sugishita once again carried the Dragons, winning three games, pitching thirty-eight and two-thirds of the possible sixty-one innings, and posting a 1.38 ERA. Not surprisingly, Sugishita won the Japan Series Most Valuable Player Award. He also beat out Yonamine for the Central League MVP. Wally was a strong contender for the honor as he led the league with 93 runs scored, 172 hits, and 40 doubles as well as capturing the batting title. He also hit 6 triples, 10 home runs, knocked in 69, and stole 20 bases. Had the Giants won the pennant, Wally might have won the coveted award. He was, however, named to the Central League Best Nine team. Jyun Hirota was also named to the Best Nine team as was Tatsuro Hirooka, who won the Rookie of the Year Award, and Mitsuo Uno of the Swallows.

After the long and disappointing season, Wally and the other Nisei would have liked to go home, but they had agreed to accompany the Giants on a tour of Australia to help spread the game and improve Japanese-Australian relations.

12
World Travelers

After the success of the spring training in Santa Maria and witnessing the goodwill generated by the Major League tours of Japan, Yomiuri's management decided to send the Giants abroad to sharpen their baseball skills and help heal the wounds of World War II. Yomiuri first focused on Australia. The country had a long baseball history but had never really taken to the game. Yomiuri hoped that a baseball tour would spark interest and be viewed as a symbol of Japanese goodwill. Once again, Yomiuri asked Lefty O'Doul for his advice, and he enthusiastically supported the idea and planned to accompany the team.

American merchants and expatriates introduced baseball to Australia in the mid-1850s, well before the game arrived in Japan. The earliest recorded games took place in Melbourne in 1857 as the Collingwood team challenged Richmond for a three-game series. The 350–230 score of the second game suggests that players did not follow rules common in the United States, but instead combined rules from baseball, cricket, and rounders. Americans and Australian-born cricketers continued to play sporadically during the next few decades, but the game did not become well known until Albert Spalding and his players stopped in Sydney, Melbourne, and Adelaide during their 1888 World Tour. Thousands of spectators came to watch the American professionals, and the press covered the visitors and the games extensively.

On January 7, 1888, Spalding's entourage left Australia, but Harry Simpson, a young man from New Jersey, stayed behind to promote the game. Over the next few years, Simpson tirelessly introduced the game to cricketers, established baseball clubs, and set up leagues. He wrote to the *Sporting News* in 1890 to announce that an Australian team would be ready to tour the United States in 1893. It looked as if Australia might actually adopt the American national pastime, but a year later Simpson died of typhoid at the age of twenty-seven.

With Simpson's death, the growth of baseball in Australia waned. Many cricketers, however, continued to play the American game in the off-season to keep in shape, and by the early twentieth century, there were approximately six hundred ballplayers in Sydney alone. Amateur baseball slowly grew throughout the 1920s and 1930s as teams from across the country competed annually for the Claxton Shield, the ultimate prize of Australian baseball. The presence of American military personnel during World War II helped spread the game even further. By the late 1940s, the country could field hundreds of amateur nines.

With this spurt in popularity, both the Yomiuri Giants and O'Doul felt that it was time to try to increase the level of play and popularity of the game in Australia. The Giants contacted the Australian Baseball Commission Council to arrange a tour for November 1954, and in early November, O'Doul left California to accompany the Japanese to Australia. As he departed, Lefty told reporters that he expected the trip to raise baseball's popularity greatly.

Unfortunately, both Yomiuri and O'Doul underestimated the Australian World War II veterans' hatred for the Japanese. During the war, the Japanese military committed numerous atrocities toward Australian servicemen, including the murder of approximately 160 POWs at Tol Plantation in Papua New Guinea in February 1942 and the beheading of fifty-five POWs on Ambon Island the following February. Prisoners who were not killed outright were confined in the infamous Japanese prison camps, where they were denied medical treatment and adequate food and routinely beaten and tortured. After experiencing or witnessing this brutality, few veterans were willing to forgive the Japanese, even if they came in peace to play ball. The Returned Servicemen's League (RSL) raised objections as soon as the plans for the tour were announced and officially condemned the proposed visit. Reg Darling, the secretary of the Australian Baseball

Commission Council retorted, "We will play any team irrespective of what country they come from."

The Giants left Tokyo on November 8 and flew on a Qantas plane to Australia. At the last minute, O'Doul was unable to accompany the team. They arrived at Perth on November 11, which, unbeknownst to them, was Remembrance Day, the national holiday to commemorate Australian soldiers killed in World Wars I and II. Members of the outraged Returned Servicemen's League waited for the Giants on the runway. Cappy Harada, who acted as the team's general manager during the tour, told the players to remain on the airplane as he went to speak with the protesters.

As Harada approached the group, one of the leaders growled, "You have a lot of nerve bringing Japanese ballplayers here, after what they did to us!"

"Wait a minute," Harada responded, "we have four American citizens on our team."

"What do you mean by American citizens? They're all Japanese."

"No. They're Japanese American." He ticked off the names: Wally Yonamine, Dick Kashiwaeda, Jyun Hirota, and Doug Matsuoka. "They are all from Hawaii and were born in the United States, but are officially members of the Tokyo Giants. So what's wrong with that?" The delegation begrudgingly let the players disembark without incident but continued to plague the team throughout the trip.

The Giants' tour began with a 10–1 victory against Queensland, but only five hundred came to watch the match. The team then traveled to Sydney, where attendance was even worse. The *Chicago Tribune* noted, "Tokyo's baseball Giants scored a run for almost everybody in the crowd today [November 16] as they beat New South Wales 20 to 1. The paid attendance was 33."

"At that time," Yonamine recalls, "the Australians didn't know baseball at all. When we hit long fly balls, they would misjudge them and the balls would be ten feet over their heads. They were cricket players, so they could run, throw, and had good bat speed. I knew that eventually they would produce some good ballplayers."

Dick Kashiwaeda remembers Australia fondly. He not only made lifelong friendships with three Australian players, but the tour helped him gain a lucrative contract. Kashiwaeda had hit poorly during the '54 season, but prior to the trip Shoji Yasuda told him that if his hitting improved during the tour that he might get a raise. As there were few baseball diamonds in Australia, the Giants played on converted cricket fields. Cricket fields are oblong, so right field was always short and left field extremely deep. As a left-handed batter, Dick just had to pull the ball in the air for a home run. On top of that, the Australian baseball was a little larger than the Japanese ball. The Giants used the Japanese ball when on defense, and faced the Australian ball when hitting. The bigger ball was both a bigger target and did not break as sharply, making it easy for the Japanese to hit. Kashiwaeda hit four or five home runs and got his raise.

On November 17, the Giants played the Australian national team in a "test match" at Sydney. The Returned Servicemen's League tried to prevent fans from reaching the ballpark by stopping the streetcars, but the game was held nonetheless. For ten innings the Australians held their own, before the Giants won the game 14–8 with a six-run eleventh inning. Yomiuri moved on to Canberra, where Prime Minister Robert Menzies held a reception in the team's honor. Attendance at the games, however, remained low and the tour's promoter was losing money. Faced with little prospect of recovering expenses and the persistent opposition of the Returned Servicemen's League, the promoter cancelled the remaining games in Melbourne, Perth, and Adelaide.

On the return trip to Japan, the Giants stopped in Manila. Before World War II, the Philippines had been a baseball hotbed. The game came to the islands in 1898 with the crews of American battleships, and a few years later, U.S. military forces had a thriving league in the newly acquired territory. Thousands of Filipino fans followed the games and soon were playing baseball themselves. In 1913, the Manila Baseball Club, an all-Filipino team, toured the United States, Japan, and Hawaii. That same year, the Filipinos finished second to a Meiji

University team in the Far Eastern Games baseball tournament. Two years later, the Filipinos captured the tournament championship and added five of the next six Far Eastern Games titles to their trophy case. Baseball continued to thrive in the 1930s, and foreign teams often stopped on their way from Japan to challenge the Filipinos. Babe Ruth and the Major League All-Stars played in Manila in 1934 and the Tokyo Giants came in both 1935 and 1936. The heavy fighting during World War II, however, disrupted Filipino baseball and the game never regained its prewar popularity.

"There was still a lot of anti-Japanese feeling there as well," Harada remembers. The Japanese military were particularly brutal during the invasion and occupation of the Philippines—over one hundred thousand civilians were massacred during the four-year occupation. Yonamine adds, "I remember coming out of the hotel one morning, and a Filipino with a big Bowie knife came up to me and asked, 'Are you a Jap?' I said, 'Oh no, I'm not a Jap, I'm American!' 'If you're an American, ok,' he muttered. Then he turned to my teammate Fukashi Minanimura and he said, 'Are you a Jap?' 'No, no. I'm Korean!' replied Minanimura. I don't think he was Korean."

The Giants played two games in Manila—one against the Philippine University All-Stars and another against the Manila Baseball League All-Stars. The Giants won both as eight thousand fans packed the stadium.

Finally on December 1, Wally, Dick, Jyun, and Doug Matsuoka returned home to Honolulu. The winter break was short, however. They needed to be back in Tokyo by January 10, for the team's 1955 spring training tour of Latin America.

Mexican industrialist Alejo Peralta, a future billionaire, had just formed a new franchise in the Mexican Baseball League. Known as the Mexico City Tigers, they would begin play in April 1955. Seeking publicity for his new team, Peralta contacted Shoji Yasuda at the *Yomiuri Shimbun* and invited the Tokyo Giants to Latin America. Yasuda agreed and appointed Cappy Harada as the tour's general manager. Together Harada and Peralta's representatives arranged a tour that would take the Giants across six Latin American countries in four weeks.

In early February 1955, the Giants flew to the United States and traveled down to Mexico City. In the Mexican capital, they acclimated to the time change and climate, saw the sites, and practiced. The Mexican winter league season was still in progress, so the Giants had no games scheduled for the first week. They would return to Mexico in March to challenge local teams.

After roughly a week in Mexico, the team traveled to Panama. They stopped to watch ships traverse the canal before continuing on to Panama City. Just five weeks earlier, assassins had gunned down the Panamanian president, José Antonio Remon, at the Juan Franco Racetrack. Vice president Jose Ramón Guizado briefly took the presidency before being indicted in the assassination plot. The second vice president, Ricardo Arias Espinoza, now held office, but the fear of violence was widespread, and Panama was under martial law. Nonetheless, the games on February 7, 8, and 9 were held and spectators packed the stadium.

The Giants dropped the first game, 2–3, to the Panamanian champion Carta Vieja Yankees. The next day, they faced off against Spur Cola. Like most Latin American teams, Spur Cola was mixed race. The roster included Clyde Paris, Leon Kellam, and Granville Gladstone, who had played in the North American Negro Leagues, as well as lighter-skinned Latin Americans. Two of their roster, pitcher Humberto Robinson and outfielder Héctor López, went on to play in the Major Leagues.

Pitching dominated the game. Nakao and Otomo of the Giants were shutting out the Panamanians when an urgent telegram arrived for Shigeru Mizuhara. Mizuhara opened it to find unexpected news. Shoji Yasuda, the team's chain-smoking general manager, had died after a brief illness. Mizuhara called time out and shared the news with his team and the umpires. Some of the Giants cried openly. Yasuda had been well liked and had befriended many of the players. Wally, in particular, was close to Yasuda. The umpires announced the death and called for two minutes of silence in Yasuda's memory. When the game commenced, Mizuhara quietly stated, "We have to win this game." The pitchers duel continued until the Giants pushed a run across in the top of the eighth to win 1–0.

The following day, Yomiuri won a close game with a run in the tenth against Chesterfield before packing their bags and leaving for Colombia. Unlike Mexico and Panama, Colombia produced just one Major Leaguer prior to 1975. Luis "Jud" Castro was the first Latino to join the Majors but had learned the game in the U.S., where he attended school. Although born in Medellín, Castro signed with the Philadelphia Athletics in 1902, one year prior to his homeland's first organized baseball game. Baseball remained a low-key amateur sport in Colombia until 1948, when the professional winter league Licobal was formed. The league relied on low-level minor leaguers in search of winter employment and was not particularly successful. It did, however, survive until the late 1950s.

The Giants set up base at Cartagena in a dumpy hotel on the beach with spectacular views. The team had four games scheduled in Cartagena and three in nearby cities, which they would reach by bus. The Giants dropped three games to a squad of Colombian All-Stars before defeating the nearby town of Barranquilla's local team 4–0 behind the outstanding pitching of Takumi Otomo. The momentum carried over to the next game, as the Giants finally overcame the Colombian All-Stars 2–1 in Cartagena. Wally played well in the victory, going 2 for 2 with two walks. After the game, the teams left for the nation's capital, Bogotá.

The Giants boarded a small, rickety bus, no more than a wooden box set on a truck body. It was too cramped for all the players to sit inside, so the younger players rode on the roof with the luggage. Tadashi Iwamoto remembers clinging for dear life as the bus sputtered along the bumpy, steep mountain passes toward Bogotá. The Japanese found the high Andean air uncomfortably thin, but during the game the ball flew off the bats. The Giants racked up seven runs on eight hits, including two long home runs by Tetsuharu Kawakami. Mizuhara gave Hawaiian Doug Matsuoka a rare start, but the Colombians hit him hard, scoring five runs in the first inning, and went on to win 9–7.

The Giants were scheduled to play the next day in Cartagena, so after the game they began the long trip back down the mountains. The team planned to spend the night on the road at the luxurious-sounding American Hotel in the town of Montería. Cappy Harada recalls, "We figured that the American Hotel in Montería might be a really nice place because of the name, so we were all looking forward to it. When we got to Montería, the bus headed toward downtown and all of a sudden stopped between two small buildings. I said to the bus driver, 'Hey, let's get going! We're tired and we want to get to the hotel.' 'This is the hotel,' he replied."

The grand American Hotel was a little adobe house surrounded by a wooden fence. Chickens and pigs ran around the small yard and nearly a dozen buzzards perched on the roof. The older Giants got out of the bus, as the younger players clambered off the roof, and together they peered inside. There was just one room with a dirt floor. A stack of folding cots stood in the corner. Flies buzzed everywhere.

The hungry players asked the hotel manager for dinner and in the far corner of the hall, a cook began the meal. Soon, a foul-smelling mutton stew simmered away. With bloody hands, the cook began preparing a large black-feathered bird. Cappy Harada looked over to Yonamine.

"Hey Wally, do you know what he's cooking?"

"What?"

"Look up," Harada responded, pointing to a buzzard perched just outside the hall.

Gagging, Wally ran outside.

"We're not staying here tonight," Mizuhara announced, and around 9:00 p.m. the team piled back into, and on top of, the bus. Even though it was many hours away, they headed back to Cartagena. After several hours, the bus came to a sudden halt in a cane field. The dozing Giants woke up and began asking why they had stopped. But the driver had left. Eventually, they found him on the roof taking a nap. An hour or so later, they resumed the trip and reached the outskirts of Cartagena in the middle of the night.

The older section of the city, where the hotel stood, was built on a spit of land reaching into the Caribbean. A ferry service provided the only access to this section of town, and unfortunately for the Giants, the ferries did not operate at night. So they sat by the water, longing for the hotel they had previously complained about. Many players left the bus, found what blankets, or clothes, they could and slept on the ground. Dawn finally arrived, and the exhausted Japanese champions took the ferry back to their hotel. Later that day, they played Barranquilla's local team again. Somehow, the tired Giants won 6–1.

The Giants were supposed to visit Venezuela next, but at the last minute the trip was cancelled. Instead, on February 21, they left for the Dominican Republic. On the way, the team stopped overnight in Kingston, Jamaica. In the airport, just after customs, the players noticed several large casks full of pineapple slices. Thirsty after their flight, they helped themselves to ample handfuls, slurping them down quickly, only to find that they had been soaked in rum. By the time the team bus got to the hotel, half the players were asleep.

The Giants arrived in the Dominican Republic the next day and settled in a hotel owned by the country's baseball-loving dictator, Rafael Trujillo. They stayed for five days, playing each day against an All-Star team known simply as Dominica. The Dominicans have a long history of both professional and amateur baseball. In the 1870s refugees from the Cuban struggles for independence from Spain brought the game with them when they settled on the coast surrounding the towns of San Pedro de Macorís and La Romana. Amateur baseball leagues were established at the beginning of the twentieth century, and in 1912 teams fought for the first national championship. Soon the teams began importing Cuban stars to bolster their chances, and greats such as Martín Dihigo and Alejandro Oms appeared on the amateur teams' rosters. The importation of ringers hit its pinnacle in 1937 when dictator Rafael Trujillo packed his Ciudad Trujillo team with Negro League superstars, including Satchel Page and Josh Gibson. Trujillo supposedly paid thirty thousand dollars for the two future Hall of Famers and seven of their teammates. Officials suspended the championship the following season.

In 1951 Trujillo organized the country's first openly professional league. It consisted of four teams, but unlike the other Latin American leagues, games were held in the summer rather than winter months. This decision doomed the league. Other Latin American leagues maintained a high quality of play and fan enthusiasm by importing Negro, minor league, and Major League players during the North American off-season. As these players were unavailable during the summer months, the quality of the Dominican league remained low and led to its reorganization as a winter league in late 1955.

When the Yomiuri Giants arrived in February, the summer league had played its final season in 1954 and the new winter league would not start for nine months. As a result, the Giants faced a team of Dominican players unsigned by the other Latin American leagues. Nonetheless, the Dominicans took four of the five games from the visiting Japanese. Yonamine had a poor series, gaining just two hits in fourteen at bats. The Giants' sole victory came in the opening game, as they scored twice in the ninth to send the game into extra innings. In the top of the tenth, the Giants scored five to win the game as the young catcher Shigeru Fujio homered off the star Dominican pitcher Diomedes "Guayubín" Olivo. Olivo reigned as his nation's greatest player. He dominated both the Dominican and Mexican leagues, winning 147 games against only 69 losses. Fifty years later, he still holds the Dominican records for most strikeouts in a season, most strikeouts in a career, and games won. Eventually, he made the Major Leagues, becoming the oldest rookie ever at age forty-one in 1960. Far past his prime, Olivo pitched well, but not spectacularly, for three seasons in the Majors.

By the end of the five days, the Giants were tired and eager to move on to their next stop—the baseball powerhouse, Cuba. Of all the Latin American countries, Cuba has the longest and most prestigious baseball history. Students brought the game back from the United States in the early 1860s, and the first league tournament was held in 1878. By the turn of the twentieth century, Cuba had both professional and amateur leagues producing outstanding players. According to New York Giants' manager John McGraw, Cubans José Méndez and Cristobal Torriente were among the best players in the world, but were barred from the Major Leagues because of their African heritage. From 1913 to 1916, both Méndez and Torriente barnstormed across the United States with the All Nations squad—a team made up of players from around the world—that included a Waseda University graduate named Goro Mikami, who played under the name Jap Mikado.

Cuba became the center for winter baseball by the early twentieth century. The racially integrated winter league soon became one of the strongest leagues in the world. Major League, Negro League, and Latin American stars congregated each winter to hone their skills and earn an extra paycheck. Recognizing an untapped market with loyal fans, the Florida International League (Class C) expanded into Cuba in 1946 by placing a franchise in Havana. The team won four consecutive championships between 1946 and 1950 before the franchise transformed into the Cuban Sugar Kings of the AAA International League in 1954. Bobby Maduro, the Sugar Kings' owner, had invited the Yomiuri Giants to Havana for a three-game series.

The day after arriving in Havana, the Giants played their first of three games against the Sugar Kings at El Cerro Stadium. The Sugar Kings were beginning their spring training for the upcoming International League season and were not yet at full strength. The American players, such as former Major Leaguers Clint Hartung, Johnny Lipon, and Ken Raffensberger, did not play against Yomiuri.

In the opener, the Cubans put Raul Sánchez on the mound. Sánchez had pitched briefly with the Washington Senators in 1952 and would later pitch for the Cincinnati Reds. He went the distance, holding the Giants to seven hits and just one run, as the Sugar Kings won 4–1. Wally, however, did well, getting two hits off the Cuban star. The Havana newspapers commented, "the Japanese played with class and were also surprisingly talented as fielders, even if they weren't much as hitters."

The newspaper writers needed to reassess their views after the second game. Takumi Otomo, with his underhanded delivery, shut out the Sugar Kings on just three hits. On the other side of the diamond, Yomiuri got six hits and drew twelve walks as they scored five times. Wally had a particularly good day, with two hits, a walk, and two runs scored. But Sugar King fans did not remain disappointed for long as the Cubans handed the Giants an embarrassing 11–1 loss the next afternoon.

The players were now dog-tired. They had covered four countries in four weeks and played eighteen games. They also had trouble adapting to Latin American cuisine. Much of the food was too spicy or not of high enough quality, and they missed Japanese rice. Occasionally, they would meet a Japanese émigré who would bring them Japanese food. For example, in Colombia an old man showed up with rice balls, but there were not enough to go around. The pitchers were given one each, but the position players had to split the remaining treats.

After the loss to the Sugar Kings, the Giants boarded a plane to Mexico—their final stop before traveling home. To a man, they were now sick of baseball and looking forward to finishing the trip. The Pan American flight landed in Mérida, Mexico, after dark. The team ambled onto a bus, looking forward to resting at the hotel. But instead of driving toward the city, the driver headed into the countryside. Outside the windows, it was pitch black except for an occasional farmhouse light as the bus drove through fields. All of a sudden, bright lights flooded through the windows. There, in the middle of nowhere, stood a ballpark packed full of people. "What's going on?" Harada asked the local guide.

"Well," he responded, "we've got to play a game."

Fukashi Minanimura protested, "What kind of crazy schedule is this!"

Some of the ballplayers didn't want to take the field, but Cappy and Shigeo Mizuhara explained that they had no choice. The team left the bus, suited up, and played, but the less than enthusiastic Giants lost 4–0 to the Mérida Lions.

The Mexican leg of the tour went by in a blur. The Giants played eight games in seven days in four different cities. The tired Japanese could barely focus on the games and lost all but the final encounter. After two games with the Mérida Lions, the Giants traveled to Mexico City. There, they challenged a Mexican All-Star team in what was probably the first game played in the newly constructed Parque del Seguro Social, which Alejo Peralta had built for his Mexico City Tigers. The All-Stars won the first five games easily. The lopsided scores suggest that the Giants faced some of Mexico's top professional players, who were the equivalent of Double-A and Triple-A Minor League players. Yonamine only collected one hit in twelve at bats against the Mexican All-Stars before turning his ankle on March 10 and sitting on the bench for the tour's final two games.

With an 8–7 win over the All-Stars at Mazatlán on March 12, the Giants' tour of Latin America was over. The team flew to Los Angeles and traveled back to Tokyo via Honolulu in shifts over the next few days. "When we arrived in Los Angeles, it was a hell of a treat to have a nice hotel and a good solid hot meal!" Harada recalls.

The Giants won only eight of the twenty-six games during the tour, leaving little doubt that the Latin Americans played a higher caliber of baseball. Yet, the Giants had made a good showing. They had played in a different climate, in poor conditions, and mostly against All-Star teams that often included Major League players.

When asked about the Latin American trip today, the former Giants just shake their heads and laugh. The trip was badly organized, the food poor, accommodations often worse, and the travel conditions almost intolerable. But the experience brought the players closer together and made them tougher. During the upcoming 1955 season, they used the memories of the trip as a rallying cry. If they could survive the bus trip to Bogotá, then surely they could defeat the Hanshin Tigers.

13

Hard Labor

The Giants returned to Tokyo in mid-March of 1955 exhausted. Wally told reporters, "It was a really rough trip. Every player lost weight. I myself dropped fifteen pounds. We are all fagged out." As the players settled in and prepared for the April 5 season opener with the Kokutetsu Swallows, tragedy struck Japanese baseball. On April 2, seventy thousand fans waited outside Koshien Stadium for the opening game of the twenty-seventh annual All-Japan High School Baseball Spring Invitational Tournament. The stadium had room for fifty-five thousand but few reserved seats, forcing patrons to jockey for the best locations in the bleachers. When the stadium gate opened, the crowd surged forward. Some began to push and run to get the best seats. The crowd was soon out of control and stampeded forward, crushing and trampling hundreds. In all, four died and twenty-seven were seriously injured.

Despite the tragedy, the professional season started on schedule. The Giants beat the Swallows in the first two games, but then the tired team went into a skid, losing four of their next six. They fell as low as third place before rebounding into first by May 1. In the long run, the trip to Latin America helped the Giants. The hardships gave the players a resolve that had been lacking the previous season when the Dragons captured the pennant. Wally's teammates seemed tougher, and the team continually came from behind to win close games. The Giants won nine in a row during May and reeled off thirteen straight in June. By the All-Star break, they had a nine-game lead over the second-place Tigers with an outstanding 45-17 record.

Much of Yomiuri's success was due to Andy Miyamoto, a new Nisei player Wally had helped recruit. Born on Maui, Miyamoto was a high school football MVP before he joined the Asahi as a catcher. He was a powerful man, standing 5 feet 10 inches tall and weighing nearly 190 pounds. He led the AJA Senior League in Honolulu in home runs in the 1955 season. The Giants still lacked a true power hitter, and Wally believed that Miyamoto could fill the gap. Cappy Harada signed the well-built Hawaiian, who would start as soon as he completed his military service. Andy arrived in Tokyo on May 6 and immediately went to the Korakuen Stadium, where Shigeru Mizuhara welcomed him and told him to be ready to play the next day. At the time, the Giants were in first place by only a game and were about to begin a three-game series against the third-place Hanshin Tigers.

Miyamoto sat on the bench the next day watching the Tigers beat the Giants. The Giants were down 4–3 in the bottom of the ninth with two outs, when Mizuhara told Andy to grab a bat and see what he could do. Miyamoto nervously went to the plate. The Hanshin hurler, Shozo Watanabe, went into the windup and threw inside for a ball. The next delivery came on the outside corner for a strike. Andy didn't know Watanabe's pitching pattern, but guessed that he would try to hit the outside corner again. The rookie guessed right, connected with a loud crack, and the ball disappeared over the right-field fence to tie the score. The sellout crowd roared and Andy circled the bases with wobbly knees, hoping that he wouldn't stumble. In the top of the tenth, Mizuhara sent Andy out to right field, a position that he had never played before at any level. Miyamoto spent the inning hoping that the ball wouldn't come his way. His wish came true and the Giants scored again in the bottom of the tenth to win the game. Reporters crowded around Miyamoto after the game firing questions at him. As Andy didn't understand Japanese, Yonamine and Jyun Hirota translated for him as Andy flashed a big toothy smile that would soon be known in the Japanese press as "the million dollar smile." Despite Miyamoto's inexperience in the outfield, he became the Giants' starting right fielder the next day.

Yomiuri now had too many foreign players on their roster. The commissioner's office, concerned that a plethora of *gaijin* would hamper the development of Japanese players, decided to limit each team to three. With the addition of Miyamoto, the Giants now had five: Andy, Jyun Hirota, Dick Kashiwaeda, Doug Matsuoka, and Bill Nishita, who had returned to the Giants in 1955 after completing his military service. Oddly enough, Wally Yonamine did not count toward the limit of foreigners, as the commissioner gave him special status for being the first one in the league.

Yet Yomiuri found a loophole—they kept all five *gaijin* under contract by relegating two to their farm team, which was not covered by the new rule. Throughout the season, the Giants would promote and relegate different foreigners based on their immediate needs. For example, when the Giants' pitching was strong, Nishita and Matsuoka would stay with the farm team, but if the starters began to tire, Nishita would be called up and Miyamoto or Kashiwaeda would be sent down.

Wally was having another fine season, hitting just over .300 and leading the team with eight home runs at the All-Star break. His family had settled into their house in Meguro and Jane was expecting their second child any day. In his fifth season in Japan, Wally's exploits no longer grabbed the headlines. He was now accepted by the media and most fans as just another member of the Giants. Japanese had seen enough American baseball from touring Major League teams and the many other foreigners in the league that Yonamine's aggressive playing style, once considered dirty, was now rarely commented upon. He was still, however, less popular than similarly talented Japanese players. For example, he finished fourth among outfielders in the 1955 All-Star voting and rarely received endorsement offers.

Although the Chunichi Dragons had won the pennant in 1954, their skipper, Shunichi Amachi, had retired after the season and would be unable to manage the Central League All-Stars. League officials decided to let Shigeru Mizuhara manage the team instead. Despite not being elected by the fans, Mizuhara placed Wally on the Central League All-Star team as a reserve. The first of the two All-Star games was scheduled for July 2 in Osaka. As Wally prepared to leave for the trip, Jane went into labor. At 6:30 in the morning on July 1, Wally phoned Mizuhara.

"My wife is having labor pains. I want to take her to the hospital. Is it alright if I take an airplane afterwards?"

"Wally, are you a midwife?" responded the manager. "When did you become one? What use would you be at the hospital? You'd be useless. Get on our train as scheduled!"

Fuming, Wally told Jane of Mizuhara's response and they arranged for a friend to drive her to the hospital. Only an hour later, their second daughter Wallis Keiko was born. Wally, however, was already on the train to Osaka and would not see his new daughter until later in the week.

Wallis was a healthy baby but was born with her knee facing the wrong direction. As soon as Jane and the little girl were strong enough, they returned with Amy to Honolulu to have doctors examine the knee. Dr. Nobuyuki Nakasone, a longtime friend, recommended that Wallis have corrective surgery, so Jane and the girls remained in Honolulu for the remainder of 1955.

The Giants continued to play well in July, winning twelve of their first seventeen games. On July 27, they had a ten-game lead over the second-place Dragons, and then the team inexplicably began to lose. From July 28 to August 7, they lost five out of six and the lead dwindled to just four and a half games. Over the next three weeks, the Giants regained their winning ways, but the Dragons were better and closed the gap to three and a half games. Mizuhara decided it was time for some new blood and called Bill Nishita up from the minors. He faced the Whales on July 28 in his first start for the Giants since 1952.

Yonamine hit a solo homer in the top of the first to give Nishita the lead. The righty was throwing hard and had good control as he faced the Whales in the bottom of the first. He got two quick outs before a pop fly went into shallow right field. Chiba sprinted over laterally from second base as Kawakami raced backward from first. Kawakami called for the ball, stretched out, and missed it as it fell in for a single. With the better angle, Chiba probably would have made the catch. From that point on, Nishita shut down the Whales, not allowing a hit for the remainder of the game. He had come within a few inches of pitching a no-hitter in his first game after his two-year absence. The Giants believed that the promising Hawaiian would finally emerge as a star. But they were wrong. The one-hitter was Nishita's only win of the season. He lost his next two starts before being relegated to relief duty.

Two days after Nishita's one-hitter, Takehiko Bessho shut out the Swallows 2–0. Then, after two days off, Bessho took the mound again and pitched a complete game for a victory over the Carp. The Giants now had a five-and-a-half-game lead over the Dragons, and Yonamine felt confident. He was beginning to swing the bat well, was fourth in the league with a .311 average, and led the Giants with eleven home runs. Kawakami still led the batting race, but Wally believed that he would catch him and win back-to-back batting titles.

The Giants were playing the second game of a doubleheader in Hiroshima on September 4 when in the bottom of the second inning Tomio Hirooka of the Carp hit a bloop into shallow center field. Wally charged in for the ball and shortstop Saburo Hirai raced backward. Second baseman Shigeru Chiba yelled, "Wally, Wally!" so Yonamine assumed that he was supposed to get it and focused on the dropping ball.

"I was going to have to make a shoestring catch, so I slid and tried to scoop the ball up. But at the last minute Hirai also drove for the ball." They collided. Wally saw stars and fell unconscious. In the mid-1950s, before batting helmets were used, some players wore hats reinforced with steel bands in both the cap and visor. Hirai's reinforced visor sliced straight into Wally's jaw, cutting him badly. The Giants carried Wally from the field and brought him to an infirmary at the nearby branch of *Yomiuri Shimbun*. There, the doctors took X-rays and told Yonamine that nothing had been broken. But the intense pain told Wally otherwise. "I knew that something must be wrong. Even in football, I was never hit that hard."

Returning to Tokyo, Wally went directly to the Giants' doctor. He took another X-ray and found nothing amiss. Skeptical, Yonamine went to Jikei Medical College to have an American-trained Nisei specialist examine him. The doctor found two hairline fractures in Wally's jaw, one in his face and another in his forehead. The doctor ordered Wally to catch the next plane to Hawaii so that his family could take care of him.

Yonamine informed the Giants of his condition and immediate departure. Highly concerned, the front office pointed out that twenty-three games still remained on the schedule and Yomiuri was in a tight pennant race. The Giants were about to face the second-place Dragons for a three-game series, couldn't he stay for a few more days and play in this crucial series? Flabbergasted, Wally refused.

With his jaw badly swollen and immobilized, Wally was unable to telephone Jane to tell her about the accident. Unbelievably, the ball club also did not call Jane. Instead, Jane learned of the accident on September 6, when she went to the supermarket and saw the headline in the *Hawaii Times*: "Wally Yonamine Suffers Broken Jaw in Ball Game." Surprised and worried, she read the article and discovered that her husband would arrive in Honolulu that very day.

As soon as Wally arrived, he went to Kuakini Hospital for more X-rays and tests. The doctors confirmed the four fractures and operated the next day. "I was in a cast for two months," Wally recalls of that exceedingly painful time. "I couldn't eat anything, so Jane would grind up beef and shove it into my mouth because I couldn't chew. Even today, it hurts if I open my jaw wide."

With Wally's departure, the Giants put Dick Kashiwaeda into the starting lineup in the third slot. He hit well, and the Giants won ten in a row. The team coasted to the Central League pennant with a 92-37-1 record, fifteen games in front of the second-place Dragons. Tetsuharu Kawakami won the batting title with a .338 average, while Yonamine finished in fourth place. Kawakami also won the RBI crown and the Central League's Most Valuable Player Award. Kawakami, Wally, Jyun Hirota, and Takehiko Bessho were named to the Central League's Best Nine team.

Once again, the Giants faced the Nankai Hawks in the Japan Series.

Without Yonamine, it was a close contest. The Hawks won three of the first four games and looked to finally capture the championship, when Mizuhara decided that the Giants looked old and tired. In Game 5, he benched veterans Shigeru Chiba, Jyun Hirota, and Kazuo Higasa and started the much younger Hirofumi Naito, Shigeru Fujio, and Minoru Kakurai in their stead. The younger players led the Giants to victories in the next three games to steal the title from Nankai.

Immediately after the Japan Series, the New York Yankees arrived in Japan for sixteen exhibition games. Huge crowds gathered along the Ginza to welcome the American League pennant winners to Tokyo. Each game was sold out with a total of 463,000 fans coming to watch the famed Bronx Bombers. The Yankees handled the Japanese All-Star teams and clubs set against them easily, winning fifteen games with one tie. Overall, New York hit .308 with 31 home runs off Japanese pitching while holding the Japanese hitters to a .173 average with just 4 homers. "The Japanese were very surprised how far the Yankees could hit the ball," Dick Kashiwaeda remembers. "In batting practice," adds Andy Miyamoto, "they were hitting them like golf balls. Hank Bauer, the right fielder, hit a home run in Korakuen Stadium to left center that went over the scoreboard and out of the park!"

Between games, the New Yorkers dined well and visited cultural sites. Casey Stengel's wife, Edna, commented, "Home was never like this. We had more excitement in Japan than six World Series. Crowds up to seventy-five thousand saw our games; there were parades, dinners and flowers in our hotel room until we nearly hung out a florist sign."

Despite the lopsided scores, several of the Japanese players impressed Stengel. After the tour, he signed Bozo Wakabayashi to scout Japanese talent for the Yankees. Stengel told reporters, "It may be four or five years, but I think the next great innovation in American baseball will be a Japanese star. . . . Japanese baseball is developing fast. I saw about five fellows over there who could hit our boys' pitching, and when I say hit, I mean they whanged that ball 395 to 410 feet. And remember, we had the lowest ERA in the American League."

Back in Honolulu, Wally's broken bones healed slowly. In January

Cappy Harada flew to Honolulu and signed Yonamine, Jyun Hirota, and Dick Kashiwaeda for the 1956 season. Andy Miyamoto was already signed. Bill Nishita and Doug Matsuoka were, however, released. Nishita signed with the Brooklyn Dodgers and entered their Minor League system. After signing the Hawaiians, Cappy announced that he would retire from the Yomiuri Giants and focus on his business interests. Later, he would become a scout with the San Francisco Giants and was instrumental in bringing the first Japanese to the Major Leagues when Masanori Murakami joined the Giants in 1964.

Yomiuri's remaining Nisei players met to assess their futures with the Giants. Mizuhara's reliance on the young players during the Japan Series concerned them. Wally worried that he might not regain his old form after the injury and would have to fight hard for a starting position. Jyun's role as starting catcher was in jeopardy. The young catcher, Shigeru Fujio, had hit .296 in 1954 and was looking increasingly comfortable behind the plate. Dick had just been moved into the starting lineup at third base the previous September and, of course, wanted to maintain the position. Only Andy seemed to have a slot in the starting lineup locked up. The four agreed that they would report to the Giants on the first day of spring training.

The Hawaiians arrived at the Giants' camp in Akashi in early February. To keep warm, the players lit fires in five-gallon cans filled with charcoal, where they warmed their hands and cold and brittle bats over the coals. Shigeru Mizuhara had decided to work on the team's defense. He hit fungo after fungo to each player. Soon, the sandy infield became rutted. The sharply hit fungoes took bad bounces and ricocheted off players' gloves, legs, and stomachs. At third base, Dick Kashiwaeda was having a particularly difficult time. Third basemen have little time to react to hard-hit balls, and the pocked surface made fielding dangerous. As he bobbled ball after ball, Dick began to worry that a bad bounce might break his glasses, which led him to boot even more. Mizuhara, who expected Kashiwaeda to be his starting third baseman, started screaming at him. "If you can't field a grounder, then pack up your things and go back to Hawaii!"

Dick bristled and vowed to show the old manager how well he could play. As he fielded the grounders, he threw to first with all his might. Blam!, went the first baseman's glove. Again and again, Dick threw with all his might. By the end of practice his arm ached.

Wally had overheard Mizuhara's taunts and after practice went to him to protest. "If you send Dick back to Hawaii, I'm going too!" he found himself saying, much to his own surprise. Mizuhara was surprised, too. He looked at Yonamine and growled "What a fool thing to say." Then he walked away. This made Wally even angrier and he actually began to contemplate returning to Hawaii when Shigeru Chiba and Tetsuharu Kawakami approached him. "Mizuhara-san isn't serious. He's just trying to give Dick a jolt," they explained. Wally wasn't completely sure about that, but it was enough to calm him down. Mizuhara never mentioned the threat again.

Wally and Jyun Hirota were also having difficult springs. Wally was not swinging the bat well and hit poorly in exhibition games, but he was not worried. It usually took him a while to find his swing and he had trouble playing in the cold. Once the season started, he knew that he would be okay. Jyun's problems were different. As feared, Mizuhara was grooming Shigeru Fujio to become the Giants' starting catcher. Fujio started most of the preseason games and was hitting well. As both Hirota's arm and hitting had begun to deteriorate, it looked as though the Hawaiian would become the backup catcher.

The Giants broke camp in mid-March and headed back to Tokyo for their opener on March 21. Jane and the girls were staying in Honolulu until Wallis finished the treatment on her knee, so Wally decided to stay at an inn near the ballpark where Dick and Andy lived. Even with his friends under the same roof, Wally felt lonely without his family. He wrote them every day, and nearly every morning a letter would arrive from Jane.

The season began with a doubleheader against the Kokutetsu Swallows. As usual, Masaichi Kaneda pitched the opener for the Swallows. The Giants countered with Takahiko Bessho, winner of the previous season's Sawamura Award for the best pitcher. Despite his poor spring,

Wally led off the Giants' batting order. Shigeru Chiba, who had also had a poor spring, sat on the bench. The veteran second baseman would be thirty-seven in two months, and his skills had slowly deteriorated during the past two years. Hirofumi Naito, the longtime utility player and Wally's close friend, took Chiba's place.

In the bottom of the first, Yonamine dug in against Kaneda. As always, the powerful pitcher challenged Wally and the first two pitches came in for strikes. Wally shortened up his grip, determined not to begin the year with a strikeout. Kaneda placed one on the corner and Wally expertly fouled it off. Two more pitches, two more fouls. Wally had faced Kaneda hundreds of times over the last five seasons, so he knew a curve would be coming. It came, low and slow. Wally swung hard and lashed it over the right-field wall. The season began with a home run—definitely a good sign. For the second consecutive season Wally had homered off Kaneda in the opener.

The Giants dropped the second game of the doubleheader and another game against the Dragons. On March 25 they were about to lose to Chunichi again, trailing 0–3 in the bottom of the ninth, when the first two batters got on. Shigeru Sugishita emerged from the bullpen to close the game. He forced Tatsuro Hirooka to hit an infield grounder, perfect for a double play—but the ball was bobbled, leaving the bases loaded with no outs. After Fujio struck out, pinch-hitter Kazuo Higasa homered to win the game 4–3. It was the first sayonara (walk-off) grand slam in the history of Japanese baseball.

The Giants played poorly over the next two weeks, losing six of eleven games and falling into third place. Meanwhile, Dick Kashiwaeda's arm continued to ache. Realizing the seriousness of the injury, the Giants took Dick off the active roster. He stayed in Tokyo, waiting for his arm to heal, but it did not. His professional baseball career was over. "I was thirty-two years old," Kashiwaeda recalls, "I should've been smart enough not to try to show off to Mizuhara, but sometimes pride is too strong." At the end of the season, he returned to Hawaii and became an insurance agent with Equitable. Dick eventually returned to the game he loved. After the arm healed, he played for the

Asahi for nearly ten years and now, over eighty years old, still plays competitive softball several times a week.

Still stuck in third place on April 22, Kazuo Higasa once again came through in the clutch. In the bottom of the tenth inning, the Giants and Tigers were knotted at five. With two outs, Mizuhara sent in Higasa to pinch hit against future Hall of Famer Masaaki Koyama. Higasa hammered a *shuto* over the fence for his second sayonara home run of the season. Laughing with joy, the normally reserved Mizuhara ran to Higasa, hugged him around the neck, and planted a big kiss on the cheek. "Was that truly their manager?" some players must have wondered.

Higasa's big hit revitalized the team. They won six of the next seven and moved into first place on April 29. But they could not pull away from the Tigers. Hanshin remained within a game throughout early May. When the Giants arrived in Hiroshima on May 19, the two teams were even in the standings. The hapless Carp were having another dismal season, and the three-game series was just what the Giants needed to recapture first place. Sure enough, the Carp succumbed easily as Andy Miyamoto hit a home run in each of the Giants' three victories.

As usual, the Hiroshima fans taunted the Giants during the series, but as Yomiuri completed their 10–1 victory in the third game, the hostile crowd erupted. Seat cushions and glass bottles rained down on the players as they ran for their dugout. A bottle hit relief pitcher Yoshinori Kido, leaving a deep gash in his right shin. He was quickly brought to the first-aid room and later to the hospital. The Giants retreated toward their bus, as Hiroshima fans threw more bottles and started to kick Shigeru Mizuhara. Mizuhara reached the safety of the bus, but mob didn't relent. They surrounded the bus, breaking windows as it pulled away.

It was the third riot that Wally had witnessed in Hiroshima. Yomiuri finally had enough and announced that they would no longer play there. As the loss of revenue from the cancelled Giants' games would bankrupt the Carp, league officials met with the respective owners, politicians, and the Hiroshima police to try to appease the Giants. At last, Yomiuri relented. In return, the Carp offered an official apology and banned the sale of bottles in the stadium.

The Giants left Hiroshima with a game and a half lead over the Tigers. In the following game, Andy Miyamoto homered again. His four home runs in four days tied a Japanese record, and his smiling face appeared on the front page of the sports dailies. A week later, Tetsuharu Kawakami recorded his two thousandth career hit, becoming the first player in Japan to reach this mark. Since the Japanese seasons are somewhat shorter than Major League campaigns, 2,000 lifetime hits there has become the equivalent of 3,000 hits in the United States. Players who reach that benchmark are now honored with membership in the Meikyukai (The Golden Players Club), a player-run organization founded in 1978 that is similar to a Hall of Fame.

By the first week of June, the Giants' lead over the Tigers had increased to two games. Wally was hitting particularly well and on June 19 led the Central League with a .331 average, twenty-one points over second-place hitter Noboru Inoue of the Dragons.

Andy was also having a great season. His mammoth home runs continued to propel the Giants to victories—often when it looked like Yomiuri had no chance. On June 13, the second-place Tigers were leading the Giants 3–0 in the ninth at Koshien Stadium with the Giants only managing four hits off starter Shozo Watanabe. Tadashi Iwamoto and Yonamine, however, led off with back-to-back singles, and Watanabe accidentally hit pinch hitter Masahiko Mori in the face. Mori had to be removed from the field on a stretcher, but would recover and go on to become one of the best catchers and managers in the history of Japanese baseball. The Tigers brought in Mitsuo Osaki to face Andy Miyamoto with the bases loaded. With a ball and two strikes, Osaki came in with a slider, high and tight, but Andy didn't flinch and slammed it over the left-field wall to give the Giants a 4–3 lead and the eventual victory. By the All-Star break, Andy led the team with eleven home runs.

Just prior to the break, Wally went on a home run binge of his own. He hit his sixth homer of the season to lead off the first game of a doubleheader against the Swallows on June 24, and led off the second game with another home run. It was the first time a lead-off batter had ever begun consecutive games that way. After a day off, Yonamine hit his eighth and ninth home runs against the Whales. He was now third in the league in that category, trailing Andy Miyamoto and Noboru Aota, who had fourteen.

With each home run, Jane received a present. "Korakuen Stadium used to have advertising signs in the outfield—one advertised hair oil and another toasters. If a player hit a home run over a sign, they would get a free product. Wally always hit his home runs to right field over the sign for the pink toasters, or a little to the left over the hair oil sign—that stuff was so stinky you couldn't sit next to someone using it! I would get about a dozen pink toasters every year. So I gave all my friends pink toasters. It wasn't even the type where the bread popped out, you had to open it. So we ended up with a lot of burnt toast!"

This season the Japanese fans rewarded Wally for his accomplishments in the All-Star voting. Previously, the fans had elected Yonamine to just one All-Star team, and Shigeru Mizuhara had to add him to the roster. In 1956, however, they gave Wally a resounding 202,859 votes, making him the most popular player in the competition. He led Noboru Aota, his nearest competition among the outfielders, by almost 50,000 votes. Andy Miyamoto finished fourth among the outfielders with 42,697, and Mizuhara added Andy to the roster as a reserve. Neither Hawaiian had a good All-Star series. Yonamine started both games in center field, getting a hit and a walk in eight at bats, while Miyamoto picked up one hit and a walk in four at bats.

Yomiuri began the second half of the season with four straight losses, erasing the small lead they had built over the Tigers in June. Yonamine continued to hit well, and by July 18 his average rose to .352. On July 19, for only the third time in his career, Wally got into an argument with an umpire. In the third inning against the Dragons, Tatsuro Hirooka laid down a squeeze bunt and Wally came racing home. Shigeru Sugishita came off the mound, fielded the bunt, and threw to the plate. Yonamine came in hard but the catcher held the ball. Behind the plate, umpire Hidenosuke Shima called Wally out. According to the *New York Times*, which picked up the story from the Associated Press, "Yonamine lumbered to his feet, stuck his face to within an inch of the umpire's mask, and chewed him out in ringing tones that could be heard in the bleachers. The astonished umpire stuck to his decision but let Yonamine stay in the game."

In previous seasons, the Japanese press would have seized on Wally's tantrum to portray him as an aggressive American and a dirty player, but not now. They had grown accustomed to Wally's hard play and now admired him. Most of the papers ignored Yonamine's previous two arguments with umpires and noted that "it was the first time Yonamine had shown any temper or raised his voice in six years of play with the Tokyo Giants." At least one paper portrayed Wally's behavior as laudable. "When Yonamine slid into home plate in the third inning, he flared up at the umpire calling him out. Typical of his American style, he bore down on Umpire Shima, stomping his feet. The fighting spirit exemplified in this protest seemed to represent the spirit of the Giants."

July was a difficult month for Wally. Jane and the girls remained in Hawaii, and he missed them terribly. The loneliness began to wear on him, perhaps explaining why he exploded at Shima. His average dipped into the .340s, but more significantly, the Giants weren't playing well. They dropped two games to the Tigers and one each to the Whales and Carp. On July 29, they fell from first place. At this point, Wally's old mentor and friend, Shigeru Chiba, approached Mizuhara. Chiba had only played sporadically that season and had never regained his batting form. The former All-Star second baseman told Mizuhara, "Only guys with real ability should be in the dugout. There should be some young, lively player sitting there on the bench in my place." He then asked to be demoted to the farm team. Mizuhara gracefully agreed and Chiba left the team. His absence made Wally even sadder. Chiba had always been there to offer wise advice or take him to dinner when he was down. True, Wally now had many friends, both Japanese and Hawaiian, on the team, but Chiba was the lone veteran player who had reached out to him.

The Giants finished off July with a three-game series against the first-place Tigers at Koshien Stadium. The first game was tied at zero in the sixth inning when the umpire called the Tigers' outfielder Kenjiro Tamiya safe on a close play at the plate. Mizuhara charged out of the dugout, went face to face with the bespectacled ump and yelled, "Your glasses don't fit your eyes, do they? Show them to me!" And then to everybody's surprise, Mizuhara reached over and grabbed the umpire's glasses off his nose. The umpire promptly threw Mizuhara out of the game, but not before they scuffled some more. The Tigers won the game 4–0 and were ahead again the next day when Tamiya swung at and missed a Bessho curve that broke down sharply and hit his foot. As the umpire signaled for Tamiya to take first base, Bessho complained that Tamiya had missed the pitch and only his momentum had caused him to come into the pitch's path. The ump disagreed and soon the two began a heated argument. Fans started to shout and jeer, "Giants go home!" A bottle came flying onto the field, followed by another. The players hastily retreated toward the dugouts as fans jumped onto the field, hurling insults and anything they could lay their hands on at the Giants. Just as the Giants reached their bench, somebody tossed a large snake in front of the dugout. It raised its head and slithered toward the team. The umpires finally restored order, the marauding reptile was captured, and the game resumed. The Tigers triumphed again and a week later held a five-game lead over the Giants.

In mid-August Jane, Amy, and Wallis finally returned to Japan. With his family around him, Wally relaxed and began to hit even better. About the same time, the Giants overcame their slump. They took two straight from the Whales and were three games out of first place when the Tigers came to Korakuen for a three-game series on August 18. Takumi Otomo and the Tigers' ace Mitsuo Osaki dueled in the first game, taking shutouts into the bottom of the eleventh. Then, for the second time in the season, Andy Miyamoto blasted a sayonara home run off Osaki. The dramatic win revitalized the Giants. They won the next two games comfortably, and the Tigers left Tokyo even with the Giants in the standings. The Giants next swept a pair of doubleheaders from the Swallows with Andy hitting another sayonara home run and Wally picking up five hits, including a home run. With the nine-game winning streak, the Giants had moved back into first place.

The Giants slowly padded their lead in late August and early September. On September 5, Wally raised his batting average to .351. His nearest competitor for the batting title was rival Tetsuharu Kawakami, who lagged 35 points behind with a .316 average. Andy's 18 home runs placed him second behind Noboru Aota for the home run crown. Aota had 21, but twenty games remained on the schedule. Miyamoto was also in the running for the RBI crown, as Kawakami, Aota, and Andy all hovered around 60 RBI.

In mid-September, the Giants won seven in a row, increasing their lead over the Tigers to five games and clinching the pennant on September 23. Five days before, Wally had clinched the batting crown. Sportswriters now tried to predict the league's Most Valuable Player. There were four prominent candidates: Tetsuharu Kawakami, who would finish second in batting and RBI; Takehiko Bessho, who led the league in wins; Andy Miyamoto, who would win the RBI crown and finish second in home runs; and Wally, the batting champion. The *Hawaii Times* believed that Yonamine was the best candidate, but other newspapers waffled. *Sports Nippon* reported, "Yonamine . . . has a good chance of becoming the MVP. Although it cannot be denied that the strength of his legs and shoulders have decreased, his natural instinct and senses are outstanding."

With the pennant clinched, Yomiuri rested for two weeks and followed the Pacific League pennant race. The Nankai Hawks seemed assured of another trip to the Japan Series. They had led the league since June, but the team was aging and seemed to tire in the season's final weeks. The Nishitetsu Lions, composed of young, hungry players and led by a maverick manager named Osamu Mihara, narrowed the

gap and overtook the Hawks in the final days of the season to win by
just half a game.

Mihara was Shigeru Mizuhara's longtime rival. The two had grown
up together on Shikoku Island, playing for opposing schools. After
high school, Mizuhara had enrolled at Keio University, becoming a
star third baseman and pitcher, while Mihara went to Waseda. Their
rivalry intensified in 1931 when Mihara helped Keio win by stealing
home as Mizuhara went into his windup. Both players joined the 1934
All Nippon team and became original members of the Yomiuri Giants. But they played together for only three years, as Mihara entered
the military in 1938 and Mizuhara followed in 1942. Mihara returned
to Japan first and became the Giants manager, leading them to the
1949 championship; however, when Mizuhara returned from his long
internment in a Russian POW camp, management gave him the Giants'
helm in 1950 and moved Mihara into the front office. Disgruntled,
Mihara left Yomiuri the following year to manage the one-year-old
Nishitetsu franchise.

With the Lions, Mihara focused on signing and instructing young
players. He rejected much of the hierarchy prevalent on the Giants,
and forbade hazing the younger players. "Once you are on the field,
age doesn't matter as long as you have ability," he told his team. His
strategy paid off and he developed two young superstars: Futoshi Nakanishi and Yasumitsu Toyoda. The name Futoshi means "strong,"
"fat," or "robust," and Nakanishi was indeed that. A squat, powerful
third baseman, standing 5 feet 8 inches tall and weighing 205 pounds,
he won the 1952 Rookie of the Year Award and led the league in home
runs each year from 1953 to 1956. Nakanishi also had narrowly missed
winning the Triple Crown in 1953, '55, and '56, losing it by 1 RBI in
1955 and a batting margin of just .0005 in 1956. On August 29, 1953, he
hit a five-hundred-foot home run, which stood for many years as the
longest blast in Japanese pro baseball history. It began as a line drive
that passed just above the shortstop's glove and kept rising until it
went over the outfield screen and out of the park, landing at the base
of historic Fukuoka Castle, located just behind Heiwaidai Stadium.

At shortstop, young Yasumitsu Toyoda could hit for average and power and had denied Nakanishi his triple crown by winning the 1956 Pacific League batting title. To support these youngsters, Mihara brought in the veteran Hiroshi Oshita. Oshita had won three batting titles with the Flyers in the late 1940s and early 1950s—his .383 batting average in 1951 remained the Japanese record until 1970. At thirty years old, Oshita seemed like an old man to the team's young stars. "Oshita had a very strong sense of not wanting to lose," Futoshi Nakanishi recalls. "He saw us young ones hitting home runs and would come in earlier to practice and try to compete with us. Mr. Mihara was smart and arranged it so that we would feel a rivalry and be stimulated by each other. We learned from Mr. Oshita and he was pushed by us."

Mihara scrutinized baseball, dissecting all aspects of the game, but often applied his own unique brand of logic. Tadashi Iwamoto, who later played under Mihara, recalls, "The way Mr. Mihara used the players was outstanding. He was a professor and a psychologist. He'd gather all this data, put it in his head, and then go into the game. He would do unpredictable things, but his strategy was based on all his data. They called it 'Mihara magic.' For example, if a batter got a hit in each of his first three at bats, his fourth time up Mr. Mihara would pinch hit for him. Why? You see, if he's already gone three for three, the chances are against him getting another hit. That was Mr. Mihara!"

The Lions' true strength lay in their outstanding young pitching staff. The 1956 club relied on four starters, all twenty-three years old or younger. Yukio Shimabara, the oldest at twenty-three, was the workhorse. In 1956 he blossomed from an ineffectual reliever into a 25-game winner with a 1.35 ERA in 373 innings pitched. Hisafumi Kawamura, who had just turned twenty-two in August, had already proven himself the year before by going 25-12 with a 1.99 ERA. In 1956, he won 21 games with a 2.35 ERA and led the Pacific League in strikeouts and walks. Sadao Nishimura was twenty-one. He had also won over 20 games in 1955 but fell one short with 19 wins in 1956. But none of these outstanding arms compared to the chunky nineteen-year-old rookie, Kazuhisa Inao.

The son of a fisherman, Inao reportedly built up his arms by hauling his father's nets. He signed with the Lions out of high school without much publicity and made the Lions' starting rotation that spring. Inao threw hard and had superb control. "He'd throw a slider right on the black and we'd foul it off," Tadashi Iwamoto remembers. "Next, he would throw it out of the strike zone—just off the outside corner by half a ball. If I hit this, it would be another foul ball. The third ball would be just outside the plate. So he was slowly pulling us toward the outside part of the plate. Then, just when our minds were concentrating on the outside, he'd throw one on the inside! And it would all be over in an instant!" Inao took the 1956 Rookie of the Year Award as he won twenty-one games and led the league with a 1.06 ERA.

The 1956 Japan Series opened on October 10 at Korakuen Stadium. Takumi Otomo, the submariner with the buzzing fastball, took the mound for the Giants, while Mihara surprised many by passing over his young aces and starting veteran Tokuji Kawasaki. Kawasaki had been the Giants' ace during the 1947 and '48 seasons before leaving for the newly created Lions in 1950. Now near the end of his career, he pitched in only eighty-five innings in 1956. Perhaps Mihara felt the opening game of the Japan Series needed an experienced pitcher. It was a mistake. Kawasaki faced only six batters, giving up four hits and two runs, before Mihara brought in Nishimura, Shimabara, and Inao in succession to finish out the game. In the second inning, Yonamine singled home two runs to make the score 4–0, but Otomo only needed one as he shut out the Lions on four hits.

Strong winds blew from behind home plate toward center field during Game 2. Mihara went with Inao and Mizuhara countered with Bessho, but neither pitched well as the wind helped four hits leave the park. Wally rapped out two singles and stole a base, but it wasn't enough, as the Lions won 6–3.

With the series tied 1–1, the teams traveled to the southern island of Kyushu to play three games at Fukuoka's Heiwadai Stadium, Nishitetsu's home ballpark. The Giants scored four quick runs off Nishimura in the second inning of the third game to knock him out, but the Lions came back with one in the sixth and scored four off Bessho in the bottom of the eighth to go up 5–4. Inao, who had come on in relief in the eighth, shut down the Giants in the ninth for the win. Shimabara and Inao combined to shut out the Giants 2–0 in Game 4 backed by Futoshi Nakanishi's mammoth 420-foot, two-run homer off Hiroshi Nakao in the eighth inning. The Lions now needed just one more victory to capture the championship.

The Giants' bats finally awoke the next day as they pounded the Lions 12–7. Mihara used all four of his young aces as well as Kawasaki, but the Giants hit them all hard. Wally, who had gone hitless in Games 3 and 4, picked up a single and an RBI. As the teams traveled north back to Tokyo, the Giants must have been optimistic. They were returning to their home park and had proven that each of the Lions' young pitchers was far from unhittable.

Nearly twenty-eight thousand streamed into Korakuen Stadium to watch the teams' two aces duel. Takehiko Bessho took the mound for the Giants while Kazuhisa Inao threw for the Lions. Fans who expected a pitchers' duel were disappointed. Bessho gave up four hits and two runs before Mizuhara pulled him after facing just five batters. But the damage had been done. Inao had pitched in every game of the series, but didn't seem tired. He overwhelmed the Giants, allowing just four hits and a single run in nine innings. At the end of the 2–1 loss, the weary Giants trudged into their locker room as the Lions celebrated their first Japan Series title by giving Mihara a traditional victory toss.

Although Wally felt exhausted from the long season and frustrated by the loss in the Series, there were still more games to play. The Brooklyn Dodgers were in Japan for a nineteen-game goodwill tour. The National League champs had just come off a tough loss of their own to the New York Yankees in the World Series. The series had gone a full seven games, but the highlight was undoubtedly Don Larsen's famous perfect Game 5. The Dodgers brought all their stars: Duke Snider, Gil Hodges, Roy Campanella, Pee Wee Reese, Don Zimmer, Don Newcombe, a young Don Drysdale, and Jackie Robinson.

Wally was particularly looking forward to meeting Jackie Robinson. Although nobody was calling Wally "the Jackie Robinson of Japan" at this point, Wally was aware of the similarities between them. Both were converted football players; both were the first of their ethnic group to break into a professional league; both were picked because of their gentlemanly personalities; and both had to hide their true feelings since other players' futures rested on their behavior.

Dodgers' radio announcer Vin Scully recorded the team's experiences for the magazine *Sport*. "Tokyo was thick with rain and mist when we came in. But just the same it was a sight I won't soon forget. Thousands of people had jammed the airport to wait for us. . . . After that there was a parade through the streets of Tokyo, with our party riding in closed cars because of the rain. Hundreds of thousands of people lined the sidewalks, despite the bad weather, to catch a glimpse of the famous Dodgers. . . . The players, worn out from the traveling, . . . [were] led on a giddy round of parties and sightseeing that first night, and most of them didn't struggle into bed until the early hours of the morning."

The next day, or later that afternoon for many of the Dodgers, the visitors played the Yomiuri Giants. The tired Dodgers expected an easy victory, but the Japanese surprised them. "We went over there with the typical American misconceptions," wrote Scully. "We expected the local teams to be stocked with little yellow, buck-toothed men wearing thick eye-glasses. When they first walked on the field in Tokyo, I heard one of our players yell, 'Hey, fellas, we've been mousetrapped!' One of the first ballplayers out of the dugout was a pitcher who was six feet four," Scully exaggerated. . . . "Another misconception we had was that our big pitchers would be able to blow them down with fast balls. We were dead wrong. They murdered fast-ball pitching. Our guys would rear back and fire one through there and invariably the ball would come back even harder than it was thrown."

With more rain threatening, only fifteen thousand spectators came to Korakuen to watch the opening game. The Giants started Sho Horiuchi, a young second-year pitcher, who led the squad with a 1.46 ERA in 1956. The Dodgers countered with another young pitcher,

Don Drysdale. The big sidearming righty had just finished his rookie season. He had pitched well, going 5-5 with a 2.64 ERA in 99 innings, but few would have guessed that he was destined for the Hall of Fame. Yonamine led off for the Giants and greeted Drysdale with a sharp single between first and second. A batter later, Wally trotted home as Andy Miyamoto homered over the left-field wall. Kawakami homered in the third to give the Giants a 3–0 lead. Horiuchi had struck out six Dodgers before Jackie Robinson and Gil Hodges hit home runs in the fourth inning to give the Dodgers a 4–3 lead. Mizuhara immediately brought in Takumi Otomo. Like the 1953 New York Giants and the Latin American teams, the Dodgers had trouble adjusting to Otomo's underhand delivery. In the next five innings, Otomo struck out ten and held the Dodgers scoreless. In the meantime, the Giants came back to win 5–4 on a second home run by Kawakami.

The Central League All-Stars faced the Dodgers in the second game. Wally led off and played center field. Embarrassed by the loss the day before, the Dodgers hit the Japanese pitching hard and won easily 7–1. Roy Campanella led the offense with two home runs and knocked in six, while Clem Labine held the Japanese to just four hits. Wally was one of the few to gain a hit, but he was unable to score. After his single, Wally led off first base. As the next batter grounded sharply to second baseman Jim Gilliam, Wally bore down toward second. Gilliam fielded the grounder and threw to Pee Wee Reese covering second. Reese, attempting to turn the double play, dropped his arm down to throw to first, and froze. Yonamine was right in front of him. "Get your head down, Wally!" Reese screamed in frustration. Had Reese tried to complete the double play he would have hit Wally in the face. Wally had never seen a middle infielder get that low to turn a double play. The advantages were obvious, throwing from the low position forced runners to get down and not block the throw. During Major League games, runners who failed to get down were promptly hit and rarely failed to hit the dirt again. In Japan, however, a certain gentlemanly attitude toward turning the double play still existed. Middle infielders routinely tried to throw around runners, causing a plethora of errors. It was not unusual for such heaves to sail over the first baseman's head into the stands.

On their third day in Japan, the tired Dodgers played again, this time, against an All-Star team from both leagues. The fans had voted for the starting lineup, and Yonamine was the most popular player on the All-Japan roster, receiving over forty-two thousand votes. Don Newcombe took the mound for Brooklyn against Yukio Shimabara from the Lions. Wally went hitless in two at bats before Kenjiro Tamiya of the Tigers took his place in center field. Nonetheless the Japanese scored four runs against the Dodgers superstar and went on to win the game 6–1. At the time, Wally did not get to talk to Newcombe, but years later they would become friends and teammates.

After the third game, the Dodgers left Tokyo and traveled throughout Japan playing various All-Star teams. Wally remained at home and did not play again until the teams returned for a game on November 9. The Giants gave the Dodgers a tough game. Wally got a hit off Ralph Branca, and Shigeru Fujio hit an inside-the-park home run as the two teams were knotted at four in the top of the eleventh inning. Jim Gilliam led off the inning with a single off Takehiko Bessho, who had entered the game in the seventh and had held the Dodgers hitless to that point. Bessho quickly got two more outs, but Gilliam had moved to second on a ground out. As Jackie Robinson stepped to the plate, Shigeru Mizuhara called for an intentional walk. To everybody's surprise, Bessho shook off the sign. The catcher Fujio rushed to the mound to confer with Bessho, who still refused to obey Mizuhara's orders. Leaving Bessho, Fujio lumbered to the dugout, spoke with Mizuhara, and ran back to the mound to rely the manager's instructions. Bessho, however, remained obstinate and pitched to Robinson, who slammed a double into right center to put the Dodgers ahead.

The Dodgers played two more games in Japan before returning home on November 14. Brooklyn dominated the Japanese, winning 19 of the 23 games. The hosts hit only .219 off Brooklyn pitching, while their hurlers posted a fat 5.25 ERA. Yonamine, however, had hit well. He gained 4 hits and 2 walks in 11 at bats for a .364 average.

Jackie Robinson played in all but one game, hitting .327 with two home runs. Few guessed that these would be his last professional games. Roughly a month later, Dodger owner Walter O'Malley traded Robinson to the New York Giants for thirty-five thousand dollars and pitcher Dick Littlefield. Incensed, Robinson chose to retire rather than play for the crosstown rivals.

As the long season ended, the league announced the winner of the Most Valuable Player Award. Wally secretly hoped to win. He had led the Central League in runs scored as well as batting, hit thirteen home runs (sixth in the league), and stolen twenty-five bases. After receiving the most votes in both the All-Star and All-Japan team balloting, Wally had become one of the most popular players in Japan. Wally hoped that the writers were also ready to acknowledge his accomplishments, but he was disappointed. Ninety-five of the 144 voters chose Takehiko Bessho as the league's MVP. Wally received 32 votes, Kawakami 12, and Andy Miyamoto 5. Hirofumi Naito concluded, "I suppose that there was a sentiment of not wanting to give the title to anyone except a Japanese." Wally, however, accepted the slight graciously and never complained to his friends or the press.

14

Lucky Seven

Wally sat on the Giants' bench fuming. He felt frustrated and humiliated. True, he had hit poorly in that spring of 1957. He had arrived at camp with a bad cold and not in top shape. He knew he might become injured if he pushed himself too hard in the frigid weather, so he concentrated on batting techniques such as fouling off difficult pitches as he had before the 1954 season.

Shigeru Mizuhara had gone to Vero Beach, Florida, in early March along with Shigeru Fujio and Sho Horiuchi. The two young players had impressed the Dodgers during the 1956 goodwill tour, so Walter O'Malley had invited them, along with Mizuhara, to the Dodgers' spring training camp to improve their skills. With Mizuhara in Florida, Tetsuharu Kawakami had been left in charge of the training camp. Kawakami would eventually become one of Japan's most successful managers, but this was his first experience as a skipper, and he was anxious to have the team in top condition when Mizuhara returned. A special concern was Yonamine's poor hitting. The two still disliked each other, and Wally had not told Kawakami that he was fouling off pitches on purpose rather than swinging away for hits. Kawakami had telephoned Mizuhara at Vero Beach.

"Wally just can't hit the ball," fretted Kawakami. "I'm worried."

"Wally? Don't worry about him. He'll start hitting when the pennant race takes off," the manager responded.

At the time, Wally did not know about the phone call, so he continued practicing slicing the ball foul. His bat control had improved greatly and he was pleased. Mizuhara returned to Japan just before Opening Day, bringing batting helmets—presents from the Dodgers.

These hard plastic helmets had just been designed by former Dodger, and now Pirate, general manager Branch Rickey. Major Leaguers began using them in the mid-1950s but they would not be mandatory for almost two decades. Many of the Yomiuri veterans shunned the innovation, but others, like Wally, gratefully accepted the extra protection. Prior to the start of the season, Wally twisted his ankle, but it was not a serious injury. He had played with far more pain and expected to start the opener. He had honed his batting eye and felt excited about the new campaign. It would be his seventh in Japan—his lucky number.

Prior to the Opening Day ceremonies, Wally sat expectantly as Mizuhara read off the batting order. "Iwamoto, center field; Naito, second base; Miyamoto, right field; Kawakami, first base . . . " He looked up in disbelief. He was not in the starting lineup. Since his first game in 1951, he had never been benched, except when injured or sick. Mizuhara glanced at Wally and said, "Probably Kaneda will pitch today, and he's a southpaw. So Wally, rest up a bit. Your leg hasn't completely healed yet either, has it?"

"I mumbled something about my leg not being so bad, but the manager had disappeared," Yonamine remembered. "I remained in a daze like a sleepwalker, hardly able to watch the game. Certainly my left ankle was swollen and painful, but my feelings were hurt more."

Wally looked down the bench. A number of the faces had changed this year. His close friends Dick Kashiwaeda and Jyun Hirota were no longer with the team. Kashiwaeda, still unable to throw, was back in Honolulu acting as the Asahi's assistant coach. The Giants had released Hirota over the winter. Other Japanese clubs had made offers, but Jyun decided to retire and concentrate on a career in business. He told the *Honolulu Star Bulletin*, "I have a good job with the stocks and bonds department [of] Bishop Trust. At my age of thirty-four, I couldn't possibly play more than a couple of years. The job opportunities then may not be as good. Besides, my family had to be considered. My wife and sons, thirteen and eight, were not with me except during summer vacations. That arrangement wasn't good. I decided to settle down and be with my family."

His old friend, Shigeru Chiba, sat on the bench near the manager. Chiba had retired at the end of the 1956 season but stayed on as a coach. There were two new faces. Over the winter, the Giants had convinced Motoshi Fujita to join the squad. Like Mizuhara, Fujita was a graduate of Keio University and one of the school's finest pitchers. After graduation he had little interest in turning pro. Instead, he pitched for Japan in the 1956 World Amateur Baseball Tournament held in Milwaukee, where he won the award for best pitcher. After the tournament, Shigeru Mizuhara persuaded Fujita to join Yomiuri. During his 1996 Hall of Fame induction speech, Fujita explained that Mizuhara, as an older Keio alumnae and thus his *senpai*, ordered Fujita to join the Giants. Fujita felt that he could not refuse. Once news of the agreement became public, but before he signed the contract, the Chunichi Dragons offered the thin hurler a fifteen-million-yen signing bonus plus three hundred thousand yen per month. Fujita, however, remained faithful to his agreement with Mizuhara.

The second new face was hard to miss. It stood well above the others. Shohei Baba was 6 feet 6 inches tall and weighed nearly 190 pounds. The Giants had signed him after he dropped out of Sanjo Jitsugyo high school in his junior year. As a schoolboy, he was a good enough pitcher but the Giants hoped that with the proper instruction, he would take advantage of his size and become a truly intimidating hurler. Despite Yomiuri's efforts, Baba never emerged as a pro-caliber pitcher, throwing just seven innings for the Giants. After spending most of his time on the farm club, he moved to the Taiyo Whales in 1960, where an injury to his pitching hand—incurred in a fall while emerging from the team bath—ended his baseball career. He left baseball and turned to professional wrestling, where he excelled after a tortuous internship under Rikidozan. Known as "Giant Baba" and admired as much for his smiling, good-natured personality as he was for his towering ring presence and pole-axing attacks, he became the most popular wrestler in Japan, his matches regularly televised on the Yomiuri network. He eventually became an international heavyweight champion and a tireless promoter of the sport in both Japan and abroad.

Kaneda did not start the opener after all, but nonetheless Wally remained on the bench. A day later, Kaneda started and Wally once again watched from the dugout. Bessho, with help from Fujita, battled Kaneda for ten innings. In the bottom of the tenth with the score knotted at two, the Giants loaded the bases with two outs. Fujita was due up. In the third base coach's box, Mizuhara considered his options. Only left-handers remained on the bench, and Kaneda was still on the mound. Nonetheless, he had an experienced bat ready. He walked toward the dugout and told Yonamine to pinch hit. Wally grabbed his bat, placed the new steel batting helmet on his head, and strode to the plate.

Kaneda started him off with a fastball right down the middle. It went by Wally in a blur. Despite pitching eleven innings, the Swallows' ace had lost nothing. Wally got a piece of the next one, fouling it off. Strike two. After a ball, Wally got a piece of the fourth pitch, but instead of skipping backward, the ball blooped forward near the foul line between third and home. The third baseman and catcher scrambled after it, but a gust of wind yanked the popup toward the stands. The catcher dove, got his mitt on the ball, but could not capture it.

Kaneda still had the two-strike count and threw hard on the black at the inside corner. Wally flicked the ball backward again and again. The confrontation now reached its eighth pitch. This one was high and inside, but straight. "If I had let it go, it would have been a ball. But I swung with all I had, throwing my hips into the swing." The ball sailed just over the shortstop into left field for a hit. Kawakami scampered home with both arms raised in a celebration, as the Giants swarmed on to the field congratulate each other. Suddenly, Wally's left ankle began to throb, and teammate So Horiuchi helped him limp back to the locker room.

Wally rested his ankle for a game and returned to the starting lineup on April 2. He got two hits and an RBI, but the starlight belonged to Andy Miyamoto, who pounded out three home runs as the Giants demolished the Whales 10–5. But after opening the season with five straight wins, the Giants began to slump, losing five of their next ten and slipping into second place. With his ankle now fully healed, Wally played as aggressively as ever. In the first game of a doubleheader on April 14, he hit a sixth-inning triple and tried to steal home. Maybe he had lost a step in his seventh season, or maybe the Swallows were wise to his tricks, but he was thrown out. Nonetheless, the Giants won 5–2.

Two games later, Wally tried to steal home again. He led off the game with a base hit against the Carp's ace Ryohei Hasegawa. The next batter singled, sending Wally to third, but Hasegawa retired the next two. Knowing that he could score only on a hit, Wally decided to take a chance and swipe home. Once again, Wally slid home too late and was called out to end the inning. Hasegawa bore down on the Giants and did not allow a hit for the remainder of the game to win 1–0. Technically, Hasegawa had pitched a two-hitter, but after the second batter had retired twenty-seven straight Giants. The game sent Yomiuri into a funk, and they lost eight of their next eleven. As the Giants fell into fourth place and dipped below the .500 mark, Wally's average plummeted to .270.

In early May, Wally began to pull out of the slump. He homered on May 3 against the Hanshin Tigers to help the Giants tie the game and set up Andy Miyamoto's dramatic ninth inning sayonara shot. By May 11, Yonamine's average was back up to .306. The Giants, however, were still floundering in fourth place, five and a half games out of first and two games under .500.

That May, Wally headed down to Meiji Jingu Stadium to take in a Tokyo Big Six University League game. He bought a ticket and sat in the left-field stands to hide from the press. He was there just to watch the game and one young player in particular. Shigeo Nagashima was the biggest star Rikkio University had ever produced. The school usually finished near the bottom of the league, but Nagashima had changed that. They were now champions. The twenty-one-year-old was exciting to watch, a true five-tool player, who played with an enthusiastic flair rarely seen in Japan. He would swing with all his might and occasionally fall to the ground when he missed. Nagashima always ran hard and on defense dove for balls just out of his normal range. The articulate young man also had movie-star good looks. The press followed him everywhere and turned him into a national celebrity while he was still a student.

Just as Wally came to Jingu Stadium to watch Nagashima, the Big Six star came to Korakuen to watch Wally. Nagashima studied how Yonamine played the game and modeled his hustle and all-around play after the Hawaiian. Nagashima knew that if he could play like Wally, he would make it in professional ball.

Besides Nagashima, Rikkio had several good players, but one in particular stood out—a small, wiry bespectacled pitcher named Tadashi Sugiura. Sugiura threw submarine-style with incredible speed and could make the ball break up as well as sink. It wouldn't be long until he was getting Yonamine out at the professional level.

The Giants' luck began to change in the second match of a three-game home stand against the Tigers. In the eighth inning, Andy hit his eleventh home run of the season to propel Yomiuri over Hanshin. The following day, Wally got three hits and successfully stole home in the eighth inning to seal a 3–1 victory. The victories moved the Giants into third place and brought the team together. Led by Wally's and Andy's bats, Yomiuri won eleven of twelve games between May 22 and June 11 and captured second place, only half a game behind the Dragons. During the hot streak, Wally hit three home runs and raised his batting average to .345. He now led the Central League, as Kawakami's average had dipped from .350 on June 4 to .337 on June 8. Andy Miyamoto, however, was the headline story. His thirteen homers led the Central League and he was among the league's RBI leaders.

Kyushi Yamato, a writer for *Hochi Shimbun*, noted that Miyamoto was now one of the most popular celebrities in Japan. "Miyamoto is a big lovable boy," Yamato added in a feature article, telling Andy that fans love "your big smile with your white teeth shining when you miss a wicked swing or strike out." Miyamoto attributed his home runs to Walt Alston, the Brooklyn Dodgers' manager. "Alston watched me during the exhibition games in Japan with the Dodgers last fall and told me that I was dipping my right shoulder when I swung. He said that if I could level off when I took a cut it could boost my average a lot." Andy had also changed bats for the 1957 season. Brooklyn slugger Duke Snider had presented Andy with eight bats at the end of the fall tour. They were heavier than Andy's bats but seemed to suit his improved swing and help him drive the ball with more power. By June, however, Andy had already cracked six of the eight.

Just as it seemed the Giants would roar back into first place, they faltered. In the last two weeks of June, they lost eight of thirteen. The Dragons and Tigers also went into skids, so despite the slump, Yomiuri remained in second place, only a game and a half behind the Dragons. Wally battled the flu as well as opposing pitchers and conquered both. He ended the month with a .369 batting average, well above the other Central League hitters. Yonamine had another reason to be happy—he and Jane were expecting their third child. Jane would once again be in her third trimester during an unbearably humid Tokyo summer.

In the middle of the Giants' slump, they met the Swallows at Korakuen Stadium on June 19. For the seventh time in the season, Masaichi Kaneda took the mound against them. The intense southpaw needed only five strikeouts to break the career strikeout record of 1,960 held by Victor Starffin. Kaneda had great control and a particularly sharp curve as he struck out four Giants over the first four innings. Yonamine came to plate in the fifth and Kaneda went straight after him. It ended quickly with Wally swinging hard but missing the third strike. After the game Kaneda revealed that he had wanted to break the record against Yonamine or Kawakami and had paced himself to accomplish it. Starffin was not in the stands to congratulate the new record holder. After his retirement in 1955, the Russian had begun to drink heavily and died in an automobile accident earlier in January 1957.

Andy Miyamoto's popularity and great season brought him a starting position on the Central League All-Star team. His 193,291 votes were the highest of any player. Wally also finished among top three outfielders and made his sixth consecutive All-Star squad. Yonamine gained only one hit in five at bats during the two All-Star games, but in the second game, Andy gave the fans what they wanted with a four-hundred-foot homer to center field in the bottom of the seventh inning to break a 4–4 tie and give the Central Leaguers a 5–4 victory.

After the break, Yomiuri's woes continued. Over the next four weeks the Giants lost eleven against eight wins and two ties. Only corresponding slumps by the Dragons, Tigers, and fourth-place Carp kept the Giants in third place, five and a half games behind the leading Dragons with 93 of the 130-game schedule having been played. The Giants had never overcome this large a deficit this late in the season to win a pennant.

Tokyo sportswriters began writing off the season and casting blame. A *Yomiuri Shimbun* writer proclaimed, "Our chances are hopeless." Another writer blamed the team's failure on ineffective pitching and the slowing up of veterans. Indeed, Tetsuharu Kawakami was slumping. During June and July, his batting average had fallen forty points and was now at .310. Takehiko Bessho was 10-8, while Takumi Otomo had developed arm trouble and his effectiveness plummeted. He tossed just eighty-one innings in 1957 and posted a 3.89 ERA, more than two and a half runs above his career mark. The underhanded hurler with the buzzing curve could have been the first Japanese Major Leaguer, but his career was effectively over. He played another season for the Giants and one for the Kintetsu Buffaloes, but he pitched in only sixty-two innings during the two seasons.

One writer also listed Yonamine among the aging players responsible for the Giants' poor performance. He claimed that Yonamine, "who virtually terrorized the opposing team when he got on the bases, had aged rapidly and had slowed up so much that he was a liability instead of an asset in the outfield." He added that Yonamine's throwing arm had become so weak that "a base runner scores even on a Texas Leaguer to center." When asked about the comments, Wally responded, "I'm covering just as much territory as any other outfielder in the league. And I don't think that I have lost any speed on the bases." Shigeru Mizuhara added that Yonamine was still "probably the best fly chaser in the league." Predictably, the writer failed to mention that Wally was leading the league in hitting at the time he wrote the article.

Both Wally and Mizuhara agreed that the Giants weren't out of the pennant race yet. "I think the Giants still have a chance to win the pennant no matter what the sports writers say," Yonamine told the *Hawaii Times*. "We have thirty-seven games left on the schedule and if ... the American Giants won the pennant in 1951 after trailing thirteen games behind the top, we can certainly clip a five-and-a-half-game difference," Mizuhara confidently told reporters.

Just as the criticism reached its pinnacle, the Giants' season turned around. In the third week of August, the Dragons slumped while the Giants swept three from the Carp and split a two-game set with the Tigers. Suddenly, Yomiuri was only two and a half games from first place, with a five-game road trip to Hiroshima and Osaka coming up.

As Wally prepared for the important trip, Jane went into labor. He telephoned Mizuhara and told him, "I have to go to the hospital. Can I catch the next train? I'll be to the game on time." But the answer was the same as when Wallis was born. "Yonamine, you get to the train with the players! You get on that train to Hiroshima!"

Once again, a friend took Jane to the hospital as Wally left for the station. As Wally boarded the train to Hiroshima, Jane gave birth to a healthy seven-pound, nine-ounce boy named Paul Kaname after Jane's father and Wally. Wally fidgeted anxiously during the long ride. He would have to wait until the next morning, after the team arrived in Hiroshima, to find out how his wife and new baby were doing. He received the good news by telephone as soon as he arrived. Now elated, Wally celebrated by propelling the Giants to victory with a late-inning home run to straightaway center field against the Carp's ace Ryohei Hasegawa.

As the Giants were sweeping the Carp, the Dragons faced Masaichi Kaneda and the Swallows in Nagoya. Shigeru Sugishita threw for the Dragons, holding the Swallows scoreless for eight innings. It wasn't enough. Kaneda mowed down the Dragons, pitching eight perfect innings. The light-hitting Swallows finally pushed one across in the top of the ninth. As Kaneda retired the first Dragon in the bottom of the ninth on a check-swing strikeout, nearly a hundred angry Chunichi fans rushed onto the field and fell on the umpire, beating and kicking him furiously, before police came to his rescue. Forty minutes later, the game resumed and Kaneda quickly struck out the next two batters to finish off the fourth perfect game in the history of Japanese baseball. The shock of the embarrassing defeat sent the Dragons into a deadfall. They lost the next five games to the last-place Taiyo Whales. Meanwhile, Yonamine hit his twelfth home run as the Giants took two of three from the Tigers and moved into first place on August 24.

Wally was on another hot streak, and Jane was undoubtedly complaining about his smelly, unwashed clothes. He hit .450 during the last three weeks of August and now had a fifty-point lead over his closest rival, Kenjiro Tamiya of the Tigers, in the batting race. Andy Miyamoto, however, was in a home run drought. He had not hit one out in the five weeks since he had splintered the last of Duke Snider's bats.

The Tigers knocked Yomiuri out of first place for a few days at the beginning of September, but by mid-month the Giants regained their one-game lead. With the Giants' comeback and Wally's hitting, the fickle sportswriters were now praising the Hawaiian center fielder. On September 11, a writer for the *Tokyo Shimbun* argued that Wally deserved the coveted MVP award, not only for his batting but also for his fielding and base running. The *Asahi Shimbun* commented, "Whenever Yonamine steps up to the plate, he . . . looms like an ogre in the eyes of the pitcher."

In September Andy rediscovered his home run swing, just in time for an unusual six-game showdown with the Dragons. Due to a combination of scheduling and rain, the Giants and Dragons would play six consecutive games against each other—two in Nagoya, followed by one in Tokyo, and then three back in Nagoya. Unless the Tigers, who had now slipped into third place, went on a winning streak, the long series would decide the pennant.

As the two teams met on September 21 for the first game, they shared first place. In 1954 the Dragons had won seven of their final ten games against the Giants to capture the pennant. The Yomiuri players had not forgotten this humiliation and exacted their revenge with a thundering sweep of Chunichi. Wally contributed with a number of hits and clinched the batting title during the series, but the Giants won behind superb pitching and three game-winning home runs by Andy Miyamoto and Tatsuro Hirooka. At the end of the series, Yomiuri held a four-game lead over the second-place Hanshin Tigers; the Dragons had fallen into third. The *Hawaii Times* noted that it now "appears virtually impossible for the Tigers and Dragons to catch up," so fans were focusing on who would capture the home run crown. Takao Sato of the Kokutetsu Swallows and Noboru Aota of the Taiyo Whales led the race with twenty-one homers each, but Andy Miyamoto was just one behind with twenty.

But the season took yet another twist. After Andy tied Sato and Aota by hitting his twenty-first in a 7–0 romp over the Carp on October 8, the Giants fell apart. The weak-hitting Carp scored eight against Bessho and relievers to win the next game. The last-place Taiyo Whales then took two from the Giants, and the Tigers came away with two victories at Korakuen Stadium. Both Wally and Andy slumped as opponents outscored Yomiuri 23–8 during the five games (Andy would not hit another home run and lost the crown as Sato and Aota each ended the season with 22). Just twelve days after declaring the pennant race virtually over, the *Hawaii Times* wrote the "outcomes of both the pennant and home run races now appear almost unpredictable." Luckily for the Giants, their next five games were against the Carp and Whales, whereas the Dragons and Tigers had to play each other twice and then sit idle.

The Giants ended their tumble with a sweep of the Carp. The three wins restored the Giants' lead to two and a half games with just five left on the schedule. The final two games were against the Dragons, so the Giants needed to take at least two of their three games against the Whales. Bessho won the first with a brilliant 1–0 complete-game shutout, and after a day off, the Giants easily won the first game of

the October 21 doubleheader as the twenty-year-old lefty starter Taketoshi Yoshiwara capped his seventh victory with a grand slam. In
the nightcap, Sho Horiuchi did not allow a runner until an eighth-inning single broke up his perfect game. The Giants led 2–0 in the ninth
when Horiuchi allowed another single and a walk. The former Giant
and home run champ, Noboru Aota strode to the plate, representing
the winning run, but Mizuhara elected to stay with his young hurler.
Horiuchi reared back and fanned Aota. As the former Yomiuri star
walked dejectedly back to his dugout, the current Giants rushed to the
pitcher's mound in celebration. They hoisted Mizuhara above their
heads and gave him the traditional toss.

On October 23, the final day of the 1957 regular season, eighty
American Nisei businessmen and dignitaries arrived at the historic
Imperial Hotel in Tokyo to attend a three-day convention designed
to increase ties between Japanese ethnics across the Pacific. The
same day, Japanese sportswriters finally elected Wally Yonamine, the
most prominent Nisei sports figure in both countries, as the Central
League's Most Valuable Player. All 157 sportswriters voted for Yon-
amine, save a lone ballot for the Giants' shortstop Tatsuro Hirooka.
Wally ended with a .343 batting average, 35 points above second-place
Kenjiro Tamiya of the Tigers. He led the league with 160 hits, was
second with 7 triples, and hit 12 home runs. The writers also elected
Wally to the Central League Best Nine for the sixth straight season.

"This is my seventh baseball year in Japan," Wally commented. "I
am happy to have won the most valuable player honors. Now I have
a good present to bring home to Hawaii. . . . I hit with the same con-
sistency throughout the season, for which credit goes to my wife for
her cooking! I would like to share my joy with my family for it is they
who sacrificed themselves permitting me to practice at the Tamagawa
grounds on rest days."

Three days later, the 1957 Japan Series opened at Heiwadai Stadium
in Fukuoka. The Nishitetsu Lions had won the Pacific League pennant
by a comfortable seven games. Kazuhisa Inao had matured into one
of the top hurlers in Japan, winning the Pacific League MVP, amassing

35 wins and a 1.37 ERA. Appearing in 68 of the Lions' 132 games and throwing 373⅔ innings, the press gave Inao the banal nickname "The Iron Arm."

Baseball attendance in Japan hit an all-time high in 1957, and millions of pro ball fans eagerly awaited the series. The anticipation was especially high following the exciting 1956 series and the continuation of the famed Mizuhara-Mihara rivalry. The *Japan Times* reported that the Lions were three-to-two favorites. The Giants were not the team they used to be, the newspaper pointed out. The "pitching corps has no mainstay [and] in batting, Wally Yonamine alone was constantly good throughout the season while Tetsuharu Kawakami, the symbol of the old and powerful Giants, seemed to be on his way out and young power hitters like Andy Miyamoto and Tatsuro Hirooka lacked steadiness."

Mizuhara decided to start the lefty Taketoshi Yoshiwara against Inao in the opening game. Yoshiwara pitched well for five innings but relievers Takumi Otomo and Yoshinori Kido couldn't hold back the Nishitetsu offense as the Lions prevailed 3–2. Sho Horiuchi and Hisafumi Kawamura battled in the second game, shutting down their opponents for eight innings. In the top of the ninth, Andy Miyamoto homered to put the Giants ahead 1–0, and Mizuhara brought in the rookie Motoshi Fujita to close out the win. Fujita had adapted well to professional ball, winning Rookie of the Year honors with a 17–13 record and a 2.48 ERA. This was not his day, however. The Lions manufactured two runs on two singles and a hit batsman to win 2–1.

Three days later, the series continued at Korakuen Stadium. In the late morning, "the narrow, winding streets leading to the stadium were a bedlam of honking automobiles, three wheelers, bicycles and motorcycles" as the fans arrived for the game. During the two hours of pregame ceremonies, Wally and other award winners lined up on the infield received their trophies and each said a few words of gratitude. Finally, the Giants and Lions paraded through the field "with beautiful Japanese queens in western-style dress leading the way with large signs topped by clusters of balloons" as fireworks exploded overhead.

The deputy governor of Tokyo threw out the first pitch at 1:30 and the game began. Taketoshi Yoshiwara took the mound for the Giants and retired the Lions in the first. Wally led off the bottom of the inning for the Giants. On the hill, Kazuhisa Inao stared down at him with the cockiness of a twenty-year-old who had just wrapped up league MVP honors. His demeanor was temporarily shaken seconds later when Yonamine arced a ball into the right-field stands and circled the bases. An article in the *New York Times* described the moment. "Immediately a half-dozen characters with polka-dotted headbands and yellow ribbons around their chests jumped on top of the Giants' dugout and started waving huge banners while blowing horns, banging iron plates, beating drums and blowing whistles." The Giants scored again on a Nishitetsu error and led 2–0 through the fifth, before the Lions came roaring back with home runs by Hiroshi Oshita and Seiji Sekiguchi, and Yasumitsu Toyoda's two-run triple. Down 5–2, Andy Miyamoto homered in the eighth to bring the Giants within one, but Inao stranded a runner on third in the bottom of the ninth for the complete-game victory. The Giants now faced a three-game deficit. With another win, Mihara's Lions would be repeat champions.

The fourth game was uniquely Japanese. The game began on time at 1:30 but dragged on and on, as both teams' pitchers nibbled at the corners and went deep into the counts, terrified of giving up a big hit. Wally had banged out three singles in his four at bats but his teammates could not get him home. As they entered the tenth inning, still scoreless, the sky began to darken. By the end of the inning, it was too dark to see. Although Korakuen Stadium was equipped with lights, the electricity was expensive and no money had been budgeted for their use during the Japan Series. The umpires, therefore, called the game due to darkness, ending it in a 0–0 tie.

The teams tried again on November 1. With his younger pitchers tired from the two previous games, Mizuhara decided to go with experience and start Takehiko Bessho. Bessho never made it out of the first inning. Two outs, two hits, and a run later, Mizuhara pulled his old ace for Fujita. The Giants went ahead by a run in the fifth, but

Hiromi Wada, a part-time catcher who hit just .214 during the regular season, hit two home runs and knocked in four to put the Lions on top for good. Mihara's Lions had swept the mighty Giants by coming from behind in all four victories. It was the first Japan Series sweep and the Giants trudged into the locker room embarrassed.

15

Young Giants

When Wally and Andy arrived for spring training in March 1958, reporters, photographers, and screaming fans packed the Giants' normally quiet camp. Most came to watch the rookie phenomenon, Shigeo Nagashima—the same young man that Wally had paid to watch play at Meiji Jingu Stadium. The Giants had lured the Rikkio University star with a forty-eight-thousand-dollar signing bonus—by far the largest in the history of Japanese baseball. The reporters and photographers followed Nagashima everywhere, noting everything he did and continually getting in the way of the other players.

The attention lavished on the rookie annoyed some of the veterans, who grumbled that he had yet to see a professional pitch. At first these players didn't care much for Nagashima, but the *senpai* never subjected him to any sort of hazing or demeaning tasks like Hirofumi Naito had to endure in 1948. Nagashima was already a star and had so much class that such treatment was almost unthinkable. Surprisingly, Kawakami was not one of the veterans upset by Nagashima's popularity. As a younger man, the Giants' captain had jealously guarded his position as the league's premier star by hassling rivals like Yonamine, Chiba, and Noboru Aota, but now he went out of his way to help Nagashima, driving him to and from the ballpark and discussing hitting technique with him.

As the vets watched Nagashima practice, they realized that he was already one of the best players in Japan. Everything seemed to come easily to him. "I thought he was such a natural that he didn't have to practice that much," Wally recalls. "But I found out later that he would practice by himself at night in the dark when nobody was watching." Hirofumi Naito adds, "Nagashima would run very early in the morning or late at night along the Tamagawa River. The only ones who knew about it were the old men who fished in the river." With his every move scrutinized since his college days, Nagashima practiced in secrecy so that he could concentrate and work on his skills without distractions and interruptions from the press or fans. As his teammates began to know the young man better, they couldn't help but like him. He was friendly, kind, and despite all the fame, not arrogant, but down to earth. In fact, Wally always thought that Nagashima was a little shy.

On the field, however, Nagashima was anything but shy. "He was a showman!" Wally exclaimed. "He was very flamboyant and would do things for the fans to make the game more exciting, like spiking the ball. He made his hat one size too big so that it would fly off and make plays more exciting. He was one of the few players to show his emotions on the field and the fans loved it."

Nagashima would have a spectacular career. Most former players rate him as the best player in the history of Japanese baseball. But his career had an inglorious beginning, one that older fans still discuss today. The Giants opened the season as usual against the Kokutetsu Swallows with Masaichi Kaneda on the mound. Nagashima faced Kaneda four times and each time went down swinging. After the final strike, he slammed the barrel of his bat on the ground in frustration. Yet Nagashima overcame his embarrassing debut quickly, getting his first professional hit the next day, and his first home run three games later.

The Giants languished in fourth place for most of April and moved into third in early May, before capturing first place on May 18. Wally once again was fighting for the batting title. In mid-April, he was second in the league with a .326 average and briefly captured the lead with a .336 average in mid-May. On May 26, he tallied his one thousandth career hit with an eighth-inning single.

To most people's surprise, the Kokutetsu Swallows, led by Masaichi Kaneda, had matched Yomiuri's record and shared the top spot in the standings. Kaneda pitched brilliantly. He began by beating the Giants in both the opener and the second game of the season. Two weeks later he beat Yomiuri again. By April 23, the Swallows had eight wins—all by Kaneda! His eight victories had come in a space of just eighteen days as he both started and relieved. Nearly a month later, Kaneda faced the Giants again, taking a no-hitter into the ninth inning before Tadashi Iwamoto singled. Kaneda still won the game 2–0, increasing his record to 14 wins and 1 loss, and it was only mid-May. At the end of the game, he had not given up a run for 42 consecutive innings. Four days later, Kaneda shut out the Taiyo Whales, extending his scoreless streak to 51 innings and breaking the previous Japanese record of 49 held by Takehiko Bessho. Several days later, however, the Swallows lost two games to the Hanshin Tigers and dropped out of first place.

That spring, Andy Miyamoto broke the hearts of millions of female fans by announcing his engagement to Hirofumi Naito's sister, Kimiko. Earlier that year Wally had called over to Naito, "Hey, Naito-san, Andy should take out your sister."

"No way!" replied Naito. "You Hawaiian ballplayers are rascals!"

"Yeah," piped up Andy, "I'll take out your sister. They talk a lot about her."

"No way a Hawaiian ballplayer is going to take out my sister," Naito repeated.

Weeks later, Naito approached Miyamoto, "Are you sure that you want to take her out?"

"Yeah," Andy said.

In a later interview, Miyamoto discussed his unusual courting technique, "I picked her up and we went to dinner and then to see *The King and I* on the second floor in an old wooden theatre in Hibiya. We were watching the movie when the fire alarm went off. I thought that old wooden theatre would burn right down, so I just stood up and took off, right out the front entrance and left her in the theatre! I was waiting for her in front, but she didn't come. She finally came down and told me that it was a false alarm so we went back and watched the movie. She wasn't very happy that I had left her, but we still went out a few more times and then I proposed. If we waited until after the season to get married, by the time she could get her passport and papers to come to Hawaii, I would have to return to Japan for spring training, so we got married on June 6 at the U.S. Military Tokyo Chapel Center." Wally and Jane were the best man and matron of honor. "We had no honeymoon. The next day, I had to go to Kawasaki to play baseball! The fans really got on me! You can just imagine the things they were yelling!"

Several hundred Chunichi Dragons fans had nearly caused the wedding to be postponed. On May 29, Miyamoto threw out Dragons' shortstop Mitsui Imasu while trying to stretch a double into a triple. Angered by the umpire's call, Chunichi fans pelted Andy with bottles and stones while he stood in right field. Then, nearly a dozen men jumped on to the field and began threatening him. Kawakami immediately led the team into the dugout for protection, but the angry fans followed. Finally, police rushed onto the field to remove the fans and stood guard for the remainder of the game.

By the All-Star break, the Giants were firmly entrenched in first place, five games in front of the second place Tigers. The Swallows had slipped to third, but Kaneda still continued his winning ways. On July 16, he won his twenty-fifth game, becoming the first pitcher in Japanese history to reach that level in four consecutive seasons.

The Giants' new phenomenon Shigeo Nagashima had somehow even exceeded expectations. At the midway point, Nagashima led the Central League with 16 homers, 52 RBI, 52 runs scored, 82 hits, 158 total bases, and 24 stolen bases. His .289 batting average was fifth in the league behind Kenjiro Tamiya of the Tigers (.315), Noboru Inoue of the Dragons (.314), Yonamine (.302), and Yoshio Yoshida of the Tigers (.293). He also shone on defense. The "Golden Boy," as some called him, was now even more popular with the fans. He received 220,134 All-Star votes, while his nearest rival, Hideji Miyake of the Tigers, received just 41,054. It would be the first of seventeen consecutive times the fans would select Nagashima as the Central League's starting third baseman. The fans also elected Wally, Andy Miyamoto, Shigeru Fujio, and Tetsuharu Kawakami to the starting team. Wally was third in the batting race and, due to a power surge in early July, had clouted six homers. His average was down nearly forty points from the previous season, but knowledgeable fans and reporters knew that this was not a cause for concern as averages were down throughout the league.

The balance of Japanese baseball had changed over the past few seasons. Pitching now dominated the game. When Wally first arrived in 1951, Central League batters hit an aggregate .264, while the league ERA stood at 3.85. At the end of the 1958 season, batters hit only .231, while the league ERA had plummeted to 2.68. The top batting average in the Central league also fell during the 1950s from Tetsuharu Kawakami's .377 in 1951 to Kenjiro Tamiya's .320 in 1958. Although Central League pitchers' ERA declined gradually from 1951 to 1954, they dropped one-half run in 1955. Likewise, the league batting average fell from .254 in 1954 to .236 in '55. A corresponding fall in ERA and averages did not occur in the Pacific League until the 1956 season. The exact reason for this change is unknown, but it may be due to the limited talent pool and the number of teams in each league. The Central League contracted from eight teams in 1950 to seven in the '52 and '53 seasons to six teams in 1954. The Pacific League contained seven franchises between 1950 and '53, eight from '54 to '56, seven in 1957, and finally went down to six in 1958. As the number of teams diminished so did the leagues' aggregate ERAS.

With Nagashima's success, attendance soared. By June 7, over three million fans had already attended professional games. Baseball officials had estimated that more than eight and a half million fans would attend games in 1958—a 9 percent increase from the record-setting 1957 attendance marks. Thanks in great measure to the Giants, Central League teams routinely outdrew their Pacific League rivals. It should be noted, however, that teams routinely inflated their attendance figures. This was rampant among the less popular teams, where a crowd of ten thousand or less might be reported as twenty thousand.

Wally started the first All-Star game in left field. Tadashi Sugiura,

Nagashima's former teammate at Rikkio University, took the mound for the Pacific Leaguers. The tiny hurler had signed with the Nankai Hawks for a forty-one-thousand-dollar bonus; like Nagashima, he had exceeded expectations. At the All-Star break, he led the Pacific League with a 17-3 record. Glenn Mickens, who had a brief trial with the 1953 Brooklyn Dodgers and spent five seasons in Japan, recalls, "Sugiura threw three-quarters underhand, so he wasn't a complete submarine pitcher. He could turn the ball over and make it sink from the letters down to your knees. The ball would just explode! Then he could turn his wrist and make the ball explode up because he was coming from down underneath. He wore glasses, must have weighed 155 pounds at most, and stood only 5 feet 8, but he was the most dominating pitcher I've seen."

Wally faced Sugiura for the first time in the top of the second inning. "I usually hit underhanded pitchers pretty well. Under-handers often have a late-breaking curve, and I could stay back on the ball and wait for it. But Sugiura was different. He was so fast! He probably threw in the upper nineties." Wally got around late on the ball and grounded out to third base. His Central League teammates, however, had better luck against the rookie and sent him to the *furo* (Japanese bath) later in the inning after scoring two runs. In subsequent at bats, Yonamine singled off Takao Kajimoto of the Braves and grounded out to second base twice. In the ninth inning, Bill Nishita, Wally's old Asahi and Yomiuri teammate, came in to pitch for the Pacific League. After playing in the Brooklyn Dodgers farm system, Nishita had returned to Japan with the Toei Flyers. He moved straight into the Flyers starting rotation and would end the season with a 2.30 ERA and a 16-19 record for the second-to-last-place Flyers. In the second All-Star game, Wally came in as a pinch hitter to face Nishita in the eighth inning with fellow Nisei Fibber Hirayama on third. Wally grounded out but Hirayama scampered home for the run.

Immediately after the All-Star break, the Giants slumped. As they lost eight of their next fourteen games, the comfortable six-game lead over the second-place Tigers dwindled to half a game. Yomiuri, however, recovered with a nine-game winning streak that reestablished their margin. The 1958 Giants were no longer the aging team that stumbled in the hot Augusts of 1956 and '57. Only Wally and Kawakami remained from the starting lineup of the great squads of the early 1950s. Shigeru Chiba had, of course, retired after the 1956 season and was coaching the team. Tatsuro Hirooka had taken over Saburo Hirai's spot at shortstop after Hirai had retired prior to the start of the 1958 season. Mitsuo Uno still managed the Swallows, and Nagashima now played third. In the outfield, Fukashi Minanimura had retired the previous year, and Tadashi Iwamoto was in the process of being replaced by a young slugger straight from Naniwa Shogyo High School named Kazuhiko Sakazaki. Sakazaki often played center field with Wally moving to left field. Andy Miyamoto patrolled right field. Behind the plate, Shigeru Fujio had emerged as a true All-Star, but a squat catcher named Masahiko Mori was also showing promise. Kawakami, even though he was elected to the starting All-Star squad, was having a terrible season. Now thirty-eight years old and in his nineteenth professional season, his skills had deteriorated. The "God of Batting" was hitting around .250, and 1958 would be his last campaign.

Only Takehiko Bessho remained from the early '50s rotation of Bessho, Otomo, Fujimoto, Nakao, and Matsuda. Fujimoto and Nakao had retired after long, successful careers. Both would eventually be inducted into the Japanese Baseball Hall of Fame. Kiyoshi Matsuda was traded to the Swallows in 1956; Otomo, recovering from an arm injury, pitched just 41 innings in 1958. Now thirty-five years old, Bessho was still effective, but no longer the staff ace. He started just 20 games in 1958, pitching only 126 innings.

Motoshi Fujita now led a revamped rotation. Fujita emerged in 1958 as a superstar. By the All-Star break, he had already won twenty-one games against just six losses. He would end up pitching in nearly half of the Giants' games for a total of 359 innings, while holding the opposition to just 1.53 earned runs per game. Behind Fujita were twenty-two-year-old Sho Horiuchi, twenty-two-year-old Tatsuyoshi Yasuhara, twenty-year-old Taketoshi Yoshiwara, and Bessho. Although Horiuchi and Yoshiwara had several strong seasons, they never developed into the star pitchers the Giants had expected. Without the strong rotation he had in the early 1950s, Mizuhara relied more and more on Fujita. Fujita would later say, "I just couldn't say no to Mizuhara," but he would return from the ballpark so exhausted that he would occasionally collapse just inside his doorway. The workload destroyed his arm after just seven seasons, forcing him into an early retirement.

From late August to early October, the Giants maintained a four- to six-game lead in the Central League. The races for individual Central League crowns also lacked drama. Nagashima led the league in home runs and RBI by a large margin, and Kenjiro Tamiya seemed certain to capture the batting crown with an average in the .320s. Trailing Tamiya were Nagashima, hitting in the low .300s, and Yonamine, hitting in the high .290s. Both Masaichi Kaneda and Motoshi Fujita had cooled off since the All-Star break, but Kaneda was on pace to win thirty games, and Fujita was just behind him. Nonetheless, the race for most victories was not enough to hold fan interest. Outside of Tokyo attendance fell off sharply. On October 4, a record low seven hundred patrons showed up to watch the second-place Osaka Tigers beat the last-place Taiyo Whales at Koshien Stadium.

The Giants finally clinched the pennant on October 2, but the celebration was restrained. Days before, a massive typhoon had hit Tokyo and the Izu Peninsula, dropping a foot of rain in just nineteen hours. Most of the damage centered south of Tokyo in the small coastal villages, where the flooding and one-hundred-mile-per-hour winds left over 442,000 people homeless and killed at least 300. Two days after the storm, over a thousand people remained missing.

At the end of the regular season, the sportswriters announced the season's awards. As the Most Valuable Player Award in Japan usually is presented to a player from the championship team, the writers bestowed it upon Motoshi Fujita. Masaichi Kaneda, who had a better season, won the Sawamura Award for best pitcher. Wally received 149 votes from the 153 cast ballots to make his seventh consecutive Best

Nine team. Nagashima and Shigeru Fujio were also elected to the Best
Nine, as was Tetsuharu Kawakami. As Kawakami finished the season
with a .246 batting average, nearly seventy points below his career
mark, his unusual inclusion on the Best Nine was out of respect for
his career accomplishments rather than his current productivity.

Two days after the league announced the awards, the Giants and
Lions met in a legendary Japan Series. The Nishitetsu Lions had captured the Pacific League pennant from the Nankai Hawks by a single
game. Tadashi Sugiura and the Hawks had led for most of the season,
but down the stretch Kazuhisa Inao and Futoshi Nakanishi brought
the Lions roaring back. Inao pitched in each of the Lions' last nine
games to bring home the pennant. He ended up topping Sugiura in all
major pitching categories, winning thirty-three and leading the league
with a 1.42 ERA. Nakanishi won the batting and home run crowns,
but was just one RBI short of winning the Triple Crown. Once again,
Mihara's Lions were favored over the Giants.

The rematch of the 1957 series began at Korakuen Stadium with the
two aces facing off. Neither, however, reached the fifth inning. Seven
hits, three runs, and a Tatsuro Hirooka home run sent Inao to the
showers in the fourth. Fujita left in the fifth after surrendering one run
and six hits. The Giants led 3–1 when Wally, batting in the third slot,
singled and scored on a Nagashima home run. Yomiuri went on to
win 9–2 as Takumi Otomo picked up the victory in relief. The Giants
crushed the Lions again the following day 7–3. All seven runs came in
the first inning before Nishitetsu starter Yukio Shimabara could get
a single out. Both Wally and Andy singled during the rally. Directly
after the game both teams boarded an express train to Fukuoka.

The aces, Inao and Fujita, faced off again in Game 3 and produced
the pitchers' duel they were unable to fashion in their first meeting.
Each pitched a full nine innings. Inao surrendered just three hits and
one run, but Fujita held the Lions scoreless while scattering four singles. The Giants were on the verge of avenging the sweep of the previous year.

It rained hard that night, but the storm passed by daybreak. Although the sun shined and fans lined up outside the stadium expecting a game, Nishitetsu officials used their prerogative as the home team to declare the field unplayable. The trick postponed Game 4 until the following day, thereby allowing the Lions to rest their ace. With a full day's rest, Inao took the mound again. The Giants greeted the weary ace with three runs in the first two innings. Mizuhara decided to start Otomo, who had pitched so well in relief during the first game, but his comeback was short-lived. The Lions tied the score in the bottom of the second, and the Giants' manager brought in Fujita. Yasumitsu Toyoda homered in the fifth and seventh to put the Lions ahead, and despite Wally's three hits, Inao kept the Giants at bay for the complete game win.

The next day, Yomiuri scored three off Sadao Nishimura in the first inning as Wally homered with two runners on base. Horiuchi held the Lions scoreless through six, and it seemed that Yomiuri would wrap up the series. In the fourth, Inao had come in to keep the Giants at three. He did, allowing just one hit for the remainder of the game. Horiuchi gave up two in the seventh, but the Giants entered the ninth with a 3–2 lead. Mizuhara brought in Fujita to close the game and the season, but destiny stood in his way. With two outs, Yasumitsu Toyoda slammed a ground ball down the line past third. The Giants breathed a sigh of relief—foul ball. But no! The umpire signaled fair and Toyoda cruised into second base with a double. Mizuhara charged on to the field to argue, but the play stood. Futoshi Nakanishi then stroked a single to center to send the game into extra innings. The Giants failed to score off Inao in the top of the tenth, and Mizuhara gave the ball to Otomo for the bottom half of the inning. He had to face the bottom of the Lions order: probably a pinch-hitter for the weak-hitting catcher Hiromi Wada, a pinch-hitter for Inao, and then second baseman Akira Ohgi. Otomo quickly retired the first pinch-hitter, but in a surprising move Mihara sent Inao to the plate to bat for himself. Inao hit well for a pitcher but had already pitched seven innings, nine innings the day before, and another nine innings two days before that. As it was time to take him out of the game, a better hitter should have replaced him. But Mihara Magic struck, as Inao lofted a homer into the left-field stands to win the game.

The teams traveled back to Tokyo to resume the series, but rain postponed Game 6 another day. With a full two days off, Inao took the mound again to duel with Fujita. The Lions scored quickly on a two-run homer by Nakanishi in the first, but Fujita shut them out thereafter. Unfortunately for Wally and his teammates, Inao was nearly untouchable. He struck out nine and gave up just three hits during the complete-game shutout.

The Giants were tense. They had lost the previous two championships to Mihara's Lions and with just one win could regain the crown. "The Giants were saying, 'We can't lose this series. We've got to win!'" Futoshi Nakanishi later explained. "But we remained relaxed, saying, 'Let's just play our normal game, and do it.'"

Inao started Game 7 despite having thrown a complete game the previous day. Mizuhara countered with So Horiuchi, but the Lions made short work of the young pitcher as Nakanishi's three-run homer sent him to the showers after recording just one out. In the bottom of the first, Wally singled and tried to get the Giants' offense moving by stealing second, but was thrown out to end the inning. It was the last chance the Giants had. Inao pitched magnificently again, shutting out the Giants for eight innings as the Lions tacked on three more runs. In the ninth, Nagashima hit a long fly over the center fielder's head and sped around the bases before they could catch him, but the inside-the-park home run was meaningless. Two batters later, Inao finished off the Giants and the Lions tossed Mihara in the air for the third consecutive year.

In a postgame ceremony, Inao received a thirty-nine-hundred-dollar Toyopet automobile as he was unanimously selected the series MVP. His accomplishments in the series are still viewed as one of the top feats in Japanese baseball history. He pitched in 47 of the possible 62 innings, including 4 complete games, in just eleven days; won 4, lost 2, and posted a 1.53 ERA. "There's a saying," Nakanishi reflected, which symbolizes the Japanese approach to sports, "a cherry blossom comes

out for only a short time. Let it blossom, and show its stuff. Well, it
was the moment of Inao's career, and we let him show his stuff!"

After the last game, the Giants trudged morosely into the locker
room. Tetsuharu Kawakami slowly began removing the items in his
locker as reporters gathered around and cameras flashed. After a
twenty-year career, "the God of Batting" called it quits. "I feel," he told
the reporters, "that the time has come for me to retire from active
playing with the Tokyo Giants and that the team should be cored by
younger players. As I have been bothered by an injured right ankle
for the past eight years, I do not have the confidence that I can keep
myself in the best condition and go all out in every game."

Although they didn't know it yet, Yomiuri had already found
Kawakami's replacement. Three weeks earlier, the Giants had signed
a high school pitcher named Sadaharu Oh. Oh had led his school to
the national championship his junior year by pitching complete game
victories throughout the tournament despite a painfully sore arm. His
team was eliminated after two games during his senior year, but Oh
had homered in both games, becoming the first player in the decades-
old tournament to hit a home run in consecutive games.

A few days after the Japan Series ended, the St. Louis Cardinals
began a sixteen-game goodwill tour of Japan. This time, all of the
visitors' games would be against a Japanese All-Star team composed
of the best players from both leagues. Wally played in nine games, but
only came to the plate thirteen times. In the mist of the Cardinals'
tour, Kazue Shinagawa, the president of the Giants, made a historic
announcement. "Japanese baseball should be played by Japanese players and we have no intention of signing up new foreign players in
the future." Shinagawa added that as members of the current team,
Wally and Andy would both be offered contracts for the upcoming
season. After eight years of being leaders in importing foreign talent, the Giants had reversed their policy. They would now build an
all-Japanese team around Nagashima and Fujita to hopefully rival
American teams.

The Giants' rebuilding continued the following spring when Sadaharu Oh arrived at camp. Yomiuri expected much from Oh. At the press conference to announce his signing, they presented him with a jersey with the number 1 on the back—a number meant for a star. During spring training, they quartered him in the veterans' dormitory and assigned him to room with Nagashima. Yet in all other ways he was treated like a normal rookie. The Giants had signed Oh as a pitcher, but his hitting prowess intrigued them. When he was not pitching, Oh had played outfield in high school, and many believed he would develop into a stronger position player than hurler.

"The coaching staff of the Giants was meanwhile puzzling how exactly to use me," Oh explained in his autobiography. "I practiced with pitchers and hitters and fielders. . . . In the middle of one set of drills, somebody would come over to me and say, 'Go to the bullpen,' and I'd run off to the bullpen. In the bullpen, someone would come over to me and say, 'Go join the outfielders for fly-ball drill,' and I'd trot off to the outfield. In the outfield, somebody would come over and order me to take the thousand-ground-ball drill as a first baseman—and off I'd go again. When I stood down in the bullpen, though, and watched the Giant pitchers warming up, I knew in my heart that I was no pitcher. The velocity with which they threw the ball was simply astonishing to me, far beyond what I could do. . . . I also knew . . . that I wasn't quite the pitcher everyone thought I was. And if I really needed any confirmation of that, I was simply clobbered when I finally wound up pitching in a Red-White intrasquad game that spring."

It soon became obvious that Oh needed to become a position player. Although he had played outfield as a high schooler, he was too slow to break into the Giants' starting outfield. With Kawakami retired, there was an opening at first base, but Mizuhara had planned to play Yonamine there, thereby keeping the former MVP's bat in the lineup but replacing him in the outfield with a younger, faster player. The Giants remained in a quandary as to what to do with Oh, but Wally came up with the solution when Kazuhiko Sakazaki, the starting center fielder, developed an injury during spring training.

"Wally Yonamine—whose autograph I still cherished with intense

and secret joy," Oh explains, "told the coaches that I was too good a
hitter not to be in the lineup. He said that I already knew how to hit
to left field, something that had taken him many years of study to
achieve. His suggestion, therefore, was to use me at first base and send
him to the outfield. Though I believe his own future with the Giants
may have been at stake in this decision, he unequivocally urged it and
stood behind it. By the end of camp, I was a first baseman and my
pitching days were behind me."

Under the tutelage of Kawakami, who had become the Giants' head
coach, Oh practiced first base and worked on his hitting. By the end
of spring training, his bat seemed ready. In the first exhibition game
after the Giants returned to Tokyo in late March, Oh hit a sayonara
home run in the bottom of the tenth to conquer the Nankai Hawks.
His fielding, however, was not as polished—the green first baseman
committed two errors in the game.

The appointment of Kawakami as head coach caused dissension
among the coaching staff. Despite being teammates together for
twenty years, Kawakami and Shigeru Chiba disliked each other. Chiba
had served as a Giants' coach since his retirement at the end of the
1956 season, but soon after Kawakami's appointment was announced,
he left Yomiuri to manage the Kintetsu Pearls in the Pacific League, a
team that had not finished above fourth place since its inception in
1950. To honor their famous new manager, the team changed their
name and adopted Chiba's nickname. From then on, they would be
known as the Buffaloes. Chiba took Wally's old friend and roommate
Hirofumi Naito with him to Kintetsu. Wally's other old friend Tadashi
Iwamoto also left the Giants. Iwamoto's college coach, Shigeo Mori,
had taken over the helm of the Taiyo Whales and had promptly acquired Iwamoto from the Giants.

Wally was certainly saddened by his friends' departures and missed
them throughout the season, but he was now one of the team's veterans. Instead of being an inexperienced foreigner on the outside of the
team's social circles, he now acted as a mentor to the younger players.
He took the new players out to eat, just as Shigeru Chiba had once

done for him. Wally also entertained his teammates American-style. In Japan, men rarely entertain clients or colleagues at home, but Wally and Jane threw parties, or luaus as they called them, and invited the players. "When it was my birthday, or one of my children's birthdays, Jane would throw a party and invite all the young players, like Nagashima and Oh, and all my friends." "We did it Hawaiian style," Jane adds. "Everybody brought something, so it was a potluck. We had a nice big house and it was just one big fat Hawaiian party. Wally had a friend from Maui who used to play the ukulele, so people would bring guitars and sing. All the young ballplayers loved it." One of the highlights was Jane's pies. Pie à la mode was Wally's favorite dessert, but good apple pie was difficult to find in Japan so Jane baked them on special occasions and to welcome Wally home at the end of long road trips. Rolling pins were not available so Jane had to improvise. She would scrub down one of Wally's baseball bats and after it was clean, dust it with flour. Jane would then carefully roll the dough out in a fanlike motion since the bat was not even on both ends.

The season opened on April 11 at Korakuen Stadium against the Swallows, but the day before few people were thinking about baseball. The players, and much of Japan, sat glued to their televisions as the Crown Prince Akihito married Michiko Shoda. Wally and Jane watched the pageantry closely, taking pictures off the television. For the first time in Japanese history, a Crown Prince was marrying a commoner, albeit the daughter of a distinguished businessman. This marked a significant change, as just fifteen years before most Japanese people considered the emperor to be divine. The union, considered a love match, created a frenzy in Japanese popular culture. Opinion polls showed that 87 percent of the population approved of the marriage and more than fifteen million people watched the traditional ceremony and open horse-and-carriage parade on television, making it one of the most watched TV events in Japanese history.

For the third time in five seasons, Masaichi Kaneda beat the Giants in the opener, but the following day, Wally doubled and tripled as the Giants swept both games of a doubleheader to begin an eight-game winning streak. Yomiuri captured first place with their fourth win and remained in the top spot for good.

Wally hit well to begin the new season, and by May stood fourth in the league with a .319 average. Sadaharu Oh, on the other hand, began miserably. Like Nagashima the year before, Oh started his professional career by striking out against Kaneda, but game after game went by without Oh gaining a hit. "I could not understand why I was doing that badly," Oh recalls. "I would feel all right in practice, I would work hard before the game—sometimes I even got up with the farm team at eight in the morning to work out with them before afternoon practice prior to our evening game—but nothing seemed to work." On April 26, the Swallows came into Korakuen Stadium for a doubleheader. So Horiuchi pitched a gem in the opening game. After the Swallows' lead-off hitter beat out a slow roller back to the mound, Horiuchi held them hitless. Meanwhile Swallows hurler Yoshio Kitagawa shut down the Giants for six innings before Yomiuri scored a lone run to win. The pitching duels continued in the second game. With the scored tied at zero in the seventh, Oh broke his 0 for 26 slump by lofting a high fly ball into the first row of the right-field stands for his first hit and the first of 868 career home runs.

Unfortunately for Oh, the home run did not end his batting slump—hits remained elusive during May and June. Mizuhara, however, left Oh in the lineup. As Yomiuri remained at least five games up on the second-place Dragons during these months, Mizuhara could afford to let Oh gain some experience. The fans, however, were less tolerant. As Oh's strikeouts mounted, witty fans started yelling, "Oh! Oh! Sanshin Oh!" The Chinese character (kanji) that Oh used to write his last name also meant "king," so the chant's double meaning was "Oh! Oh! Strikeout King!" "Soon, every time I came to bat," Oh recalls "I would hear the chant, until thousands of people at the same time were all joining in. . . . The chant followed me from one stadium to the next, across Japan."

As May turned into June, Wally's average fell into the low .270s. Even with Yonamine and Oh not hitting, the Giants increased their lead to ten games on the eve of the most famous game ever played in Japan. Japanese called it "The Emperor's Game" because it marked the first time that Emperor Hirohito attended a professional match. It pitted the Giants against the Hanshin Tigers at Korakuen Stadium on June 25.

Most of the players were nervous on game day. Nagashima barely slept the night before. Even the Americans felt privileged to be in the lineup. Prior to the game, Mizuhara tried to calm his players, "You were all swinging well in batting practice. If you play as though this were just another game, the results are sure to be good." Then he undermined his opening lines by adding, "It's just that—well, we have to win today. In order to win we'll all have to do our best. We're all excited about their Majesties being here, so let's try to put our excitement to work to win the game."

Mizuhara sent Motoshi Fujita to the mound and the Tigers countered with Masaaki Koyama, one of Japan's most consistent hurlers. Koyama threw in the upper eighties with pinpoint control and would eventually place third among all Japanese pitchers in both career wins and strikeouts.

Tension hung on each pitch. For many of the players, performing in front of the Emperor was more significant than playing in the Japan Series. The score swung back and forth. Nagashima homered in the third to put the Giants ahead 2–1, but the Tigers took a 4–2 lead in the sixth. Oh, still mired in his slump, homered in the seventh to tie the game. "The fans were going crazy every two minutes," Wally recalls. "Instead of watching the ball game, I think that they were all looking at the Emperor and Empress." In the eighth, the Tigers' rookie sensation Minoru Murayama replaced Koyama on the mound.

Murayama retired the Giants in order, looking untouchable. After Fujita held the Tigers in the top of the ninth, Nagashima led off the bottom of the ninth. "With Murayama at the peak of his form, it was beginning to look like extra innings," writes Robert Whiting in *The Chrysanthemum and the Bat*.

If so, the Imperial Couple, whose scheduled time of departure was 9:30, would miss the end of the game. No one wanted that to happen. The Emperor stayed to see Nagashima bat one last time. He only had to watch five more pitches. With the count at 2-2, Nagashima took a deep breath as Murayama went into his windup and threw the most famous pitch of his career—an inside fastball that Nagashima saw coming all the way. The Emperor leaned forward in his seat and watched the ball sail ten rows into the left-field stands. Rounding second base, Nagashima glanced up at the royal box and then trotted to home plate to be mobbed by his teammates. Everyone wanted to touch him, as if some of his incredible magic might rub off on them. The Emperor and Empress stood in their box and smiled. Then, bowing ever so slightly toward the players milling around plate, they prepared to leave the stadium. The scoreboard clock read 9:40. The greatest game ever played in Japan was history. And Shigeo Nagashima had won it for his team.

"It had to be Nagashima to hit that home run," Wally adds. "When he hit that ball to left field, he didn't know if it was going to be fair or foul, so he just stood at home plate and watched. Then, when he figured that the ball would be fair, he started running. Nagashima was the best clutch hitter in Japan. In an important game like that, he would always come through for us."

The Emperor's Game was also the first time Oh and Nagashima homered in the same game. Unlike Americans, the Japanese have a special term for when a team's top two sluggers homer in the same game. They call these *abekku homuran*: which is intended to represent *avec* home runs. Why the Japanese have borrowed the French word for "with" to create this term is a mystery. By the end of their careers together, the "Cannon," as the duo became known, hit 106 *abekku homuran*.

During spring training, Andy Miyamoto had injured his leg and subsequently had missed the first two months of the season. By late June he had moved back into the starting lineup and hit his first home run on June 30 against the Taiyo Whales. Two days later, a Giants-Whales game became the first baseball game in Japan broadcast in color. Wally regained his batting eye in July, and his average rose steadily back into the .280s. If he had his usual late-summer hot streak, his average might climb past .300 and put him in contention for another batting title.

Yonamine's resurgence suffered a setback in a doubleheader against the Tigers on July 19. Wally reached first base in the third inning of the opening game. As he edged off first base, Tigers pitcher Shozo Watanabe eyed him warily. Although Wally might have lost a step in recent years, he was still a threat on the base paths. Suddenly, Watanabe snapped a throw to first. It came in high and struck Yonamine squarely in the face. Pain shot through his jaw, but he shook it off and stayed in the game. Upon further reflection, Wally thought that Watanabe might have intentionally thrown at his head. There had been no need to keep him close, as Wally had a very short lead and got back to the bag easily without sliding. Furthermore, the throw should have been down so that the first baseman could tag his leg, not head-high. There was bad blood between the Tigers and Giants and opponents often looked for ways to pay Wally back for his aggressive sliding.

After the game, the Giants took Wally to the hospital, where X-rays revealed a cracked bone in his cheek. The doctors told Wally he would need two weeks to recover. Yonamine, however, vividly remembered how he had stepped into the starting team as a freshman at Lahainaluna High School when the first-string running back broke his thumb. He did not want to lose his spot on the Giants in a similar manner. A few days later, he was back on the field, hitting his first home run of the season on July 25, two days before the All-Star break.

For the first time in four years, the fans did not elect Wally to the starting lineup. He was not having a great year, but was certainly hitting well enough to make the starting team. Yet he placed a distant sixth in the fan balloting with just 28,141 votes. The leading outfielder, Toru Mori of the Dragons, received 91,478.

The fans wanted to see the league's new stars. In 1958 and 1959, an incredibly talented crop of exciting rookies entered Japanese professional baseball. These players did not play the slow, passive game of the 1940s. They had grown up watching Yonamine and his Giants while playing high school and college ball during the 1950s. They were faster, stronger, and more aggressive than their predecessors—and the fans loved them. Nagashima reigned supreme over these young players, but the rookie classes of 1958 and '59 contained six other future Hall of Famers, including Japan's all-time hit leader Isao Harimoto and its all-time home run and RBI king Sadaharu Oh. A gaggle of other new stars helped captivate Japanese fans. Still, Mizuhara added Wally to the roster as a reserve once again. Despite his fractured cheek, Wally pinch hit in the first game and started in left field in the second game but went hitless.

With the responsibilities of motherhood, Jane had stopped attending most games, but she sometimes brought the children to Korakuen Stadium to watch Wally play. In the late '50s, however, a rash of kidnappings, especially of celebrity children, hit Japan. "Our kids," Jane recalls, "would stand out like a sore thumb at the ballpark because they dressed differently from the Japanese. When I was sitting with the kids, people would come down and give them candies. It got frightening. Of course, it was just because they were happy to recognize Wally's kids, but you don't think like that when you see a total stranger who knows your children. It was pretty scary so I quit taking them." Security became an important issue for the Yonamines. They ended up hiring a second maid to help watch the children and employing a driver to take the girls to school.

Instead of watching the games at Korakuen, the Yonamines would join Wally when the Giants practiced at the Tamagawa facility. As the Giants ran and went through drills, Jane and the kids would spread a picnic blanket and watch from the sidelines. The children enjoyed the open fields and country air. The picnics must have raised some eyebrows among the Japanese, who would never have brought their families to a practice, but nobody complained.

The Giants maintained their large lead in the Central League and

clinched the pennant with eleven games left in the season. Sadaharu
Oh had never found his batting stroke. Although he hit seven home
runs in just 193 at bats, his batting average did not rise above .200,
and he ended the season at a dismal .161. By the late summer, Oh sat
on the bench and Mizuhara had Yonamine playing first base. Wally
continued to hit around .280, but he was not driving the ball as he
had in past seasons. His slugging percentage was down; until the last
week of September he had just one home run. His power picked up
in late September, however, as he hit two more homers and a rash of
extra-base hits. Andy Miyamoto also regained his powerful swing in
the summer heat. With his ankle injury healed, he hit six homers after
July 29. Shigeo Nagashima once again led the league in total bases,
hits, batting average, and slugging percentage. With their best hitters
in top form, the Giants entered the Japan Series against the Nankai
Hawks as clear favorites.

In the four years since the aging Hawks had lost to the Giants in the
1955 Japan Series, Kazuto Tsuruoka had rebuilt the club. Only two
of the starting position players and none of the top five pitchers remained from the 1955 team. The young, well-balanced squad led the
Pacific League in batting average and runs scored as well as ERA in
1959. They had power from a morose-looking backstop named Katsuya Nomura, who according to American Daryl Spencer stood in
the batter's box like a "wet rag," but would generate enough power
to hit 657 home runs; speed from the lightning-fast Yoshinori Hirose
and Hawaiian-born Nisei Carlton Hanta; and outstanding pitching
from Mutsuo Minagawa and Nagashima's college teammate Tadashi
Sugiura.

   The Hawks quickly showed that they were more than a match for
the Giants as they erupted with five runs in the first inning to win
Game 1 behind Sugiura's unspectacular but effective eight innings.
Mizuhara turned to Motoshi Fujita for Game 2. Fujita had another
fine season for the Giants, winning the Central League MVP award
with a 27-11 record. Tsuruoka rested Sugiura and the Giants chased

his replacement, Yoshio Tasawa, from the game with two runs in the first. Sugiura eventually came in for the last five innings and won the game as the Hawks scored six off Fujita. After a day off, the managers returned their aces to the mound in Game 3. Fans finally watched a wonderful pitchers' duel as Sugiura and Fujita each gave up two before the Hawks won with a single run in the top of the tenth.

Sugiura had won each of the first three games and pitched 23 innings in just four days, but after an off day, Tsuruoka started him again in Game 4. Down three games to none, Mizuhara had little choice but to bring back Fujita to oppose the Hawks' ace. Fujita pitched well, giving up six hits and three runs in eight innings, but Sugiura was phenomenal. He spotted a devastating change-up among his underhanded curves and fastballs to shut out the Giants for the complete-game win. For the second consecutive year, a single dominating pitcher beat the Giants in the Japan Series.

Wally left Tokyo soon after the series finished. Unable to predict Sugiura's pitching sequences, he had a miserable series with just two hits in sixteen at bats. For the first time since 1952, the sportswriters did not name Wally to the Central League Best Nine. He had the fourth-highest batting average in the league and might have made the team had his name been Kawakami instead of Yonamine, or had he not split his time between two positions. He finished third in the balloting for top first baseman and just missed the team by finishing fourth among the outfielders. Although saddened by not getting the award, in typical Wally Yonamine fashion he rested the blame squarely on his own shoulders and vowed to do better next season.

16
End of an Era

For the first time in years, Wally reported to the Giants on the opening day of spring training. He needed 1960 to be a good year. It was his tenth year of professional ball in Japan and, like all ten-year players under the rules in effect at the time, he would become a free agent at the end of the season. At the end of the '59 season, Kenjiro Tamiya of the Hanshin Tigers had tested the free agent market and signed with the Daimai Orions of the Pacific League for an eighty-three-thousand-dollar bonus. Team owners and league officials promptly put a cap on free agent bonuses at double the player's base salary, but even so, as one of the highest-paid players in Japan, Wally hoped that a good year would enable him to sign a lucrative contract. Coming off his relatively poor showing in 1959, Yonamine was extra diligent in preparing for the 1960 season. Jane told the *Japan Times*, "He is taking good care of himself. He is even watching his diet and I sometimes feel sorry for him."

The season began well. After two straight opening-day loses to Kokutetsu, the Giants were finally able to beat Masaichi Kaneda, chasing him from the mound in the first inning as they won 8–1. Wally doubled in the middle of a four-run first inning rally and later tripled. His hitting, however, did not remain sharp. Acclimated to the warm climate of Hawaii, Yonamine usually started slowly during the cool Japanese Aprils and gradually hit better as the weather warmed. The spring of 1960, however, was unusually cool and rainy. In late May, Wally's batting average hovered just above .200. Giants fans and sportswriters alike became concerned. The *Japan Times* ran an interview with him focusing on the slump. "I'll have to fatten my batting average pretty fast. Otherwise, I'll end up the season far below three hundred. Right now I'm hitting somewhere around two hundred, which isn't my style of play." The Times noted that "Wally's pronouncement was not meant to be cocky; it was his usual way of oozing confidence. As a matter of fact," said the writer, "Wally is one of the most likable and modest fellows we've ever met." When asked if he was slowing down due to age, Wally responded, "Well, I don't believe so. I [expect to play in Japan for] two more years." Then, he added, "I might try a hand at coaching or managing a ball team in Japan. My first and last love is baseball and I love this country. And I get along fine with the youngsters."

Despite Yonamine's slow start, the Giants captured first place ten days into the season and remained on top until late May. As the weather warmed, Wally's hitting picked up somewhat. He hit homers in consecutive games against the Carp in early June and again two weeks later against the Whales. But his average remained in the low .200s.

Whereas in past years, Wally would have been infuriated by his poor hitting, he took the off-year in stride. "During my first nine years, when I went 0 for 4, I got upset because I knew that I could do better. If I didn't do well in a game, I would come home grumpy, and not talk to Jane. I shouldn't have done that, but baseball was my life and if I didn't do well, I wouldn't earn enough to send my kids to college. Nineteen sixty was different. Jane told me later how surprised she was because I used to come home smiling even if I went 0 for 4. You see, deep down I knew that I didn't have it anymore, so I didn't get as upset."

By the All-Star break, the Giants had fallen into second place, two games behind the Dragons. Wally received thirty-eight thousand votes for the fans' team, placing him fifth among the Central League outfielders. The votes were more of a tribute to his popularity and past greatness than a reward for his current performance. This time, however, Mizuhara did not select Wally as a reserve—for the first time since his rookie year, he could relax with his family during the break.

The Yonamines had enrolled Amy and Wallis, now seven and four years old, at the American School of Japan. Wally and Jane never considered sending the children to a Japanese school. They wanted them to get a strong education in English since they would probably end up living in the United States. All three children, however, grew up speaking Japanese. Although they spoke English at home, just by living in the country, watching television, and playing with friends in the neighborhood, they learned the native language before starting school. Yet, because they learned Japanese through friends and television, they had trouble reading kanji. "Strangers used to get irritated with me," Amy recalls, "because I looked Japanese and spoke without an accent, but asked for help reading signs at the train station. They would say, 'Why don't you just read it yourself?' I always felt like a foreigner in Japan. We may have been raised in Japan, look Japanese, and speak without an accent, but we always considered ourselves foreigners."

As a young girl, Amy already showed signs of becoming a successful businesswoman. She came home from school one day and told her father that her friends wanted his autograph. Wally dutifully signed page after page of Amy's small notebook. The next morning, she skipped off to school notebook in hand. Later that day, the school principal called Jane. Although they really appreciated that Mr. Yonamine was a famous baseball player and had many fans, the principal began, they would nonetheless like Amy not to sell his autograph at school!

Tokyo had changed greatly in the ten years since Wally had joined the Giants. Gone were the rows of wooden stalls lining the major streets, the charcoal-driven cars, and the unsanitary conditions. During the 1950s Japan's economy rebounded strongly and Tokyo saw major changes. New concrete housing, modern shopping centers, subways, freeways, and office buildings covered the city. A large, state-of-the-art amusement park now stood next to Korakuen Stadium, and in 1958 the Tokyo Tower, a massive steel edifice resembling the Eiffel Tower, was completed. The tallest structure in Japan served little purpose other than attracting tourists and soon became a symbol of the Japanese economic recovery. Tokyo had become a modern industrial city able to rival Western capitals in infrastructure and amenities. It also surpassed most Western cities in air pollution, and its poor air quality became legendary.

Despite the increase in wealth and infrastructure, social unrest still occasionally rocked the city. Throughout the early part of May, there had been daily demonstrations against the upcoming renewal of the Security Treaty between Japan and the United States, which allowed for the stationing of some one hundred thousand troops on Japanese soil. Among those protesting against the treaty were students, leftists, and ordinary citizens who did not believe the presence of American soldiers offered much protection—especially in the event of a nuclear attack. The protests increased in size and intensity, highlighted by Zengakuren (All Student Group) snake-dancing through the streets of Central Tokyo and frequent clashes with police. They peaked with a million-man march on the night of May 19, when the treaty was re-endorsed by the Japanese parliament. In that final angry rally in front of the National Diet, a student from Tokyo University was trampled to death. Throughout the protests and riots, baseball continued.

The Giants remained in second place, just a handful of games behind the Dragons, until the Taiyo Whales made a surprising leap into the top spot in mid-August. Since their formation in 1950, the Whales had been one of the Central League's worst teams. Owned by a fisheries company and based in the polluted city of Kawasaki (located between Tokyo and Yokohama), the Whales played at Kawasaki Stadium, the smallest, dirtiest ballpark in either league. In their first ten years of existence, they finished above .500 once and had finished last in each of the past six seasons. At the end of the 1959 season, however, the Whales offered the helm to Osamu Mihara, who had just been fired by the Nishitetsu Lions. Mihara worked his magic on the group of young men, devoid of superstars.

Wally's old teammate Tadashi Iwamoto now played for Mihara's Whales. "The difference in the level of play between the Giants and Whales was really big. The level was very low at the Taiyo Whales at that time. A number of players had come straight out of the universities and had only been playing professionally one or two years, but Mr. Mihara used the athletes very well."

After dropping into third for August, Yomiuri moved back into second place in early September. For the first time in a decade, the Giants couldn't seem to hit. Every season since Wally had joined the team in 1951, Yomiuri had the highest team batting average in the league. In 1960, however, the team's average hovered at .230, two points below the league's average. Yonamine was not the only cold starter—six of the eight position players were hitting below .240. Only Nagashima and Oh were swinging the bat well. Nagashima led the league with an average in the .330s, while Oh was having a solid second year, hitting in the .270s. Still, Yomiuri remained just two games out of first place. A hot streak by Wally, or any of the other slumping starters, could push the Giants back into first.

But the desired streak never materialized, and the Whales captured the title in the final days of the season. Mihara became known as "The Miracle Man" for being the first manager in Japan to bring a team from last to first place. The miracle continued in the Japan Series as the Whales overcame the highly favored Daimai Orions in four straight games. Soon after the series finished, Yomiuri dismissed Shigeru Mizuhara. Although Mizuhara had led the Giants to eight pennants and five championships in eleven seasons, Yomiuri had not captured a Japan Series since 1955. Both management and the fans wanted a change. On November 19, the Giants named Tetsuharu Kawakami their new manager.

"As soon as they named Kawakami," Wally recalls, "I knew that I would be fired. It was the end of my tenth year so I could negotiate a new contract. When I went into the front office to meet with the new team president, Atsumi Sasaki, they didn't even give me a chance to get a word in. They just said I would have to take a cut of forty to sixty percent next year. Was I ever surprised! In the States they trade players left and right, but when a player does well for nine years and has one bad season they still give him a break. They made it plain that they didn't want me around.

"When I came out of the meeting, Kawakami was standing there and said, 'How was the meeting?' I didn't even talk to him. I just walked away. I knew he was the guy who really wanted to let me go."

Yomiuri announced their decision in a derogatory and untruthful press statement issued on November 25. According to the *Japan Times*,

> *Atsumi Sasaki, new owner representative of the ball club, said the decision was made not to renew Yonamine's contract because the thirty-four-year-old Hawaiian Nisei ballplayer had demanded the same terms as his 1960 contract although his performance has deteriorated during the last three years. "Yonamine has been unable to check the continuous weakening in his throwing arm and legs," Sasaki said. "Since we have rounded up a good outfield and there appears no chance for Yonamine to get into the lineup, we decided not to renew his contract." Sasaki said that the club had considered retaining Yonamine as a coach, but disregarded it because of Yonamine's "language difficulty."*

"I didn't think Japanese people would ever treat me like that," Wally told the *Hawaii Times* several days later. Wally still felt that he could play for another year or two and found the comment about his "language difficulty" insulting. He had, after all, been living with and playing alongside his Japanese teammates for ten years.

At the time the Giants let Wally go, he had the highest career batting average in Japanese baseball history. In 4,138 at bats, Wally had 1,308 hits for a .316 average. His longtime rival Tetsuharu Kawakami was second with a .313 lifetime mark. Hiroshi Oshita, who had retired in 1959, was third at .303.

"When I was fired from the Giants, I didn't know what to do. I went home but the media was surrounding my home and the phone kept ringing. So Jane and I decided to go out and see a movie. It just happened that one of my good friends from Nagoya, named Nimi-san, was at the movie theatre."

"Wally, you look so sad," Nimi-san said.

"Well, I just got fired today," Yonamine responded.

"Do you want to play with the Dragons?" his friend asked.

Wally didn't have to think hard. "Well, I'm out of a job, so if I can get a job someplace else, I'm willing to go."

"Give me a couple days," Nimi said.

About three days later, Nimi called to say that the Dragons were interested. Wally immediately went to Nagoya and signed a two-year contract.

After finishing first, second, or third from 1950 to 1959, the Dragons had fallen to fifth place in 1960. Chunichi fired manager Shigeru Sugishita (their lanky former ace pitcher had taken over the Dragons' helm in 1958), and hired Wataru Nonin. Nonin was an unusual choice for Sugishita's replacement. Most Japanese managers are recently retired star players or former professional coaches. Nonin had played professionally from 1936 to 1943 and briefly in 1948, yet he was anything but a star with a career .212 average. After leaving pro ball, he played and later managed in the industrial leagues throughout the 1950s. This appointment to the Dragons' helm would be his first professional managerial experience, but the Dragons wanted new blood to help them rebuild. Many of their starters were young; a veteran like Yonamine would provide valuable maturity and guidance.

Wally stated at the press conference to announce the contract, "It is said that I have slowed down somewhat, but I'll make it up with skill and headwork. I am determined to set a good record next season." He returned to Hawaii on December 17 and immediately began intensive workouts, determined to be in top condition for the upcoming season.

When Wally reported to the Dragons' training camp in January 1961, he almost felt like a rookie again. "I didn't know how the players felt about me, since I was a star player with the Giants for ten years. I knew that whatever I had accomplished in the past didn't matter. So I decided to do all the drills and conditioning the other players did. I was nearly thirty-six years old so if I had taken a rest here or there, I would have stayed healthier. Yet, I was afraid the players might have thought I was a prima donna if I didn't finish all of the workouts, and I really wanted to fit in with my new team."

By the end of spring training, Wally was driving the ball all over the field and looking particularly sharp. During his years with the Giants, Wally rarely hit above .300 in spring training. He knew that he would be a starter when the season began, so he usually focused on individual skills, such as slicing the ball foul or sliding, until a few weeks before the end of spring training when he would begin to prepare for opening day. With the Dragons, however, he arrived in good shape and immediately played hard in the exhibition games. For the first time, he hit above .300 in spring training. Wally was particularly motivated that spring. The Dragons would open their season against the Giants at Korakuen Stadium and Wally was determined to show the Giants and Kawakami that they had made a mistake by not renewing his contract.

Thirty-four thousand fans jammed the stands at Korakuen on opening day. The Giants had just returned from Vero Beach, Florida, where they had been training with the Los Angeles Dodgers. After the Major League spring training, the Giants felt confident about the upcoming season. Wataru Nonin started Wally at first base and put him third in the batting order. The game featured a superb pitching duel between chipmunk-faced curve ball artist Minoru Nakamura of the Giants and the Dragons' Eiji Bando. Entering the ninth inning, the score remained deadlocked at one.

Nakamura had surrendered just four hits and still looked strong as Wally walked slowly from the on-deck circle toward the left-handed batters' box. The familiar number 7 no longer adorned his back, as Wally's lucky number already belonged to the slugger Toru Mori. Instead, Wally took number 37, his old high school football number. Yonamine approached the box casually, as if he was about to take batting practice. He held his bat at the top of the handle allowing the barrel to trail behind him, almost touching the ground. Before entering the box, he took three casual practice swings in rapid succession and then dug in.

So far, Wally had looked unimpressive, going hitless in three at bats. Nakamura went into his full windup, reaching above his head with both hands, before bringing his knee high above his waist and then driving toward the plate. The Hawaiian turned on the pitch and with a loud crack sent the ball into the right-field bleachers. Wally's new teammates came out of the dugout to greet him at home plate, but more significantly, "as I jogged home, the Yomiuri fans, who had watched me for ten years, all stood and clapped for me. That was one of the best feelings in my life." The next morning, the newspapers heralded the feat as a samurai ronin getting revenge on the master who had discarded him.

Wally's great start continued the following day as the Dragons and Giants split a doubleheader. Yonamine hit three singles in four at bats in the first game and had two walks in the nightcap. Wally hit well that April, but in May, his hitting began to tail off. He no longer drove the ball with authority. "I worked so hard in spring training that after about two months I got tired and my average started to go down," he later recalled. Nonin rested Wally, using him mostly as a pinch hitter and spot starter. Coming off the bench for the first time in his baseball career was difficult. "When you come off the bench as a pinch hitter, you're cold. It's hard to read the pitcher and figure out what they are going to throw you. I couldn't break out of my slump and I became very frustrated."

By June, Chunichi, Yomiuri and the Kokutetsu Swallows were locked in a tight pennant race. The three teams leapfrogged back and forth among the top three positions in the standings. The Dragons' young offense played well, finishing second in the league in batting average and runs scored, but the secret to Chunichi's success was the rookie pitcher Hiroshi Gondo. The twenty-two-year-old right-hander had not attended college but refined his game in Japan's industrial leagues. By the time he came to Chunichi in 1961, Gondo had a strong fastball, a change-up, and a very good drop curve. He quickly became the ace of the staff, and Nonin used him at every opportunity. He would pitch in 69 of the Dragons' 130 games for an astounding total of 429 innings. Gondo dominated the league, winning the pitching Triple Crown with 35 wins, 310 strikeouts, and a 1.70 ERA. He also won both the Rookie of the Year and the Sawamura Awards.

Gondo's success, however, was short-lived. Two seasons of overuse led to arm trouble. He pitched 1,011 innings in his first three seasons but had to stop pitching after his fourth year. He stayed with the Dragons as a utility infielder for three subsequent seasons before attempting, unsuccessfully, to revive his pitching career in 1968. He later told writer Robert Whiting, "I couldn't say no if the manger asked me to pitch, even though many times my fingers and arms were pained and numb. The code of Bushido was very strong at that time." But another factor may have contributed to the extraordinary number of innings Gondo pitched. In the late 1950s, teams began awarding cash bonuses after each game for outstanding play. At first, the prizes were small, but they soon grew so substantial that some players banked their entire salaries and lived off the fight money. According to Yonamine, Gondo would pitch at every opportunity to earn more fight money. Wally tried to dissuade him, pointing out that with more rest his career would last longer and he would earn more money in the long run, but Gondo did not listen.

Entering September, the Swallows had dropped back into third place, but Chunichi and Yomiuri remained tied for first. Wally had no difficulty playing against his former teammates and friends. "I was so mad at the Giants. I had worked so hard for them for all those years and then they let me go. When I went to the Dragons, I told myself that if anybody on the Giants got in my way, I would just knock them down. I wanted to beat the Giants so badly."

The Dragons played the Giants well all year, winning fifteen of the twenty-six meetings, but Yomiuri pounded their other opponents and in the final days of September led the Dragons by four and a half games. The season seemed over for Wally and his new teammates, but then a near-miracle occurred. The Giants started to lose. They dropped one to Kokutetsu, tied the last-place Whales, gave up two to the Dragons, and finished the season with three straight losses to the lowly Hiroshima Carp. Without a win in their final seven games, the Giants' lead evaporated, but somehow Chunichi couldn't capitalize. Another win or two in the final two weeks would have given the Dragons the pennant—but they couldn't quite catch the Giants, losing by a single game.

Wally never recovered from his slump and finished with a disappointing .178 average in 146 at bats. With the poor season, his career average had slipped to .311, putting him two percentage points behind Tetsuharu Kawakami for the highest lifetime batting average. At this point, even Wally had to acknowledge that he had slowed down significantly and that his career as an active player was nearly over. He still had another year left in his contract with Chunichi, but when he returned to Honolulu in November, Wally's focus was not on preparing for the 1962 season but on searching for a post-baseball career.

"My friends in Hawaii told me that it was time to think about entering the business world. They said, "Don't be one of those athletes who have no other skills and have to drive a truck after they retire." Wally was friendly with the chairman of Aloha Airlines and already did occasional publicity appearances for them. The airline was considering expanding into Tokyo, so Wally discussed working for them full-time and spent many of his off days visiting travel agents on the airline's behalf.

When the 1962 season began, Nonin once again used Wally as a pinch-hitter and defense replacement. Wally's poor hitting continued and he was batting just .214 when Nonin approached him in late April. "He asked me to retire and become the batting coach. At first, I refused. I told him that I didn't want to be the batting coach, I wanted to play. 'If you want to play, I may have to put you down on the farm team,' he responded. I said, 'That's fine. I'll go down to the farm team. That's okay with me.' I figured that on the farm team, I could work out, get some playing time, and get out of my slump. But they decided not to send me down after all. After sitting on the bench some more, I decided that I might as well accept the job as batting coach." Without fanfare, Wally's playing days had ended.

17

Coach

The Dragons stood at attention along the first base line eyeing warily Coach Yonamine's new drill. Two players stood on either side of the base path, about fifteen feet from first base. They held a wire between them, just above waist height. Most runners have the tendency to straighten up too early, Yonamine was explaining. They need to remain crouched longer, like sprinters do when they begin a race. "Hai! [Yes!]" the players agreed in unison. Taking turns, the team began to sprint to second keeping their heads low to avoid the wire. At first several players, perhaps fearing decapitation, stayed too low, nearly pitching forward as they ran. Others ran straight into the wire. But by the time they slumped exhausted to the ground forty minutes later, most had mastered the technique. A few, however, would be at it for days until they got it right. As Yonamine dismissed them, some of the younger players bowed to thank him before heading for the clubhouse.

Coaches in Japan have far more authority and responsibility than their American counterparts. In the Major Leagues, coaches are primarily advisors. Players seek them out for advice and to create workout routines, but they remain free to accept or reject this counsel. Not so in Japan—coaches are expected to critique all players, who are *required* to obey the instructions. Japanese view a player's success or failure as a direct result of the coaching he receives. The coach is usually blamed and often fired for poor results.

These basic differences stem from divergent beliefs in athletic ability. Americans tend to stress natural talent and view a coach's role as helping players reach their potential. Japanese believe that dedication and practice create great athletes. Therefore, drawing on the martial arts traditions, coaches and players form a master-student relationship. This gives Japanese coaches disciplinary powers unheard of in the Majors. For example, they can strike negligent players or berate them with abusive language. They routinely scrutinize players' personal lives, too. For young players living in the team dormitory, coaches become surrogate fathers, controlling all aspects of their lives. They tell the players when to sleep, eat, and practice, also monitoring their leisure time.

When Wally Yonamine first became the Dragons' batting coach, most Japanese coaches had turned pro in the 1940s and lacked an understanding of the basic fundamentals taught to every American Minor Leaguer. Few knew which foot to pivot on when chasing a deep fly ball, the correct way to hook slide, and the finer techniques of batting. "When I was a ballplayer," Yonamine states, "I was very fortunate to have coaches like Lefty O'Doul, who taught me the correct way to do things. Then, I practiced over and over again so that during a game, I didn't have to think about form. That's how I became a .300 hitter. When I was a coach, I followed the same approach. I taught my players the fundamentals through repetition. Japanese players aren't home run hitters like Major Leaguers so I taught them how to hit line drives and hit to the opposite field. I focused on how to hit the inside pitch, how to hit the outside pitch, and most importantly the inside-out swing."

Wally's instruction helped many players to improve their hitting, and his teams were routinely among the league leaders in batting. During his four seasons with Chunichi, the Dragons had the highest team batting average in the Central League twice, and finished a close second and third in the other two years. In 1966 Wally moved to the struggling Tokyo Orions, which had the fourth-highest team average in the Pacific League. Under Wally's eye, the team finished with the league's highest average during the next three seasons. They did particularly well in 1968, finishing fourteen percentage points above the second-best hitting team and sixteen points above the league batting average.

"Hiroyuki Yamazaki was one of my best pupils," Yonamine adds. "When I first went to the Orions, he was just a .200 hitter. By our second year together he was hitting .250, and the third year he became a .300 hitter." Eventually, Yamazaki would reach two thousand career hits and become a member of the prestigious Meikyukai club. "When Arturo Lopez first came to Japan in 1968, he used to go after many bad pitches. So every day I would send him to the bullpen and have him just stand there for fifteen minutes while the pitcher threw, so he would get used to the strike zone. Once he knew the strike zone, he became a .300 hitter."

Roughly a month after Wataru Nonin appointed Wally as his batting coach, Don Newcombe joined the Dragons, followed a month later by Larry Doby. Both joined Chunichi as part of a State Department–approved plan to improve international relations by sending athletes across the globe to teach their skills. Although previously an ace pitcher, Newcombe—always a strong hitter—played first base in Japan. Doby, still hampered by a broken ankle suffered in 1959, nonetheless manned his regular outfield position. Newk (age thirty-five) had been out of the Majors for a year and Doby (thirty-eight) for two. Even so, they were the first big-league stars to play in the Japanese leagues and needed special attention. Formerly, *gaijin* players had been young Nisei or Triple-A-level Americans who were eager for a chance to play professionally and willing to adapt to Japanese baseball and culture. Doby and Newcombe were respectful to their hosts, but neither made strong efforts to understand Japanese baseball or get to know their new teammates. Wally, therefore, found himself acting as Doby's and Newcombe's cultural advisor as well as being the batting coach. He soon realized that these new responsibilities were crucial and made special efforts for the rest of his career to help American players adjust to Japan.

"A lot of times the *gaijin* players didn't know what was going on, so I always tried to explain. At night, I would often take them out to keep them company. The interpreters are with the players at the ballpark but after the games, they go home to their families and the Ameri-

can players are left on their own with nothing to do. I always tried to
be there when they needed somebody to talk to—especially after the
tough games. When Americans do poorly, they usually need to talk it
out. With some players, I would go out after the games nearly every
night that we were on the road and talk to them for hours."

   "We couldn't have gotten along without Wally," Don Newcombe recalls. "He was very helpful and always a gentleman. He kept me from
getting into trouble in Hiroshima. There was always tension there between Americans and Japanese even though it was 1962. I was scoring
from second base on a single from Larry Doby and the catcher decided to block home plate. The ball and I got there at the same time.
Being a pitcher, I never learned how to slide, so I just ran over him
and my knee hit him in the ribs. I broke a couple of his ribs and they
carried him off the field on a stretcher. In Japan, they don't boo you
but they throw bottles and cushions and whatever else. I was playing
right field that night so I went and sat in the dugout and so did Larry
Doby. We sat there for about an hour and a half. Then Wally came to
us and said, 'Don, if you don't go out and apologize in the middle of
the field to those people, we might not leave Hiroshima tonight.' So I
got up, went out into the middle of the field and apologized—bowing
to the crowd. They stopped protesting and cleared the field and we
finished the game."

While Wally played and coached with Chunichi, Jane and the kids
remained in Tokyo. As Nagoya, a midsized city on the eastern coast
of Honshu, lacked an international school, the children would receive
a better education in the capital. Also, the Dragons were in Tokyo
almost as much as they were in Nagoya. Tokyo had three teams, the
Whales, the Giants, and the Swallows, so when the Dragons came to
town, they would usually play each team and would often stay for
ten days. When he was in town, Wally woke up early every morning,
despite being out late each night, to have breakfast with his children,
since they were in bed by the time he came home after the games. He
called every night when he was on the road. "When my mom said

that he was on the phone," Wallis remembers, "we had to drop what we were doing and all line up to talk to him. He always knew who was having a test the next day, and the following day, we would have to tell him how we did. So we never felt like he was really away."

During long home stands in Nagoya, Jane would sometimes take the children down after school on Friday and stay for the weekend. This got much easier in 1964 when the high-speed bullet trains went into operation, just in time for the Tokyo Olympics, cutting the trip between Tokyo and Nagoya down to just two hours. The road trips to visit her father are some of Amy's fondest memories. "Sometimes, my mother would put my sister and me on the *shinkansen* and we would go on our own. My dad would be waiting on the platform for us. We would go stay with him for a couple of weeks in the dorm with the players. That was such a special treat because we spent so much time with him. The team would have to leave early each day to practice, so they would have a car pick us up at the dorm and take us to the game. They put us in the press box, where we would sit with the reporters and watch the game. After the game, they brought us near the locker room and we would ride the bus with the players and our dad back to the dorm.

"One time, the Dragons had just won and the fans were going wild. We were on the bus and I was sitting by the window when one of the fans climbed up and grabbed my arm! He was pulling on me, and hurting me because he was so excited. He just wouldn't let go. My father looked panicked and had to pry this man's fingers off of my wrist. From then on, I had to sit on the inside of the bus seat."

While Wally coached in Nagoya, Jane made a decision that would change the Yonamine family's future. For years, she had acted as tour guide for the many friends who visited the family in Tokyo. After seeing the sights, visitors wanted to shop and especially buy Japanese pearls. Soon, Jane knew all the best shops, how to judge fine pearls, and what they were worth. Dr. Hung Wo Ching, a family friend, suggested that Jane open her own shop and offered to help with the capital. The Yonamines knew that coaches rarely last long in Japanese baseball and the family would eventually need another income source, so Jane decided to try the idea.

She rented a small room in the rear of a tailor shop and hired the family's driver to help string pearls. As the business needed more capital than was available to buy stock, she began by accepting pearls on consignment. Major dealers loaned the jewelry to Jane, who either sold the pieces for a commission or returned them after a specified amount of time for new items. Through this method, Jane earned enough to buy her own stock.

Wally's celebrity status and the family's connections within the foreign community helped the business get off the ground, but it was Jane's talent that caused the enterprise to boom. Jane treated her customers, who often included celebrities visiting Japan and important diplomats, especially well. "Every customer has become a friend," Jane told the *Honolulu Star-Bulletin* in 1969. "Customers are served tea and coffee. We don't just try to sell but we give personalized service. . . . We try to remember what a customer has and suggest what she might like to add." Jane expanded her business by exporting pearls to the United States as well as South Africa, South America, and Europe. Within a few years, the shop encompassed the entire second floor above the tailor shop and employed five people.

The Dragons had a good team in 1962 but were not strong enough to compete for the pennant. The Hanshin Tigers, led by the dominating pitchers Masaaki Koyama and Minoru Murayama, took their first pennant since 1947. Chunichi finished third, five games behind the Tigers, but three games in front of the fourth-place Giants, who had their worst season since finishing fifth in 1947. The Dragons' offense led the league in batting average, home runs, and runs scored. If their pitching had been better (they were fourth in the league in ERA), or if Newcombe and Doby had been more productive, Chunichi might have contended. Doby hit just .225 with ten home runs, while Newcombe did better at .261 with twelve homers. Both had joined the Dragons after the season began and took a while to adjust to the

Japanese game. "Larry Doby had broken his ankle before coming to Japan," Wally recalls, "and he could hardly run. His ankle started to get better near the end of the season, and then he began to hit much better. He was so strong that when he hit home runs, the ball would just fly out of sight. I was hoping that the Dragons would give him another year because I think he would have done much better the following season, but they didn't." Doby wasn't the only Dragon not asked to return. Disappointed with a third-place finish, Chunichi fired Wataru Nonin and appointed Kiyoshi Sugiura manager.

Sugiura reappointed Yonamine as batting coach and brought in three Americans, Billy Klaus, Jim Marshall, and Bob Nieman, to replace Doby and Newcombe. Each of the three new Americans was a journeyman with extensive Major League experience, and all were younger than Newcombe and Doby. Chunichi hoped that the three *gaijin* in the center of their lineup would provide enough power to propel the team to the pennant. This was nearly the case. Jim Marshall hit 28 home runs and Bob Nieman hit 13, but Billy Klaus hit only 3 and became a part-time player.

Under Sugiura, the Dragons' winning percentage was .584—normally enough to capture the pennant, but Kawakami's Giants had an outstanding year and won by two and a half games. Prior to the '63 season, the Giants traded Andy Miyamoto to the Swallows, eliminating the last of their foreign players. Kawakami felt that Japanese baseball would improve only if the country developed its own stars and did not rely on *gaijin*. For the next twelve years the Giants would not hire another American. They did, however, field Asian nationals. Sadaharu Oh, although born and brought up in Tokyo, was ethnically Chinese and still carries a Taiwanese passport but was not considered a *gaijin* player because he had graduated from a Japanese high school. In 1965 Masaichi Kaneda left the Swallows and joined the Giants. Kaneda was ethnically Korean, but like Oh had attended a Japanese high school.

Sugiura returned as skipper the following season, but he had lost his touch. The Dragons began the season by losing seven of their first nine and remained in the cellar thereafter. On June 9, the front office fired Sugiura. To fill the void, Chunichi decided to promote one of the team's coaches, either Dragons legend Michio Nishizawa or Yonamine. Several newspapers argued that Wally was more qualified and would make the better manager, but the front office chose Nishizawa, claiming that Wally's Japanese was not strong enough to lead the club. Wally was, however, promoted to head coach. Hawaiian newspaper writers bristled. Kenneth Tanaka wrote: "I have known Wally for many, many years and . . . he may not be able to speak the language as fluently as the people in Japan but I know definitely that he is good and can converse with any ballplayer or Japanese for that matter. I personally think that it was a rather poor excuse." Wally accepted Nishizawa's appointment with his usual humbleness, telling reporters that Nishizawa would make a fine manager and he would do his best as head coach to help the team.

Prior to being fired, Sugiura had appointed Sadao Kondo as his pitching coach. During the war years, Kondo had been the Giants' top right-handed hurler, but in 1946, after he had won twenty-three games, Kondo was struck by a U.S. Army jeep and knocked into a ditch. He cut his wrist and severed the tendon in his right middle finger. Unable to bend an important digit on his pitching hand, Kondo was subsequently released by the Giants and was so despondent that he considered committing suicide by jumping off the Maruko Bridge into the Tamagawa River. In 1948, however, Chunichi hired him as a pinch runner–pinch hitter and a miracle happened. While playing catch with his bad right hand, he found that his pitches curved like a real palm ball. He became a pitcher again for Chunichi, winning a total of twenty-four games in three years—victories which he said were "far more important to him than his twenty-three wins with the Giants." He played for the Dragons until retiring in 1954.

Having rescued his own career through hard work and mental discipline, Kondo made his pitchers throw often and used his aces at every opportunity. This practice cut ace pitcher Hiroshi Gondo's career short. Realizing that overuse had destroyed his top pitcher, Kondo decided to revamp his pitching staff in 1964. He converted an ineffective spot-starter named Eiji Bando into a stopper. The term stopper originally meant an ace pitcher who could be counted on to stop a losing streak, but during the 1960s and '70s its meaning changed to denote a top reliever. Unlike today's closers, who pitch for an inning, stoppers were expected to pitch two to three innings, and sometimes start important games. Kondo also set up a four-man rotation. Other Japanese teams soon followed suit, although some teams did not rely on a true rotation until the mid-1970s.

Kondo's innovation did not help Nishizawa raise the Dragons from the cellar in '64, but in '65 Chunichi was once again in the pennant race. Under Kondo's tutelage the pitching staff's ERA improved from the league's worst in '64 to the third best in '65. Wally's instruction helped the Dragons lead the league in hitting, but the combined might of Shigeo Nagashima and Sadaharu Oh was too much for Chunichi; the Giants won the pennant by thirteen games.

After the season finished, Wally took three promising young Dragons to the Florida Instructional League for seasoning. Second baseman Morimichi Takagi, catcher Tatsuhiko Kimata, and pitcher Tasumi Yamanaka joined the Washington Senators' prospects for several weeks. The young Japanese compared well to their American counterparts. Bob Addie of the *Washington Post* noted that Takagi "was the best player on the field against the Reds."

While in Florida, Masaichi Nagata, the owner of the Tokyo Orions, tried to contact Yonamine, but Wally, who was still under contract with the Dragons and knew the rules governing contract tampering, refused to return his calls. Realizing why Yonamine was not taking his calls, Nagata called Jane and explained that he wished to hire Wally. Jane, of course, repeated the conversation for her husband. Wally declined to discuss the offer with Nagata until his contract expired, but as soon as the season ended accepted a coaching job with the Tokyo-based Orions so that he could spend more time with his family.

Wally was especially needed at home in 1967. Despite the corrective surgery Wallis had as an infant, she still had problems with her knee. Her kneecap never set properly and would occasionally slip out of place. Wally brought her to the team's trainer, who would ease it back into the socket and wrap it to keep it in place, but this was only a temporary solution. In 1967, twelve-year-old Wallis and Jane went to the United States for another round of surgery. Dr. Robert Samuelson of Children's Hospital in San Francisco tried an innovative procedure— tying the cartilage from behind the knee around the kneecap to hold it in place. The operation was completely successful, but Wallis needed to stay in San Francisco for a half year of physical therapy. As Amy and Paul were still in school in Tokyo, Jane constantly flew back and forth between Japan and California. Luckily the Hosodas (the same family that adopted Wally when he was with the 49ers) lived near the hospital and invited Wallis to live with them.

Wally stayed with the Orions for three years. The first year, the team finished in fifth place, fourteen games out of first. The team had only one major star, Koichi Enomoto, a standoffish first baseman with a .303 lifetime batting average. Enomoto led the team with a .290 batting average, but the anemic overall offense hit just .240 with a league low 87 home runs. Under Wally, the Orions' average increased 22 points the following season to lead the Pacific League. The Orions also topped the circuit with 155 home runs. Still starved for pitching, however, the Orions finished third in '68, thirteen games out of first. They finished third again in 1969, but this time they narrowed the gap to five and a half games. The Orions now had a strong core of young hitters. Future Meikyukai members Michio Arito and Hiroyuki Yamazaki had emerged as All-Stars, and two powerful Americans, George Altman and Arturo Lopez, bolstered the center of the lineup. Their pitching had also improved. The Orions were ready to challenge for the pennant, but Wally did not stay to enjoy the fruits of his labor.

During Wally's absence, the Chunichi Dragons finished in second in 1968 under Michio Nishizawa, but the following season Shigeru Sugishita took over the helm and the team finished dead last, with a winning percentage of just .385. It was their worst finish since 1948, and Sugishita was dismissed. In his stead, Chunichi hired sixty-year-old Shigeru Mizuhara, who after being fired from the Giants had managed the Tokyu Flyers for seven seasons. Mizuhara asked Yonamine to join him as head coach, and out of loyalty for his former manager and mentor, Wally accepted.

The Dragons improved under Mizuhara and Yonamine, finishing fourth in 1969. The staff's ERA dropped sixty points from the previous season and it looked like the Dragons might contend for the pennant in 1970, but the team suffered a major setback on May 6 when police arrested the team's ace, Kentaro Ogawa, for attempting to fix motorcycle races. Ogawa later received a lifetime ban from professional baseball. Without their top hurler, the Dragons finished in fifth place. It was but one incident in the so-called Black Mist Scandals that tainted baseball that year. An investigation by police and the national Diet revealed that game fixing had taken place involving a handful of players and organized crime gambling groups. Among those punished was Nishitetsu Lions ace Masaaki Ikenaga, who, at the age of twenty-five, was banned for life. He spent the next three decades trying to be reinstated and eventually succeeded.

The 1971 season began much like the previous season had ended—poorly. From April to mid-June, the Dragons flip-flopped between fifth and last place. The team consisted of young raw players and veterans past their prime. Morimichi Takagi and Tatsuhiko Kimata, the young players Wally took to Florida in 1965, were now starters but were not yet at the top of their game. Joining Takagi and Kimata in the starting lineup were Kinji Shimatani and Kenichi Yazawa, two young power hitters with promise. On the mound, twenty-four-year-old Senichi Hoshino also had potential. He was stubborn, proud, and ready for any challenge. In late June, the team started to win and slowly moved up the standings. By July 1, they reached fourth place. A month later, they captured third and a final spurt in September brought them into second, where they finished six and a half games behind the Giants.

Just prior to the end of the season, Yonamine was sleeping in his room at the Castle Hotel in Nagoya when the telephone rang. It was after midnight and Wally naturally feared an emergency. It was a member of the Dragons' front office explaining that the club president, Takeo Koyama, wanted to see him right away. A car picked Yonamine up and whisked him downtown to the International Hotel. Inside the room, Koyama got quickly to the point. Shigeru Mizuhara was going to resign as manager after the season and the board of directors wanted Yonamine to take over. They wanted to sign Wally to an open ended contract—he could manage as long as he wished to stay. Wally smiled to himself. He knew that trick. Japanese teams were famous for firing managers after just one bad season. "No, but I would consider a three-year guaranteed contract so I can build up the team," Wally countered. Koyama agreed to discuss it with the board. A few weeks later, they confirmed the appointment. Wally finally had his chance to lead a team.

18

Yonamine Kantoku

The Dragons celebrated Wally's accession to *kantoku* (manager) with a lavish party in the Chunichi newspaper's main hall. During the many speeches, Takeo Koyama, the club's president, told the gathering, "This is the year we will win the championship!" The board of directors felt that after finishing second in 1971, Yonamine had a legitimate shot at capturing the pennant. But Wally knew otherwise. "We were lucky to finish second," he thought. Later, he explained to Koyama, "There's no way. We're not ready yet. Give me three years. I'm going to teach these guys fundamentals and I will want to make a couple of trades." Yonamine knew that it would be hard to beat the Giants that season, with Oh and Nagashima in their prime, but Nagashima would turn thirty-six years old that year. In two or three years, Yomiuri would be vulnerable.

Wally got right to work training his players in the fundamentals of defense as well as hitting. He hired Sadao Kondo, the palm-ball artist who had revamped Chunichi's pitching staff in 1964, as his pitching coach. Kondo brought with him Hiroshi Gondo, the man whose career he helped ruin, as his assistant pitching coach. Perhaps his former boss felt guilty for helping to bring Gondo's career to a premature end. The Dragons worked hard under Yonamine. He felt that repetition would cement the fundamentals and turn the Dragons into a championship team. The team spent hours practicing details, such as how to properly go back on a fly ball hit over one's head. Wally kept hard candy in his uniform pocket and would give some to players as a reward for using the proper technique. They would do the drills over and over until they could do the tasks correctly without thinking about it.

Many Americans state that the Japanese practice too much. "I believe that the Japanese put more emphasis on practice than actually
playing the game," said Gene Martin, who later played for Yonamine.
Leron Lee, who played for the Orions during the 1980s, adds, "To show
their fighting spirit, the Japanese would focus on how hard they could
practice and how long they could practice. . . . So when they would get
into the ball game, they couldn't really perform up to their abilities."

Yonamine agrees that many Japanese managers at that time conducted drills that accomplished little. He especially disliked the thousand ground ball drill, pointing out that as players tired they abandoned their fundamentals. At best, it led the players off track. At
worst, it led to bad habits that affected their play.

Wally, however, argues that Japanese players then, and now, need to
practice more than Major Leaguers. In the United States, most players learn baseball basics in high school, college, or at the latest in the
instructional league—the first rung of the Minor League ladder. They
then fine-tune their skills as they ascend through the extensive Minor
League system. During this time, the young players practice hard so
that when they become Major Leaguers, proper technique is auto-
matic. Most Japanese, on the other hand, have not been taught proper
fundamentals in high school and college. They enter the professional
league as raw players with much to learn. There is no equivalent of
the American instructional league in Japan, and each club has only
one minor league squad. Young Japanese players therefore rarely get
enough drill before they are promoted to the main team. As a result,
Japanese managers need to constantly instruct their players and improve their skills even after they become starters on the parent club.

As Yonamine had been head coach for the two previous years, as well
as the batting coach from 1962 to 1967, he knew most of the Chunichi
players well and was friendly with many. Unlike most Japanese managers, who try to distance themselves from their players to maintain
their authority, Wally fostered his previous friendships and attempted
to befriend the players he knew less well. Twice a year, Jane and Wally

would invite the players to their Tokyo home for a Hawaiian-style luau—just as they had thrown when Wally played for the Giants. Even by the end of their first spring training together, Yonamine noted that the Dragons "were just like a family." Of course, "sometimes I had to show them who was boss, but usually we were all very friendly."

Yonamine was strict about punctuality and fined players who were late to practice. "Wally ran a tight ship. He'd get on your butt," Gene Martin found out when he showed up a few minutes late one afternoon. The Japanese players were already on the field doing their running when Martin strolled out of the clubhouse. The runners paused and started watching their manager closely. Even though they liked Martin, there was always tension between Japanese and *gaijin* players. If *gaijin* were treated specially, the Japanese would grumble. Wally knew that to maintain discipline and team morale he would have to make an example of Martin. So, he stopped supervising the running, walked directly to Martin and asked him why he was late. "I had to tape up my hands," the large American replied. "Gene," Wally began, "if you knew that you had to tape up your hands, why didn't you come in ten minutes earlier? Then you would be ready when the other players were ready to go. Now, I have to fine you." The fine was a paltry ten thousand yen, which Martin paid without complaint, but the Japanese were thrilled that Wally held the American to the team rules.

Yonamine made a point of treating all of his players—rookies, stars, and Americans—the same. During one game, his captain and star shortstop Morimichi Takagi missed a bunt sign, but swung away and hit a two-run homer to win the game. The following morning, before the team meeting, he called Takagi to his hotel room.

"Look," Wally told him, "you hit a two-run home run yesterday and we won the game—terrific—but you missed a sign. What should I do?" Without hesitation, Takagi replied, "Fine me." Yonamine smiled. He had been expecting that answer. He went on to explain that the normal fine for missing a sign was ten thousand yen, but since Takagi was the captain, he would be fined twenty thousand. The shortstop nodded in agreement.

Before the pregame meeting, the Dragons speculated on what would happen to Takagi. Most seemed to think that he should be fined, but few expected it would happen—after all he had won the game with his home run and he was the captain. When Wally announced the punishment, many players actually cheered the decision. They were thrilled that no player was above the team rules.

Although Yonamine was a strict disciplinarian, he never berated his players to the press, a common tactic Japanese managers use to motivate their teams. Instead, if he had an issue with a particular player, he took him aside and spoke to him in private. Wally understood the psychology of his players and knew how to motivate them as individuals. "I studied my players because human beings don't think alike and ballplayers can get moody. I had to motivate players in different ways." If a player reacted poorly to criticism, he would refrain from scolding them but instead praised their accomplishments and their hustle. Other players needed to be angry to play well. These players he would challenge and scold to bring out their abilities. Once in a while, Wally would have to take drastic measures to motivate a player. In the early 1970s the Dragons drafted Takamasa Suzuki, a young pitcher with a great fastball but little self-confidence. Early in his career, he was beating the Yakult Swallows 1–0 when the American slugger Roger Repoz hit a home run off him to put the Swallows ahead. At the end of the inning, Suzuki returned to the dugout hanging his head. Yonamine took one look at him and realized that his self-confidence was shot. "I didn't want him to stay discouraged and not have any guts when he took the mound," Wally remembers. "So I went over and gave him a good whack on his left shoulder (because I didn't want to hit him on his pitching arm) and growled, 'What you up to? You're a good pitcher! You can't put your head down!' I gave him one more smack. Whack! And that got him out of his funk. I told him, 'I want you to go out there and pitch a good game!'" Suzuki returned to the mound and shut out the Swallows for the remainder of the game. A few years later, he became a star pitcher, winning 124 games during a seventeen-season career.

Many wondered how Wally, with his gentlemanly and mild demeanor, could be a successful manager. But Yonamine managed with the same intensity that he played the game. His mild manners disappeared once he entered the dugout. Years later, reporters asked star pitcher Senichi Hoshino to tell them something about each manager he had played under. When the reporters came to Yonamine, Hoshino responded, "Fight! Fight!" Wally was a fiery leader, often charging from the dugout to argue with umpires or occasionally fight opposing players. "When my players got into fights, I would be right in there with them," Wally explains. "One time against Yakult, Hoshino slid home and hit the catcher in the face. Three or four guys ran out of the Yakult dugout toward him, so I charged them and threw a body block—a football block—and all four went down. A Chunichi writer told me, 'You are the manager, you are supposed to stop the fights, not fight along with your players.' But I wanted the guys to know that I was one hundred percent behind them. They had confidence in me and gave me one hundred percent in return."

Yonamine also went to the other extreme. Japanese managers are usually reserved with their players, emphasizing the hierarchy with formal mannerisms. The ideal manager is stoic, like a Zen master. Wally, however, was rarely stoic. He constantly yelled encouragements from the bench, congratulated players after good plays, and when truly excited would give a player a bear-hug, or plant a kiss on his cheek. The kisses surprised, perhaps even shocked, some players, but they soon became used to their emotional American manager.

Many writers mistakenly identify Yonamine as the first American manager in Japanese professional baseball. Just as Yonamine was not technically the first American to play in Japan after World War II, other Nisei had managed prior to Wally. Hawaiian-born Bozo Wakabayashi had managed the Tigers from 1942–44 and 1947–49 and the Orions in 1953, while Kaiser Tanaka skippered the Tigers in 1958 and '59. Wally was, however, the first man with professional baseball experience in the United States to manage in Japan. As a result, his managerial style was part Japanese and part American.

Yonamine adopted American attitudes toward pitching, played percentage baseball, and did not play the typical passive Japanese game. Motoh Ando, who played for the Hanshin Tigers from 1962 to 1973 and managed the team from 1982 to 1984, recalls, "Japanese managers do things in a certain way, but when Wally was managing he would do things a bit differently. So we had a hard time figuring out what he was going to do and we often didn't know how to defend against his moves."

"For example," Ando continued, "Yonamine-san hated to bunt early in the game." Japanese argue that the team that scores first is more likely to win the game. As Japanese games tend to be low-scoring, managers fight for the first run by sacrificing whenever a lead-off batter reaches first. This tactic moves the runner into scoring position and removes the likelihood of a double play. American managers, on the other hand, rarely sacrifice early in a game, but instead try to get a big inning that might lead to an easy victory. Many American managers also point out that sacrificing the lead-off runner to second base often results in the third hitter being walked to set up a double play, thereby taking the bat out of the hands of one of the team's top hitters.

Yonamine played more of an American-style game. Under his direction, the Dragons usually sacrificed less than other Central League teams. In 1972, for example, Chunichi laid down 62 successful sacrifices, almost half of the Swallows' league-leading 120. Wally relied on the percentages and chose when to sacrifice carefully. "I would sometimes bunt in the first inning if two really good pitchers were going at it, and there weren't going to be a lot of runs. Occasionally, I'd even use my pinch hitter in the first inning if I felt that an early run was important."

Playing the percentages sometimes led Yonamine to sound but unusual tactics. In one particular game, the Dragons led by three in the ninth inning when the Giants loaded the bases. Sadaharu Oh came to the plate. "He was so patient, so disciplined, such a really good hitter that I knew he could win the game. So I walked him purposely and gave them one run. Oh couldn't believe it. It was the first time it had ever happened to him." After the walk, the Dragons remained two runs ahead and promptly retired the next batter to win the game.

Yonamine was also sensitive about overusing his pitchers. With his pitching coach, Sadao Kondo, he set up a four-man rotation, thus giving his ace pitcher more rest between starts. Yonamine's ace pitchers routinely threw fewer innings than other teams' aces. From 1972 to 1977, the Dragons' ace threw an average of 241 innings per season (Misuo Inaba's 261 innings in 1972 were the most logged by a Chunichi pitcher during the period). The Central League leader during this time usually threw about 300 innings. In the first few years of his managerial career, Wally occasionally used his best starters as relievers in important situations. Later, he began using a true stopper and allowed his starters to get their full rest between starts.

One week before Chunichi promoted Yonamine to manager, *Sports Hochi* assigned Ryozo Kotoh to cover the Chunichi Dragons. Kotoh's passion for sports had not vanished since the day he sat on the roof of his school discussing Yonamine's debut with his friends. When he turned sixteen, Kotoh decided that he wanted to be a sportswriter. He focused on his dream and after graduating college went to work for *Sports Hochi*, a daily newspaper owned by Yomiuri. Like most young Japanese salarymen, Kotoh started at the bottom. He first covered the 1964 Tokyo Olympics and then boxing before being transferred to the more prestigious baseball beat. Covering the Dragons was not as distinguished as covering the Yomiuri Giants, but it was a good position. Only fifteen to twenty writers covered the Dragons, as opposed to the nearly three hundred reporters who followed the Giants, often causing strife between the media and the players and manager.

As he readied himself for his new assignment, Kotoh heard the thrilling news that his childhood hero, Wally Yonamine, would be the Dragons' new manager. The Dragons' front office naturally wanted reporters from their own Chunichi newspaper to get preferential treatment and inside scoops, but Yonamine was drawn to Kotoh even though he wrote for the rival *Sports Hochi*. The two soon became close friends and dined together often. Yonamine spoke openly with Kotoh about the Dragons' problems, but nothing he said in confidence ever appeared in print.

The Yonamine family once again did not relocate to Nagoya—now recognized around the world as the home of the Toyota car company. Jane's pearl business was thriving. The shop had become a stop for visiting dignitaries on sightseeing tours, and the family relied on the enterprise as a source of income. It made little sense for Jane to close up shop and move to Nagoya. Both Amy and Wallis were in California attending college, but Paul, now in his teens, remained at home and attended St. Mary's International School. He was a talented ballplayer, making the regional All-Star team during the school year in Japan, and winning the state championship during the summer in Hawaii. Pros, scouts, and media watched him closely and constantly compared him to his father. A professional baseball career, however, was not in Paul's future as he eventually stopped playing to concentrate on academics.

During his years as manager, Wally lived at the Hotel Castle, a deluxe hotel located across the street from the centuries-old Nagoya Castle—in the heart of that industrialized and polluted town. There, the staff pampered him. "The hotel manager took such good care of Wally and knew exactly what to do," Jane comments, "like not serving the same type of food two days in a row if the team lost. I would have been jealous if he was a woman!"

Chunichi's Yonamine era began well as the Dragons swept the first six games of the 1972 season. Bart Shirley, the Dragons' American shortstop, who was known more for his glove than bat, propelled the team with a flurry of home runs. "They tried pitching me inside and I kept pulling the ball," Shirley remembers. "It was one of the best starts I ever had. I was up there in home runs with Sadaharu Oh for a few weeks." Wally especially relished the two victories over Kawakami's Giants on April 14 and 16. By the end of April, the Dragons held first place with a 15-5 record.

May, however, was as disappointing as April was exhilarating. Shirley began to slump and Chunichi lost fourteen of their sixteen games. They fell into fourth place and remained there for most of the season. A final spurt during the last six weeks, however, brought the Dragons into third at season's end. Yonamine had pleased Chunichi management and fans by starting many of the Dragons' younger players on an everyday basis. Kenichi Yazawa, Yasunori Oshima, Tatsuhiko Kimata, and Kinji Shimatani were not quite ready, but all showed signs of becoming stars. With the inexperienced lineup, the Dragons' record had actually improved from 65 wins in 1971 to 67 in 1972. Wait until next year, Chunichi fans said.

In the off-season, Yonamine orchestrated two trades that solidified his team. He picked up twenty-eight-year-old Hiroaki Inoue from the Hiroshima Carp in exchange for a journeyman pitcher named Kazuhito Kawabata. Inoue had posted five unimpressive seasons in Hiroshima as a utility player. For the past three years, his average had hovered around .200, but Wally believed that with proper instruction, Inoue could become a productive hitter. Yonamine also swapped four nonessential players to the Lotte Orions for Osamu Hirose and two young pitchers. Hirose was a typical no-hit great-fielding shortstop, but when paired with Gold Glove second baseman Morimichi Takagi, he gave the Dragons dependability in the middle of the infield.

The Dragons' year finally seemed to arrive in 1973. The season began well, with the club winning over 60 percent of its games during the first seven weeks. The Whales and Carp, who would finish fourth and last, kept pace with the Dragons for a few months, but by mid-July Chunichi sat comfortably on top of the division. The Giants were languishing in fifth, well out of the race. The Dragons' lead slowly dwindled throughout the summer until Hanshin overcame them in mid-August. Yomiuri meanwhile began to slowly climb through the standings, moved into first place in early September, and maintained a slim lead until the end of the season. From top to bottom, it was the closest pennant race in Japanese history—it almost seemed that no team wanted to win. The Giants ended up on top, with the lowest winning percentage in Central League history, by half a game over the

Tigers, a game and a half over Chunichi, and six and one half over the last-place Hiroshima Carp.

Wally's preseason moves had paid off. Inoue, starting in left field, hit .271 with sixteen home runs, while Hirose gave them solid defense. The Dragons, however, lacked power overall and finished fourth in the league in home runs. Kinji Shimatani led the team with just twenty-one. With a true power hitter in the middle of their lineup, the Dragons might have captured the pennant.

By capturing the pennant, Wally's old rival, Tetsuharu Kawakami, had turned the Giants into one of the best sports teams in history. Since he took the reins in 1961, Yomiuri had won eleven pennants in thirteen years, including nine straight Japanese championships from 1965 to 1973. Kawakami developed a managerial philosophy called *kanri yakyu* (controlled baseball), where he took Shigeru Mizuhara's practices one step further. Like Mizuhara, Kawakami was an autocratic disciplinarian. Both on and off the field, Kawakami required his players to behave in a dignified manner. Reading comic books in public, for example, was banned for being unprofessional. In practice, Kawakami pushed his players to their physical and mental limits to strengthen both body and mind.

During games, Kawakami did not delegate responsibility but called every play from the bench. He advocated the sacrifice bunt and relied on a small number of talented pitchers rather than using a set rotation. As the manager of the Yomiuri Giants and an intelligent, articulate man, Kawakami's theories on baseball were constantly disseminated in the media. He also wrote numerous magazine articles and several books promoting his ideas. Giving Kawakami's success with the Giants and Yomiuri's domination of the Japanese media, it is not surprising that his views were adopted throughout Japanese baseball.

Kawakami's success is undeniable but it may have been more a product of Shigeo Nagashima and Sadaharu Oh rather than his managerial philosophy. Wally's former teammates had matured into Japan's greatest players. After Sadaharu Oh developed his famous flamingo batting stance in 1962, he won every home run crown between

1962 and 1973. Together Oh and Nagashima won 11 MVP awards, 13 home run crowns, 12 RBI titles, and 8 batting titles during Kawakami's tenure from 1961 to 1973.

Yet Wally's prediction was coming true. The Giants were gradually weakening. Shigeo Nagashima would turn thirty-eight in 1974, and his batting average had gradually decreased over the past few seasons. Masahiko Mori, who had been the starting catcher for fifteen straight seasons, would turn thirty-seven and was also slowing down. After winning the pennant by such a slim margin in 1973, Wally knew the Giants' dynasty was ready to fall.

19

Sometimes Nice Guys Do Finish First

Chunichi fans expected big things for the 1974 season, and it looked as if the Dragons would pull off the greatest coup in the history of Japanese pro ball. In December 1973, the *Nikkan Sports* announced that the Dragons had offered Boston Red Sox superstar Carl Yastrzemski one hundred thousand dollars for the 1974 season. Accompanying the article was a photograph of Yastrzemski meeting with Yonamine in Tokyo. For a week, Japanese sports papers created a frenzy, especially after they spotted Yaz meeting with Yonamine and Dragons' president Takeo Koyama at a Tokyo hotel. Reporters hounded Wally, camping outside his home, hoping for news about the reported contract.

Realizing the problems he was causing for Wally, Yastrzemski squashed the rumors in a lengthy interview with the *Stars and Stripes*. "I haven't talked to anyone here in Japan [about] any type of contract," Yaz stated. "They're speculating falsely and it's getting Wally in trouble. . . . The Yonamines are great people and have helped us overcome the language barrier. They have shown us places in Japan tourists don't usually see. They've made our visit here in Japan much more enjoyable. Once we were spotted together—the first day in Japan—three separate photos were taken. Those pictures had to be spliced together to get Wally and I together, because at no time were we photographed together. Everything just mushroomed into crazy things. . . . The whole thing is crazy."

Wally did meet with Yaz and Takeo Koyama to discuss the personalities of several Major Leaguers the Dragons were considering for the upcoming season. The club understood that an American's ability to adapt to Japan was often more important than pure baseball talent.

The previous season, the Yakult Atoms had signed former Yankee star Joe Pepitone for seventy thousand dollars, but Pepitone saw action in just fourteen games before developing suspicious injuries and refusing to play further. The Dragons settled on Gene Martin, a Triple-A outfielder who had played with the Washington Senators. Martin was no Carl Yastrzemski, but he was a solid power hitter with a good attitude and a level head on his shoulders.

Although Yonamine and Chunichi fans felt that the Dragons were pennant contenders, the *Japan Times* disagreed. The newspaper staff predicted the team would finish fourth because of their lack of pitching. The conclusion was not unfounded. Chunichi would end up with the second-worst ERA in the league, but it was offense and determination that would carry the team. Japanese teams routinely adopt official mottos each season. Wally chose "Never Give Up!" and throughout the season, the Dragons continually came from behind to overcome their opponents.

The season began with a dramatic come-from-behind victory. Losing 4–5 to the Carp in the seventh inning, the Dragons put two men on before Tatsuhiko Kimata homered to give Chunichi a 7–5 lead. The fiery Senichi Hoshino, whom Yonamine used as a both a reliever and spot starter, shut down Hiroshima for the victory. Yonamine's Dragons went on to win ten of their first fourteen games and held a two-and-a-half-game lead over the Hanshin Tigers and Yomiuri Giants at the end of April. Wally managed aggressively. In a 3–2 victory over the Tigers on April 24, Chunichi scored twice in the second on two singles and two squeeze plays. In the fourth inning, the Dragons gained a third run on another squeeze play! In important games like this, Yonamine turned to his most consistent starter, Yukitsura Matsumoto, and then brought in Hoshino to protect the lead.

The Dragons had chosen well by hiring Gene Martin. He participated in the Japanese workouts without grumbling and got along well with his new teammates and manager. He also feasted on Japanese pitching, hitting eight home runs in the first four weeks of the season. The Dragons remained in first until May 15, when the Hanshin Tigers, in the midst of a five-game winning streak, took over the top slot. The two teams met on May 18. Determined to regain the lead, Yonamine started Hoshino, who held the Tigers to two runs through seven innings. The teams entered the ninth inning tied at two. Wally, borrowing one of Mizuhara's dubious strategies, brought in his number one starter, Yukitsura Matsumoto to pitch the ninth. The ace retired the first two batters before giving up a game-winning homer to Bobby Taylor, who had played for the Dragons the previous season. The following day, Yonamine started Matsumoto. Perhaps angered by his loss the night before, Matsumoto pitched a three-hit shutout and snapped Hanshin's winning streak at seven. The Dragons were now just half a game out of first place. Yet after Matsumoto's stellar performance, they went into a tailspin, losing four of their next five and then three of the following four. By June 10, Chunichi had fallen into third place, five games behind the Tigers.

As the losses piled up, the media questioned Yonamine's reliance on a rotation. They argued that the Dragons would have won more games if Yonamine had rested his struggling pitchers and only started those who were consistently pitching well. Wally, however, explained that the pennant race is a long-distance event and that he needed to conserve his frontliners. He stuck with the rotation and weathered the slump.

The Dragons recaptured second place in late June, and a six-game winning streak in early July brought Wally's team within two games of the Tigers. But Yomiuri was also making a move. The 1974 Giants were long in the tooth and not the dominating team of the late 1960s. Shigeo Nagashima, now thirty-eight years old, was hitting below .250 for the first time in his career. Masahiko Mori, who had been the starting catcher for fifteen straight seasons, was now thirty-seven and relegated to the bench. Other standouts from the "V-9" era, such as second baseman Shozo Doi, shortstop Yukinobu Kuroe, and outfielder Shigeru Takada, were having poor seasons. Sadaharu Oh, however, carried the sickly offense. He would end up with his second consecutive Triple Crown, hitting .332 with 49 home runs and 107 RBI. Oh and

Yomiuri's outstanding pitching staff, led by ten-year veteran Tsuneo Horiuchi, who was coming off his best season ever with twenty-five wins, made the team a formidable opponent.

Each year in August the national high school baseball tournament is held at Koshien Stadium. Forty-nine prefectural finalists journey to Osaka for the single-elimination competition. The event is Japan's most closely followed sporting event and takes approximately two weeks to complete. During the tournament, the Hanshin Tigers embark on an extended road trip, known as *shi-no-rodo* (Road of Death). The players find the long journey exhausting and their performances often suffer. On August 6, Hanshin began its 1974 Road of Death. They left Osaka in first place, three games in front of the Dragons and three and a half games up on the Giants; they returned on August 26 firmly in third place, five games behind the first-place Giants. They had lost ten of their twelve away games and failed to score a run in the final thirty-five innings of the trip. Meanwhile, Yomiuri had won ten in a row to grab the lead.

August ended with the Giants beating Chunichi 4–1 on a three-run sayonara home run by Toshio Yanagida off Hoshino at Korakuen Stadium. The Dragons were now three games behind the seemingly unstoppable Giants. As Yomiuri's next six games were against the league's worst three teams, it looked like they would soon wrap up their tenth straight pennant. Yet, just as the Giants seized first place during Hanshin's losing streak, a slump of their own knocked them out. They dropped five of six to the Swallows, Whales, and Carp, as Chunichi went on a seven-game winning streak. On September 3, Yukio Iida hit a pinch-hit grand slam in the bottom of the ninth to give the Dragons a dramatic come-from-behind victory over the Carp and move them into a tie for first place. Four days later, a grand slam by Yasunori Oshima propelled the Dragons over the Whales and gave them a one-and-a-half-game lead over the Giants. By the time the Giants traveled to Nagoya on September 28 for a three-game series, the Dragons had stretched their lead to five games.

Tsuneo Horiuchi and Yukiharu Shibuya faced off in the Saturday

night series opener. Sadaharu Oh homered as the Giants went out to
a quick 4–0 lead, but Chunichi battled back to knock out Horiuchi
and tie the score in the fourth. The game eventually ended in a 6–6
tie as the slugfest went past the allotted time. The next afternoon, the
Dragons sat in the clubhouse wondering who the opposing pitcher
would be. Like many Japanese managers, Kawakami kept the identity
of his starter secret until the lineup cards were exchanged prior to the
game. This strategy was designed to keep the opposing manager from
tailoring his lineup against a specific starter. Gene Martin recalls, "We
were going, 'Maybe it will be this guy, or maybe that guy.' Well, I'll
be darned if Horiuchi didn't come out and start the game. I kid you
not. He never pitched well after that. I mean never again." That afternoon, however, Horiuchi pitched brilliantly. He surrendered just six
hits during the complete-game win. But Martin was right. It would be
Horiuchi's last good year. After being one of the league's most dominant pitchers for nine seasons, Horiuchi lost eighteen games in 1975,
and his ERA remained above 3.50 for the next nine seasons.

Yomiuri also won the third game of the series to pull within three
games of the Dragons. The Giants returned home to Tokyo and won
six of their next eight. Still, they could not catch Chunichi. As pennant fever had seized Nagoya, the Dragons were determined to win
and fought hard in each game, often coming from behind to win crucial contests.

"My players had never won the pennant before," says Yonamine.
"They had no experience in being in a pennant race. I told them in
the meetings, 'Fight! Fight! If anybody is in your way, knock them
down!' Especially when the Giants were in town, the players got really nervous. I told them, 'Don't be afraid of the Giants. You are just
as good.' I wanted them to realize that the Giants were not the Giants
of five years before. With Nagashima no longer much of a threat, we
could pitch around Oh. When we played the Giants, I would sometimes stand right at the edge of the dugout and yell to my pitcher,
'Bean him! Bean him!' I wasn't actually calling for the pitcher to hit
the batter, but I wanted the Giants to hear me so that they wouldn't

get comfortable at the plate and also know that if they hit us, that we would pay them back. Hoshino was a big help because he wasn't afraid to throw inside, right below the chin."

With a week to go, the pennant race was still undecided, but Chunichi had an edge. The Dragons needed to win three of their remaining five games, while Yomiuri had to win all three of their final games and have the Dragons lose at least three. To heighten the drama, the two teams would play a doubleheader against each other on the last day of the season.

The Dragons reduced their magic number to two by tying Yakult on October 11 and met the Taiyo Whales the following day for a doubleheader at Nagoya Stadium. A sellout crowd watched Yukitsura Matsumoto scatter ten hits and win his twentieth game as the Dragons easily defeated the Whales 9–2 in the opener. Wally turned to Hoshino in the nightcap with the pennant on the line. Hoshino pitched brilliantly. He held the Whales scoreless through the first five innings as the Dragons built a 3–0 lead. The Whales scored one in the top of the sixth but in the bottom half of the inning Kinji Shimatani and Hiroaki Inoue each homered to give Chunichi a 6–1 lead.

As the game progressed, the Chunichi fans became louder and louder until the noise was deafening. With two outs in the top of the ninth, Wally removed his eyeglasses and handed them to the traveling secretary so that they wouldn't get lost in the celebration. Seconds later, Daisuke Yamashita connected with a Hoshino fastball and lined it hard above third base. Kinji Shimatani leapt high into the air, stabbing the liner in his outstretched glove. He thrust his other arm toward the sky and ran toward Hoshino with both arms raised in victory. The Dragons' bench stormed the mound with Wally, completely carried away by emotion, leading the pack. As the players mobbed Hoshino, thousands of fans jumped onto the field. Soon, fans, players, and reporters mobbed the infield, jumping in excitement and pounding each others' backs and heads. Reporters holding their cameras aloft tried to photograph the celebration as streamers fell from the upper reaches of the stands behind home plate. The players never had a chance to give Wally his traditional victory toss. Instead, the mob grabbed him, held the skipper prostrate above their heads and tossed him up and down across a sea of fans, players, and reporters. Despite the rough treatment and the realization that crazed strangers, rather than his players, were tossing him, Wally's face bore a huge grin of pure joy.

It took Wally nearly a half an hour to push his way back to the clubhouse as excited fans, desperate to congratulate him, thwarted his progress. The celebration continued inside as the players, howling with delight, began shaking up beer bottles and letting the foam explode into the air. Soon after Yonamine entered and retrieved his eyeglasses, Shimatani ran toward him shaking a bottle, and dumped the foamy beer over his skipper's head. Both laughed hilariously. Just as he recovered from the first attack, another player sneaked up from behind and doused Wally again. His eyes burning from the alcohol, Wally removed his glasses and wiped his face. Nearby, Yukio Iida planted a big kiss on Gene Martin's balding crown as his teammates hugged each other and continued to cover themselves in beer. After a few minutes, Wally excused himself and telephoned Tokyo and California to share the news with his family.

With the victory, the season-ending doubleheader against the Giants had no meaning. Yomiuri had notified the press that Shigeo Nagashima would be honored at the games and at their conclusion would announce his retirement. Fretting that Nagashima's retirement would push their championship off the headlines, Chunichi's management decided to hold the victory parade the day after clinching the pennant even through the Dragons were scheduled to travel to Tokyo that morning. The front office decided to send the reserve players to Tokyo and keep the starters behind for the parade. Wally immediately called his old friend to apologize for not being able to attend his farewell game. "Oh no, don't worry about it," Nagashima replied. "Don't worry about my game, your parade is more important."

Fifty thousand fans crowded the motorcade of open-top cars bearing the Dragons. Wally, wearing a yellow lei around his neck, rode in the first car along with his pitching coach, Sadao Kondo. As confetti floated down from office buildings lining the street, Wally stood in the back seat shaking hands as they were thrust into the car. By the end of the parade his hand was swollen and painful.

The Giants swept the afternoon doubleheader, televised nationally, and true to form, Nagashima homered on the last day of his career. At the end of the day, the third baseman stood alone on the pitcher's mound, a spotlight illuminating him in the growing early evening dusk, and addressed the crowd. He wept freely as he announced his retirement and thanked his fans. The scene, which drew far more attention throughout the country than the Dragons' victory parade, is one of Japanese baseball's most touching and famous moments. Even today, many fans are filled with sadness as they watch rebroadcasts of the speech.

Wally, however, admits, "Even though it was a sad moment, every time I see Nagashima making that speech, I remember the great feeling of beating Kawakami's Giants to win the championship. I won a lot of pennants as a player, but when Shimatani leapt up and caught that last ball, I just couldn't believe the feeling. It was much better than when I was a player."

By sweeping the doubleheader, Yomiuri had won seventy-one games, one more than Chunichi, but they had also lost one more than the Dragons. Yonamine's Dragons had captured the pennant by tying two more games than the Giants, giving them the narrowest possible lead—a .588 winning percentage to the Giants' .587.

The Dragons would face the Lotte Orions in the Japan Series in Nagoya on October 16. Masaichi Kaneda, the former ace left-hander for the Kokutetsu Swallows, now managed Wally's old team. The Orions had won the Pacific League by just half a game over the Hankyu Braves but had swept Hankyu in the newly established Pacific League playoff. Many of Yonamine's former pupils were still on the squad. Michiyo Arito, George Altman, and Hiroyuki Yamazaki hit in the middle of the powerful lineup he helped create.

Just as the series was about to start, Wally received devastating news—Senichi Hoshino would not be available as a starting pitcher. Hoshino had turned his ankle toward the end of the season. Although he had pitched brilliantly in the pennant-clinching game against the Whales, the stress of throwing nine innings had aggravated the injury. Wally had hoped to rely primarily on Hoshino and Matsumoto as starters throughout the series, but now Hoshino would be restricted to limited duty as a reliever.

Hoshino's injury hampered Yonamine throughout the series as Chunichi's starters were ineffective. Matsumoto lasted just two innings in the series opener, gave up four runs in seven and two-thirds innings in Game 3, and pitched only four and one-third innings in Game 6. With Hoshino not able to start, Wally turned to twenty-year-old Takamasa Suzuki, a reliever who only started three games all season, to start Games 2 and 5. Suzuki pitched well but failed to gain a victory. Yet the Dragons' offense kept the series close through tenacity and clutch hitting. Chunichi won the opener as Morimichi Takagi doubled home the tying and winning runs with one out in the bottom of the ninth. They led the second game 5–1 before the injured Hoshino came on in relief in the eighth and promptly gave up four runs to lose. Three home runs gave the Dragons a 5–0 lead and an eventual 5–4 victory in Game 3. But the offense suffered a grievous blow during a 6–3 defeat in Game 4 when Takagi hit a foul ball off his ankle in the fifth inning, although it was not broken as doctors had initially believed, Takagi was forced to sit out Game 5 as Masaaki Kitaru shut out the Dragons 2–0. He returned in the lead-off slot for Game 6 and slapped a sharp single to center in his first at bat.

With the Orions one victory away from winning the series, Yonamine turned to Matsumoto, but once again the ace pitched poorly. After giving up eight hits in just four and a half innings, Wally brought in Hoshino, having now regained much of the strength in his ankle. Hoshino held the Orions scoreless for five innings as the Dragons tied the score at two. In the tenth inning, however, the Orions finally scored an unearned run off Hoshino to win both the game and the series.

Losing the series was certainly a disappointment, but Wally remained proud of his players' perseverance. The media recognized Yonamine's accomplishments with the Manager of the Year Award. They lauded him for his leadership, strategy, and especially his use of the starting pitching rotation. One writer argued, "Yonamine is perhaps the best manager Japan has had in 30 years. The Dragons' organization has the most progressive training methods in the country. He doesn't overwork his players in training—especially the pitchers."

For winning the pennant, Chunichi's board of directors gave the team two rewards. The first was a new clubhouse. The old clubhouse had a filthy old floor, no heat, and no air conditioning. In the spring and fall, steam would come off the players as they left the bath and walked through the cold air to their lockers. In the summer, the humidity was nearly unbearable. The new clubhouse was a modern facility with all the amenities.

The second was a trip to Florida for spring training. Yonamine made arrangements with Joe Brown, Pittsburgh's general manager, for the Dragons to train with the Pirates. The Dragons arrived in March, already in shape from their February camp at Hamamatsu, and played exhibition games against the Pirates and nearby Major League teams. Though everybody knew that the American teams were not yet in top form, Chunichi did well, taking two of three games against Pittsburgh and beating the Chicago White Sox 1–0.

The primary reason for coming to Florida, however, was to study Major League techniques. The players improved their skills while Yonamine and his coaching staff conferred with Pirates' manager Danny Murtaugh on strategy. Based on these discussions, Yonamine and Kondo decided to convert the young and talented Takamasa Suzuki into a late-inning stopper. Previously, they had used Senichi Hoshino as both a stopper and spot starter for important games. By using Suzuki as a stopper, they could make Hoshino a full-time starter and allow their new stopper to concentrate on relief.

Yonamine had high hopes for the 1975 season. In Hoshino and Matsumoto, he now had two ace starters as well as Suzuki in the bullpen. Chunichi had hired outfielder Ron Woods, a six-year Major League veteran, to join their already powerful lineup. To compete with the Dragons, both the Giants and Carp had made significant managerial changes. After the second-place finish in 1974, Tetsuharu Kawakami retired as Yomiuri's manager, and Shigeo Nagashima took the helm. Many reporters and fans expected Nagashima to lead the Giants to another pennant, despite his lack of experience. Japanese teams routinely hire retired stars as managers, believing that their greatness will carry over from the field to the dugout and that their cachet will bring fans to the ballpark. Although most former players coach for a year or two before taking over as manager, Nagashima would not have the luxury of testing his theories and strategies before taking over the most popular and closely watched team in Japan.

The Hiroshima Carp, for their part, tried something completely different. The Carp had finished last for the past three seasons but had a talented young team. Koji Yamamoto, probably the best all-around player in Japan, played center field. He usually hit around .300, averaged 30 home runs per season, stole 15 to 20 bases, and played Gold Glove defense. Their third baseman, Sachio Kinugasa, would eventually break Lou Gehrig's record for consecutive games played and would hit over five hundred home runs. Bookending these young Japanese stars were two proven American power hitters, Gail Hopkins and Richie Scheinblum. Hiroshima had tried a series of former Japanese greats as managers with no success, so they made a radical move and named American Joe Lutz as manager. Lutz had served as a Carp coach in 1974 but did not speak Japanese. Many criticized the appointment, but some saw it as a bold move that would help modernize Japanese baseball.

Neither managerial move paid off, and both the Giants and Carp fell straight to the bottom of the standings. Lutz lasted less than a month. His inability to communicate directly with his players, his continual arguing with umpires, and his attempts to Americanize his team led to a strong rift between the skipper and his players. Deciding that he was not receiving the support he needed from the front office, Lutz resigned and returned to the United States. Almost immediately, the Carp began to win and were soon in the thick of the pennant race.

The Dragons, however, had not been able to take advantage of the Giants' and Carps' early misfortunes and also fell into the second division. In early June, the team righted itself, started playing above .500, and began their ascent through the standings. Suzuki emerged into an outstanding stopper and would lead the Central League with twenty-one saves, more than twice his nearest competitor. Freed from his relief work, Hoshino would win seventeen games and, as expected, teamed with Matsumoto to anchor a strong rotation. By the All-Star break, the Dragons had moved into second place and briefly took first in early August. The Dragons, Carp, and Tigers fought for the title throughout August and September—most days only a game or two separated the three teams in the standings. As the pennant race intensified, the fans became edgy. On September 10 in Hiroshima, when Carp shortstop Toshiyuki Mimura was tagged out at the plate in the bottom of the ninth to end the game and deliver a key victory to the Dragons, angry Carp fans charged the field and rushed into the Dragons dugout, assaulting players left and right. In the melee, they injured Ron Woods and three others before police dispersed the mob and restored order. After that riot, which seemed, in some strange way, to inspire the Carp nine, Hiroshima surged forward during the season's final weeks to capture their first pennant ever. Wally and team had to settle for second place.

The Giants' last place finish was an even bigger story than Hiroshima's first championship. Yomiuri finished twenty-seven games out with a .382 winning percentage—the worst record in franchise history. Without Nagashima to protect Sadaharu Oh, opponents pitched around the great slugger, limiting the damage he could do. For the first time in thirteen years, Oh failed to win the home run crown. The Giants had tried to find suitable protection for Oh by hiring Dave Johnson, a power-hitting infielder, who had played for Earl Weaver's great Baltimore Orioles teams and later the Atlanta Braves. But, as the first American on the Giants since 1962 and the first Caucasian since

Victor Starffin left the team in 1944, Johnson came under constant attack from the media. Unable to adapt to Japanese baseball or the pressure of playing for the Giants, and hampered by a shoulder injury, Johnson floundered at the plate, hitting just .197.

After the '75 season, Yomiuri made significant changes. In four separate trades, they swapped seven players in return for six new faces. The most important addition was Isao Harimoto, the seven-time Pacific League batting champion. Harimoto had a traumatic childhood. A native of Hiroshima, he lost a sister in the atomic bombing. The year before the attack, he had received a severe burn on his right hand, making it difficult for him to grip any object. Harimoto loved baseball, however, and through constant practice overcame the disability to become one of Japan's greatest hitters and the only player to ever reach three thousand hits. Yomiuri hoped that Harimoto, although now thirty-six years old, would offer Oh the protection needed to bring the Giants another pennant.

Chunichi, with the league's most potent attack in '75 and the second-best ERA, made no significant roster changes. Having just missed the pennant in '75, Yonamine believed he had a good chance at the championship in '76. He hired Bart Shirley, the Dragons' *gaijin* shortstop in 1971 and '72, as a coach to help refine the players' skills and tutor them in American-style baseball.

Prior to the start of each season, the Dragons would go to a Buddhist temple to pray for success. The tradition put Yonamine in an awkward position. "As the manager I was supposed to be in front leading the team, but as a Catholic I didn't want to pray to another God. So I asked my head coach to lead the team and I would stay in the back. I would go to the temple to show my respect, but I wouldn't actually pray along with them."

The 1976 season began well for the Dragons, as they captured first place at the end of the second week of play. But things went quickly downhill. Two weeks later, Chunichi fell into fifth with a losing record. The Dragons' once-mighty offense was floundering. The team's batting average fell from the league's best to third best, and they hit

the second-fewest home runs in the league. Several key starters, such
as Yasunori Oshima and Hiroaki Inoue, had poor seasons, while Ron
Woods slumped throughout the spring. Chunichi released Woods
in midseason, leaving them with a serious gap in the lineup. Yet the
Dragons' real problem was pitching. They had the worst ERA in the
league. Hoshino and Matsumoto, who nearly brought Chunichi the
pennant the year before, had terrible years—each had an ERA close to
4.00, over a run higher than the year before.

Mired in fourth place from June onward, Yonamine decided to try
something new. Stealing signs was against the rules of Japanese baseball, but the practice was nonetheless widespread. Tactics ranged from
trying to glimpse the catcher's signals from the coaches' boxes to listening to opponents' strategies with electronic devices planted in the
dugouts. Yonamine had abstained from sign-stealing during his first
four years as manager but now figured that since other teams were doing it, he should try as well. His plan was simple. Wally stationed two
coaches in center field. One used binoculars to steal signs from the
catcher, the other stayed inside the scoreboard. When the first coach
saw the sign for a curve ball, he would tell the second coach, who
would tip off the batter by shaking the "D" (which stood for Dragons)
on the scoreboard. If the "D" remained still, batters knew that a fastball was coming. "What's amazing," notes Wally, "is that when you do
something right out in the open like that, nobody notices." Wally tried
the tactic for a couple of weeks before abandoning the idea. Knowing
what type of pitch was coming did not help the Dragons win more
games. In fact, the signals ended up confusing the hitters and caused
them to hit worse.

The Dragons never recovered and finished fourth, twenty-one and
a half games behind the Giants. Yomiuri's roster moves had paid off
as Harimoto hit .355 with 22 home runs and Dave Johnson rebounded
from his miserable first year to hit .275 with 26 homers.

Prior to the start of the 1977 season, a newspaper contacted Jane and
asked for an interview. Jane emphatically told them that she would

not discuss baseball because that was Wally's occupation, not hers. "No, no," the reporter told her. "We are doing a story on weddings and we want to interview you because it's your twenty-fifth wedding anniversary." "Okay," she responded. Three weeks into the season, the article appeared under the title, "Chunichi will take the championship, I should know because I've been married to him for twenty-five years." Jane was furious. There is a deep-rooted superstition in Japanese baseball that is bad luck to say that you will win the pennant. "How am I going to face Wally?" she thought. When Wally telephoned from Hiroshima that night, Jane reluctantly asked him, "Did you hear about the newspaper article?"

"Yeah," Wally responded with surprising enthusiasm. "The club president was really happy! He came all the way down to Hiroshima to tell the team, 'That's the way you guys should be feeling, just like Mrs. Yonamine!'"

Although the Dragons really needed pitching, Chunichi's front office decided that another strong bat could propel them back into the pennant race. In a major coup, they were able to sign Willie Davis, a bona fide Major League star. Davis had played for the Los Angeles Dodgers for fourteen seasons as well as four other clubs at the end of his career. He was a former All-Star with postseason experience and 2,561 career hits. He also possessed blazing speed—something the Dragons lacked. Although Davis was nearly thirty-seven years old, he had played in 132 games the previous season with the San Diego Padres, hitting .268 with five home runs and ten triples. The Dragons felt that his experience, speed, and hitting would bring potent dimensions to their lineup.

Davis came to Japan enthusiastically. He had recently become a follower of the Soka Gakkai Nichiren Buddhist sect and embraced the chance to continue his baseball career in a country where the sect emerged. Wally was excited by the possibilities Davis would give him. With Davis's speed, he could be more aggressive—stealing bases and using the hit and run more. Little did he know that his new weapon would be among his greatest challenges as a manager.

Although friendly and outgoing, Davis could not fit in with his Japanese teammates. He inadvertently managed to upset his teammates by continually defying cultural norms. Soon after he joined the team, Davis forgot his lessons in bathing etiquette. In a Japanese communal bath, individuals wash with soap and rinse before entering the tub. Davis finished his afternoon running early and went into the clubhouse before his Japanese teammates. "We had a seven-hundred-gallon stainless steel bathtub in the clubhouse," Gene Martin remembers, "and Willie just dove right in! He didn't wash off or anything. He just dove right in and started soaping up! Boy, the Japanese went nuts!" The players sought out Yonamine and explained what Davis had done. Wally called him over and explained how to use the bath. Davis apologized and said that he understood. But the next day, Davis went into the tub with his slippers on. Once again the Japanese would not enter the fouled tub and complained to Yonamine. "Oh man," Wally exclaimed in exasperation as he explained this breach of etiquette to Davis.

Davis pounded Japanese pitching. "One time, he hit a ball to the right-field fence," Yonamine remembers, "and it ricocheted off the wall. He started running and when he ran, boy could he run. He went to first, and then to second and third, and he was coming around third base so damn fast that I didn't want to stop him, so I sent him in. He was safe easily with an inside-the-park home run."

Davis, however, would occasionally decide not to play. "Willie would come to the ballpark," Martin recalls, "and say, 'I don't feel like playing,' and go home! Other times, he would show up at the ballpark five minutes before game time, put on his uniform, and walk out onto the field with his shoes off."

At one point, Davis slumped at the plate for a few games so Yonamine decided to rest him. When told that he would not start, Davis looked annoyed but said nothing. Partway through the game, Chunichi's center fielder became injured. Wally looked down his bench for Davis but he was nowhere to be seen. "Where's Davis-san?" he asked. "In the bullpen," his players responded. Yonamine grabbed the dugout phone and called the bullpen.

"Willie, you're going in."

"No. No, I'm not playing," Davis told his manager.

"What do you mean?"

"I didn't like the way you talked to me." Frustrated, Wally slammed down the phone. It was not the time to comfort a bruised ego.

The next morning, however, Yonamine called him into his office. "Look Willie, why didn't you play yesterday?"

"I didn't like the way you spoke to me," the star answered.

"What do you mean?"

"You have to ask me nicely if I want to play."

Holding back an exasperated sigh, Wally said, "No problem."

"I realized then that I couldn't give him a rough time or he would just quit on me. So I started spending a lot of time with him. At night, he'd sit alone at the hotel restaurants so I began joining him, for two hours every night, just talking to him because I didn't want him to get out of line."

Davis also annoyed his teammates with boisterous comments from the bench and his flamboyant dress. Instead of donning the requisite jacket and tie when the team traveled, Davis would sport one of his brightly-colored designer copies of his Chunichi training suit. Yet, ironically it was his devotion to his Japanese-born religion that upset the team the most. Following the teachings of Soka Gakkai, Davis continually chanted *Namu Myoho renge-kyo, namu Myoho renge-kyo, namu Myoho renge-kyo*. He chanted on the team bus, in the locker room, in the on-deck circle, and in his hotel room. On road trips, "he would keep you up all night with this chanting from the room next to you," Martin complained. The Japanese players soon had enough. Morimichi Takagi, the captain, approached Yonamine and begged him to get Davis to stop. "It sounds like we are going to a funeral," Takagi explained. Once again, Wally spoke to the quirky outfielder about his behavior. "I'm just praying that nobody gets hurt," Willie explained. He tried to be quieter but the chanting, which was important to him, continued.

By August, Davis was hitting over .300 with twenty-five home runs in less than three hundred at bats, but Chunichi was in fifth place, well out of the pennant race. The team was floundering when the veteran crashed into an outfield wall and broke his wrist. The injury sidelined Davis for the rest of the season. Almost immediately, the Dragons began to win. Over the final two months, Chunichi had the best record in the league and finished in third place, just half a game out of second.

Many thought that the turnaround stemmed from Davis's absence. Although he had put up impressive offensive numbers, his behavior disrupted team harmony—what Robert Whiting terms *wa*—thus causing more problems than his production could overcome. Without Davis, the Japanese relaxed and functioned together as a team. Gene Martin adds, "Things really livened up when Willie was there, but he wasn't good for the team. They didn't care for him at all. He was a real thorn in Wally's side."

The turnaround, however, happened too late in the season to save Wally. During the August 2–4 trip to Hiroshima, the club's president paid Yonamine a surprise visit. Takeo Koyama, who had hired Wally six years earlier, explained that the board of directors had decided not to retain him as manager for the following season. Yonamine understood. Koyama was under a lot of pressure to win the championship, and the Dragons were floundering in fifth place. They had to fire somebody. The decision was supposed to be a secret but somehow the players found out. Instead of giving up, Wally's players rallied behind him and tried to save his job. They worked extra hard, began to win, and finished in third, only half a game away from second place. But Chunichi's board of directors did not reconsider.

After the last game, the players and writers gathered in a back room for Yonamine's sayonara speech. "I kept on telling myself, 'I'm not going to cry. I'm not going to cry.' I tried to be really strong during my speech, but I looked up into the corner and there was Morimichi Takagi and Senichi Hoshino, those two stubborn, tough, gutsy guys, crying like babies! When I saw them crying, I lost control. But thank God they let me go when they did. I went home and had a thorough physical. The doctor told me, 'You're lucky you got fired because you were about to get ulcers.' So, it was a good time for me to leave the Dragons!" Predictably, Wally did not spend time relaxing, but instead broke tradition again as he moved into the next stage of his career.

20

Suketto

Japanese often call foreign players *gaijin suketto* (foreign helpers). The role is explicit—to support their Japanese teammates. Ironically, they are also expected to be among the most productive members of the squad and are intensely criticized if they fail to meet expectations. Indeed, they are often blamed for a team's failure even when they play well. Successful *gaijin suketto* should not expect much praise. Their contributions are usually downplayed and sometimes even ignored by both the media and their team's front office. The 1980s were an especially difficult time for these helpers. Japanese economic success led to increased tension between Japan and the United States and a rise in ethnocentrism. *Gaijin* players were hired begrudgingly amid calls from the media and even the commissioner's office to bar them from baseball altogether.

After leading the Dragons to their first pennant in twenty years, producing five winning seasons, and posting a .526 winning percentage, Yonamine was once again a *gaijin suketto*. He would spend the next ten years helping managers capture championships but never again led a team himself. But Wally rarely complained. He coached for three of the most fascinating managers of the decade, imparting his knowledge to a new generation of Japanese players.

Soon after Wally returned to Tokyo in October 1978, Shigeo Nagashima asked him to join the Giants as a coach. He accepted without hesitation although it was unusual for an ousted manager to return the following season as a coach for another team. Most men were too proud to accept the lower position after managing—at least until a number of years had passed. Yonamine's decision surprised many within Japanese baseball and the media, but the supposed loss of face did not worry him. "I loved the game so I wanted to remain in baseball. I also wanted to share my knowledge with the younger players. I put my pride aside and was able to listen to others."

Nagashima appointed Yonamine the outfield and base-running coach and also used him as the third base coach. Wally was pleased to be back with the Giants and working closely with Nagashima. The coaching staff included several old friends. Hirofumi Naito, his one-time roommate, and Tadashi Iwamoto were there, as was his old rival Shigeru Sugishita, the former Dragons ace. Wally also rejoined Ryozo Kotoh of *Sports Hochi*. Kotoh had been promoted a couple of years earlier and was now covering the Giants. It was nice to be among his old friends again, but more importantly Wally could now live at home. All three children were living in California. Amy had married Theodore Roper, who was studying to become an attorney, in 1977. Wallis would be married to her college boyfriend Dennis Yamamoto within a year. Unbeknownst to the Yonamines, Dennis' father was friendly with Wally's old friend from San Francisco Bill Mizuno: Mizuno received a wedding invitation from both the bride's and groom's parents. Paul was enrolled at the University of San Francisco. Occasionally, the children would return to Tokyo during the summer months. Now that he was with the Giants and also relieved of the duties of running a baseball club, Wally spent more time with his family during the height of the baseball season.

Yomiuri's 1979 season opened in Nagoya, and Yonamine coached third base. As he stood there in the Giants uniform, Dragons fans began slinging insults at Wally. "Why, Yonamine," others asked in bewilderment, "Why would you wear the Giants' uniform?" Many fans were unaware that Chunichi had fired Wally. The official announcement had been carefully worded to suggest that Wally had left on his own accord. Most fans were therefore under the impression that he had quit managing the Dragons to become a Yomiuri coach.

As a manager, Nagashima could inspire his players. John Sipin, a former San Diego Padre who played with the Giants from 1978 to

1980 after five years with the Taiyo Whales, recalls, "Nagashima was a great leader. He was a legend and had extremely high energy. Unlike most managers, he would not go into the dugout and sit down. He was always on the field, hitting fly balls or ground balls." Nagashima especially liked aggressive players who showed "fighting spirit" and rewarded them with compliments and playing time. His enthusiasm was infectious and most of his players trained and played hard for him.

Nagashima's ability as a strategist, however, did not match his enthusiasm. He rarely played percentage baseball. Instead, he relied on a bizarre combination of traditional conservative Japanese baseball tactics and irrational hunches. After a lead-off hitter reached base, Nagashima routinely used the second batter to bunt the runner over, even when the Giants trailed by large margins. He rarely employed pinch runners, even when a slow catcher representing the tying run stood on second in the late innings. He bunched his like-handed hitters together in the lineup, instead of interspersing lefties with righties. Most importantly, he did not stick to a steady pitching rotation. He often started pitchers who were throwing well on short rest and continually used starters in relief. Nagashima was also intolerant of pitching mistakes and routinely pulled pitchers at the first sign of trouble.

Yet, the Giants' talent and Nagashima's charismatic leadership made up for his tactical blunders. Yomiuri won back-to-back pennants in 1976 and '77, albeit losing two consecutive Japan Series to the Hankyu Braves. In Wally's first year as coach, they nearly captured the pennant again, finishing just three games behind the Yakult Swallows. By '79, however, the Giants lineup was beginning to show its age. Six of the eight starting position players were over thirty years old. All-Star center fielder Isao Shibata was thirty-five, while superstars Sadaharu Oh and Isao Harimoto were now thirty-eight. Bothered by a bad back, Harimoto sat out much of the season and hit just .263 when he was in the lineup. The team's batting average fell eleven points from the previous year, and they finished fifth in the division in runs scored. With the poor offense, Yomiuri finished in fifth place with a .483 winning percentage. It was just the third losing record in franchise history, and Nagashima was responsible for two of them. Despite his popularity with the fans and players, there was a growing feeling that his days as the Giants' manager might be numbered.

That fall, instead of playing the usual series of exhibition games, known as the Aki Riigu, or Fall League, Nagashima put the team through a grueling fall camp on the Izu peninsula, some one hundred miles south of Tokyo. It lasted nearly a month and featured a dawn-to-dusk regimen replete with thousand fungo drills, endless batting swings, marathon runs, nighttime workouts, baseball lectures, and a sprinkling of physical abuse. Billed as the "Izu Hell Camp" by the Japanese press, it was the first autumn training camp in the postwar history of pro ball.

The following summer, Nagashima began to phase out his older stars and give his prospects much-needed playing time. Discounting Oh and the *gaijin* Roy White, all of the starting position players in 1980 were under twenty-nine and averaged just twenty-five years old. The pitching staff was also full of talented young arms. The top three, Suguru Egawa, Takashi Nishimoto, and Shoji Sadaoka, were between twenty-three and twenty-four years old. The team showed improvement, finishing in third place, one game above .500, but fourteen games behind the champion Hiroshima Carp, a result which pleased Nagashima, if not those in the front office. Near the end of the season, Nagashima and Yonamine went to the Tamagawa training facility. As they watched the impressive, rapidly maturing squad of players practice, Nagashima told Wally, "Next year, we're going to win the championship." The Hawaiian agreed.

Yet Nagashima never had the chance to lead his new team to the title. Soon after the 1980 season, the Yomiuri brain trust, increasingly critical of some of Nagashima's bizarre on-field moves, forced him to resign and replaced him with Motoshi Fujita, the ace of the 1957–59 teams. Following Japanese custom, Yonamine resigned his coaching position as well. Nagashima's predictions were correct. Fujita won the pennant by a comfortable six games. Egawa finished at 20–4, and up-and-coming third baseman Kiyoshi Nakahata hit .322. Nakahata, who would go on to become team captain, often cited that Izu fall camp for making him into a better player. From that time on, other managers began copying Nagashima's autumn camps.

Yonamine did not remain unemployed for long. Don Blasingame, who had just been appointed the Nankai Hawks' new manager, offered Wally the head coach position. Wally happily accepted. After Wally, and fellow Hawaiians Bozo Wakabayashi and Kaiser Tanaka, Blasingame had remained in Japanese baseball longer than any other American. He had first visited Japan in 1958 as a member of the touring St. Louis Cardinals. "Blazer" led the Cards with a .385 batting average against the Japanese All-Stars that included Yonamine and Nagashima. Two years later, he was back again as a member of the touring San Francisco Giants. He enjoyed his visits, but the thought of playing in the Japanese leagues never crossed his mind until Daryl Spencer of the Hankyu Braves told him that the Nankai Hawks were looking for an American second baseman in the fall of 1966. Blasingame decided to give Japan a try. He played three seasons for the Hawks, making the Pacific League Best Nine twice. When the Hawks' superstar catcher Katsuya Nomura became a playing manager in 1970, he asked Blasingame to become his head coach. The American agreed and stayed with the Hawks for another eight seasons. Nomura left the Hawks in 1978, and Blazer coached for the Hiroshima Carp for a season before the Hanshin Tigers bravely hired him as their manager in 1979.

Once in charge, Blasingame tried to Americanize the Tigers. He attempted to cut down practice time and make the time on the field more efficient. His efforts, however, were doomed to failure. "The Japanese spend long hours at work to show their dedication to their jobs and respect and appreciation for their employers," Blasingame observed. "That has spilled over into baseball, so they spent long hours practicing. I decided that I wasn't going to step on their culture. Things that didn't particularly pertain to winning or losing, I left alone. But once the game started, I played the game my way."

The Tigers improved quickly under Blasingame's direction. After finishing last in 1978, thirty and a half games out of first place, they won twenty more games in '79 and finished fourth, just eight games out of first and only two games away from second place. Expectations were high for 1980, as the Tigers had drafted Akinobu Okada, the superstar of the Big Six University League. Yet rather than being a savior, Okada was Blasingame's undoing. Okada was a talented third baseman, but the Tigers already had a superstar at third base named Masayuki Kakefu, who had hit .327 with forty-eight home runs in '79. Blasingame decided to convert Okada into a second baseman, but the transition was slow. He did not want to undermine Okada's confidence by playing him at a new position before he was ready. Accordingly, the American manager picked up Dave Hilton from the Yakult Swallows to play second in the meantime. The Hanshin fans, media, and even his front office were outraged. They longed to watch the Okada and hoped that the youngster would lead the Tigers to the pennant. Instead, the *gaijin* manager had brought in another foreigner and relegated their promising rookie to the bench. Under the intense pressure, Hilton cracked and went into a prolonged slump. In May, Blasingame released Hilton and resigned as manager.

After decades as one of the top teams in the Pacific League, the Nankai Hawks had finished in fifth or sixth place from 1978 to 1980. To help rebuild the team, Nankai hired Blasingame for the 1981 season. He immediately brought in Wally as his head coach and Barney Schultz, a former Major League hurler, as his pitching coach. The team was not talented, but with American-style managing and coaching they could be made respectable. Blasingame gave Wally free rein on teaching the fundamentals of hitting and fielding, while Schultz tried to put the woeful pitching staff on an American-style rotation. At the time, Japanese pitchers threw roughly a hundred practice pitches each day, whereas American pitchers would rest for two days after a start before practicing again. Throwing every day had its advantages—supposedly it helped the Japanese develop their famous pinpoint control—but all too often Japanese pitchers damaged their arms through overuse. Schultz tried to conserve his pitchers' arms by telling them not to throw for the first two days following a start, but the players sneaked down to the farm team's training facility and threw their hundred pitches behind their American manager's and coaches' backs. Eventually, the Americans had to concede defeat and let the pitchers train in the Japanese style.

"I really enjoyed working with Don because he was different from the Japanese managers," Wally remembers. "There were no two-hour meetings. He didn't want to fool around. He just took charge. He was the best manager that I coached for and was such a nice guy." Blasingame and his American coaches moved the team out of the cellar in 1981 as the Hawks won five more games than they had the previous season, but they still had a losing record and finished firmly in fifth place.

In the off-season, Blasingame wanted to make some trades and made several suggestions to the Hawks' management, but no deals were forthcoming. The team won the same number of games in 1982 as they had the year before, but this time finished last. Nankai management concluded that their American manager and coaches would not be able to turn the team around and dismissed them.

Within a month, Wally's old teammate Tatsuro Hirooka, the Giants' shortstop from 1954 to 1965, offered him a job on the Seibu Lions' coaching staff. Wally would be the team's outfield and base-running coach as well as the batting instructor for Seibu's farm team. Known as the Iron Shogun, Hirooka was the most controversial manager in Japanese baseball in the postwar era. His prickly personality, control over his players' behavior on and off the field, and demanding workouts made him both the most disliked and successful manager since Kawakami's V-9 Giants.

Like Yonamine, Hirooka believed that championship teams were built on baseball fundamentals, practice, and sound strategy. Hirooka had played for Kawakami's Giants for six seasons, but the two never got along, and Hirooka left the Giants upon retirement. After coaching for Hiroshima, Hirooka went to the United States to study how the game was played in America. He instituted many of the things he learned when he became manager of the Yakult Swallows in 1976. One year after taking control of the perennial losers, Hirooka guided them to second place and won the pennant the following year.

Prior to the 1979 season, hotel magnate Yoshiaki Tsutsumi purchased the Fukuoka Crown Lighter Lions (formerly the Nishitetsu Lions), renamed them the Seibu Lions, and moved the franchise to the suburbs of Tokyo. Determined to build the Lions into an enterprise that would rival the Yomiuri Giants, both on the field and in profits, Tsutsumi began rebuilding the team. In 1982, he brought in Hirooka as manager.

"When I went to Seibu, they were a veteran team," Hirooka relates. "They had the skills but had never won. To win they had to get in good shape, so I started off with their diet. I tried to get them to eat unpolished rice, vegetables, and less meat. The mass media distorted what I tried to do. For example, they claimed that I would not allow the players to eat meat at all, which was untrue. The players didn't accept the new diet easily and we had to reach some compromises. For example, I eventually had to serve a mixture of unpolished and polished rice."

Hirooka also set a strict eleven o'clock curfew. "I tried to teach them that sleep and diet would help them stay in good condition without getting hurt," he noted. But many players bristled at the loss of liberty. American Terry Whitfield complained, "After the game was over, there would be our postgame meeting and we would eat our dinner. So it's already eleven o'clock. There's no time. I feel that as adults, as grown men, we should be able to have some time of our own."

On the training grounds, Hirooka pushed his players hard—even by Japanese standards. The team routinely practiced for three hours under the hot afternoon sun before night games. If driving rain cancelled a game, the team practiced indoors instead.

Hirooka also rarely praised his players. He constantly focused on negatives. In the nightly postgame meetings, he went over each mistake and chastised the responsible players, whether or not the Lions had won the game. Even more offensive to some players, Hirooka openly criticized his players to members of the media.

"The funny thing is that Hirooka united the team," says the team's former third baseman Steve Ontiveros, "because everybody disliked him to some extent. Often in Japan, Japanese and foreign players practice differently, which causes tension between the groups. But under Hirooka, we were all doing the same things and were all bitching about it to each other."

Under his austere leadership, Hirooka took the Lions to the pennant and Japan Series title in his first year as manager. When Yonamine became available after the 1982 season, Hirooka wasted little time signing the Hawaiian to a two-year contract. "If he had been free, I would have hired Wally right away to teach the Lions real baseball." The two men's personalities couldn't be more different. In contrast to Wally's friendly, happy-go-lucky demeanor, Hirooka rarely smiled and didn't laugh. He was extremely uptight with a regal bearing. Yet, the manager and new coach respected each other and got along well. Both shared a passion for baseball and an understanding of the finer points of the game. "Hirooka was a good baseball manger," Wally proclaims. "He knew his fundamentals pretty well. He had studied hitting and although he wasn't a good hitter himself, he was a great teacher. He would spend hours working out with the guys. A lot of players didn't like him because he controlled everything about their lives, but they also respected him. On the playing field, he was the boss."

Wally enthusiastically taught his new pupils the finer points of base running and playing the outfield. Through constant repetition during Hirooka's grueling practices, the Seibu players became proficient in all aspects of the game. Former Yankee and Yomiuri Giant Roy White explained that Seibu "was like watching a well-oiled, smoothly working machine in operation. They were good at using the delayed steal and the push bunt—small things that gave them the edge." During Wally's first season with Seibu, the Lions dominated the Pacific League, winning the championship by seventeen games. They led the league in batting, home runs, ERA, and fewest errors committed.

In the second year of Yonamine's contract, the Lions' head coach, Masahiko Mori, and fellow coach Akihito Kondo began acting strangely. Both refused to acknowledge Yonamine's presence. They did not return salutations and would walk by Wally as if he did not exist. During coaches' meetings with Hirooka, Mori and Kondo directed their comments toward their manager and never spoke directly with Yonamine. As a former manager and a natural teacher, Yonamine had taken charge of instructing the players on the finer points of the game. Mori had spent nearly twenty years as the Giants' catcher and understood baseball strategy well but was a poor teacher of baseball fundamentals. He had difficulty spotting mistakes in technique and even more trouble helping players improve their game. He undoubtedly resented Wally's teaching skill and the manner in which the Hawaiian took control during practice. Perhaps Mori felt that his position as head coach or future manager was at stake.

Not surprisingly, Wally found Mori and Kondo's behavior infuriating. But true to his personality, he did not confront his antagonists but instead modified his own behavior. He began to step back from teaching the players. Soon Wally was acting more like an American coach, waiting for players to ask for advice rather than taking control and instructing his charges. Yonamine now sees this as a mistake. In 2004, he apologized to Hirooka, "you hired me to teach the players fundamentals, but because of Mori and Kondo, I backed off and didn't do what you asked me to and for that I am sorry." According to Steve Ontiveros, the tension between the coaches did not disrupt the team. Yet Seibu finished in third place, fourteen and a half games behind the Hankyu Braves. It was the only season between 1982 and 1988 when Seibu would not win the pennant.

After the 1984 season, Wally's contract with Seibu expired. Shigeru Takada, whom Yonamine had coached while with the Giants in 1979 and '80, had just been named the Nippon Ham Fighters manager and asked Wally to become his head coach. Although Seibu would probably offer him a contract extension, Wally decided that his relationship with Mori and Kondo was interfering with his effectiveness and making Seibu an unpleasant place to coach. Accordingly, Yonamine accepted the offer to coach for Nippon Ham.

As a player, Takada was aggressive on the base paths, stealing two hundred bases during his career. He wanted to build a team around speed, but the Fighters' front office did not procure the appropriate players. Prior to the seasonal amateur draft, Takada would tell the front office whom he wanted but they ignored his requests. As a result, Takada and Yonamine were unable to turn Nippon Ham into a strong team. They finished fifth twice before capturing third place with a winning record in 1987. In 1988, however, the team dipped under .500 again and Takada resigned as manager. Following custom, Wally also turned in his resignation.

Unemployed once again, Yonamine was considering his options for the upcoming season when his old friend Ryozo Kotoh offered him some advice. "You had better retire and get out of uniform now," Kotoh began. "To be eligible for the Hall of Fame, you have to be out of uniform for five years. You should retire now while there are sportswriters who still remember your playing career because you need to be on seventy-five percent of the ballots to make it." Wally thought about it. Although he wished to stay in baseball and continue coaching, he wanted to be in the Hall of Fame. He was now sixty-three years old and had been in uniform for thirty-eight years. Perhaps it was time to retire.

21
Hall of Fame

It was hot—very hot. We bought ice cream to cool off, but it melted faster than we could eat it, turning our hands sticky. Napkins weren't common at Seibu Stadium (they were hard to find throughout Japan for that matter), so we tried to wipe off the mess with an old newspaper. I sat next to my wife and our friend Masanori "Max" Ninomiya at the top of the left-field stands waiting for the 1994 All-Star game to begin. Seibu Stadium is now covered with a dome, but in July 1994 it was an idyllic field nestled in a hollow surrounded by trees. The stadium fit into the landscape, with the uppermost seats at ground level and the playing field far below at the bottom of the depression.

Prior to the game, a voice announced that the newest members of the Japanese Baseball Hall of Fame would be inducted in a pregame ceremony. I had been to the Hall of Fame in the basement of the Tokyo Dome many times to view the relics of past Japanese greats and was thrilled to watch the ceremony. First they honored Tomoo Hirooka, who helped make baseball an Olympic sport. Next came Sadaharu Oh, one of my favorite players. Finally, they introduced Wally Yonamine.

I knew of Yonamine from Robert Whiting's books *The Chrysanthemum and the Bat* and *You Gotta Have Wa* as well as from old *menko* baseball cards. I clapped my still-sticky hands and cheered. As an American living in Japan, I naturally empathized with Wally. He, like I, was thrust into a foreign culture without knowing the language. Even the simplest tasks could become difficult. I was quite proud, for example, of purchasing these tickets from a hard-to-find ticket outlet in the basement of the Seibu Department Store. It took me an hour to locate the outlet and an awkward conversation in broken Japanese punctuated with hand signals to pick out the seats, but the game would be worth it. At that point, I had never spoken to a professional ballplayer for longer than it took to ask for an autograph. The idea that ten years later I would know Wally Yonamine well and write his biography would have been laughable.

As they announced his name, Yonamine left an office near the stadium entrance behind home plate and descended the long flight of steps to the field. "What a fantastic feeling to have the entire crowd of twenty-five thousand focus on you as you walk down those steps," he would say later. Wearing a dark suit and tie that contrasted with his silver hair and a large red chrysanthemum in his lapel, he approached the pitcher's mound and took his place next to a pedestal displaying his Hall of Fame plaque. As he stood listening to the ceremony, he thought about his parents. They had worked hard to scratch out a living and raise his family on the sugar plantation. They had taught him dedication, perseverance, and compassion. He had always been proud of them and missed them dearly since they passed away. He wished that they could have seen this day. Blinking back tears, Wally stepped forward to receive his award.

After bowing to the presenter and returning to his position, Wally's thoughts turned to his family. Without Jane, he would not have made it this far. She allowed him to concentrate on baseball by taking care of the family. She fixed things around the house so that he wouldn't injure himself and even pitched to him from across the living room to improve his timing. Her business sense also allowed the family to live comfortably since he had retired. Their children had grown into wonderful people. Amy and Wallis were both living in California with families of their own, while Paul remained in Tokyo. He now had five grandchildren: T.J., Lesley Ann, Ryan, Lauren, and Bryan. Two more, John and Andrea, would be born in the next two years. He felt truly blessed.

Not everything in the past five years had been easy, however. In late 1991, Amy developed leukemia. Paul provided his sister with his bone marrow, and Amy received the transplant in February 1992. Both Wally and Jane relocated to California during the months following the operation. Wally, who had attended church on Sundays, began attending mass each morning—a practice that he continues to this day. Amy's body accepted the transplant and she recovered relatively quickly. By June she could function well on her own, and Wally and Jane returned home. The disease had been conquered.

The ceremony concluded and Yonamine climbed the steps to re-join his family. Jane and Paul were there, but Amy and Wallis were in California, unable to make the trip. Wally sat back and watched the game. A young fireballer named Hideki Irabu took the mound for the Pacific League and threw a 98.8 mile per hour fastball past another future New York Yankee, Hideki Matsui.

The country and the game had changed so much since Yonamine first arrived forty-three years ago. In 1951 Japan was still recovering from the war. It was poor, dirty, and occupied by a foreign army. Wally remembered the inedible food, the absence of public sewers in parts of Osaka, and the lack of air conditioning in the summer and heat in the winter. Today, Japan was an economic powerhouse, fastidiously clean in most places, and at the forefront of technology.

The players had it much easier now. There was no more sleeping on the floors of third-class trains or staying in run-down inns. Every-thing was now first class: the nicest forms of transportation, hotels, and restaurants. And, of course, they made a lot more money. Had Yo-namine played today, he would have made millions each season. Wally was envious—but only to a degree. Actually, he reflected, "I'm happy for them. They should be paid what they deserve. As long as they re-alize how lucky they are and play hard." He was especially pleased to see so many Americans in Japan. Over four hundred so far had fol-lowed him over the Pacific Ocean. Each team filled its quota of three foreigners (two position players and one pitcher). But *gaijin* players still faced prejudice. They rarely got endorsements, and just a decade earlier in the mid 1980s, the commissioner of Japanese baseball stated that *gaijin* should be banned. Wally worried that a few prima donna

Americans, who gave their organizations too much trouble, might lead the commissioner to actually enact this ban. He made a point of cautioning the Americans he met, "Play hard and be respectful so that other Americans can come to Japan after you."

The way the Japanese played the game had also changed since the early 1950s. The players were more aggressive now. They broke up double plays and slid hard into bases, but they were still more cautious than Major Leaguers. Japanese rarely went from first to third on a single to right field and almost never bowled over the catcher on a close play at home. Strategy had changed more. Today, managers rarely based their decisions on hunches. Most played percentage baseball, basing their lineups and maneuvers on scouting reports, video analysis, and a myriad of statistics. Many skippers still sacrificed too often and employed the hit and run too little for Wally's taste, but at least all the teams had switched to a true pitching rotation and were using closers. The more adventuresome were even experimenting with setup men after watching Cito Gaston of the Toronto Blue Jays use the strategy so effectively in the 1993 World Series.

A loud noise disrupted Wally's thoughts. Smoke billowed forth from the center-field bleachers. Several Hanshin Tigers fans had set off smoke bombs and had even thrown one on the field. "Well," he mused wryly, "some things never change." At least the Tigers' fans weren't throwing things at him anymore. On the whole, he felt, the fans were better behaved now. They were less rowdy, but noisier. Instead of three male cheerleaders performing on the tops of the dugouts, organized cheering sections with brass bands, drums, and flag bearers packed the outfield stands. They played fight songs or chants for each player as they came to bat. The noise could be deafening, but often had little correlation to action on the field. They could be just as loud with nobody on and one out in the third as with bases loaded and two outs in the ninth.

By the sixth inning, the Pacific League had a 7–1 lead, and the Yonamines got up to leave. It had been an emotional, tiring day. As Wally turned and climbed the stairs toward the exit, a young hurler named Hideo Nomo took the mound. Just as Wally had changed the game forty-three years earlier, within the year Nomo would radically change Japanese baseball.

Nomo was pitching with a sore arm and was disgruntled with his manager, Keishi Suzuki, for overusing him. After the season, he would retire from the Kintetsu Buffaloes and sign with the Los Angeles Dodgers, becoming the first Japanese to play in the U.S. Major Leagues since Masanori Murakami pitched for the San Francisco Giants in 1964 and '65. Nomo would become a sensation—starting the All-Star game for the National League and winning the Rookie of the Year Award. The Tornado's success spurred other Japanese players to follow him to the Majors.

Within ten years, five of the ten pitchers from this All-Star game would leave Japan. Besides Nomo, Irabu would join the Yankees, Masato Yoshii the Mets, Keiichi Yabu the Athletics, and Shingo Takatsu the White Sox. Over ten other pitchers would also jump ship, and in 2001 Ichiro Suzuki would become the first position player to leave Japan for the Majors. He would delight American fans and win both the American League Rookie of the Year and Most Valuable Players Awards. Two other starters in the 1994 All-Star game, outfielders Tsuyoshi Shinjo and Hideki Matsui, would join Ichiro in the Majors. The departures would leave Japanese baseball in a crisis.

"When I was playing and coaching," Yonamine notes, "my dream was to one day see a real World Series between Japan and the United States. But once the stars started to leave for the Major Leagues, I knew it was no longer possible. The quality of Japanese ball has fallen down too far. If you pick one to two stars from each team, like they did for the World Baseball Classic, the Japanese can field a good team. But each franchise has only a few ballplayers at that level so overall the teams drop down to Double-A level. My dream will never happen unless Japanese baseball makes major changes to raise the quality of play. I think the only way they can do this now is by importing more American ballplayers to strengthen the teams."

By 2003 Major League baseball was broadcast daily in Japan, and newspapers started reporting on the games in detail. Millions of Japanese started following the Majors closely, and attendance as well as television ratings for Japanese games plummeted. In an effort to bring back the fans, Japanese baseball instituted interleague play in 2005, created franchises in the northern cities of Sapporo and Sendai, and set up a playoff system in the Pacific League. These initiatives have brought in fans, but the future of the Japanese league still is unclear. Will it become an unofficial minor league, seasoning players until they leave for the Majors? Or will they raise the level of play, becoming a rival of Major League Baseball with the national champions meeting in a true World Series?

Wally Yonamine will turn eighty-three in 2008 and Jane will turn seventy-eight. The couple split their time between their homes in Honolulu and Tokyo. Although Wally is retired, Jane continues to work hard at the pearl shop, which has now grown into one of the most successful pearl retailers in Tokyo. It has seven employees and continues to attract visitors from all over the world for the exquisite jewelry and exemplary customer service. Amy and Wallis operate the California branch, now located in Redondo Beach. Paul and his family live in Tokyo, where he is the president and CEO of Hitachi Consulting.

Wally has spent his retirement quietly helping the causes close to his heart. Despite his fifty-plus years living in Japan, Wally's love for his native land remains strong. He returned to Hawaii every winter during his baseball career and since retiring spends most of his time in Honolulu. When tourism to Hawaii dropped dramatically after the Japanese economic bubble burst in the early '90s, Wally began using his celebrity status and baseball connections to help attract more Japanese tourists. In 1998 Hawaiian Governor Benjamin Cayetano appointed him a "special advisor for sports promotion" at a salary of one dollar per year. At the time of the appointment, Wally stated, "basically I'm donating my services to the state. Hawaii, Japan, and baseball have been so good to me. I'm happy to be able to give something back." They planned to build a $27 million baseball training camp that included six diamonds and a 4,500-seat stadium on 55 acres in the town of Waipahu, approximately 24 miles west of Waikiki. They hoped that the state-of-the-art facility would attract Japanese teams to Hawaii for spring training as well as thousands of Japanese fans. Unfortunately, the governor cancelled the project in late 1999. "I think that was a big mistake," Yonamine concludes, "the complex would have really helped the economy of Hawaii. If two or three Japanese teams were to come for spring training, they could have had exhibition games at the stadium and a lot of Japanese fans would have come over to see them play."

As athletics allowed Yonamine to escape a life of hard labor on Maui sugar plantations, Wally wanted to give Hawaiian children the opportunity to develop their athletic skills. Accordingly, Paul created the Wally Yonamine Foundation in 1990. After a few years, Wally's nephew Dean Yonamine became the organization's director. The foundation's mission is "to promote the youth of Hawaii through athletics." The Yonamines do this through several avenues. They hold clinics throughout the islands to instruct both players and coaches. Often, the foundation pays for former big league stars such as Maury Wills, Mike Fetters, and Kazuhiro Sasaki to come to Hawaii and teach the kids. The foundation also donates money to equip Little League and other community teams that lack the funds for their own equipment. Since 1997 the Yonamines have also donated ten thousand dollars each year to fund the Hawaii state high school baseball tournament. In recognition of this generosity, the Hawaii High School Athletic Association renamed the tournament the Wally Yonamine Foundation State Baseball Championship. In June 2006 the family made an unprecedented two hundred thousand dollar donation to create an endowment for the tournament.

For his charity work and former prowess on the athletic fields, Wally has received many accolades in the past ten years. He is an inaugural inductee in the Hawaiian Sports Hall of Fame, the Hawaiian High School Football Hall of Fame, and The Japanese American Sports Hall of Fame (sponsored by The Japanese Cultural and Community

Center of Northern California). He has also been honored by Major League Baseball for his role in Japanese-American relations, as well as by the San Francisco 49ers. In 2006 the 49ers created the Perry-Yonamine Award to be given annually to a player, youth football coach, and a local company who demonstrate an exceptional commitment to promoting unity with their team and community. The year before, the city of Honolulu included Yonamine among the list of the "100 people who have made long-lasting contributions to Honolulu over its 100-year history."

But the greatest honor came in 1998, when the Japanese government presented Yonamine with one of its highest awards: Zuihôsho, the Order of the Sacred Treasure, Gold Rays with Rosette (fourth class) for "outstanding service and achievements in strengthening the bonds of friendship between Japan and Hawaii." The honor could be bestowed at a lavish ceremony in Tokyo or in Honolulu by the consul-general. Yonamine chose Hawaii. "I want to bring as much attention and positive publicity to Hawaii as I can," he reiterated. "The economy is not good there right now. Tourism is down, especially from the Japanese."

Despite the many honors, not all of the last ten years have been joyous. During a routine physical examination in 2001, Yonamine's doctor discovered evidence of prostate cancer. Further tests confirmed the findings, and Wally began treatment that is still ongoing. Around the same time, Wally went to visit an eye, ear, and nose specialist in Honolulu for a minor problem. After the appointment, Jane asked the doctor to look at a lump she found on her neck. A biopsy revealed that she too had cancer. Jane had the tumor removed immediately and underwent radiation therapy. The cancer was extracted and has not returned.

Typically, Wally and Jane turned their personal hardships into an opportunity to help others. Wally spoke publicly about prostate cancer to promote awareness about early prevention and to convince men to get tested. The couple also donated generously to cancer and leukemia foundations as well as creating the Wally Yonamine Leukemia Research Fund at the Memorial Sloane Kettering Cancer Center in New York.

In an age when professional athletes are reaching new heights of egocentricity and selfishness, Wally Yonamine is refreshing. He remains humble, friendly, and even a little bit shy. "I'm just a boy from Olowalu, Maui. I've never forgotten my roots and where I started. When I was just a teenager with the Plebs club in Maui, our Coach Seke Sasaki taught us not only baseball but also how to be a gentleman on and off the field. These lessons were always on my mind when I played for him, for the 49ers, for the Giants, and even today. People tell me that I'm a living legend and a big star, but inside I don't feel that I'm different from anybody else. I'm just one of the guys—the same person I was growing up. I've been fortunate, so I'm just happy that I can give something back to Hawaii and help others fulfill their dreams."

Wally Yonamine reminds us all how a true sports hero should behave.

Appendix

Wally Kaname Yonamine (bats left, throws left)

Year	Team	G	AB	R	H	2B	3B	HR	RBI	K	BB	SB	AVE
1951	Giants	54	181	47	64	17	5	1	26	18	28	26	.354
1952	Giants	116	474	104	163	33	5	10	53	38	47	38	.344
1953	Giants	104	365	58	112	24	2	6	54	33	57	13	.307
1954	Giants	125	477	93	172	40	6	10	69	56	69	20	.361
1955	Giants	107	424	68	132	22	2	13	65	66	49	10	.311
1956	Giants	123	452	86	153	20	4	13	47	72	63	25	.338
1957	Giants	126	467	55	160	20	7	12	48	62	35	10	.343
1958	Giants	128	467	64	137	21	3	8	58	77	51	8	.293
1959	Giants	117	432	67	124	16	8	3	26	52	49	6	.287
1960	Giants	126	399	48	91	19	3	5	26	55	43	6	.228
1961	Dragons	76	146	17	26	6	0	1	9	24	28	1	.178
1962	Dragons	17	14	0	3	0	0	0	1	0	3	0	.214
Totals		1219	4298	707	1337	238	45	82	482	553	522	163	.311

Bibliographic Essay

Extensive interviews with Wally Yonamine, his family, friends, and teammates as well as local newspaper stories provide most of the information for this book. From 2003 to 2006, I interviewed Motoh Ando, Arthur Arnold, Don Blasingame, Joel Franks, Garland Gregory, Carlton Hanta, Cappy Harada, Tatsuro Hirooka, Satoru Hosoda, Tadashi Iwamoto, Dick Kashiwaeda, Walter Kirumitsu, Ryozo Kotoh, Gene Martin, Glenn Mickens, Andy Miyamoto, Bill Mizuno, Kerry Yo Nakagawa, Futoshi Nakanishi, Hirofumi Naito, Don Newcombe, Steve Ontiveros, Amy Yonamine Roper, Bart Shirley, Don Sinn, John Sipin, Lou Spadia, Shigeru Sugishita, Sumi Hosoda Tanabe, Robert Whiting, Clyde Wright, Isamu Uchio, Larry Yaji, Wallis Yonamine Yamamoto, Akira Yonamine, Dean Yonamine, Jane Iwashita Yonamine, and Paul Yonamine. The recollections of these individuals were invaluable for reconstructing events and adding color.

As a major sports figure, Yonamine's careers in football and baseball were closely reported in the *Maui News, Honolulu Advertiser, Hawaii Times, Honolulu Star Bulletin, Hawaii Herald, Hawaii Hochi, Pacific Citizen, San Francisco Chronicle, Sports Hochi, Nippon Times,* and *Japan Times.* Occasionally, Wally's exploits reached the *New York Times, Los Angeles Times, Washington Post, Chicago Daily Tribune,* and *Pacific Stars and Stripes.*

The history of Japanese baseball is well documented in Robert Whiting's three books *The Chrysanthemum and the Bat* (Permanent Press, 1977); *You Gotta Have Wa* (Macmillan, 1989); and *The Meaning of Ichiro: The New Wave from Japan and the Transformation of Our National Pastime* (Warner Books, 2004); Joseph Reaves's *Taking in* a Game, A History of Baseball in Asia (University of Nebraska Press, 2002); and my own *Remembering Japanese Baseball: An Oral History of the Game* (Southern Illinois University Press, 2005). Japanese baseball statistics were drawn from *The Official Baseball Encyclopedia* (Baseball Magazine, 2004); Hiroshi Morioka's *Biographical Dictionary of Japan Professional Baseball Players 1936–2001* (Nichigai, 2001); the *Tokyo Yomiuri Giants 50th Anniversary History* (Yomiuri Shimbun, 1985); Daniel E. Johnson's *Japanese Baseball: A Statistical Handbook* (McFarland, 1999); Hirokazu Yokoo's *Dream Games History Since 1951* (Baseball Magazine, 2001); *Baseball Magazine*, vol. 17, no. 4 (1993); and Gary Garland's Web site Japanbaseballdaily.com.

General background on post–World War II Japan and Tokyo was gleaned from John Dower's *Embracing Defeat: Japan in the Wake of World War II* (Norton, 1999); Takemae Eiji's *The Allied Occupation of Japan* (Continuum, 2003); Edward Seidensticker's *Tokyo Rising: The City Since the Great Earthquake* (Alfred A. Knopf, 1990); Shodo Taki's *Japan Today: A Pictorial Guide* (Society for Japanese Cultural Information, 1950); and Robert Whiting's *Tokyo Underworld: The Fast Times and Hard Life of an American Gangster in Japan* (Vintage, 1999).

Wally Yonamine's Japanese autobiography (written with Shigeru Yamamoto), *The Innovator in the Ball Park* (Baseball Magazine, 1992), was an invaluable source. An unpublished translation of the first 221 pages by Sen Nishiyama is in the Yonamine family's possession.

Joel S. Franks, professor of Asian studies at San Jose State University, has written about Yonamine several times. See his "Pacific Crossings and Baseball: Comments on Hawaii and America's National Pastime and the Great Wally Yonamine," *NINE*, vol. 8, no. 1 (1999); and *Crossing Sidelines, Crossing Cultures: Sport and Asian Pacific American Cultural Citizenship* (University Press of America, 2000).

Prologue

Details of the meeting between Harada, Shoriki, and Yasuda come from interviews with Cappy Harada. For more on Harada's fascinating life see Fitts, *Remembering Japanese Baseball*, and Harada's biography, *A Bridge Across the Pacific* (Baseball Magazine, 1980), published in Japanese. Details of Shoriki's life are from Edward Uhlan and Dana L. Thomas's *Shoriki: Miracle Man of Japan* (Exposition Press, 1957).

Chapter 1

For discussions of immigration to Hawaii and life on the plantations, see Yukiko Kimura's *Issei: Japanese Immigrants in Hawaii* (University of Hawaii Press, 1988); John F. McDermott Jr., Wen-Shing Tseng, and Thomas W. Maretzki's *People and Cultures of Hawaii: A Psychocultural Profile* (University of Hawaii Press, 1980); Dennis Ogawa's *Jan Ken Po: The World of Hawaii's Japanese Americans* (University of Hawaii Press, 1973); Jonathan Okamura's *The Japanese American Historical Experience in Hawaii* (Kendall/Hunt, 2001); and Ronald Takaki's *Pau Hana: Plantation Life and Labor in Hawaii* (University of Hawaii Press, 1983). The quote on page 8 "life on the plantations . . ." is from Takaki, *Pau Hana*, p. 123. The 1910, 1920, and 1930 federal census reports provide details on Olowalu and its inhabitants. The Kashiwaeda quote on page 13 is from Michael Okihiro's *AJA Baseball in Hawaii* (Hawaii Ho-chi, 1999), p. 33. See the *Lahainaluna High School 150th Anniversary Commemorative Book* (privately published, 1981) for a history of the school. On Herman Wedemeyer see The Herman Wedemeyer Home Page (http://www.wedey.usanethosting.com/wedey.htm) and Bill Kwan's "December 7 was a Special day for Herman Wedemeyer," *Honolulu Star-Bulletin*, Dec. 7, 1996.

Chapter 2

The history of Honolulu Stadium is presented in Arthur Suehiro's *Honolulu Stadium: Where Hawaii Played* (Watermark, 1995); quotes from Al Michaels and Stuart Ho are from pp. vii and 21 of that book. Statistics on the 442nd Regimental Combat Team's casualties and honors come from the Katonk.com Web site. Biographical details on Sunderland come from Eric Kiner's "Who is Jock Sutherland" in *American Football Monthly*, Sep. 2002. The letter from Sunderland to Wally is in the Yonamines' possession. Yonamine's quote on pages 32–

33 is from the *Honolulu Advertiser*, May 6, 1947. Shaw's quote on page 33 is from the *Honolulu Advertiser*, May 14, 1947, p. 14.

Chapter 3

Sources for the history of San Francisco's Nihonbashi and its residents' forced relocation during World War II include the following Web sites: Manzanar Historic Site (www.nps.gov/archive/manz/history.htm); Topaz Camp (www.millardcounty.com/topazcamp.html); Topaz Museum (www.topazmuseum.org); and the Virtual Museum of the City of San Francisco (www.sfmuseum.org/war/evactxt.html). The history of the San Francisco 49ers is found in Joseph Hession's *Forty Niners: Collector's Edition* (Foghorn, 1993). See also Steve Dimitry's *Extinct Sports Leagues* (www.geocities.com/Colosseum/Arena/6925/aafc.html). The Beals quote on page 37 is from Hession, *Forty Niners*, p. 10. The Shaw quotes on page 43 are from the *San Francisco Chronicle*, Sep. 1, 1947. Yonamine's statistics come from *Total Football II: The Official Encyclopedia of the National Football League* (Collins, 1999), p. 1434.

Chapter 4

On the Asahi see Michael Okihiro's *AJA Baseball in Hawaii* (Hawaii Hochi, 1999); Carl Machado's "Hawaii Nisei in Baseball," *Nisei*, 1948 no. 2, p. 16, and "The Athletics," *Nisei*, 1949 no. 2, p. 14; and Karleen Chinen's "Hawaii's AJAS Play Ball" in *More Than a Game: Sport in the Japanese American Community*, edited by Brian Niiya, (Japanese American National Museum, 2000), pp. 110–23. Jyun Hirota's story comes from his unpublished manuscript "The Country Boy from Ewa Plantation." More on Dick Kashiwaeda can be found in Fitts, *Remembering Japanese Baseball*. Yonamine's quote on page 51 is from the *Honolulu Advertiser*, July 17, 1948. On the PCPFL see Bob Gill's "PCPFL: 1940–45," *The Coffin Corner*, vol. 4 (1982), and "The End of the PCPFL," *The Coffin Corner*, vol. 5 (1983). The Yonamine quote on page 56 is from the *Hawaii Times*, June 4, 1949. The quotes on page 57 "he shot . . ." and "there have been . . ." are from Hal Wood, "Yonamine, Pancheco

Released by 49ers," an article from an unknown newspaper in the Yonamine family scrapbook. On Lefty O'Doul see Richard Leutzinger's
wonderful *Lefty O'Doul: The Legend that Baseball Nearly Forgot* (Car-
mel Bay, 1997).

Chapter 5

Yonamine's final stats come from the *Pacific Citizen*, Sep. 16, 1950.

Chapter 6

The Leishman quote on page 74 is from the *Pacific Citizen*, Jan. 20,
1951. The quote on page 75 "a salary . . ." is from the *Pacific Citizen*,
Mar. 3, 1951. Information on Wakabayashi is drawn from Fred Miike's
Baseball Mad Japan (privately published, 1955) and Robert Fitts and
Gary Engel's *Japanese Baseball Superstars* (privately published, 2001).
Wakabayashi's quote on page 77 "A letter . . ." is from the *Hawaii Times*,
Mar. 13, 1951. On Sam Uyehara see Eddie Tanaka's "Smile Leagues: Sam
Uyehara Promotes Sports to Develop Good Citizens," *Nisei*, 1948 no.
4, pp. 19–26, and the *Hawaii Herald*, June 20, 1951. For information on
Americans playing professional baseball in Japan before Yonamine,
see Ralph Pearce's "Foreign Players 1936–1949," *The Japanese Baseball
Enthusiast*, vol. 2, no. 3.

Chapter 7

Many writers have discussed the differences between American and
Japanese baseball. See works by Whiting, Reaves, and Fitts as well as
William Kelly's "Blood and Guts in Japanese Professional Baseball,"
in *The Culture of Japan as Seen through its Leisure*, edited by Sepp
Linhart and Sabine Fruhstuck (State University of New York Press,
1998), pp. 95–112.

Chapter 8

The Chiba quote on page 93 is from Yonamine, *Innovator*, p. 23. For
more on Naito see Fitts, *Remembering Japanese Baseball*. The Yonamine quote on page 94 "to tell the truth . . ." is from his *Innova-*

tor, p. 19. Yonamine's quote on page 97 is from his *Innovator*, p. 21. Brian Maitland's quote on pages 98–99 is from his book *Japanese Baseball: A Fan's Guide* (Charles E. Tuttle, 1991), p. 60. The nickname "the alps" was coined by a Japanese alpinist who stated that the many white-shirted fans sitting in the steep section gave the impression of a snow-capped mountain. The quote on page 99 "just didn't like . . ." is from Clyde Wright in Fitts, *Remembering Japanese Baseball*, p. 204. Yonamine's quote on page 103 "I was tempted . . ." is from Ferd Lewis's "Yonamine reshaped Baseball in Japan," *Honolulu Advertiser*, Apr. 7, 1985. Aota's quote on page 104 is from Yonamine, *Innovator*, p. 34. The quotes from Oh on page 107 are from Sadaharu Oh and David Falkner's *Sadaharu Oh: A Zen Way of Baseball* (Kodansha, 1984), pp. 20–21. The quote on page 109 "like he was dancing" by Takashi Iwamoto is from Fitts, *Remembering Japanese Baseball*, p. 48. The Reaves quote on page 110 is from *Taking in a Game*, p. 82. Writers referring to Yonamine as a Jackie Robinson include Robert Whiting, James Floto (Wally Yonamine, "The Nisei Jackie Robinson," Thediamondangle .com/archive/may01/yonamine.html), and Jerry Izenberg ("Another Side of the Rising Sun," the *Star Ledger*, July 13, 1997).

Chapter 9

Background on Newberry and Britton is from James A. Riley's *The Biographical Encyclopedia of the Negro Baseball Leagues* (Carroll & Graf, 1994). Jane Yonamine's quote on page 119 is from Yonamine, *Innovator*, p. 66. On the relationship between martial arts and baseball in Japan see Whiting, *Meaning of Ichiro*, pp. 51–57, and Kelly, "Blood and Guts." The quote on page 123 "He's got . . ." is from the *Pacific Citizen*, Apr. 29, 1950. Mizuhara's quote on page 126 is from the *Pacific Citizen*, May 24, 1952. Hirota's quote on page 127 is from Hirota, "The Country Boy," p. 8. On Starffin see Richard Puff's "The Amazing Story of Victor Starffin," *The National Pastime*, no. 12 (1992); and Miike, *Japanese Baseball Superstars*. The Nakamura quote on pages 132–33 is from the *Pacific Citizen*, Sep. 20, 1952.

Chapter 10

The O'Doul quote on page 137 is from the *Japan Times*, Oct. 19, 1952. The quote on page 138 "given a rousing . . ." is from the *Pacific Citizen*, Feb. 20, 1953. Information on Zenimura is taken from Kerry Yo Nakagawa's *Through A Diamond: 100 Years of Japanese American Baseball* (Rudi, 2001), pp. 84–85. The Harada quotes on page 140 are from the *Hawaii Times*, Mar. 25, 26, and 28, 1953. The Yonamine quote on page 141 is from the *Hawaii Times*, Mar. 26, 1953. The quote "puffed up . . ." on page 141 is from the *Los Angeles Times*, Mar. 23, 1953. Quotes from the *Hawaii Times* on page 142 are from Apr. 1, 1953. An interview with Dick Kashiwaeda is reproduced in Fitts, *Remembering Japanese Baseball*. Quotes from the discussion of the Namba riot are taken from interviews with Yonamine and from his *Innovator*, pp. 103–7. The Chiba quote on page 151 is from Yonamine, *Innovator*, p. 78. The Shoriki quote on page 153 is from Whiting's *Tokyo Underworld*. The quote "Manager Shigeru Mizuhara . . ." on page 157 is from the *Hawaii Times*, Oct. 16, 1953. Nakamura's quote on page 157 is from the *Hawaii Times*, Oct. 16, 1953. The *Nippon Times* quote on page 158 is from Oct. 17, 1953.

Chapter 11

The Kawakami quote on page 165 is from Yonamine, *Innovator*, p. 129. Yonamine's quote on page 165 is from his *Innovator*, p. 130. On Witt and Profitt's study see "Jessica Witt Study Correlates Perceived Ball Size with Batting Average," *Medical News Today*, Dec. 15, 2005; and Jessica WK. Witt and Dennis R. Proffitt, "See the Ball, Hit the Ball," *Psychological Science*, vol. 16, no. 12 (2005), pp. 937–38. The quote "I was batting . . ." on page 167 is from Yonamine, *Innovator*, p. 134. On Larry Raines see "Land of Rising Sun to Miss Raines in '55," *Chicago Daily Tribune*, Nov. 27, 1954, p. B4.

Chapter 12

On the history of Australian baseball see Joe Clark's *A History of Australian Baseball* (University of Nebraska Press, 2003). The quote from Reg Darling on page 176 is from the *Nippon Times*, Oct. 28, 1954. The *Chicago Tribune* quote on page 176 is from Nov. 17, 1954. Background on Latin American baseball is drawn from Peter Bjarkman's *Diamonds Around the Globe* (Greenwood, 2005). Mizuhara's quote on page 180 is from Yonamine, *Innovator*, pp. 149–50. For more on Page and Gibson going to Cuba, see John Holway's *Josh and Satch* (Carroll & Graff, 1991), p. 90.

Chapter 13

The Stengel quotes beginning on page 193 are from "Stengel Interested in Japanese Players," *Los Angeles Times*, Jan. 17, 1956, p. c2. The *New York Times* quote on page 200 is from July 21, 1956, p. 12. On page 200, the quote "it was the first time . . ." is from the *Hawaii Times*, July 10, 1956; the quote "when Yonamine . . ." is from Yonamine, *Innovator*, p. 185. Chiba's quote on page 200 is from Yonamine, *Innovator*, pp. 193–94. The *Sports Nippon* report on page 202 is quoted from Yonamine, *Innovator*, p. 201. Mihara's quote on page 203 is from Fitts, *Remembering Japanese Baseball*, p. 34. Vin Scully's quotes on page 207 are from "The Dodgers in Japan," *Sport*, Apr. 1957, pp. 26–93.

Chapter 14

The Mizuhara and Yonamine quotes on pages 211–12 are from Yonamine, *Innovator*, p. 218. Hirota's quote on page 212 is from the *Honolulu Star Bulletin*, Jan. 10, 1957. Yonamine's quote on page 214 is from his *Innovator*, pp. 217–20. The Miyamoto quote on page 216 is from the *Hawaii Times*, May 29, 1957. Quotes from Japanese newspapers on page 218 come from the *Hawaii Times*, Aug. 14, 1957. Quotes by an unnamed Japanese sportswriter on page 218, as well as Yonamine's and Mizuhara's responses, are from the *Hawaii Times*, Aug. 21, 1957. Yonamine's quote on page 219 is from the *Honolulu Advertiser*, Aug. 21, 1957. Mizuhara's quote on page 219 is from the *Hawaii Times*, Aug. 21,

1957. The *Asahi Shimbun* quote on page 220 is taken from the *Hawaii Times*, Sep. 11, 1957. The *Hawaii Times* quote on page 221 is from Oct. 4, 1957. The second *Hawaii Times* quote on page 221 is from Oct. 16, 1957. Yonamine's quote on page 222 is from the *Hawaii Times*, Oct. 26, 1957. The *Japan Times* quote on page 223 is from Oct. 26, 1957. The quote on page 223 "the narrow . . ." is from the *New York Times*, Oct. 31, 1957. The quote on page 223 "with beautiful . . ." is from the *Hawaii Times*, Oct. 30, 1957. The quote on page 224 "immediately a half-dozen . . ." is from the *New York Times*, Oct. 31, 1957.

Chapter 15

Mickens's quotes on page 231 are from Fitts, *Remembering Japanese Baseball*, pp. 70–71. Kawakami's quote on page 237 is from the *Hawaii Times*, Oct. 21, 1958. Shinagawa's quote on page 237 is from the *Hawaii Times*, Oct. 30, 1958. The Oh quotes on pages 238–39 are from Oh, *Sadaharu Oh*, pp. 58, 77–78, and 85–86. The Whiting quote on pages 242–43 is from his *Chrysanthemum*, pp. 98–100.

Chapter 16

The quote from the *Japan Times* on page 248 is from May 23, 1960. The *Japan Times* quote on page 253 is from Nov. 27, 1960. Yonamine's quote on page 253 is from the *Hawaii Times*, Dec. 5, 1960. Yonamine's quote on page 254 is from the *Hawaii Times*, Dec. 7, 1960.

Chapter 17

For more on the differences between American and Japanese coaching, see Whiting, *You Gotta Have Wa*, especially p. 60. Jane Yonamine's quote on page 264 is from the *Honolulu Star-Bulletin*, Feb. 25, 1969. Tanaka's quote on page 266 is from "Tips from Japan," 1964, a clipping from an unknown newspaper in the Yonamine family scrapbook. On Kondo see his obituary at japanbaseballdaily.com, Obituaries, Jan. 2, 2006. The Addie quote on page 267 is from the *Washington Post*, Nov. 25, 1965, p. E2.

Chapter 18

Lee's quote on page 272 is from Fitts, *Remembering Japanese Baseball*, p. 135. For more on Kawakami's philosophy see Kelly, "Blood and Guts," and Whiting, *Meaning of Ichiro*, pp. 62–63.

Chapter 19

Yaz's quote on page 282 is from "Yastrzemski Spikes Talk of Rich Offer to Play in Japan," *Stars and Stripes*, Dec. 9, 1973. The quote on page 291 "Yonamine is perhaps . . ." is from Whiting, *Chrysanthemum*, p. 206.

Chapter 20

For more on Don Blasingame see Whiting, *You Gotta Have Wa*, pp. 144–60, and Fitts, *Remembering Japanese Baseball*, pp. 109–16. The Whitfield quote on page 308 is from Whiting, *You Gotta Have Wa*, p. 231; the White quote on page 309 is from *You Gotta Have Wa*, p. 233.

Chapter 21

Yonamine's quote on page 317 is from the *Honolulu Star Bulletin*, Apr. 8, 1998. His quote on page 319 is from Marty Kuehnert's "From Humble Roots to Imperial Honors," an article from an unknown newspaper in the Yonamine family scrapbook.

Index

CPSIA information can be obtained at www.ICGtesting.com
Printed in the USA
BVOW021149170412

287816BV00002B/1/P